Louis Tracy

The Lost Provinces

How Vansittart Came Back to France

Louis Tracy

The Lost Provinces
How Vansittart Came Back to France

ISBN/EAN: 9783744665858

Printed in Europe, USA, Canada, Australia, Japan

Cover: Foto ©ninafisch / pixelio.de

More available books at **www.hansebooks.com**

" ' Move and I fire,' he shrieked."

See page 108.

HOW VANSITTART CAME BACK
TO FRANCE

BY

LOUIS TRACY

Author of "The Final War," "An American Emperor," etc.

———

ILLUSTRATED

———

G. P. PUTNAM'S SONS
NEW YORK AND LONDON
The Knickerbocker Press
1898

The Knickerbocker Press, New York

CONTENTS.

iv Contents.

ILLUSTRATIONS.

THE LOST PROVINCES

THE LOST PROVINCES

CHAPTER I

A KING AND TWO EMPERORS

"SO history repeats itself. The war of 1870 is to be fought again, and with, I fear, the same issue."

"Is there no hope of a peaceful settlement?"

"How can there be peace between a robber and his victim? Germany is resolved that France must be crushed. Crushed she will be to the utmost bounds of humiliation unless——"

"Unless you go back again, guv'nor, and take a hand in the game."

The interruption came from Arizona Jim, who was sitting with Vansittart and Evelyn in a canoe lying motionless on a silvery lake in the heart of the Adirondacks.

For a moment no one spoke. It would seem that this privileged adherent had blurted out the millionaire's secret thought, and the possibility alarmed Evelyn. In sharper tones than was her wont she cried, after a quick glance at her husband : "Don't say such foolish things, Bates. Your master has given enough to France without adding his life to the debt of gratitude. Twenty years hence you will suggest that Henry should follow in the same cause. The sole object of your existence is to seek danger and trouble."

The allusion to her three-year-old son softened her voice

to breaking point. Her eyes glistened with tears as she looked wistfully from one to the other of her hearers.

Arizona Jim was astounded at this outburst. The use of his surname conveyed far more reproach than mere words. He worshipped Evelyn with dog-like fidelity, and now, in mute pain, he sought, with a look, encouragement from Vansittart. But Jerome steadily watched a spiral of smoke from his cigar curling into shapelessness in the still air. So Jim essayed to defend himself.

" Well, mum, there was a time when I used ter fool round lookin' for trouble. But I kinder thought that bad ole time had passed. The biggest trouble I did n't allow for, an' that is for you to be vexed with me. As for danger, I 'm sorter fixed in the notion as how it ain't in our hands. Kings an' sparrows run under the same rules."

" Oh, Jim, I 'm not angry with you. But you don't understand—you don't understand," and Evelyn's repressed tears forthwith became downright sobs.

If her wayward mood amazed Bates, it was quite comprehensible to Jerome, who now silently admonished the other to leave matters where they were. In very truth, the impulsive Texan had but placed into words the thought which for days past had thrown a shadow upon Evelyn's bright existence.

Sensational statements in the press, backed by the better-informed confidential reports constantly supplied to Vansittart by the French Ambassador at Washington, proved beyond doubt that Germany was seeking a pretext for a rapid and irresistible attack upon her prosperous neighbour. Bismarck's policy still prevailed in Berlin, though his domineering presence was removed from the council chamber. " A strong France is a menace to Teutonic aspirations." " In European disputes the bayonet is the court of appeal." " Blessed are those who possess." These were his aphorisms, and the hot-headed ruler of the German nation considered them to be still as vital to the longevity of his empire as in the troublous period when the first Chancellor proclaimed the reign of blood and iron.

France had thriven amazingly since Vansittart converted the arid Sahara into a panorama of cornlands and vineyards. The commercial prosperity of the people brought with it expansion in the trade marts of the world. Germany, soured by the uselessness of her own colonial efforts, experienced the novel sensation of being heedlessly elbowed to one side by her mercurial neighbour. Frenchmen were taught reason by contentment. The Russian alliance was no longer coveted, bickerings against England became spasmodic and feeble, whilst the last man that Henri V. regarded as an antagonist was the German Emperor. France, in her dream of peace, was even forgetting the Lost Provinces ! But the King and his advisers should have read the open book supplied by the recorded utterances of their greatest enemy.

" Every state," said Bismarck, " must recognise that its security rests on its own sword." Henri did well to enrich his people, but ill to neglect the safeguards of French independence. And now that there was open alarm at the disclosure of German designs after years of secret and well-planned preparation, France was unready : heroic sacrifice might out-stay the impending doom. These were the plain facts, divested of diplomatic trappings. On the surface there was an apparently commonplace dispute concerning customs duties on German importations to the new African domain. Beneath lay the rancorous hatred of the Teuton for the Frank, intensified daily by battles fought in the counting-house, and territories won or lost in the world-wide kingdom of trade.

The New York press explained the situation with point and flippancy. " Germany must fight or give up," wrote one of the chief papers. " The Kaiser must either throttle France or be drummed out of power by an impoverished people famishing and mutinous. The nation is sinking beneath ever-increasing military burdens which must be met out of a falling revenue. The alternative, to the German

Emperor's thinking, is simple. The rest of the world desires peace ; he must have war—and every other interest but that of the house of Hohenzollern may go hang."

The London newspapers were more moderate. But even as they spoke of conciliation, they obviously dreaded the outbreak of hostilities at any hour. The *Times*—straining after an amicable settlement—could only suggest that an international committee should revise the offending tariff as a *modus vivendi* for twelve months. One might, with equal futility, ask the wolf to stay his spring until the lamb had sought the shelter of the fold.

No wonder, then, that Evelyn Vansittart was sad at heart in the midst of pleasant surroundings, or that her emotions were not in harmony with the joyous springtide in the hills. She knew full well that France, sore pressed, would, in the hour of extremity, appeal to the one man in whom the populace placed unbounded faith. And she herself would be the first to admit that duty and honour alike offered her husband but one course of action. He must return. They must leave their Garden of Eden. It was bitter, and her soul rose in revolt against the warlike and unscrupulous Kaiser.

After all, money does not bring happiness. The millionaire and the man in the street are separated only by some bricks and mortar. Their lives are very similar when viewed through the telescopes of the gods.

Five minutes of quiet thought revealed the situation more clearly to Arizona Jim. When Evelyn had calmed somewhat, in response to Jerome's half-jocular, half-sympathetic raillery, Jim ventured to say :

" It 's like this, mum. It 'll do no good for the guv'nor to fight, anyhow. This is a business for armies, an' big ones at that. But the French want someone to do the thinkin' for 'em. That 's more 'n half the game, an' alluz hez been ever since the days of Nebbycodnezzer."

Jerome laughed outright at the extraordinary simile ; even his wife smiled as she dried her eyes.

" Why on earth do you drag in Nebuchadnezzar, Jim ? " cried Vansittart when he was able to speak.

" 'Cos he thought he could live on grass, an' it kep' him goin' for seven bloomin' years."

The conceit put them in better humour. They were about to resume their interrupted fishing when Jerome caught sight of Harland walking towards them, down the hill on which stood their summer residence. They watched him in silence until he reached the verge of the lake. Then he put his hands to his mouth and shouted :

" Cablegram for Evelyn."

" A cablegram for me ! " repeated Evelyn, in astonishment. " From whom, I wonder ? Paddle in at once, Jerry. Surely there is nothing amiss with mother, or aunt. I had a letter only yesterday. Why does n't Dick call out its contents ? " Had she been on shore she certainly would have examined the printed envelope to see if it gave any indications of the nature of the interior message.

She did not wait to land before she cried :

" Whom is it from, Dick ? "

" From the Queen of France."

" What is it about ? "

" It will best convey its own message. Thinking it was from home I opened it. It is written in the private code used by the King, Liancourt, and Jerome, so I have translated it and here is a fair copy."

Evelyn took the manuscript, and read it aloud :

" DEAR AND TRUE FRIEND,—The expected has happened this time. Germany has forced a pretext for war upon us. Acting under the specific instructions of the Kaiser, a German gunboat accompanied a trading vessel to Gabes, and attempted to land a cargo of goods in defiance of our customs regulations. The officials invoked the aid of the captain of one of our warships on duty at the port, and he ordered the Germans to desist. This they refused to do unless compelled by force, whereupon our officer fired a blank cartridge by way of warning. It was sufficient, but there cannot be the slightest doubt that this paltry incident will be made a cause of war. We are, God

knows, ill prepared for a campaign, though we have strained every
nerve to strengthen our resources since our enemy's cruel design
became apparent. We are alone in this quarrel. We cannot expect
England to interfere, and Russian friendship has suddenly become
frozen. Oh, my dear Evelyn, do not you desert us! I ask you to spare
your husband to aid us in this terrible crisis. I know not what to
urge in behalf of my request, but the need of my beloved France
impels me to prefer it, if necessary on my knees. The King or Liancourt would have cabled to Mr. Vansittart, but I told them to leave
the appeal to me, for I am assured that the decision will rest with you.
I cannot think that you will deny me. With Mr. Vansittart directing affairs, my people will be hopeful. In his absence, they will
march to death, brave but despairing.

> "Your afflicted
> "HONORINE."

When the familiar name left her lips, Evelyn turned, and
hid her face against her husband's shoulder. Jerome put
his arm round her:

" It has come sooner than we thought, old girl," was the
best he could find to say.

Dick Harland dug his hands into his pockets, and looked
at them fixedly, but Arizona Jim felt that he required sus-
tenance, so he took a surreptitious bite at a plug of tobacco.
At last, Evelyn regained her self-control. She said quite
firmly:

" *Does* the decision rest with me, Jerry? "

" Yes."

" Then we start for France at the earliest moment."

" We? "

" Yes, we; I refuse to remain behind. If you go without
me I will follow by the next steamer."

" My dear girl, there is the boy to think of."

" He will be well looked after during our absence. My
place is with you."

" So be it, sweetheart. This war will make an old man
of me, so we will age together. Dick, wire to New York
and ask when the *Seafarer* can sail for Europe."

" And at the same time I will answer the Queen."

Evelyn was grit right through.

The day was Tuesday, early in May. An hour later they learned that the *Seafarer* would be ready for sea at two o'clock on Thursday afternoon.

" Then Thursday afternoon at two o'clock we sail," cried Jerome, cheerily. " Now, Dick, I have been making a few plans already. How can I best purchase, for the speediest shipment, twenty thousand strong, well-conditioned horses? They must be up to weight and sound in wind and limb. Anything over fifteen hands and between five and eight years old will meet my requirements."

.   .   .   .

The difference in sun time between the Adirondack region in New York State and the capital city of the German Empire is about seven hours. At the precise hour, therefore, when the momentous question of Vansittart's return to France was decided, it was already night in Berlin.

In a room of the Imperial palace that stands on the famous boulevard, Unter den Linden, was gathered a notable conclave. The Emperor—impulsive, exuberant, brave to rashness, and daring in thought—sat at the head of the council table. With him were the chief officers of the army and the responsible Ministers of State. There was nothing of doubt or hesitation in the Kaiser's words, nor did his manner belie him. He had chosen this chamber for the conference, because here, if anywhere in that royal abode, dwelt the spirit of his renowned grandfather. From that historical corner window, the great founder of the modern German Empire had looked to the last upon his faithful people and his beloved army.

The old warrior king believed in himself and in his mission. " A Hohenzollern," he said, " should not only be the first citizen of his land, but its first soldier and defender." In the closing days of his nonogenarian life, William I. would never discard his uniform. His only pleasure was to watch the daily march of the Guards down the broad avenue of the lime trees. A few hours before the end came, he declared with dignity that he had " no time to be tired," when some faithful attendant suggested a rest from the routine duties of the day.

The restless activity of William I. was reborn in his ambitious and domineering grandson. But a faith in the one had changed into a mania in the other. " Germany free and united " had transmuted itself into " Germany supreme and world-compelling."

This council of war lords had assembled to make the vainglorious dream a sordid fact. Someone had suggested a further sounding of the views held by the great Powers.

" Great Powers ! " cried the Emperor. " Great Weaknesses, rather ! Which of them will stir ship or soldier to aid France ? No. The quarrel will be left to us, in the hope that the struggle will weaken both. Already Austria and Italy have taken care to declare their neutrality, and from Petersburgh I hear that Russia is resolute in keeping aloof. England will not interfere. A hint that Egypt and the Transvaal shall be her portion of the spoil will render her complaisant—until I tell her that triumphant Germany has assumed the rights of conquered France on the Nile. But enough : we are resolved. When will the three army corps be mobilised, General von Waldersee ? "

The officer addressed, the Chief of the Staff, instantly replied :

" We can commence to throw one hundred and fifty thousand men across the frontier on Thursday night at nine o'clock, your Majesty."

" Why at night ? Is there no fear of uncertainty or confusion ? "

" None, sire, for us ; much for the enemy."

" Then I lead the first regiment of the centre column ! "

" That must not be." It was Prince Hohenlohe, the Imperial Chancellor, who spoke so emphatically.

" How ! Must not ! These are hardly fitting words to me."

" Possibly, sire, but I cannot school my tongue to conceal my thoughts. Your Majesty's impetuosity and carelessness of danger are too well known to me that I should lend my voice to a proceeding which might risk your person in a frontier affray at the very inception of our enterprise."

Emboldened by the Chancellor's outspokenness, several officers concurred with him.

" Well, well," and the Emperor turned to a map with an air of annoyance. " You are right, I suppose. But mark me. Not always will I yield to these grandmotherly precautions. I had thought it would inspirit the troops to know that their leader led from the front and not from the rear."

" The project is worthy of your Majesty, but the gain is not to be measured against the possible loss."

Who, then, will act as my personal representative ? The Emperor's deputy, at least, must be the first soldier to set foot on French soil."

" Surely no man's name can contend the right with mine."

All eyes turned upon the new speaker, Colonel von Moltke, nephew of the renowned strategist, who manœuvred the German armies with such faultless skill during the war of 1870.

" And none shall," cried the Kaiser, enthusiastically. " Yours be the honour to lead the column, Colonel, and Friday's sun shall see you major-general."

Prince Hohenlohe's cold accents broke in upon the buzz of comment evoked by the Emperor's stirring phrase."

" When will your Majesty declare war ? "

" Ah ! I had forgotten. Telegraph to our Ambassador in Paris that he is to demand his passports on Thursday evening."

" But he will not be able to cross the frontier before the outposts are met and all trains are stopped."

"*Himmel!* he can come through Brussels."

So it will be seen that, whilst the King of France left affairs of vast importance to his Royal Consort, the Emperor of Germany also launched his thunderbolt by deputy.

The other Emperor, Vansittart, was the only one who actually travelled to the front at that fateful hour on Thursday.

CHAPTER II

THE three German army corps entered France simultaneously at different points.

One line of march, from Metz by way of Gravelotte, Mars-la-Tour, and Fresnes-en-Woevre, followed the historic route of the last war. Here the French had set up a formidable barrier of men and guns, backed by the splendid fortress of Verdun.

The second attack had also been foreseen. The concentration of Bavarians at Thionville, or Diedenhofen, as it is rechristened by the Germans, caused the French Staff to expect and prepare for an immediate junction of the two corps in French territory. In the result they were not mistaken.

But the third was unpleasantly new. Vast quantities of troops were gathered at both Strasburg and Mulhausen. From each of these centres the natural advance across the frontier was, in one case, by Snarburg, north of the Vosges mountains, towards Lunéville and Nancy; in the other, through Alt Munsterol toward strongly fortified Belfort.

In either event the French would have opposed a bold front to the invaders. General Daubisson, who in his capacity as Governor of Paris was Commander-in-chief under the supreme control of the King, was chagrined rather than alarmed when he found that the southern German column had secretly detrained at Markirch, and was able to push cavalry vedettes through the heart of the Vosges as far as Farize, almost without striking a blow.

On the Friday morning the eyes of the world were bent on Paris and Berlin. The two cities comported themselves according to their moods, Paris yelping with excitement, the German capital throbbing with earnestness.

The King of France bore himself bravely before his people. In the comparative secrecy of the rebuilded Tuileries he showed alone the agonised apprehension that possessed him. His one thought was that Vansittart would arrive too late.

" We were at least warned soon enough to have prevented this misfortune," he cried. " Why did we not bring him here a fortnight ago ? "

" Your Majesty forgets," said Liancourt, " that Mr. Vansittart believed, as we did, that Germany would not commit this outrage upon humanity without even plausible excuse."

" Yes, yes," murmured Henri, " but the best of explanations will not disguise the fact. One short week of his counsel and presence would have achieved so much. One short week too soon, rather than too late ! "

" Your Majesty cannot believe that the armies of France will be beaten from the field within a week ? "

" Liancourt," and the King turned to his faithful minister with keen emotion in his face, " let us not deceive each other. You know, better than I, perhaps, what our enemies can accomplish, even in that brief period. It is for my brave soldiers, unready, ill-equipped, worse fed, that I grieve. You and I, my friend, can die at their head, but what will that avail France ! France, my country—so happy, so prosperous, so little deserving this wretched fate ! "

Liancourt could only urge the King to abandon useless regrets and do all within his power to repair defects. He realised, in their full bitterness, the truth of Henri's words.

In the palace near the lindens, William II., who, for all his dash and waywardness, is a methodical German, had retired to rest and slept soundly after the telegrams arrived announcing the departure of the three columns. He rose early, fresh and vigorous, ready to proceed to the front as soon as he learned that the left bank of the Meuse was in possession of his troops.

General von Gossler waited upon him the moment he appeared.

" 'T is fitting," cried the Kaiser, " that on this, of all days, I should be greeted by the War Minister. What news, Von Gossler ? "

" Excellent, sire. The fight is in the enemy's country. We have seized the desired positions, the armies are consolidating, and probably the first battle will be in progress by the time your Majesty reaches the frontier."

Yet the General's visage was not as cheerful as his intelligence, and the Emperor's quick eye noted the discrepancy.

" Is aught amiss then ? "

" In one respect I have tidings that your Majesty will regret to——"

" Quick. What has happened ? "

" Colonel von Moltke was shot by the French picket as he drove them over the Woevre bridge."

" Shot. Wounded you mean, I trust."

" No, sire. Shot through the brain."

" The only place to hit a Moltke ! Yet I would have given much that this had not occurred."

" Yes. I fear that the men will regard it as an evil omen."

" Omen ! There is no such word in the drill-book. And if there were, what better omen than that a Moltke should be the first to give his life for the Fatherland ? "

" I hope the army will view it in that light, but ——"

" Pish ! You grow superstitious, General. What say the papers about the war ? " The Emperor, who was more deeply moved than he cared to admit, picked up a copy of the *Zeitung*, and turned to the columns of foreign intelligence. The first paragraph that met his eyes caused him to utter an exclamation that had better be left in the maze of syllables that make up the German language.

Vansittart, when he first quitted the States to found an empire in France, had escaped the notice of the American press. Even he could not accomplish this feat twice. Every New York paper turned the X-ray intelligence of a skilled reporter upon the *Seafarer* and her inmates when it became known that she was getting ready for a voyage. Hence Reuter's correspondent was able to cable the following message :

"New York, Thursday.—Shortly before it became known that Germany had declared war against France, Mr. and Mrs. Vansittart and suite sailed for Europe on board their yacht, the *Seafarer*. The famous millionaire's sympathies for France—indeed he remains a naturalised French citizen—coupled with the fact that the yacht's destination was kept a secret, render it practically certain that he is bound for Havre, or Cherbourg. He left his summer home in the Adirondacks most unexpectedly. Information concerning his intentions is absolutely refused at his New York estate office. In any case he cannot cross the Atlantic under eight days, as the *Seafarer* is a sixteen-knot boat."

General von Gossler wondered what had so disturbed his royal master, but he was not long left in doubt.

Turning upon him with a face of fury, Wilhelm roared :

" Why was I not told of this sooner ? "

" Of w-w-what, sire ? "

" Of the departure of this Yankee adventurer, blockhead. Send Vice-Admiral Hollmann here at once. Quick, if you would retain your portfolio."

Utterly at a loss to know what this storm portended, the General rushed from the room, and the Kaiser strode to and fro in a towering rage.

He had not forgotten the way in which Vansittart, when President of the French, had played political poker with him. He wanted no more " raising " at his hands, and had cooled somewhat by the time the Secretary for the Navy raced back with the flurried Von Gossler.

" Admiral," he shouted, " there are four well-defined routes across the Atlantic ? "

" Yes, sire."

" Read this. Order a fast cruiser to proceed along each route and bring this man Vansittart, with or without his ship, to Hamburg. The commission of each captain depends upon the success of one of them. They must start forthwith and avoid conflicts with French vessels at any cost. Do you follow me ? "

" I have no doubt I will fully comprehend your Majesty's commands when I have read the news which has caused your Majesty's agitation," answered the imperturbable sailor.

" Agitation! I am not agitated; only emphatic." Nevertheless the Emperor regretted that he had betrayed such deep feeling before his subordinates. He condescended to explain himself more coherently.

It was thus that Jerome's departure was heralded in the hostile camps.

Twelve hours after the *Seafarer* passed the Sandy Hook lightship and turned her smart figure-head eastward, four fast and well-armed German cruisers sailed from Hamburg and Bremerhaven intent upon her capture or destruction.

The Stars and Stripes fluttered in the breeze over the taff-rail as the gallant little ship plunged steadily onwards through the long Atlantic rollers. Reuter's correspondent was not mistaken in describing her as a sixteen-knot ship. Her small size (2000 tons) and her owner's desire to be able to voyage in her anywhere precluded a higher engine-power. To drive her at twenty knots through a heavy sea would be not only dangerous, but destructive of all comfort to those on board, this speed being with difficulty maintained by an ocean colossus five or six times her tonnage.

The party accommodated themselves with varying emotions to the vagaries of the continent of seas which constitute the North Atlantic. On the third day out, although on a

southerly course, they plunged into the heel of a fog that
had swept down from the Newfoundland Banks. But to
Evelyn the chilly mist was refreshing, and she walked the
deck leaning on her husband's arm with a sense of exhilara-
tion at the vastness of their enterprise. Her first feeling of
resentment had passed. They were now committed, for good
or evil, to the fortunes of France, and her keen sense of
justice rebelled against the wanton cruelty of the Germans
in seeking to cripple their great neighbour in the hour of
progress and prosperity.

She noted, too, with quiet pride that Jerome had regained
his old-time bearing of command and self-reliance. Even
emperors stagnate in disuse. Vansittart had, to her eyes,
grown taller since he quitted lake-fishing for the great game
of empire.

During his brief halt in New York he had done much.
Not every man can contrive to expend twenty-five millions
sterling in half that number of hours, but he had done this,
to the huge benefit of France, as will be seen hereafter.

Now he spent most of his time in reading the records of
the war of '70-71, together with much poring over maps
and jotting down of memoranda. This evening Evelyn protested against so much preoccupation, and carried him off for
a constitutional before dinner. During their walk they
noticed Arizona Jim leaning against a ventilator away forward, gazing fixedly into the wall of fog. Jim was wrapped
in a brown study, and looked so serious that they both
laughed.

"What are you thinking about so deeply, Jim?" inquired
the millionaire.

Bates started.

"I was thinkin', boss, that things air tolerable thick
ahead."

"Here, do you mean?"

"Nit, s'long as we keep tootin' the foghorn I guess we 're
all right, if the other feller does the same."

" In France, then ? "

" Yes, guv'nor, that 's the locality. You won't find no Injun signs on rocks to help fix this business."

" Why, Jim, you are the one man in the world I should not suspect of doubting the future. Have you lost faith in me ? "

" No, guv'nor. Not I. Nary a bit. What you sez goes. But you 'll have to kill off a blamed lot of Germans."

Evelyn clutched Jerome's arm more tightly. Bates had an unpleasant knack of revealing the truth without any circumlocution. For the first time she realised that the conquest of men meant carnage—that her husband might be called upon to direct red and horrible war.

Next morning, whilst Evelyn was pouring out a third cup of coffee for Jerome and Dick, the captain of the *Seafarer* hurriedly entered the saloon.

" There 's a British man-of-war about three miles ahead on the port bow, sir, and she has signalled us to stop," he said.

" To stop ? An English ship ? Are you quite sure she is English ? " cried Jerome.

" Quite certain, sir. She is the fast cruiser *Hawke*. I know her well by sight. What shall we do ? "

" Obey the signal by all means. What 's up now, I wonder ? "

They went on deck and scrutinised the handsome warship, for the overnight fog had wholly disappeared, and the fine vessel supplied a human interest to the vast panorama of blue rolling sea and sunlit sky. The *Hawke*, first-class cruiser, 7350 tons, of 12,000 horse-power, and carrying twelve guns, was evidently in earnest. She slightly altered her course in order to come nearer, and when half a mile ahead, slowed down to lower a boat. An officer took his seat in the stern sheets, and the steady pull of eight strong-armed blue-jackets soon brought him alongside the *Seafarer*.

Within hailing distance he cried :

" Is Mr. Vansittart aboard ? "

2

" Yes," replied Jerome ; " I am he."

" I am very glad I have fallen in with you. I wish to speak with you privately."

Suiting the action to the words, he quickly climbed the rope ladder which had been lowered, and gained the deck of the *Seafarer*.

With smiling courtesy he introduced himself : " I am Captain des Vœux Hamilton, of H.M.S. *Hawke*, which you see there. I have information of great importance for you. Shall we go to the saloon ? "

Jerome led the way, saying :

" My wife and brother-in-law may accompany us ? "

" Assuredly, Mr. Vansittart."

Once out of earshot of others, the officer explained his strange appearance in mid-Atlantic. He began with a question.

" Do you know that war has broken out between Germany and France ? "

Evelyn uttered an involuntary exclamation. Even Vansittart was staggered by the suddenness of the announcement.

" Surely matters have not reached that stage already ? " he exclaimed.

" There can be no doubt about it. The German armies commenced an invasion of France on Thursday night. I left Portsmouth at noon on Friday, and several slight affairs had already taken place on the frontier, whilst in military circles it was generally believed that the first pitched battle would take place yesterday, Sunday, somewhere in the neighbourhood of Mars-la-Tour."

Jerome was powerfully moved, but his anger at this catastrophe only manifested itself by a tightening of the lips as he said :

" This is indeed grave news for me, Captain Hamilton."

" I fear my next item will be even more unpleasant, in so far as it affects you personally. Our Foreign Office is naturally keeping a very close watch on all naval movements at this moment. A trustworthy Hamburg correspondent warned Whitehall, by secret telegraphic code, that four German cruisers put out to sea, in a great hurry, early on Friday. He learned by some means that their object was to catch you and prevent you, at all hazards, from landing in France. Your yacht is an American ship, but defenceless, and you are reported to be a French citizen. Nice diplomatic differences can, however, be adjusted months hence, and even large personal indemnities paid. Meanwhile, you would be accommodated with a residence in some remote German castle. I think you follow me. You have friends in Whitehall, Mr. Vansittart, so here I am."

" Captain Hamilton," said the millionaire, warmly, " I am immensely indebted to the British Government, and to you personally. But tell me. At sea I am helpless. The *Seafarer* is not a fast boat. I may presumably expect capture at any moment."

" Hardly. The *Hawke* can slip away from anything the Germans have got, and we had, say, a couple of hours' start from Portsmouth. But one of the quartette will certainly fall in with you this afternoon or evening."

" Are they entitled to board my yacht and seize her ? "

" They are not. But I know what I or you would do under similar circumstances—leave others to settle the rights of the case, eh, Mr. Vansittart ? "

The Anglo-Saxon is very much alike on both sides of the Atlantic. They all, even Evelyn, grinned in concert.

" What are your orders, Captain ? " said Jerome, after a pause.

" My orders are to find you, and assist you."

" Without qualifications ? "

" Absolutely ! "

" In the absence of an American man-of-war I am justified in asking your protection under circumstances that savour of piracy."

" Well, you see it is this way. I can stand by you, and help you if appealed to, but—again regarding events from the German point of view—a single shell would probably settle your business during the argument."

Dick Harland now broke in.

" It strikes me that the *Seafarer* is hardly a safe place within the meaning of the act."

" What act ? " said Evelyn, innocently.

The question raised a laugh. Their absurd position was comically serious. Then a light broke upon Vansittart.

" Would it inconvenience you too much, Captain Hamilton, if I were to ask you to find quarters for a small household of five on board your ship during the next few days ? "

" When I get the request in writing," said the sailor, with dry humour, " you will come with me to quarters already prepared."

Then, with a smile, he turned to Evelyn. " You will not find a cruiser quite so comfortable as this magnificent vessel, Mrs. Vansittart, but my officers and myself will be delighted to entertain you."

" I cannot express my gratitude," began Jerome.

" No need, sir. But time presses."

A bustle of stewards, some agonised moments for a French maid, a few instructions to the captain of the *Seafarer*, and the whole party were seated in the *Hawke's* gig, which bounded willingly towards the warship.

All that morning and afternoon there was much jubilant activity on board the *Hawke*.

" Strike me stiff," said a sturdy Jackie who was hoisting ammunition from the forward magazine. " I did n't play for a shindy this trip, but you never knows yer luck."

" If things goes right to-day we 'll have a fair old beano, Bill," growled his mate, hoarse with the effect of nearly swallowing a quid when he caught the gunnery lieutenant's eye fixed on a suspicious lump in the side of his cheek.

Arizona Jim sighed as he listened. A six-chambered revolver was a trivial thing beside a six-inch rapid-firing gun. For the only time in his life he envied his fellow-men.

At three bells in the first dog watch, or, in shore phrase, 5.30 P.M., the *Seafarer*, having ignored previous signals, was compelled to shut off steam in obedience to a gun fired across her bows by the German belted cruiser *Das Rheinland*, 6500 tons, ten guns, commanded temporarily by Vice-Admiral von Grudenau. The order was imperative, and the matter at issue important, as the distinguished officer himself, escorted by an armed boat's crew, pulled off towards the *Seafarer*, and the watchers from the *Hawke* could easily distinguish an animated colloquy in progress on her deck between Von Grudenau and the Yankee skipper. It soon ended. The German did not return to his own vessel, but rapidly approached the *Hawke*. He was received with ceremonious courtesy.

After compliments, as they say in the East, he explained :

" My imperial master, the German Emperor, being at war with France, demands the person of a French subject, one Monsieur Jerome K. Vansittart, who, I am informed, is on board this ship, which flies the flag of Great Britain, a neutral nation." He spoke as a man incensed at being set back in the moment of success.

" I beg to refer your imperial master, the German Emperor, to my royal mistress, the Queen of England," was Captain Hamilton's suave reply.

" This, sir, is a subterfuge, and you know it," cried the Vice-Admiral, pale with suppressed anger. " I emphatically demand the delivery to my custody of this gentleman whom I see standing here."

" And I as emphatically refuse to comply with your demand."

" On what grounds, sir ? "

" Firstly, because Mr. Vansittart, his wife, and brother-in-law are the honoured guests of H.M.S. *Hawke*, and consequently of the British Government. Secondly, because you fail to adduce proof that Mr. Vansittart is a French citizen. Thirdly, if he were, and on board this ship, it would, under the circumstances, require the whole German navy to take him off it."

"Bully for you, Cap," murmured Jim Bates, who stood close behind the British officer. Captain Hamilton, electrified at such a remark on his own quarter-deck, turned half angrily to the speaker, but a glance at Jim softened his expression. The German was ready to burst with rage. Full well he knew that he had been tricked by a specious artifice arising from wholly unexpected conditions. Yet he dared not, and would not, return to Bremerhaven without attempting to serve his country in this ticklish affair. Why not strive, at the sacrifice of his life, to rid Germany of one potent enemy. He involuntarily made a half-step forward, whilst his right arm crossed to his sword, but Captain Hamilton and another officer sprang in front of him, and Arizona Jim's hand fell to his hip. There are times when a six-shooter is more convenient than even a six-inch gun.

The incident passed so quickly that it might have been imaginary were it not accentuated by Evelyn's slight cry of alarm.

Von Grudenau, with a rigid bow, said : "Further conversation is useless. I must obey my orders. With your permission, sir, I will return to my vessel."

As he spoke his eyes wandered along the lines of the *Hawke*. He could not fail to see that she was in fighting trim.

Captain Hamilton followed his glance and smiled.

"Will you not do me the honour of prolonging your visit and inspecting the ship? She will bear scrutiny, I can assure you."

The other politely waved the offer aside.

"I have no option but to try what force can do," he said.

"Any course you may see fit to adopt will afford me equal pleasure. But this is not a personal matter, sir. I am in duty bound to tell you that your ship is over-matched. You are rashly risking a useful vessel and the lives of your crew in striving to carry out your unreasonable instructions."

Again Von Grudenau bowed, and without further speech quitted the *Hawke*. Not until he was well clear of her did he notice that the British man-of-war was now interposed between the *Seafarer* and *Das Rheinland*.

Captain Hamilton at once turned to Jerome. "Mr. Vansittart, all non-combatants must be taken to safer quarters."

The millionaire had expected some such request. "Well," he said, "if I turn my back on the Germans this time it is only that I may have a better look at them afterwards."

The *Seafarer* now made off as fast as her screw could revolve. By the time Von Grudenau reached his own ship she was out of practical range, and the *Hawke* was slowly moving ahead. The frame of the fine cruiser seemed to throb with suppressed excitement. There was almost enough electricity in the bodies of officers and men to polarise her compasses.

The British commander was not mistaken as to the enemy's intent. There was no nonsense about firing preliminary shells as range-finders. Trusting to possible forgetfulness, the first German projectile fairly struck the companion-way near which Vansittart had stood. Iron splinters and shattered woodwork kicked up a rare commotion in the locality, but Hamilton's nice calculation of Von Grudenau's objective was equally successful in averting loss of life or limb among his officers and men.

Thereafter—for two minutes that seemed like hours—the listeners in an oil-lit cabin, near the engine-room, heard a series of violent explosions, erratic snorts of steam, a din of electric bells, and an indescribable rattle of machinery, whilst five times in rapid succession came a clang of battered iron accompanied by a staggering thud.

Then there was silence, vague, terrifying, maddening quietude, when the strained ear listened for the least sound with the agonised intensity of one who mysteriously wakes in the dead of night and strives to penetrate impenetrable gloom by the unaided sense of hearing.

Evelyn clung desperately to her husband. The French maid, huddled up in a corner, sobbed hysterically ; and the three men each confessed afterwards that they expected the top of the cylinder to blow off.

Suddenly the door opened, and Lieutenant Blomfield entered.

" Captain Hamilton wishes you to come on deck," he said. " If Mrs. Vansittart will allow me to hold her arm I will take care of her."

From the calmness of his tone he might have been conducting them to witness a regatta, but Evelyn's arm bore the marks of his grip for days. The people on the *Hawke* had just passed through an extremely sensational and diverting performance. In such moments it is hard to differentiate between the sleeve of a gown and an iron stanchion.

Events soon became intelligible.

The third shell from the *Hawke* had smashed *Das Rheinland's* rudder, and when Captain Hamilton had discovered his opponent's helplessness he ordered the " cease fire."

The *Hawke's* casualties amounted to three men killed and ten wounded, together with some broken plates and wrecked top hamper.

Von Grudenau lost everything, as he was captured in La Manche by a small French squadron, sent out for the purpose of interviewing him and his three consorts.

CHAPTER III

A COUNCIL OF WAR

"WHAT shall I tell the people, sir?" said the representative of the *Figaro* when he met Vansittart on board the *Seafarer* as she swung to her berth in the inner harbour at Havre.

"Tell them," said Jerome, "that France and I conquered the Sahara; surely, then, we are equal to the lesser task set us by Germany."

"May I be informed as to your personal intentions?"

"Only this, that I go direct to Paris to consult with the King. But, Monsieur, a word in your ear. Make much of the help given me by the British warship. Quote it as an earnest of English goodwill to France. This war will not be an affair of moments, and when the stress comes it will be well to have England at our back. Do you understand?"

"Fully, Monsieur. Your wishes are law to every patriotic Frenchman."

"And now," said Vansittart, "let us change *rôles*. What news have you?"

The journalist glanced round nervously to make sure he was not overheard. "Ill, Monsieur! France is unprepared. The newspapers claim victories won for our arms, but each such victory heralds a German advance. I fear the worst, and have abandoned hope. Who can extricate us from this miserable position?"

The journalist forgot his mission in his patriotism. But the millionaire had long ago measured the French character, and knew how to mould it to his will. " I have come from America to make a strong effort, Monsieur. Confidence begets success. Tell France to be confident."

The *Figaro* used the phrase as a headline next day.

Vansittart could, had he chosen, have driven to Paris over the prostrate bodies of his admirers. There was no need to ask the public to trust him. He was their idol. No intelligence, not even the unexpected declaration of war, had created such a thrill of excitement throughout the country as the announcemnt of Jerome's landing. And when the labouring wires bore to every centre of population the full details of his sensational escape in mid-Atlantic, coupled with his first cheerful words of encouragement, excitement passed from fever heat to delirium.

The magnetism of the hour spread to the army. Next day the northern German column sustained a severe check in the vicinity of Verdun. When an apparently impregnable flank was turned by a French brigade, each member of which fought with a vigour and determination that upset the scientific calculations of their opponents, the rallying cry of the fighting line was : " We are sent by the Emperor ! "

The routed Bavarians were sent by the Emperor too: but they had not the same measure of belief in their commander.

Paris wept with joy.

When Vansittart reached the Gare St. Lazare, he found soldiers and populace in imminent danger of conflict. The authorities had detailed thousands of men to line the streets, and three regiments of cavalry to assist the infantry. But the people would not be repressed. They wanted to see, to cheer, to touch their idol, and for a little while their frenzy threatened to end in bloodshed.

Vansittart grasped something of the ferment from the anxiety displayed by the commander of his escort. He settled the question by mounting an officer's charger, and himself leading the cavalcade at a walking pace through the streets. Everybody saw him, everybody cheered him, and all were supremely delighted.

This was one side of the question; the other presented itself when, an hour after, he reached the Tuileries, and joined the King and his principal officers of State in the council chamber. Here gloom took the place of jubilation. With downcast and saddened faces the chief men in France made him cognisant of the bitter truth. They seemed to invite reproach by their words. A neglected army, a depleted navy, deficiency in guns and stores, skeleton divisions and inferior commissariat—these were the rusty weapons they opposed to the burnished panoply of Germany. A plethoric treasury was their worst indictment. Money was being lavished now, but was it not too late?

Only once did Vansittart betray resentment. When he heard of the meagreness in munitions and supplies he said, doubtingly and surprised:

"Can this be possible with Pompier at the head of the department?"

Silence followed this question. The members of the council looked at each other, until the King passionately explained:

"I protested against it, Vansittart, but Court influences were too strong for me. Admiral Pompier was placed on the retired list, the department was split up into naval and military branches, and they are controlled by the Comte de la Feray-Metier and Baron de Champmai, respectively."

"Are these gentlemen at present discharging the same responsible duties?" said Vansittart, with asperity in his tone.

"Yes."

"It is not their fault, probably. Liancourt, will you see to it that Pompier is recalled, by telegram, and given complete control. If he thinks these titled nonentities can help him, let them be retained. If not, they can be provided for elsewhere."

Liancourt smiled. This man, inscrutable to others, was

an open book to Vansittart. It was easy to see that he rejoiced at the end of palace intrigues.

One member of the council was not pleased at this first indication of the millionaire's methods. The fat, pompous, fussy Duc de Tangier, who became Secretary of the Navy because he owned a successful yacht, rose and protested angrily.

"Your Majesty, it is a matter of precedent that in such a serious resolve as that involved by the purposed change the opinion of the responsible authorities should be sought. I, as head of the naval service, protest against Mr. Vansittart's method of dealing with this council, headed as it is by your Majesty in person."

"Who are you?" said Jerome, coolly. He felt assured that he must speedily assert himself, else he would be thwarted constantly by every jack-in-office who had sprung into existence beneath this mushroom monarchy.

"The Duc de Tangier, sir."

"Was it upon your recommendation that Admiral Pompier was removed from the office to which I appointed him?"

"Yes, it was. Let me add, sir, that your words——"

"Are generally obeyed. Monsieur le Duc, I give you the alternative of sitting down with a closed mouth, or being dismissed from your post."

The Duc sat down.

Vansittart continued : "Lest there be any doubt concerning my attitude, I now tell you plainly that in the present desperate state of France there must be one commander-in-chief. If I am to fill that important place I will listen to your counsel, but my orders cannot be questioned. Insubordination here means dismissal ; in the field, death. Are these your terms, or do I return to the United States?"

The King, who had cultivated some degree of tact since he ascended the throne, cried :

"If you leave us, Vansittart, you must take the Queen and me with you. We shall not be wanted in France.

Come, Tangier, cry ' *Peccavi.*' If I am the King, do not forget that Mr. Vansittart is ' the Emperor.' "

The crestfallen Duc apologised, handsomely enough. Thenceforth he was the millionaire's keenest supporter.

"And now, Liancourt," said Jerome, "what is the position ? "

Liancourt unfolded a map. "Ten days ago," he said, "the German Emperor simultaneously threw three army corps across the frontier. Three severe battles have been fought, besides several minor engagements. Although not routed, the French troops have been beaten by superior numbers, by superb concentration, and, particularly, by overwhelming artillery fire.

"The northern German column, commanded by General Kreuznach, occupy the right bank of the Meuse, and have lodged a division across the river at Montfaucon. The centre attack, led by the Emperor in person, is also in possession of the Meuse, Verdun being threatened, and in momentary danger of investment.

"General Daubisson has, however, offered stout resistance on both lines of advance. He was admirably served by the railway companies, and has thus been able to check the enemy's progress much more than they anticipated. Their southern column has, unfortunately, been more successful. It has repelled, almost disastrously, two attacks from Nancy and Épinal, and we fear that the diversion of a large force from Belfort will mean the immediate launching of a fourth army corps collected at Mulhausen."

" Is that all ? "

" No. The worst has yet to be stated. The only efficiently mobilised troops in France are already at the front. The German armies have halted to consolidate and bring up reserves. Here they are vastly superior to us. Supposing that their next forward move be effectual, I fail to see how we can hope to arrest their march on Paris."

" You summarise affairs rapidly," cried the King, with

some bitterness.   He resented this terse version of his own convictions.

" Your Majesty, we may deceive the enemy ; but, as you have said, we cannot deceive ourselves."

" Where is the fleet ? " inquired Jerome.

" Protecting the Gabes Canal, massed in squadrons at Marseilles, Toulon, Brest, and Cherbourg, and patrolling the Channel," broke in the Duc de Tangier.

" And the German fleet ? "

" So far as we know, resting securely behind the guns of Bremerhaven, Hamburg, and Kiel. They cannot hope to match our navy, neglected though it may have been."

Vansittart ignored the momentary sarcasm of the concluding remark.

" Let every available ship be sent from all the points you have named, monsieur, into the North Sea and the Baltic, with orders to do as much damage as possible to German commerce, ports, navy, and fortifications. Cable instructions to commanders of vessels in distant parts of the world to sail for the nearest German colony, and find occupation there. This, I think, had better be put in operation at once."

The Duc rose, but he murmured : " Even a single German cruiser in the Mediterranean can do infinite damage to the Sahara works at Gabes."

" I have not forgotten that possibility," said Jerome, quietly, and the Secretary for the Navy, in his new-born zeal, rushed impetuously from the room to his Admiralty headquarters.

Vansittart took some writing materials and began to draft a memorandum, the others watching him curiously. Without ceasing to write he inquired :

" Is the Secretary for War present ? "

" I am here," replied General Villeneuve.

" Are you well supplied with horses ? "

" On the contrary, I have had difficulty in collecting an

additional forty thousand which have been requisitioned at the front."

" But you have them ? "

" My lists are nearly complete. I intend to begin forwarding them in batches to-morrow."

" As for forage ? "

" Fortunately, we are well found in that solitary respect."

" Good. I want you to collect ten thousand horses, strong and fast, and in good condition, together with a week's supplies for them, and five thousand men, at Sedan, as soon as possible."

" At Sedan ! " broke in several voices in utter astonishment. Sedan is to the north of the present theatre of operations. In any case, it was a place of evil omen to the French mind.

Jerome paused a moment in his writing, pulled the map towards him, scrutinised it for a moment, and exclaimed :

" Yes, it is easily accessible by rail, and is just the right locality."

No one questioned him. General Villeneuve, not wishful to oppose the millionaire, yet ventured on a suggestion:

" We can hardly afford such a large number, monsieur. I pledged my word to General Daubisson that he should have forty thousand within a week."

" He will ! " said Jerome, still writing. " I bought twenty thousand before leaving the States. They will all reach Havre, Brest, or Cherbourg between to-morrow, Sunday, and Tuesday."

A general buzz of subdued comment broke out at the table. The King looked at Vansittart's thoughtful face with something like wonderment in his own. Liancourt's air was ten years younger as he murmured to his nearest neighbour : " The Emperor has not changed, then." General Villeneuve resolved to carry out instructions without comment in future.

Jerome scribbled on industriously.

" Where is Colonel le Breton ? " was his next question.

" He commands the cavalry division with the main army," said Villeneuve.

" Capital ; the right man in the right place. I am sorry that he should have to relinquish his post for a time."

At last he ended his task, and carefully revised the manuscript. The watchful council noted that he appeared to be very particular as to its phraseology. Several times he corrected it, and once sought the assistance of the King as to the exact significance of a French idiom he had used.

When quite satisfied with the production, he folded the document, and handed it to Villeneuve, saying :

" General, I entrust the execution of the task detailed therein to you, Daubisson, and Le Breton. Have accurate copies made for the instruction of both those officers. Your part of the work will make itself clear on perusal, and no one else must be cognisant of its nature. May I be assured of your implicit adherence to my instructions ? "

" What you have ordered will be done," cried the War Minister, in unconscious paraphrase of Arizona Jim's favourite declaration.

He at once quitted the assembly to attend to Vansittart's mysterious mandate.

" There," cried the millionaire with the contentment of one who has finished with a weighty undertaking, " I hope to hear the first news of that piece of work from England."

" From England ! " said Henri, with undisguised amazement.

" Yes. Your Majesty must be aware of old that I thoroughly appreciate the press. The correspondents of the enterprising English journals will, I have no doubt, inform us as to the success or failure of my first personal blow at the German host."

He explained to the council the nature of his intended *coup*, and this will be made clear to the reader in the succeeding chapter.

" I may say in conclusion," he added, " that I was not idle before I sailed from New York. My agents are buying arms, ammunition, horses and equipment, together with some special requirements of my own, at every possible centre in England and America. They are all consigned to a mythical individual named Hiram P. Sloker, of Boston, Massachusetts, but I have no doubt that they will eventually, and very soon, I hope, find their way to various French ports. The authorities must be instructed to look out for them, and the less said about these consignments the better. As I have already remarked, the press can render us great service, but it can do us even greater injury by making our secrets known to the enemy."

" You have brought us new life, my friend," said the King, seizing Vansittart's hand impulsively.

" You have plenty of life," was the cheerful answer, " but you needed rousing a bit. The catastrophe stunned you more by its suddenness than its magnitude. Believe me, France will arise from this supreme trial more powerful, more dignified than before."

" She will be bankrupt in gratitude," cried Liancourt.

" Nay, that is impossible. Of all countries, she pays most dearly for slight services. Now to protect the Sahara."

He wrote a telegram addressed to the British Foreign Secretary: " The exigencies of the campaign compel France to leave the Sahara canals at Gabes unprotected. Your interests, however, demand that they shall not be injured by any hostile power. Full explanations will be given to the British Ambassador in Paris."

" Germany will think many times before she acts once so as to impel Great Britain to actively side with us in this struggle," he explained to those present, and the message was despatched.

When the council dispersed, Jerome sought his private apartments. He missed Evelyn, and in response to his inquiries was told that the Queen, worn out with nursing her ailing child during the harass of recent events, was taking a much-needed rest, whilst his wife was looking after the infant prince ; otherwise Honorine would not have left the boy with his attendants. Jerome smiled when he reflected that even in this troublous time the two mothers would find more to say concerning the youngsters than about affairs of State. As he commenced a letter to Pompier, Arizona Jim entered.

Vansittart laid down his pen for a moment and Bates took the cue.

" There 's bin a big talkee, guv'nor ? "

" Yes, Jim, there has."

" D' you rec'llect, boss, when we started West last trip, as I said that the French could cook bully, and fight well, but were no good at thinkin', so they 'd be sure to want you ag'in ? "

" I remember it quite well."

" An' they *did* want you, I guess ? "

" Jim, when you grow too old for a fight you can set up as a prophet."

" Well, boss, afore I tackle that job I reckon on seein' you knock the stuffin' out of the Emperor William. Lordy, it 'll be more fun nor a box of monkeys."

" He is the biggest opponent I have yet encountered, Jim. He is erratic, believes implicitly in himself, and governs a stiff-necked people. The combination is a difficult one. I shall need a long rest when the job is ended."

About the same hour in the afternoon the German Emperor learned of Vansittart's arrival in France, from the same source that the latter looked to for information, the English newspapers. William II. was too physically exhausted after a protracted reconnaisance at the front to fly into a rage at this reversal of the programme he had arranged. He perused the telegram in silence, and reflected moodily for some moments before he turned to his Chief of Staff.

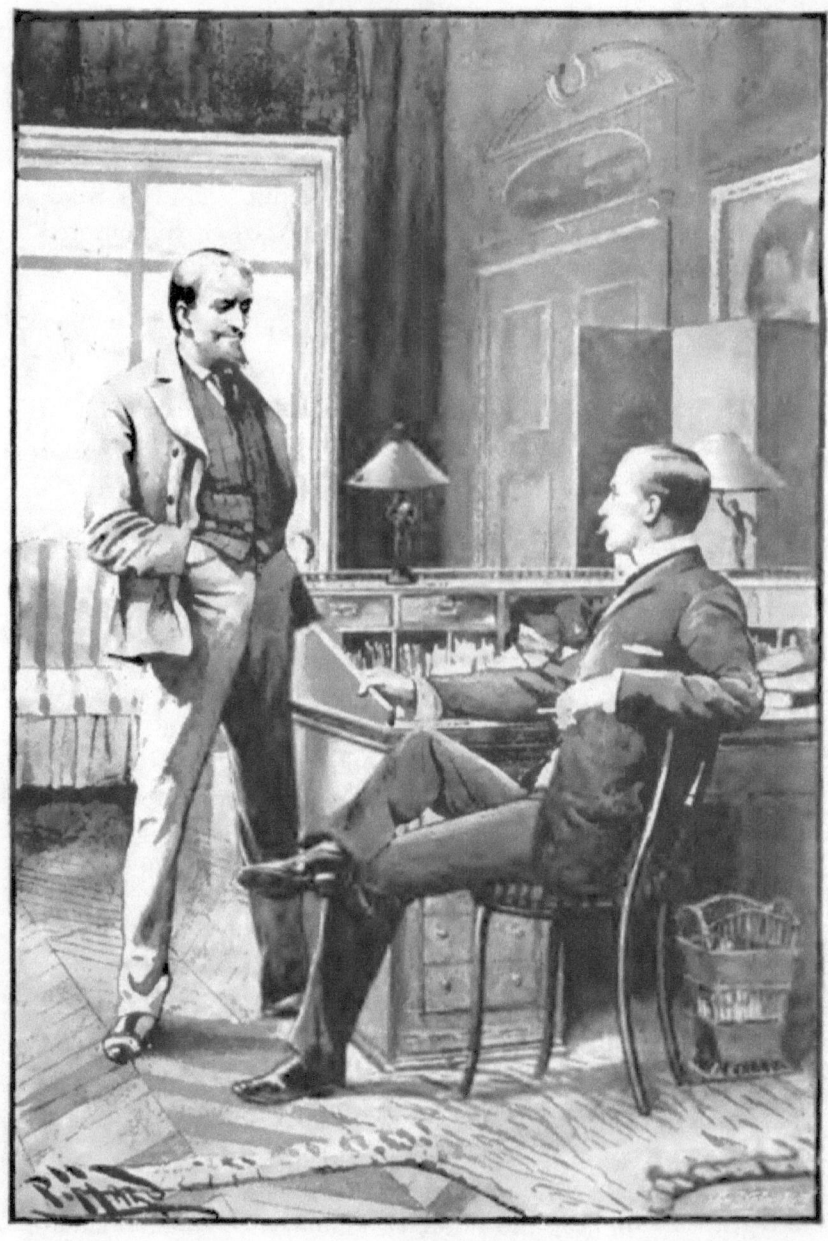

" 'Well, boss, afore I tackle that job I reckon on seein' you knock the
stuffin' out of the Emperor William.' "

" Von Waldersee, we must defeat Daubisson at the earliest opportunity."

" No doubt, sire, but it will not be judicious to cross the Meuse in force until we are reinforced."

" Nonsense ! We must attack immediately. The French have received a much stronger reinforcement than we can hope for, and we risk a great deal by delay."

" How can that be, your Majesty ? "

" That confounded American, Vansittart, has somehow eluded my cruisers, and is now in Paris. His mere presence is worth more than a couple of army corps to France. Attack ! I tell you. Let us get to Paris and then, if he has the resources of the devil, he cannot cope with us."

De Tournon said the same thing when he sought to combat Jerome in his struggle for the throne.

CHAPTER IV

WHEN the history of the War of the Revenge comes to be written, the foremost place in that remarkable work will be assigned to the ride of the five thousand.

Though soon overshadowed by the tumultuous events of the period, it was not until the incidents of the campaign began to assume their relative proportions that the true value of the first thunderbolt launched by Vansittart against the invaders was perceived and fully acknowledged. It was then deemed such an honour to have ridden with Le Breton's famous body of horse that the survivors took stringent measures to secure the accuracy of the heroic list, and the names and identity of every officer and private who accompanied their gallant leader were preserved in the official archives of France. To be a descendant of one of the five thousand was a distinction for a youth and a dowry for a maiden. No similar achievement adorned the annals of their great country.

For a proper understanding of the scope and object of this unprecedented military operation, it is necessary to quote fully the memorandum drawn up with such care by Vansittart during the meeting of the Cabinet.

It was collectively addressed to Generals Villeneuve, Daubisson, and Le Breton (the last-named having attained the rank already), and ran as follows :

It is my intention that a column shall be formed at Sedan forthwith, and dispatched, when fully equipped, for the purpose of cutting into and destroying the German lines of communication.

The column will consist of 5000 selected cavalry soldiers, artillerists, and engineers, and for the purposes of the expedition they will be supplied with two horses per officer and man engaged. The arms carried will be sabres, revolvers, carbines, and a small number of machine guns. The order of priority shows the manner of their use, which must be solely defensive.

No wheeled vehicles, ambulances, tents, or baggage can be taken. The column must, when occasion demands, be able to move at the rate of ten kilometres (seven miles) per hour. Each member of the expedition will carry food and grain for himself and his horses, but squadding arrangements will be made for the conveyance of reserve ammunition, implements, dynamite, and blasting powder.

Anything approaching an engagement with the enemy must be absolutely avoided. Fighting will be the last alternative, but if the only way lies through the hostile lines, then that is the way.

Those who fall die on behalf of France; those who live and perform their duties will have rendered their country the maximum of good service.

The object of the column is destruction. Nothing of value to the enemy must be spared. Railroads, telegraph lines, bridges, rolling-stock, commissariat trains, equipage, and stores of every description —the only exception being hospital appliances—must be wrecked, burned, or blown up.

The total distance to be covered, taking the line of the frontier from Villerupt to Markirch, and allowing for digressions, is, say, 125 miles. I will regard it as an excellent performance, if the column emerges at St. Marie aux Mines (Markirch) within three days.

General Villeneuve will provide horses, stores, and equipment, a highly important item being an abundance of good maps of the frontier. General Daubisson will supervise the selection of officers and men. General le Breton will take command of the column.

I leave to Le Breton complete discretion as to the particular route to be followed, whether in French or German territory. The measure of his success will be the loss and delay inflicted upon the enemy's lines of communication.

I would recommend, however, that he divide his force into five small brigades, that at the first halt he should explain to every officer and man the exact nature of the enterprise and the conditions governing it, that he should start on Wednesday, and that the rapidity of his advance should be governed only by the minimum of time required to destroy permanent works. The resistance offered by the enemy, when unavoidable, should never check the forward movement of the expedition.

In conclusion, I wish General le Breton and his officers and men good fortune. France commits her destinies to their hands, and I am assured they will prove worthy of the trust.

My friends—to our next meeting!

Such was the extraordinary "order of the day" that Le Breton caused to be read out to every company in his little army, when, on the evening of Wednesday, it had halted for an hour almost within sight of the charming village of Longuyon, situated at the confluence of the Crusne and the Chiers, and noteworthy as the junction of two frontier lines of rail. The expedition had gained Montmédy by rail from Sedan, thus saving horses and men a tiresome and useless march of thirty miles. It was risky, this railway trip. Longuyon, eleven miles farther on, was in the hands of the Germans, and a strong column would assuredly be detached from the northern army to attack Montmédy, thus providing security on the right flank of the invaders. Vansittart had foreseen such a move—hence his order to mobilise at Sedan.

But Le Breton judged rightly that time was more important than risk, and he was, above all things, anxious to get to work before any inkling of his approach could be obtained by the Germans. He instructed his brigadiers to give to every man the opportunity of quitting the expedition before it was too late, and to lay particular stress upon the sad necessity there was to abandon all who were so severely wounded as to be unable to ride.

Out of five thousand troopers, only one man, a private of the 18th Chasseurs in the 3rd Brigade, stood out from the ranks when his brigadier invited those who had aught to say to declare themselves. He was a native of Tarascon, a burly and muscular man, who had hitherto been regarded by his comrades as something of a fire-eater. His seeming defection was greeted with a roar of indignation by the 18th.

"Hola, Tartarin," yelled one, "thou seest a lion, then!"

"This is no picnic for a capshooter!" cried another, and the laugh at these allusions to his immortal birthplace converted the common wrath into scorn.

Pierre Laronde turned fiercely on the scoffers.

"I fought with the Emperor in the desert and rode with him to meet the President," he vehemently cried. "Those who are bellowing did neither, I should think."

The credentials were excellent. They procured silence.

"Well, what is it?" said the officer, good-humouredly. He saw that it was no recreant who approached him.

"I ask the honour of a word with the General."

"Hum, 't is contrary to discipline, but this is no time for ceremony. Come with me."

When the pair stood before Le Breton, Laronde was in no wise abashed.

"General, I see a way of doing you some service."

"Out with it, and quickly."

"When I listened to the orders I said to myself, ' Pierre, it is well thought of, but perhaps the General, in attending to many things, may have forgotten one. The Germans are well served by field telegraph, and they must be prevented at the outset from making dispositions to stop our advance by too great force.' Such was my reflection, General."

"Thy reflection is good, soldier. Hast a plan?"

"But yes. I and nine chosen comrades, two of whom can speak German and work a telegraph instrument, will, if you approve, General, try to get through the enemy's pickets at dusk, find the line to Damvillers, the headquarters of General Kreuznach, cut it, connect up again, and tell him that a reconnaissance in force is in progress along the right bank of the Meuse from Montmédy."

"Ha! Kreuznach will think we travel south rather than west?"

"So, General."

"Thy name, soldier?"

"Pierre Laronde."

"Do this, Laronde, and when you next meet me you receive your epaulettes. I like officers who can think."

The man flushed with pleasure; he needed no higher incentive.

At nine o'clock that night a message from the German commander at Longuyon, informing the headquarters staff that all was quiet on the flank, was suddenly interrupted. The operator in Longuyon, finding his instrument useless, reported the fact to his chief, who had also just received the unpleasant intelligence that two sentries had apparently been surprised and killed.

A cavalry cadet came galloping up. "Colonel, a strong body of the enemy's horse is advancing down the hill towards the bridge."

To give colour to this statement, a sputtering of rifle-fire broke out and momentarily grew in volume.

In fifteen minutes Longuyon was cleared of Uhlans and Bavarians, three bridges were destroyed, two railway viaducts blown up, and a working party was busy planting a batch of dynamite cartridges with detonating fuses in a long tunnel that pierced the hills leading to the frontier. To the Germans, confusion and chaos seemed to reign unchecked. Those who kept their senses and were in touch with the fighting, could not fail to notice that a vast body of horse, heedless of the conflict, poured headlong through the village in the direction of Diedenhofen. Meanwhile the defenders of the post were actively hunted in every direction. A troop-train, with several officers and half a battalion of Hanoverians on board, dashed off towards Spincourt, the nearest point by rail to Damvillers, and the main line of German communication; but it plunged into a ravine at a point where Pierre Laronde and his little band had thoughtfully removed a rail.

By midnight an entire division had been put in motion by

General Kreuznach, and was hastening northwards with the utmost speed, as not a word of reply could the staff get to the singular and startling message from Longuyon, which came to hand at 9.10 P.M. They encountered stragglers from the threatened flank, who announced that a French column —a division—an army corps of one hundred thousand men —had occupied Longuyon and was in full pursuit. Thereupon the commander of the relief thought it his duty to halt until daylight. He did so, marched cautiously to Longuyon, and found only the evidences of the preceding night's disaster.

At ten o'clock a dull explosion, followed by a violent earth tremor, meant that two months' hard work would scarce suffice to make the railway tunnel serviceable again, and Pierre Laronde and his comrades thought it high time to catch some riderless horses and ride fast after the main body.

Le Breton's method of advance was admirable. Every time that a bridge had to be destroyed, or a section of the parallel railway dismantled, a small party halted and began their preparations, whilst the remainder of the force pressed on through the darkness. When all had passed, the dynamite did its work, and the wreckers rode off to become the rearguard in their turn. It was like some grotesque war-dance, repeating the figures of Sir Roger de Coverley on a gigantic scale, with the clatter of horses' feet for movement, and the thunder of powerful explosives for music.

Sixteen miles from Longuyon, the head of the expedition reached Audun-le-Roman, the erstwhile French frontier custom-house. Here a small infantry guard was cut up, and two customs officers, captured in the first surprise of the invasion, set at liberty, and told to escape as best they might. Half an hour more and the sound of firing in front, instantaneously drowned in a wild outburst of cheering, proclaimed the fact to villagers, startled from their sleep, that for the first time in a generation an armed force of Frenchmen had set foot upon the soil of Lorraine. This was at Fontoy, or

Fentsch, as the Germans have re-christened it, and here Le Breton received a severe check, wholly unpremeditated on both sides.

The leading troopers cantered round a bend into the village street, and found themselves in the midst of a swarm of soldiers, infantry and artillery, being the nucleus of a division now being hastily formed in order to reinforce the main army on the Meuse. The hasty resolve of the Kaiser Wilhelm to penetrate into France, at all costs, was in process of realisation at that moment. After the first gasp of amazement, the stolid Teutons recovered themselves, and a fierce affray at once sprang up, growing instantly in volume as combatants from both sides packed into the narrow street. Here, of course, the well-drilled infantry had the advantage. In another minute volley-firing would have determined the *mêlée*, when Le Breton, who rode ever close to the advance guard, arrived. A single glance revealed the situation to him. He saw that his leading squadron must be sacrificed if he would save the rest. Spurring his horse into a furious gallop, he rode back and halted the first brigade. Reaching a cross-road, he halted the second, and planted four machine guns here, simultaneously retiring the first brigade southwards to the right. The remainder followed, but the movement had barely started when the remnant of the advance guard fell back, closely pursued by some mounted German gunners, with a mass of infantry pressing on behind.

But Le Breton's turn had come. The great advantage of the machine gun is that its fire is as destructive by night as by day, once the position of the enemy is clearly defined. In this case, all that was needed was to align the guns along a comparatively level road and blaze away, the four pouring an absolute torrent of lead into the mixed German force. Nothing could live against it. The pursuers, unable to retreat with sufficient rapidity, owing to the crowding and confusion behind, suffered frightfully. Hundreds of men fell in that slaughter-house, and those who sought to escape into

" A fierce affray at once sprang up, growing instantly in volume as combatants from both sides packed into the narrow street."

the fields were ruthlessly cut down by French cavalry posted there to prevent at all hazards a flank attack on the new line of advance.

It must be remembered that the German officers were wholly ignorant of the true position, and consequently unable to make better dispositions for assaulting this marvellous foe who had sprung from nowhere. And he disappeared as promptly as he had arrived, leaving murderous tokens of his visit in the human shambles just beyond the village, whilst a series of explosions in the distance told the listeners that every time the road crossed a stream the bridge was destroyed.

Two miles from Fontoy, Le Breton ordered a much-needed halt. It was now one o'clock. There was no immediate fear of pursuit or efficiently organised resistance, though the German staff at Damvillers and Thionville, Metz and Mars la Tour, were frenzied with annoyance at their inability to discover exactly what was going on. Orderlies raced about on horseback, field telegraphs clicked incessantly, even the Emperor at Fresnes was waked out of a sound sleep—but in vain. The incomparable German system of intelligence, which could have discovered a stray horse at any point over their fifty miles of front, was powerless to locate Le Breton and his little host, for the simple reason that he was now many miles in rear of the main body, and had already much disarranged the whole of the northerly communications. Until daybreak he was comparatively safe. Horses were picketed, some food hastily eaten, and the whole force composed itself for four hours' sleep. Beyond ascertaining that his total losses so far amounted to sixty-seven men and three officers killed and wounded, with some hundred odd horses lost, he had no fresh anxieties to deal with. His route was cut and dried and every detail settled in consultation with his officers. Events must be dealt with as they arrived ; they could not be anticipated.

" So far," growled Le Breton, as he composed himself to

rest with his saddle flap for a pillow, " I don't think Vansittart himself could have done better."

The first beams of light found the little force making its
toilette after a fashion described by the regimental wag of
the 18th as *à la mode chien*. A hearty shake and a vigorous
stretch, followed by a breakfast of tinned beef, biscuit, and
a drink of wine from the stock of a local cabaret, formed the
preliminary to an eventful day.

Whilst all hands were busy saddling up, the General called
to him the second in command, Colonel Montsaloy, a slight,
active cavalry officer, whose cheek-bones, chin, shoulders,
and elbows were all based on a well-known proposition of
Euclid affecting the properties of a right angle.

" Montsaloy," he said, " give me your map."

The other produced his military chart, and Le Breton
traced a line on it. " I have been thinking out the situation
during the last half-hour," he said, " and have decided on
an important alteration. My original intention was, as you
know, to pass southwards behind Metz, leaving it on my
right. That holds good, but if we want to avoid the certainty of being cut to pieces before the evening we must
create a diversion. They will look for us at first between
Metz and the frontier. Well, they must find you and a
brigade there."

" I understand you fully, General."

" Good. You will proceed by way of Briey, Conflans,
Mars-la-Tour, and Verny to Dieuze. If you can get there
by five o'clock I will meet you. If you cannot, well, *au
revoir !* "

Colonel Montsaloy saluted, mounted, and cantered off to
put his column in motion. A few minutes later, the dimin-
ished main body followed, but deviated to the left and quickly
gained the high road to Metz. Here they fell in with some
scouting Uhlans, riding furiously towards Diedenhofen to
discover the cause of the complete breakdown in the telegraph to that important centre. None of these gentry

escaped, else within an hour every cavalry soldier in Metz would have been in hot chase of the venturesome quarry.

Le Breton's advance now lay across country to Les Étangs, and thence to the rendezvous at Dieuze through Courcelles, Fouligny, and Foulquemont. The reader who follows the course of events on a good map of Lorraine will quickly see the General's object in splitting the force. Should the junction by any chance be effected, the two sections would have done enormous damage to no less than thirteen lines of strategic railways and twenty-four main roads. Nearly the whole of these were constructed for the sole purpose of conveying troops and war material to the frontier. It would be a phenomenal achievement to render this important section of the German communications wholly useless for a time and very inadequate for a much longer period, as even German military engineers require many days, perhaps weeks, to effectively bridge ruined viaducts, repair torn embankments, and re-lay uprooted rails. Metz, too, would be completely isolated, and this in itself was a magnificent result, the great fortress being a veritable storehouse of munitions of war.

Whilst the two columns went on with their work of devastation, the entire German host, spread over a superficial area of nearly two thousand miles, was in an uproar. The German staff was called upon to deal with, not war, but rampant lunacy. Somewhere in their midst a number of madmen, estimated variously from a regiment to an army corps, were raging about with antics similar to the struggles of a bluebottle in a spider's web. The speed of their movement, the astounding effect of their passage, the conflicting reports as to their location at any particular time, were well calculated to upset the theorists bred in the school of the last war with France.

There had been fighting in many places, that was clear. But effectual pursuit was a different matter. Infantry was useless, and neither cavalry nor guns could hope to travel rapidly along a road once Le Breton or Montsaloy had passed that way. Nevertheless, as the day wore, something akin to definiteness took the place of the frenzied statements of the night and early morning. The object of the raiders was now clear enough. Not lunacy, but superb military genius, had dictated this deadly blow at the German organisation. The authorities at Forbach and Sarrebourg hastily concerted measures to defend every important railway junction between those centres, and when General le Breton halted his troopers at two o'clock on the arid, salt-laden plain between Chateau Salins and Dieuze, the presence of numerous vedettes on the horizon warned him that his next forward step would be severely contested.

The French general was not mistaken. The salt mines at the latter town were crammed with German infantry. But they opened fire at a long range. This helped him a little, as he took ground to the right, only to find the railway line to Nancy swarming with men. At the range his machine guns were useless, and to give the necessary dramatic touch to the situation, three regiments of cavalry with six guns trotted into view right ahead, the artillery promptly trying his metal with shrapnel.

With tired men and exhausted horses, Le Breton knew that he was in a tight fix. In fact he afterwards admitted that he was quite certain his enterprise had there and then come to an untimely end. But if he despaired he did not hesitate. Riding to the head of his column he pointed with his sabre to the enemy's cavalry, and shouted :

" There lies our road, my children," and his wearied troopers made a brave effort to follow him. For the purposes of a charge they did not number two thousand, as the led horses, otherwise so useful, were now an embarrassment, and half of his men were guiding three animals apiece in the rear.

The frightful dust, too, rising from the saline plain, added to the general discomfort. In a word, everyone expected that the foray had collapsed. The German guns were on the enemy's left, which rested on some broken ground. By rare good luck for the French, the artillerists, reserve men hurrying to the front, were new to their work, and their practice was bad.

Just as the German cavalry were breaking into a gallop to meet the onset, a fearful commotion broke out on their left. Montsaloy had turned up, in the nick of time, and was now sabring the gunners and taking the horse in flank. The unequal odds of the combat swung round with a vengeance. In place of Germans carving Frenchmen it was a case of precipitate flight to avoid being carved in their turn. What puzzled Le Breton most, even in the midst of the *mêlée*, was the manner in which Montsaloy's brigade rode from out the defile. Their chargers lay to it as though taking part in a field day at Versailles. But Montsaloy soon explained :

" I came upon six trainloads of remounts on the line between here and Vic," he shouted. " I boxed them in between two broken culverts, helped myself, left a small guard, and the remainder are waiting for you."

CHAPTER V

SUCCESS is a wonderful tonic for fatigue. This wholly unexpected escape from threatened annihilation raised the spirits and dispelled the weariness of every man in the expedition.

Montsaloy's lucky find of German cavalry horses enabled the troops to replace more than half of their own wearied animals, which, by the ruthless law of war, they were compelled to shoot.

Another desperate effort enabled them, as evening fell, to gain the shelter of a defile in the Vosges Mountains. So tired were many of the troopers that they slept as they rode, and at the earliest possible moment Le Breton halted to enable them to recuperate somewhat.

Towards midnight the unpleasant inquisitiveness of the enemy's cavalry scouts forced the French commander to once more rouse his worn-out followers. For two hours they jogged steadily onward through rocky valleys shrouded in gloom by the frowning heights. Then Le Breton decided that, come what might, his men and horses should have a thorough rest, else they would be absolutely unfitted for the stern work of the following day.

The Germans, of course, were now on the alert throughout the whole of their southern lines of connection. The Emperor sent bitter and scathing telegrams to the generals of the division at Forbach and Sarrebourg, for having allowed the quarry to slip through their hands, and the latter unfortunate officer was summarily degraded in rank.

The headquarters staff felt certain, from the latest details to hand, that the French marauders would endeavour to regain the shelter of their comrades' entrenched camp at Lunéville ; imperative orders were in consequence given for a powerful force to gather in the neighbourhood of Avricourt and Blamont, in order to cut them up when they appeared. And cut up they assuredly must have been, had they tried to force this passage at any time after daybreak on Friday morning. Every hilltop was lined with scouts, every road and possible outlet crowned with furious German troops, longing for the opportunity of revenging the insults heaped upon their arms and the frightful havoc done to their communications by this intrepid body of horse. Hour after hour the Germans waited, eagerly scouring the eastern horizon for the first signs of their approaching enemies. At last they were roused into frenzied activity. The enemy had indeed arrived, but from a wholly unexpected quarter.

General Daubisson, in person, leading a strong reconnaissance of cavalry and horse artillery from Lunéville, was now forcing a passage through the new rear of the German invaders. Of this more anon.

At nine o'clock on a bright May morning, Le Breton and his brigadiers rode along the ranks of their gallant followers, addressing words of encouragement and good cheer to the men. The General had resolved upon the execution of one last bold *coup* before the final dash was made for liberty and France. There, five miles away, on the other side of the Schirmeck Pass, lay the little town of Mutzig, a great depot and manufactory of small-arms and ammunition ; but now, he learnt from the peasants, denuded of defenders save some hundreds of busily occupied workmen, most of whom were secretly enthusiastic Alsatians. Fifteen miles farther east, the Rhine flowed between vine-clad cliffs, and in the intervening country were the main line of railway between Strasburg and Colmar, two branch lines, the Rhine canal, and two main roads north and south. To ruin Mutzig and its stores, and destroy the thoroughfares by rail, road, and water, would indeed provide a glorious finale to the most remarkable achievement ever yet carried through by so small a force in a country held by such armies as owned the sway of the Kaiser.

Le Breton made no secret of his desperate enterprise, and his men applauded him as he told what he wanted them to do. After all they had already accomplished under his guidance, they would have followed him in an attack upon Metz itself.

The column had crossed the top of the pass when the rearguard saw through their glasses a solitary horseman spurring furiously after them. He was hatless, dressed in civilian attire, and obviously alone. They waited in silence until he drew near. When they halted him, he explained, with an unmistakable British accent, that he was one of the war correspondents of the *Times*, and asked to be brought before the General.

This newcomer was in strange plight. His clothes were torn and shot through in several places. Along his right cheek a bullet had torn a slight furrow, which had, nevertheless, bled profusely, and rendered him a sorry object. His horse, a fine hunter, was in the last stage of exhaustion, and barely able to support himself by propping out his forelegs when the mysterious rider dismounted. The man, too, though strongly built and hard-looking, was clearly suffering from hunger and fatigue. Yet his manner was perfectly calm, and the French soldiers marvelled whence or how he had reached them, whilst they noted, with silent approbation, that his first thought was for his horse, in whose behalf he obtained a pail of water and some food. The officer he addressed did not know how to deal with this apparition, so he promptly acceded to his request, and took him to the General.

" Whom have we here ? " was Le Breton's first question.

The Englishman produced his official pass, signed by

Villeneuve and Daubisson, setting forth that he was Mr. Herbert Fairfax, war correspondent of the *Times*, and fully accredited to accompany the French armies in the field.

"But how is this?" cried the astounded General. "Whence come you?"

"From Lunéville. I left, last night, in advance of General Daubisson's column."

"Column! What column, monsieur?"

"A cavalry reconnaissance in force, which, by this time, is breaking through the German front at St. Dié."

"With what object?"

"In order to ascertain your whereabouts, and assist you if possible."

"*Diable!* 'T is well. Yet how could Daubisson guess my position so accurately?"

"It was hardly a guess. Mr. Vansittart, informed from England and Belgium of your progress, estimated that you would be in this neighbourhood to-day, and probably hard pressed, so he asked the Commander-in-chief to try and help you."

"Monsieur, you bring good news. Nevertheless I am at a loss to know by what means you have reached me."

"Oh, I just started, and here I am."

"By Saint Denis, I see you, but my brains do not travel so quickly as my eyes. Here you are, indeed! How did you get here? Why did not the Germans stop you?"

"They tried all they knew," said Fairfax, indicating with a smile his scarred face and torn clothes. "But it is difficult to shoot straight at night, and I was better mounted than the Uhlans. I regret the necessity that compelled me to bore holes in three of them."

"Monsieur," cried Le Breton, "you are an Englishman! Let it suffice! Enough for me that you are a brave man. I welcome you. Yet must I add that you have joined us at a ticklish moment."

"I wanted something to write about," laughed the other,

" and, if all I hear be true, you are providing first-rate ' copy.' But before we proceed, General, may I suggest that a few trustworthy men, hiding among the hills, may fall in with General Daubisson, and give him definite news of your intentions ? "

The hint was acted upon with excellent effect. Mutzig was attacked at 11.30 A.M. The small body of defenders were taken by surprise, but they were able to close the gates and line the ancient fortifications on the threatened side. A vigorous use of the machine guns and carbines of dismounted troopers soon settled this effort at resistance. The sappers crossed the trench and tore the ironwork of the gate into pieces with dynamite, whereupon the Germans surrendered at discretion. Whilst this busy work was in progress, Colonel Montsaloy and his brigade again struck off across the country on a four miles' ride to Obernat, where a railway and a main road intersected each other.

In Mutsig the Frenchmen speedily dismantled the small-arms factory. The terrified townspeople, unable to escape into the country, and fearful of the destruction now being wreaked upon a colossal scale, remained in their houses, furtively peeping from their windows at the unwonted spectacle provided by French soldiers riding through their streets. The last time Frenchmen swaggered about Mutzig in uniform, the arsenal of to-day was the palace of a bishop.

Le Breton did not forget to station cavalry vedettes on all the approaches to the town. Nothing of moment occurred until two o'clock. At that hour a chasseur came riding hard to report that a troop-train was discharging an infantry regiment on the farther side of a gorge about a mile distant, where the junction line from Strasburg and Saverne crossed a turbulent stream. The viaduct had been blown up long before ; and the French officer in charge of the outpost had sent him to give the earliest warning of this hostile move. Another scout, and yet another, arrived, breathless with the news that train after train, obviously sent from Strasburg, were bringing more infantry, with horses and guns, that the German skirmishers had crossed the torrent, driving the French vedettes before them, and that a temporary bridge was in process of construction from the ruins of the viaduct for the passage of guns and horses.

It was possible at this moment for Le Breton to retreat towards Vosges, with the hope of falling in with Daubisson's relief expedition. But he had promised Montsaloy to wait for him until four o'clock. It was now 2.30. In an hour and forty minutes Mutzig would be surrounded by fresh and infuriated opponents. This, then, was the close of the brilliant raid ! That night he and his gallant comrades must be killed in battle or shot in squads afterwards. He knew well that quarter would not be given to a solitary officer or man once the Germans had them in their power. It was hard to be caught like a rat in a trap at the precise instant when there did seem to be some chance of escape.

There, towards the west, lay the unoccupied road across the Vosges to Lunéville, but not a sign from the east of Montsaloy's return. Le Breton summarised the maddening situation in a few words of emphatic colloquial French, and set himself to examining his defences. Unfortunately his zealous men had already destroyed every piece of modern ordnance, with all the ammunition, in the town. Soon a German battery, undeterred by a steady long-range fire from the walls, was laboriously hauled into position on a cliff barely three quarters of a mile distant, and the eager gunners hardly gave themselves time to align one twelve-pounder before a shell screamed through the air and struck a house in the little market-place, sending fragments of brick and mortar in all directions.

" You had better have remained with Daubisson," said Le Breton grimly to Fairfax, who was recuperating from his fatigue by sitting on an empty packing-box and smoking.

" Not I," was the cheery reply. " These chaps are afraid of you. Instead of trying to rush the place forthwith, they will proceed by set rule. And every minute they hesitate is probably worth a year's life to you."

" And you also, monsieur."

" Oh, no ; I 'm safe enough. This is too big a thing for the *Times* to miss it. I *must* get through somehow."

" I like your spirit, my friend," said the General. " But, pray, make no mistake. These Germans will spare no one attached to this party."

" General," said the other, lighting a fresh cigar, " I mean to leave Mutzig to-night with an escort of French sabres."

Fairfax was undoubtedly sanguine. Mutzig was at that moment undergoing a hailstorm of lead. Bullets swept through the streets from the neighbouring heights, and a couple of shells from the battery having smashed the defences of the northern gate, the gunners were adding to the fusillade by salvoes of shrapnell.

Le Breton's orders to his men were to seek all possible shelter and confine themselves to strictly defensive tactics, so the casualty list was not large. At last the inadequacy of the reply from the town encouraged the attackers, who were momentarily increasing in strength, to attempt a rush at the dismantled gate. But if the Frenchmen were caged, their claws were still sharp. The machine guns, drawn up at an effective angle, quickly cleared the gate and its approaches, and the Bavarian regiment that had essayed the charge left sufficient killed and wounded on their path to form two companies when they retired.

This sharp repulse showed the Germans that the assault would not be the easy matter they had assumed. A change of tactics was necessary. The town must be completely surrounded, and a plunging fire from all sides would rapidly render it untenable. Another battery arrived and started at a gallop to a point which commanded the south. The guns were unlimbered, and their first batch of shells hurtled through the streets before a burst of cheers from the defenders on that side made known to their comrades the

welcome fact that this new enemy had been somewhat disconcerted.

Whilst the German gunners were busy correcting the ad-
justment of their cannon, Colonel Montsaloy's brigade suddenly appeared over the crest of the hill, and in a few strides
the leading squadron was in the midst of the battery. No
cavalry escort had been provided or thought necessary by
the Germans, so the affair was over with the speed of a summer squall. The six guns and their attendants were literally
ridden down. A German infantry battalion, perceiving the
disaster, changed front in order to return the compliment to
the French cavalry, but Le Breton, heedless of the northern
artillery, ran his machine guns out into the open, and gave
the deploying infantry other occupation than emptying
saddles at five hundred yards.

In five minutes Montsaloy and the survivors of the brigade
—they had met with some trouble before they finally blew
up a lock in the canal—entered Mutzig. This temporary
success elated the troops, yet the most sanguine amongst
them knew full well that there was no chance of being extricated. All they could do was to sell their lives dearly.
Some hours of daylight were still at the service of the Germans. Le Breton had no plan and no hope. His only
slight glimpse of possible escape lay in a desperate dash for
the frontier when darkness fell, if he could hold out so long
—a more than doubtful postulate.

The German fire became fiercer and more effective. The
wretched inhabitants of the town suffered even more than
the soldiers. Shell after shell burst among the houses and
set them on fire, the flames driving forth those who had
escaped from the projectiles to encounter greater risk from
the bullets that flew in all directions. Wounded horses
screamed with pain and fright. The number of burning
houses increased at such a rate that all Mutzig seemed to be
enveloped in smoke and sparks. The still air became op-
pressively hot, and people fainted from sheer exhaustion

and despair. Through this pandemonium dazed men and shrieking women and children raced about wildly, seeking for some nook secure from the leaden showers, or collapsed, speechless and horror-stricken, where they chanced to fall. Truly, war may be a game for Emperors, but it is worse than a pestilence for those unfortunates who are forced to suffer its terrible realities.

Many thousands of German infantry had now reached the locality from Strasburg, and a determined attack was made upon the two available gates, whilst fresh artillery took the place of the destroyed battery. Even Fairfax was beginning to think that the *Times* would miss its most enterprising " special," when a sharp rattle of musketry and the deeper boom of cannon on the west caused the hearts of the defending force to beat with tremulous anticipation. Was it only a development of the German assault, or could it be that Daubisson—Uncertainty soon yielded to conviction. French guns were engaging the nearest German battery, dismounted French cavalry were driving back the wings of the German infantry so unexpectedly taken in flank, and French horsemen were massing in squadrons preparatory to a superb charge through the entire length of the German position on the north.

Le Breton's eyes were aflame as he roared the necessary orders to his officers. There was no time to wait for regularity or precision. Every man who could ride caught the nearest horse and slung a wounded comrade up behind him. Rabble-like, but methodically enough for their purpose, the troopers poured out of the town towards the relieving force. In five minutes Le Breton was shaking hands with Daubisson, and Fairfax was biting the end off another cigar with the equable serenity of the man who is able to say, " I told you so."

Ten minutes later the French reconnaissance column was in full retreat towards the Vosges, not forgetting to blow up every bridge they crossed in the march. The last sight of blazing Mutzig enjoyed by Le Breton and his comrades was from a hillside where the road enters the Schirmeck Pass, whence they could clearly see that their erstwhile assailants had found fresh occupation as amateur firemen.

When asked afterwards to narrate the most trying experience of the whole sensational escapade, every man who took part in the expedition said that his worst memories clustered round the misery of that final march to the frontier. Such fighting as took place—and there were hard knocks given and taken before Daubisson reached Lunéville again—did not affect the survivors of the raid. Utterly spent with the labours and excitement of the past sixty hours, too exhausted to eat, too weary to even speak, they jogged on through the night, and the strenuous efforts of their comrades were needed to keep more than half of them from lying down by the roadside. Whenever a halt was necessary it was with difficulty the men were started again. Curiously enough, the worst sufferers were those who retained their vitality to the last.

Le Breton and his Five Thousand—now, alas, little more than three !—had ridden nearly one hundred and thirty miles in sixty hours through a hostile country swarming with foes. They had fought several severe battles ; they had worked like navvies in their task of destruction ; they had slept little and eaten less. But the blow they struck at the German arms was incalculably severe. Its influence was felt throughout the war long after the merely outward signs were effaced by German enterprise and persistence. Above all else it gave Vansittart the one great essential he lacked in pitting his brains and his money against the German Emperor. Time alone, to his view, was what he required—time to recuperate the exhausted energies of France, to arouse her dormant strength. And this much-needed respite he had obtained, for though the Kaiser might bawl " To Paris ! " as loudly as he chose, his splendid army corps dared not to cross the Meuse until their shattered base was perfected again.

CHAPTER VI

THE DEAD BODY

THOSE two words, " To Paris," became, with every hour that fled, more and more a fixed idea, a spur, a mania, in the mind of Wilhelm. The delay caused by the havoc of Le Breton's ride added to his fever a touch of delirium. He desired to fly, and found it impossible to walk. He was like a man who in the night has a dream of wings and wakes in the morning with gout in his legs. Vansittart also experienced the magnetic power of the phrase. Wilhelm's dream was the American's nightmare. He dreaded the influence of every forward step of the enemy upon the volatile mind of the French nation, so prone to despair as well as to hope. " To Paris ! " cried Wilhelm when he found himself alone, with gesticulations and out-stretched right arm. " Anything but Paris ! " groaned Vansittart, turning on his bed in nightlong sleeplessness.

The splendid success of Le Breton's ride gave the million-aire a little relaxation from his agonies of unrest ; for the present, at least, Wilhelm had his work cut out, not before, but behind, him. But Vansittart's breathing-space was short. The frantic energies with which the Germans threw themselves into the task of repairing their shattered bases warned him that what he did he must do quickly. And what he had to do was this : he had to gain one great fixed battle over one or other of the German armies under circum-stances dramatic, striking, and calculated to appeal to the French imagination. It was because he had appealed chiefly to the imagination that Napoleon had been Napoleon ; he had been artist or dramatist first, and general after. From one such victory *per se*, Vansittart looked for little practical result ; but he knew well that to a nation like the French defeat at the outset meant ruin ; that success at the outset meant invincibility. And in order that the victory might be striking and dramatic, he himself must be there with the army, commanding it—he, Vansittart. Paris was no place for him. His eagerness to set out became in a few days a fever with him.

But he could not go. First of all, there was a whole world of business, a whole cosmos of organisation, which his tired brain had to arrange before he could dream of leaving the capital. Secondly, by some perfectly organised and determined hostile agency, the chief railway lines east of Paris were temporarily ruined by viaducts and bridges being blown up, notwithstanding the most elaborate precautions on behalf of the companies after the first outrage occurred. Thirdly, just as he was on the point of leaving affairs to take care of themselves in order to reach the front by a circuitous route, the body of an unknown man was found floating, all bloated and disfigured, in the Seine.

What had this water-soaked corpse to do with the millionaire, with the destinies of France ? Archimedes offered to lift the world, if someone would only provide him with a fulcrum. Fate is the fulcrum by means of which the small affairs and selfishnesses of individuals affect the general history of Man. Had the man been murdered, or was it a suicide ? That became the question. Not the *general* question, for one thought, and only one, filled the mind of the population of Paris—the War, namely, and how Vansittart and Wilhelm would severally acquit themselves therein. But the question of murder or suicide occupied for days the brain of at least one man—of Folliet, the Prefect of Police. The body was found at nine o'clock on a Tuesday morning. The same night Folliet was closeted with a detective in one of the small inner rooms of the Prefecture. His sharp,

angular features were bent in eager inquisitiveness close to
the face of his subordinate.

" Murder ? " he said.

" Oh, I suppose that 's about it," answered the other.

" No marks ? no wounds ? "

" None.   And the funny thing is the Arrondissement
doctor says the man does n't look to him as if death was
due to drowning."

" Poison, then ? "

" No—no poison, that 's certain."

" *What* was he ? "

" He looks to *me* like a German ; you know, those bullet-
headed Germans with the back of the skull all flat like a
board."

" *Where* is he ? "

" At the Morgue at present.   You can see him, if you
like."

" I will see him.   Nothing found on him ? "

" Only a little piece of wet cardboard in his pocket,
marked in red ink with a big 6.   It may be a 6 or it may
be a 9, for that matter."

" Sure he 's a German ? "

" I should say so.   Fair hair too."

" Look here, there is more in this thing than you think.
No clue at all ? ".

" I don't think it 's a clue, but there 's a German, a man
named Bach, lately disappeared."

" Ah, tell me about it ! "

" He was a lager-beer seller.   No. 1, Rue Musette.   His
description tallies very well with the body found, and at first
I felt pretty sure that they would turn out to be the same.
But so far, it does n't look as if they were."

" How so ? "

" This morning a girl came to give notice that Bach had
disappeared.   Bach 's a widower and the girl 's his sweetheart.   A little before that the body had been found, and

we took the girl to see it. She said it was n't Bach, though it was like him.''

Folliet smiled.

'' How long since Bach disappeared ? ''

'' Since Friday night.''

'' So that the body has been four days in the water, if it 's Bach ? ''

'' Yes.''

'' And very much swollen ? ''

'' Oh, yes.''

'' And the girl was frightened ? ''

'' Shuddering.''

'' Well, then, I suppose a man of your experience knows what this evidence is worth. Ten to one she only glanced at the thing, and saw a very different Bach from the one she remembers. Yet she says the body was ' like him.' ''

'' That 's so, sir. But I must point out that the girl also said that Bach never dressed like that. The clothes were wrong.''

'' Ah ! The corpse's clothes were peculiar, then ? ''

'' No, not that I could see. But his hat was a little peculiar.''

'' Then it was this hat the girl meant. In glancing in disgust at the bloated face, she caught sight of the hat. That 's it. Tell me about the hat.''

'' It was a cap with a glazed peak, turned down. It was found floating near him. Stuck between the ribbon and the side of the cap was a feather.''

'' So ? What sort of a feather ? ''

'' A fowl's, I should say, or—or—a pigeon's.''

'' What makes you think of a pigeon ? ''

'' The feather is glossy like, and has hues on it like a pigeon's.''

'' I see. Let us say a pigeon's, then. And Bach never wore a cap with a pigeon's feather stuck in it, did n't he ? But tell me about Bach all the same : he interests me. Did anything happen just before he disappeared ? ''

" No, it seems not. At seven on Friday evening the girl was with him in the parlour behind the shop. He did n't seem, she says, quite at ease—a little fidgety, perhaps—rather a nervous kind of man, she says Bach is—he kept glancing at the clock. At last he jumped up suddenly, and said he was sorry, but she must leave him that night, as he had an appointment which he must keep. So she went; and Bach has not since been seen."

" He shut up his shop to go, then ? "

" So it seems. He lived alone on the premises. It 's one of those tiny liquor shops up Montmartre way."

" It must have been a deuced important appointment this of Bach's, Carot ! " said Folliet.

" So it seems, sir."

" And in order to keep it he found it necessary to put on a cap with a pigeon's feather, eh ? "

" Yes, if Bach and the corpse are the same."

" They *are*, man. Can't you see ? If a man disappears mysteriously, and a body is found in the river, the *primâ facie* presumption is that the body belongs to the man. But how if the man and the body happen to be both German in a non-German city ? And how if the body, though bloated and disfigured, still remains something like the man ? Then the presumption gets pretty near to certainty, I think. I am surprised at you, Carot."

" No doubt you are right, sir," said Carot. " The doctor says the body has been in the water three or four days, and that is another coincidence which tallies with the time of Bach's disappearance."

" Very good. And about the girl—have you found out anything about her ? "

" Not yet."

" What 's her name ? "

" Agnès Carhaix."

" Where does she live ? "

" Rue Pigalle, No. 11."

" Good. You are to understand, Carot, that this case is now in my own hands. Come along with me. I am going to have a look at Herr Bach."

They went out together, down by the river-side, and at the Place de la Concorde stepped into an eastward-plying steamer. Near those big bathing-houses, called " Samariaine," in the neighbourhood of the Pont Neuf, Carot pointed.

" There," he said, " is the spot where the body was found —just there east of the *bain*, almost touching it."

" But the wonder is," said Folliet, " that a man getting drowned in this frequented part of the river remained unnoticed so long. The body must have been at the bottom some days, and then floated."

" I suppose that 's it, sir."

" Well, and what does that prove to you ? "

" I don't know what you would be getting at, sir."

" Well, it proves this, Carot : that the man was alive when he touched the water. A dead body thrown into a river floats, you know, if it is not weighted. A living body takes water into the stomach and sinks. If this man sank, he was living at the moment he reached the river, that 's clear."

" Which makes it rather look as if it was a suicide, sir," said Carot.

" H'm," answered Folliet, " if *you* never heard of a living man being thrown into a river without his consent, *I* have."

They came to the bridge, landed, and crossed to the island of the Cité ; then past Notre Dame, to where the little, low shed, which is the Morgue, stands gloomily facing the public street. In the centre of four other bodies, lying on raised slabs behind the air-tight glass partition, lay the man they had come to see. Folliet leant his forehead against the glass watching the horrid, still face, with musing eyes.

" Well, M. Bach," he said after ten minutes, " you are keeping your secret pretty close now, I think ; but I shall find it all the same, my man." Then to Carot : " Where 's the cap, and the ticket with the 6 or 9 ? "

" They are behind," said Carot ; " we took off the cap after the attempt at identification."

" Very well, let us have a look at them."

They proceeded at once into a room behind, where the hat hung among a host of ghastly relics on the wall. Folliet took it, and, with a magnifying glass from his pocket, commenced to examine the feather and every portion of the surface. Presently an exclamation came from him. He had found within the leather lining of the cap a small piece of wet paper folded upon itself several times.

" Ah," he said, " Bach's cap, you see, was rather too large for his head. Yet, surely, this kind of cap will fit almost anybody's head ! If he took the trouble to stuff it with paper, that shows that it must have been not only too large, but very much too large ; and that again shows that M. Bach did not purchase this particular cap for himself. How think you, Carot, that this beer-seller of Montmartre came by a cap procured by somebody else ? "

" Ah, sir, that I don't know," replied Carot.

" No, nor I neither," said Folliet, " but that is what we 've got to find out, you see. Let 's have a look at the paper."

Fold by fold he opened the damp leaf. It was ruled with red lines, and looked as if it had been torn from an account book ; on it were written some words whose blurred outlines were now all but illegible. But by the aid of the glass Folliet was able to read them, and when he read them, he smiled. The words were :

> " 3 casks bock.
> Bottled, 5 dozen absinthe.
> Lager, 17 litres."

" This, Carot, is a little bill of Bach's," said Folliet. " Suppose I tell you that it is a bill for beers and spirits, will you still doubt that the beer-seller and the corpse are the same ? "

" Well, no, sir, of course."

" All right, then I do tell you so. And now, the cardboard."

This, too, he examined. It was small—about an inch square—dry and peeling. But on it, quite legible, was the red 9, or 6 with curving tail. Folliet put it into his pocket.

" And now for M. Vansittart," he muttered.

He walked out alone, hailed a *fiacre*, and went driving westward along the river at the rapid pace of the Parisian cabmen. His brow was very thoughtful, full of wrinkles. He got out at the Louvre, and walked across the quadrangle to the rebuilded Tuileries. He was puzzled at himself. He had come to claim an interview with a man crushed under the weight of pressing affairs, and he hardly knew what the interview was to be about. He gained, of course, easy admittance. Passing along a corridor in the interior of the palace, he caught sight of a female figure rushing across it from one door to another opposite. She, too, saw him, and half stopped with an inclination of the head. Folliet bowed profoundly. It was Honorine, the Queen. She disappeared, but, before he had reached the door, returned. The part which Folliet had taken in placing her upon the throne she well knew. His presence here, she thought, might be as important as anything else could be. She had turned back to meet him. She stood before him, a head taller than he. Folliet was a somewhat wizened person, with a face dry and lean and hard. Over his brow fell his thin, iron-grey hair.

" You want to see M. Vansittart, M. Folliet?" asked Honorine.

" Your Majesty—yes."

" He is *so* overwhelmed, you know," she pleaded.

" I know, your Majesty."

" You could not tell *me* your business, could you? I am only a woman, but I promise——"

" Your Majesty has commanded," said Folliet.

" No, not that exactly, monsieur," she laughed. " But

if it can be done it may save time and poor M. Vansittart's racked brain."

"Really, your Majesty, I came more to know than to impart knowledge. There are certain points with which it is essential that I should be acquainted. The first is this : *when* exactly does M. Vansittart propose to set out for the army? "

Honorine bent closer to his ear in a kind of playful triumph.

"Soon—soon," she said.

"To-day ? "

"No."

"To-morrow ? "

"Yes ; in the afternoon."

"Who knows of his intention ? "

"Who? Why, half a dozen people, I fancy. Is there any reason why it should be a secret ? "

"There may—there may," he said gravely.

"You surprise me, monsieur. Pray tell me your meaning."

"Your Majesty must understand that there are certain kinds of intuitions, especially in the minds of investigators of crime, which cannot be imparted. We see a shadow, and at once assume a substance, but to the ordinary observer the shadow is a shadow merely. It happens that to your question I am unable to give any reply that would convince you. I will say this, however, that the time of M. Vansittart's departure ought, certainly, to be known to as few persons as possible, and I suggest, as a matter of simple precaution, that, since it is already known to be fixed for to-morrow, it be postponed till the day after."

Honorine was utterly surprised.

"You know, of course, monsieur," she said, " the gravity of the proposal you make ? Let me tell you, in your ear, that a great and possibly a decisive battle is even now impending. It is absolutely, it is urgently necessary that the departure of M. Vansittart should not be delayed an hour."

Her tone was earnest and emphatic. Folliet dropped his eyes and was silent.

" In that case, your Majesty," he said at last, " little remains to be said. To-morrow let him go. He will no doubt be accompanied to the station by a strong guard without any counsel of mine. Heaven only grant that all the enemies of your Majesty's throne may be without the walls of this palace and none within it."

" Within it, monsieur ? Have you any suspicions of such a state of things ? "

" No, your Majesty, no definite suspicion. But it is easy to see how even one unfaithful menial in the place, supposing a hostile combination outside, might be more fatal, in the way of supplying information and in other ways, than the cunning of a thousand enemies."

" That is true, monsieur ; but your words are very vague. To what hostile combination do you refer ? What can be its object ? Is not M. Vansittart the idol of all Paris ? "

" I referred to no special hostile combination, your Majesty," said Folliet, " nor do I know its object. It exists, as we know from the destruction of the railway lines. But an old ferret like me becomes, you know, in time, a kind of barometer ; he feels a change in the social atmosphere, and shivers involuntarily at the coming storm."

" Well, well, I will think over what you have said. I will find a chance to speak to M. Vansittart. As to unfaithful people in the palace, they may exist. But how can we know them ? Treachery does not print itself in red on the brow."

" Any Germans, your Majesty ? "

" Germans ? I do not think so—I do not know. There may be one, or two, or three. It is possible. But, surely, they may be our most faithful subjects."

Folliet bowed, retiring backward. Honorine extended her hand.

" Your recommendations shall not be forgotten, monsieur," she said. " Meanwhile, rest assured that we have every confidence in the hundred eyes of M. Folliet."

CHAPTER VII

IT was now growing dark. Folliet descended hurriedly from his interview with the Queen, and in the Place de la Concorde sprang into a *fiacre*. He told the *cocher* to drive to the Rue Pigalle, No. 11. This street runs north-east and south-west from the Place de la Trinité, starting from near the fine church of that name. It is narrow, and winds somewhat. The jalousied houses are large, but decayed and sombre. There is a certain mystery, a hint of squalor.

No. 11 had a gloomy exterior. It was big, and the grey jalousies were every one closed. In the courtyard there was no *concierge*. But Folliet, penetrating a few steps beyond the gate, was met by a girl some twenty years of age, well figured, with dark face, and hair in disorder. She was quietly dressed. Her eyes looked as if they had been crying.

" I want to have a talk with Agnès Carhaix," said Folliet.

" But I am she, monsieur," said the girl.

" Good. I am of the police—from the Prefecture. You called this morning, I think."

" Yes, monsieur, but——"

" I just want to have a talk with you."

" Well, monsieur—if that is so——"

Her eyes dropped. She was confused.

" What the devil," said Folliet to himself, " is the matter ? "

" If monsieur will—will step this way with me—we might sit together in the Cabaret au Vrai Bruyant just yonder outside, and there talk."

" Can't anyone enter the house, then, I wonder ? " said
Folliet to himself. Aloud he added :

" Really, but it is n't worth all that trouble, you know.
I wanted merely to ask you a question or two about your
sweetheart, M. Bach. I may tell you at once that we have
every hope of finding and restoring him to you, if we can
just get a few facts."

The girl's eyes leapt upon him.

" Of finding him—really, monsieur ? " she said.

" Yes, really—why not ? These temporary disappearances
are quite common, you know, in a place like Paris. Let us
sit in the room here a little, and talk the matter over."

Still she hesitated a moment. Then turned reluctantly
and led the way.

As Folliet moved to follow her, something slowly falling
from above through the air brushed past his nose. He
caught it quickly and quickly poked it into a pocket. It
was a feather.

The courtyard in which they had stood was dark ; but the
room on the ground floor into which Agnès Carhaix now
led him was darker still. Folliet, sitting opposite her, could
just make out her well-curved form, unconfined in corsets,
in its close robe of black. He placed his chair so that, while
he remained in absolute shadow, a dim glimmer from the
half-open door made her movements and attitude discernible.
But it was his nostrils and his ears, rather than his eyes,
which were busy. He had no sooner entered the room than
a singular odour greeted him. He had no sooner settled
himself on the chair than a singular sound fell upon his ears.
The odour was the faint, fetid odour of a stable. The sound
was a single one, resembling the stroke of a club thumping
upon boards. As it sounded through the room, the girl winced.

" Well, now, about Bach," said Folliet, with every sense
on the alert. " You will find that the questions I have to
ask you about him are not many, and easily answered.
First of all, how long have you been engaged to him ? "

Before she could answer, down came sounding the club upon the boards. The noise seemed to come from a room near. The girl winced.

" I—I——" she said, in evident confusion.

" Come now, how long ? "

" About—about two weeks."

" That all ? "

Down in answer came sounding the club upon the boards —a single blow.

" Yes—that 's all."

" And when were you to be married ? "

" In—in a week."

" So? Really? Not a very long engagement, then, all told."

" No. But what has that to do with the matter, monsieur ? "

" Well, in a case of this kind everything is of importance, you know. Just answer my questions—you will find them easy to answer. How long have you known Bach ? "

" About—about three weeks."

" That all ? He was anxious to be married quickly, then ? "

" Perhaps."

" For what reason ? "

" I do not know."

" Oh, come, now, if the man is to be found, it is clear that you must let me know the facts, you know."

" I cannot tell you."

" You won't ? "

" Ah, monsieur, do not torment me ! "

She buried her face in her hands.

" Well, then," he said, " we will start with this fact : that Bach was anxious, for some reason or other, to get married in frantic haste. Bach or you ? Which was it ? Bach or you ? "

The mysterious sound of the club came pounding in answer upon the boards. The cowering girl was silent.

" Ah, you are not open and candid, you see," said Folliet ;

" how do you expect me to find your lover for you ? Well, then, I must ask you something else. Was the appointment which Bach had to keep on the day he disappeared an important one ? "

" I suppose so."

" Only ' suppose ' ? "

" I believe so."

" Come now, that 's better. You believe so. Well, what was it all about ? "

" I don't know."

" Very well, then I shall leave you to find your lover for yourself, that 's all."

" He was going to a meeting."

" Really ? An assemblage of men ? "

" I suppose so."

" He told you so ? "

" Yes," in the faintest whisper, came from her.

" An assemblage of Germans ? "

" Oh, not necessarily Germans."

" How do you know ? "

" He did not say they were Germans. Why should you pitch upon Germans ? "

" Bach is a German ? "

" Yes—a naturalised Frenchman."

" And what was the object of this ' meeting ' ? "

" You do not suppose that M. Bach told me his secrets."

" It was a *secret* meeting, then ? "

" I suppose so."

" Why ? "

" Because—I do not know. I suppose it was secret."

" He told you it was secret ? "

" Well—I suppose—yes."

" And you know nothing of its object ? "

" How should I ? "

" Where did you first meet M. Bach ? "

" Here, in this house."

" So ?   How came he here ? "

" He was brought here by a friend of his."

" A German friend ? "

" Well—yes."

" Who knows you also ? "

" Yes—he lives here."

" A lodger ? "

" Yes."

" Have you any other lodgers ? "

" About five."

" All Germans ? "

" Most of them, I believe."

" The house is yours ? "

" Mine and my two sisters'."

" Have you always lived here ? "

" Nearly always."

" Your father's house ? "

" My uncle's."

" He is alive now ? "

" He is lately dead."

" How long ago ? "

" Three weeks ago."

" About the same time when you met Bach, then ? "

She lowered her eyes.

" Yes."

Folliet rose.   As he did so, for the twentieth time the
club sounded its solitary, strange blow upon the boards.

" Well, all I can say," he said, " is that you know a great
deal more than you choose to tell me.   It is very foolish, if
you are anxious to find him, you know.   I suppose you *are*
anxious ? "

" Ah, monsieur, find him—find him quickly for me ! "
she wailed, with hidden face.

" Well," he said, " I won't hide from you that we have a
clue—that his recovery is possible—soon—but——"

He turned sharply in surprise.   There was the swift strik-

ing of a match behind him, and the room was flooded with
light. There approached him a girl, holding a candlestick.
Her face was long, thin, and ugly ; and on her back was a
hump. A look of intense malice was stamped on her
features. Her left fist clenched with rage. Her age was
about thirty. Folliet guessed at once that she had been
listening in the dark to the whole of their talk. His eyes
keenly read her somewhat evil face.

" Why not tell the gentleman what you know of this man
Bach ? " she cried. " Your lover ! Yes, and a fine lover
for my father's child was Bach ! "

The face of Agnès was first blanched, then encrimsoned
with rage.

" Look you, Jeanne ! " she hissed, " one word—one little
word against him—and I tell every syllable I know of
whence the pigeons come ! "

" Come, now," said Folliet to himself, " this looks not ill.
Between the two sisters—you are sisters, I suppose ? " he
added aloud.

" If you can call anyone your sister who hates you, sir,"
said Agnès.

" It is *you*," replied Jeanne, venomously, " it is you who
began it ! You covetous, greedy, mercenary——"

She did not go any further. At this point her invective
was broken in upon by the shrill whinny of a horse—a
whinny fierce, and high, and strong ; it came from the
direction of the room where the club had struck the boards
and where the stable odour had arisen. Both the women
started with blanched faces. Folliet smiled.

He had long since guessed that the solitary, slow, mysterious sound was due to the restive smiting upon the bare
boards of the hoof of a high-spirited horse. Now he knew.

But he was infinitely puzzled. The plot was thickening.
He wished to be alone to think.

" Well, I won't stay to witness your family quarrels," he
said.

But it was absolutely necessary that he should return, and return by invitation. He remembered that the cause of Jeanne's sudden entrance was his promise that Bach should be found. Jeanne did not wish Bach to be found, that was clear. If he was found, she wished him, for some reason, to be guillotined or torn to pieces. So he said again :

"Well, Mdlle. Agnès, I can only promise that we shall do our best, and I think I can give you the hope of seeing your *fiancé* in three or four days at the furthest."

He bowed and passed out of the room ; he reached the courtyard and became anxious ; he reached the gate and despaired ; but as he was bending to pass through the wicket into the street, the expected happened. Jeanne touched his arm ; she had run after him.

"Come to-morrow at one, monsieur," she said in a thick whisper ; "I will be here alone, and may tell you——"

"Back—quick !" said Folliet, "your sister——"

"At one," whispered Jeanne, and ran back.

Folliet looked up and down the street, then turned to the left and walked into a small house which bore on its door the legend : "Knock and one will open." It was the Cabaret au Vrai Bruyant.

He knocked. At his entrance, a perfect hullabaloo of sound arose—stamping feet, clinking glasses, the shouts of Bedlam. Hubbub is the *raison d'être* and motive of the Vrai Bruyant. At every new entrance, the guests roar like the bulls of Bashan. In the midst of the tumult of the hall, a girl, half nude, stood on a raised place blowing a bugle.

Folliet selected a seat in the least noisy corner, and ordered a glass of beer. He sat trying to catch the eye of a big, burly fellow with long black hair combed back stiffly from his brow, dressed in black velvet, with Wellington boots, and a coarse jersey for shirt. He was the brazen-lunged proprietor of the Vrai Bruyant. Presently Folliet beckoned with a finger. The great swaggerer approached him. They knew each other.

" Sit down here, Cazalès. I want to talk to you."

Cazalès sat near.

" Who are these Carhaix young women ? "

" Carhaix ? Carhaix ? " said Cazalès, prodding remembrance.

" Yes ; they live three doors away, on this side of the street, you know. You must know them."

" Ah, yes—Carhaix—ah, yes. Three young women. Uncle lately dead."

" Tell me about them ; why do they hate each other ? "

" Hate ! Hate is n't the word for it ! It 's the uncle's fault too. They were always good friends till he died."

" Well, let me hear it—all, you know. For tip I promise you that you shall find the police all round the cabaret pretty blind for the next, say, three months."

" Honour bright ? "

" Honour bright."

" Well, you 're welcome to what I know about it from a party who should be in the swim over yonder. The whole trouble comes from the last will of the uncle. An old hermit he was, crotchety, a miser kind of dog. There are three of them : Marie, pretty little girl, flaxen-haired, about seventeen ; then Jeanne, the eldest, ugly, bitter-tempered ; and another one, I forget her name——"

" Agnès."

" That 's it. Lived happily till uncle died. Uncle in his will left the house jointly to the three, and, in addition, forty thousand francs, which are to be the sole property of the one who marries first. You can guess the result."

" I see ! " cried Folliet.

" Jeanne, at the time of uncle's death, was already engaged to be married—farmer, half-German, Lorrainer, they say. She at once writes to him to come immediately, but something prevents. Meanwhile, Agnès, in great hurry, goes and gets engaged—man named Bach—know him well—beerseller—Montmartre. What steps little Marie takes, I don't know. But the other two, frantic to be married, are tearing out each other's eyes."

"That 's all you know ? "

"That 's about it "

"Thank you, Cazalès. Sha'n't forget my promise. Find out anything else of importance to me, and I make the time six instead of three months. *Bon soir.*"

He passed out. At the first street lamp he stopped, and drew from his pocket the feather which had brushed past his nose. He took out a magnifying glass, and bent to examine it.

"Yes," he muttered. "It 's a pigeon's feather, right enough. But the horse ! the horse, living like a Christian in the house ! What—the devil—can be the meaning of that ? "

CHAPTER VIII

THE INVENTION

THE three sisters Carhaix were very different one from the other—Jeanne was ugly, Agnès was attractive, Marie, the seventeen-year-old, was lovely. In character, they were more different still—Jeanne was fierce and cunning, Agnès was profoundly selfish, but shallow and more easy-tempered, Marie was an angel.

The intense contest as to which should marry first, and so gain her uncle's wealth, was confined to only two of the sisters. Marie did not even know of this clause in the will, for the elder sisters had craftily kept it a secret from her. Yet, even so, it was a nice question as to which of the three would carry off the prize. Jeanne was plain, but she had a lover, though he was in far Lorraine ; Agnès was attractive, but her hastily acquired lover was dead, and she did not know it ; Marie had youth and beauty, but she did not know of the clause in the will, yet she, too, had a lover.

Why did not the Lorraine farmer fly as with wings to claim Jeanne and the fortune ? Day after day, she wrote letter after letter urging him to come—to leave all, and come, come ! He answered, promising to be with her soon ; but he did not come. There were affairs of far vaster importance engaging, for the time being, this man's attention. He was a German, named Hans Schwartz. He occupied, as he had told her, a small farm and homestead in the neighbourhood of Gravelotte. A great part of his life latterly had been devoted to the culture and training of pigeons. It was

77

a nice question which of the sisters *would* marry first. Agnès had only to discover that Bach was really dead in order to seek and find a new and eager lover.

An hour after Folliet had left the house of the girls, Marie came in. She was engaged during the day at a *vacherie* on the other side of the river. Her sisters had insisted that she should find employment. She walked in weary, cast her gloves listlessly on a table, and propped her fair head on a hand. She was slim and *petite*, with large and wistful eyes of clearest blue. As she sat down she glanced at a clock in the room. A lamp was on the table, and by it sat Jeanne, sewing, with tight lips. She did not speak when the other entered, but she cast upon her a look, suspicious and evil, which Marie met with a shy and timid glance. Presently, as they sat so in silence, the restless horse in a room near smote with his hoof upon the flooring.

" That dreadful horse still ? " just muttered Marie.

Jeanne rose suddenly, and leant over toward her, with her knuckles on the table.

" Yes ! " she said fiercely, " that horse *still !* Is the house yours, then ? "

" I meant no harm, Jeanne," Marie answered. " I 'm sure I meant no harm. Pray, do not ill-treat me to-night."

She said it languidly, yet not without terror. Her left fingers were touching, all the time, a note in her pocket.

" You have got to learn your place in this house, you understand ? " said Jeanne, with threatening forefinger, " or it will be a hotter place yet for you than ever it has been. Why don't you take off your hat ? "

Marie did not answer the question ; she glanced secretly at the clock. She said :

" Is there anything in the cupboard ? May I take something to eat, Jeanne ? "

" Hat off ! "

" I do not wish to take it off just now. May I take something to——"

Jeanne had edged round the table to her. Down upon the cheek of the child came a tingling slap.

At this moment Agnès entered the room.

" Don't you hear your elder sister talking to you, you little idiot ? " she said.

There was one point at least in which Jeanne and Agnès were in harmony—in their delight in habitually torturing to the verge of madness the gentle child who had usurped all their share of grace and beauty.

" I should think," sobbed Marie, " that—it does not take —two of you—to oppress a poor—miserable girl—like me——"

" Then do as you are told, will you ? Take it off now !"

" I—don't wish——"

Down upon her other cheek came the palm of Agnès, and Marie's burning face went for shelter into her covering arms. But before it did so she glanced at the clock.

" Now, perhaps you will take it off," said Agnès.

But Marie showed no sign of any such intention.

" Wait a little," said Jeanne, " there are more ways than one of making a horse——"

And with her long thin fingers she made a catch at the girl's hat. But Marie was observant through one watchful corner of an eye, and slid agilely away behind the table. On the table lay a bottle containing water. As she dodged, Agnès lifted the bottle and shot the entire mass of liquid at the child's face, but Marie, on that night of all nights, had no intention of appearing to disadvantage, and again she darted aside, escaping with only a wet shoulder.

" Oh, this child wants pounding !" said Agnès.

" And I am the one to do it," cried Jeanne, shrilly, making round the table, brandishing a long brass candlestick.

Marie ran towards the door. It was fastened, not locked. Before she could open it, Jeanne was over her. A heavy blow of the brass struck her on the shoulder near the neck.

" Now, you little beast—that hat !"

Something of despair and pride and defiance came into the hunted eyes and flushed face of the child. She cried aloud :
" I will not ! I cannot ! I don't wish to ! "

They were surprised. It was the first symptom of rebellion which her sweet nature had ever permitted.

" But why not, you little fool ! Why get beaten when you can save your pretty skin ? " said Agnès.

" Dear Agnès—have pity ! " she cried. " Oh, don't ! don't ! I cannot—I am going out ! "

" Out ! " they exclaimed together, in astonishment.

" Yes, out," she answered. " Cannot one go out if one would ? "

" Well, this is coming to something ! " said Agnès. "And where, if you please, are you going to at this hour of the night ? "

Marie averted her head. She did not answer. Ten thousand elder sisters would have found it difficult to keep her indoors that night. She had an appointment.

All this time, she held one hand behind her, on the handle of the door. In her pocket was a note which she was longing to finger, and feel, and cover with kisses.

At the announcement that Marie was going out, Jeanne, the shrewder of the two elder sisters, stood still, and turned slightly pale. Then she stepped near to Agnès, and whispered in her ear these words :

" Let her go ! "

But the injunction was useless. Even while Jeanne was whispering, Marie, who had slyly and softly turned the handle, slid fugitively through the door.

The two women looked into each other's eyes a minute. Then Jeanne, with an air of conviction :

" She 's gone to meet a man ! Wait—I 'll follow her."

And at once she, too, slid out, hatless. In Paris one does not wear a hat in the streets, if one happens to be a woman, except by way of flourish and luxury.

Down the street stole Jeanne, hiding with absolute success

and cunning in the shadows and recesses, keeping the child always in sight. First, at a corner, Marie stepped into a *lavabo*, and in five minutes came out with her pretty oval face quite tearless, and scrubbed and pink. And now, her feet winged with gladness, she sped forward, as a swallow, after long travails over seas, darts straight with joy for its summer nest. In the Rue Lafayette she leapt into a passing tram without waiting for it to stop. Jeanne got into a *fiacre*, bidding the driver keep the tram within seeing distance.

In half an hour Marie was running lightly within the gates of the Buttes-Chaumont. She had seen with alarm that she was a minute late. Behind her, toiling and panting, came Jeanne, running also.

The gardens lay sombre and umbrageous under the moonlight. They are a little bit of Switzerland in the heart of Paris. Now they were all but deserted. Only down by the waterside, amid the leafage, a few pairs of lovers cooed and kissed. This was not the point of Marie's aim. Rising high from the water is a bluff cliff crowned at the summit with a little round temple of open columns of ebony. From the bottom one ascends some rising ground, then over a rather frail and very long wooden bridge, then up some rude stone steps cut through the heart of the rock, then you are at the top, and the temple is there, with its circular wooden bench for seat, the very home of Cupid, the sanctuary of Venus. Here the moonlight was supreme. The silence and the solitude were complete.

Marie, when she reached the bridge, knew that she stood exposed to two eyes that watched for her coming. She no longer ran ; she even tried to walk slowly ; but, in reality, her pace was very rapid. In sweet, reluctant, amorous delays her wild young heart was not yet proficient. Behind her, crouching and bending, came Jeanne.

" Marie ! Marie ! " said a man's voice.

" Ah ! " in a dying sigh came fluttering from her lips.

She was on his breast.

" My soul ! " he said.

" My life ! " she whispered, but he did not hear her ; the words perished in their fainting utterance.

These two people had only known each other a few days. They had met by chance in the street. But the soul knows its own mate. In reality, their friendship dated from the old eternities. For ever they were kin.

But now, Muse of Romance, inspire my reporting pen ! They leaned together over the parapet of the little temple and saw the water and the woods, and discovered that Heaven can be nothing else than a moonlit earth, where one is always young and amorous. He, too, was young—not twenty-three—yet his forehead was bald at the temples, and down from his chin and cheeks spread a dark-red, fan-shaped beard, rough and thick, and his body was heavy and bulky. He was a ne'er-do-weel—a student, a musician, one of the wild, penniless, Latin-Quarter sort, named Armand Duprès. At the Conservatoire—everywhere—he was a marked man. One said : " He will arrive—he will be famous." But he never knew whence his dinner would come, if it came at all. If he had known whence it would come, life would have been intolerable to him at his then age. How the settled, the tame man—the clerk, the artisan—could endure to live, he could not understand. Armand reposed upon Providence. God fed him like a bird. Chance took care of him, lest at any time he dash his foot against a stone.

In one of his wild midnight revelries, with his Bohemian student friends, when coals failed to keep the fire going, they broke up one by one the few old chairs in the room and threw the pieces in the grate. One after another of the guests would rise and sup standing. Armand called this " moving out by way of the chimney." Yet this light-natured person could, when he was sober, touch a harp, or a piano, or a violin at chance moments in such a way that some heavenly dream-image would hint itself in melodious loveliness to the soul that heard it. He had a brain as keen and shrewd as lightning. And the whole world was one poem to him.

Of this poem Marie, lately found, was the climax or culminating point. Here the poem swelled into song, and music was the universe. When he looked into her eyes he saw Heaven, when she looked into his she saw Divinity.

"We will go, Marie," he said, "we will be together always, we will find a nest, and live and sing."

"Beloved!" she murmured, her face nestling by the side of his neck.

"Far away—in—where shall we say?"

"Here is Heaven, too, with you," said Marie, who lived nearer to the earth than he.

"But, Marie, one marries in the world, you know, before the Mayor. Do you know?"

"Yes, I know. But we—are we not above the world, then?"

"We are in Heaven!"

"Ah——"

"Still, Marie, in the world one marries, one sets up a *ménage*, and is practical."

"To you that were tiresome, love."

"Not with you, Marie."

"How great you are, and good! Ah, how divine! I shall die if you love me so. My heart will break."

"It is you, Marie, who are divine! All about you are rainbows and echoes of minstrelsy. I cannot at all comprehend why you love me."

"Because you are Armand."

"You are an angel!"

"You are the world!"

"You are Heaven!"

"Put your hand on my heart; feel how it bounds toward its monarch!"

"Kiss me with your lips; they are roses of flesh."

"My love!"

" My bride ! "

" My husband ! "

" My wife ! "

So, male and female, they called one to the other, singing, not speaking. Then Armand, descending somewhat again to the earth :

" Marie, we must go to the Mayor."

" Whatever you will."

" At once, Marie."

" We are poor, Armand. We have no money."

He laughed.

" Why—you housewife ! Money is of no importance."

" Sometimes, Armand. I knew a *grisette* whose child died because she had no money."

" Well, but Marie, I am so clever ! I can make money whenever I like. Only I never tried."

" How can you ? "

" How ?—I don't know. It can't be very difficult, you know, since common people do it. I am certain—if I only tried. Would you like to live in a grand house, and have jewels ? "

" I ? Not I ! It was of you only that I was thinking."

" But as to money ! " he said, with a toss of his head ; " that is easy ! Why, only last week I invented something —are you interested in the war, Marie ? "

" I *was*," she said.

" But not now ? "

" Oh, now ! What is anything to me now, but you ? "

" Sweet ! Well, but the war. I, Marie, for a week was frantic, all excited, then something happened—I had a musical fancy—it changed the current of my interest. But during that week I worked, I can tell you ! That Vansittart, the American, he seems to me so great a man. I said, ' I will invent him something more deadly than death, with which he shall destroy his enemies.' And for days, Marie, for days I kept at home, saw no one, thinking of that one thing."

" And did you invent the thing ? " she asked, with wide, wondering eyes.

" Yes ! It was not so difficult. I made a model, too —or half made it. Then I got weary of the matter—some-one came here—I went out——"

" How great you are ! "

" How sweet you are ! "

" My king ! "

" My wife ! "

" But the model, Armand ? You have it still. Is it there in your room ? "

" Yes, still."

" And you will finish it ? "

" No, it does not matter, love, now."

" You will finish it—for me ? "

" For you ? "

" Yes."

" Of course—if you tell me—why, of course."

" And, when it is finished," she said, reasoning to her-self, " then I shall know what to do. Leave the rest to me."

" So ? and what will she do, the little sweet manager, then ? "

" I will go straight to Mr. Vansittart, and I will tell him ! "

Armand caught her to him, laughing, kissing her eyes and ears and hair.

Jeanne, who was crouching a little below them at the stone steps, rose to go. She had heard all. As she lifted herself a pebble rolled down the stairway from beneath her feet, with sounds. The lovers started. They were not all alone, then ? Armand ran a little forward to see, but Jeanne had taken to her heels. They saw the dim figure scuttle across the bridge ; but Marie did not recognise it.

CHAPTER IX

FOLLIET spent a sleepless night. He sat on a hearth-rug in his own bedroom in the Rue de Maubeuge, with his arms round his knees, and his wrinkled brow sunk low in thought. The day stole into the room and found him sitting so.

Much, or at least something, had become clear to him. He was absolutely certain, now, that there was a conspiracy, an association—probably large, probably of Germans—with a secret, unlawful, political aim within the city of Paris. A man with the reasoning shrewdness of Folliet could hardly have failed, with his present knowledge, to come to that conclusion. His chain of deduction started from Bach—or rather, from Bach's cap ; from the feather in it, especially, and from the circumstance that the cap had been so very much too large for Bach. The inferences which he drew from these facts seemed to him quite clear. And they were these. The cap, with the feather in it, was a badge, a sign of membership, a symbol of association. It was very much too large for Bach, for the simple reason that it had never been specially bought for him at all, but was merely one of a lot purchased in the gross for the members of the confraternity. A faint instinct of all this had passed through his brain from the first sight of the cap. When Agnès Carhaix informed him that Bach had gone to a " meeting," and a " secret " one, he was no longer in doubt. But " a secret meeting " of Germans at such a time ? It could not be but that its object was political.

And the cardboard in Bach's pocket marked with the 6 or
9 was now no longer a matter of mystery ; 6—or 9—was
Bach's membership number. But from this fact his mind
went on to a new conclusion. He reasoned that an association whose members were known and admitted by numbered
tickets must be a large and far-reaching one—one so large
and so far-reaching that its members were not all known to
each other by sight—one requiring formality and organisation, and numerical computation. Another mind would
have reasoned : since Bach was 6 or 9, there must be at least
six or nine of them. Folliet reasoned : since Bach was
numbered at all, there must be at least six or nine hundred
of them. But if there were nine hundred of them, they must
be powerful, resourceful, strong in means to effect their end.
It takes many men and much money to destroy railways.
With this fact, then, he, the Prefect of Police in Paris, found
himself confronted.

But what was their end ? That he did not know. That
it was hostile to France was certain ; but whether this hostility was personally directed against King Henri or against
Vansittart, or merely as a general agent in favour of the
Kaiser, he could only guess.

Everywhere, after a certain point, was mystery. How
had Bach met his death ? Was it suicide ? He did not believe. How much was known to the sisters Carhaix ?
What was the significance of the symbol of the pigeon's
feather in the cap—of the pigeon's feather which had
brushed past his nose in the courtyard—of the horse stabled
in the house ?

All night his excogitation lasted, and, at the end, had he
computed the currents of his thought, he would have discovered that, in fact, it was the *horse* more than anything
else which had occupied and puzzled and excited him. The
horse ! it lay motionless—like lead—in his brain. One thing
only he decided : that he would see it that day with his own
eyes, and discover whatever was the secret associated with it.

He had till one o'clock, before his meeting with Jeanne Carhaix. He tried to devote himself to ordinary affairs, but the thought of the horse continually obtruded itself upon him. He was nervously restless ; he had a feeling that he was losing time. Sharp at one he was in front of the Carhaix gate.

Jeanne was waiting in the courtyard.

" No one in ? " said Folliet.

" No."

" Where is Agnès ? "

" Marketing."

" This her regular hour ? "

" Yes."

Folliet took a mental note of that. They passed inward, near the room where the horse had been stabled. He listened for the sound of the restless hoof, but heard nothing. Jeanne ascended a stairway before him. The whole house was dingy and close.

" Why do we ascend ? " he asked.

" Agnès may return," she said ; " I am taking you to my own room."

She led the way down a passage, and, in a rather small triangular apartment, where there was a bed, pointed to a seat. At the moment when Folliet sat, there began, on the other side of one of the three partitions, the trolling sound of some cooing bird ; at once the monody was taken up by another ; presently a perfect chorus went rolling through the air in soft rotatory joyance, with swell and fall and vibrant velvet volume.

" Well, now, we are in pigeon-land proper," muttered Folliet.

Jeanne sat opposite him, eyeing him with half-suspicious, grey under-glance. Her long, olive-coloured face was somewhat pale.

" Can you give me any news of M. Bach, sir ? " she said.

" Only this," replied Folliet, " that we as good as have

our hands on him. It is only a matter of a few hours now, and we shall be able to restore him to you and your sister."

Jeanne's pallor increased.

" Restore him to *me*, sir? *I* have nothing to do with the man. I could give you information against him, which would mean the guillotine for him the week after you find him."

" Very well, mademoiselle, go on. I am willing to hear, as you see by my presence here."

" I am a patriot, monsieur," said Jeanne.

" You are? " replied Folliet, with lifted eyebrows.

" I love my country, sir."

" Is that so? "

" What advantage should I derive if we be beaten by the Germans? I am a patriot. I prefer, on the whole, that France should be the victor. This man, Bach, is a conspirator, monsieur."

" You don't say that now? "

" He is. I can prove it."

" Well, tell me."

The cooing of the pigeons had somewhat ceased, and at this point a gentle sound of some movement, apparently accidental, came from the other side of the partition. They both heard it. Jeanne started and turned white.

" Hold! You heard a sound, sir? " she whispered.

" I? No. It is your fancy. Go on."

" I thought we were alone in the house, but some of the lodgers may have come back. They have that room there. They are Germans—they may listen——"

" Well, why not open the door and see? "

There was a door in the partition, and the key projected inward. Jeanne rose at the suggestion, turned the key, and peeped into the next room. At the first sound of her movements at the key, two men on the other side had hurriedly slipped into a spacious cupboard. While Jeanne's back was turned to him, Folliet, on his part, with the quickness of lightning drew out the key, which he could reach without rising, and pressed it deep into a lump of wax from his pocket. With swift skill he had replaced the key in the lock, and the wax in his pocket, before Jeanne again faced him with the words:

" There is no one there, sir."

" Well, now, about this conspiracy of Bach's," he said. " I need not tell you that any information you can give of importance to the Government will not go unrewarded."

" I am not seeking a Government reward, monsieur. But I make this stipulation before I go any further—that you promise me that M. Bach shall not be allowed to marry my sister until I am myself married. I am quite candid, you see, about the matter. I stipulate that."

" I see. You want him kept in prison, in case he is not guillotined, till——"

" Yes."

" Well, I promise that."

" Then, I will tell you. For why should I not be a patriot ? I ! There is a conspiracy of over fifteen hundred Germans in Paris. I know it, because——"

" Yes—tell me first its object."

" Its object, monsieur ? "

" Yes—its object ! "

" Its object is this, sir——"

She bent her lips close to his ear. But she got no further. A violent knocking was heard at the door of their entrance, a door in one of the three partitions of the room.

A cry of " Mdlle. Jeanne ! Mdlle. Jeanne ! News ! News ! Are you there ? " came from without.

Jeanne in a white scare took Folliet by the shoulders.

" Quick, monsieur ! " she hissed in flurried fright, " behind the bed-curtains—later—later I will finish——"

Folliet hurried to the hiding-place ; Jeanne to the door. She opened it, stepped outside, and closed it behind her. Two men were there awaiting her—the same two who had run hiding at her opening of the other door. To reach this side of the room they had made a wide detour through the house. They had been listening to her promise of disclosure, and hurried round in time to prevent it. They knew the means. One in his hand carried a pigeon, and a narrow strip of paper.

" Mdlle. Jeanne," he said in the lowest whisper, " sorry am I to have to tell you this——"

" What—what is it ? "

" This pigeon you see here has just arrived from the Lorrainer, and tied round its leg was this slip."

He handed her the slip. She recognised the writing of her lover Schwartz. But she could not make out its meaning ; it was in German.

" What is it ? You know I can't read it," she said.

" He says," replied the man, " that the Five Thousand sent out by Vansittart have ridden in their devastating career right through his farm, and left the place a ruin. All is trampled, harried, and desolate ; he is left penniless, Schwartz. The message is intended for you. For the present he cannot move or think of marriage."

Jeanne had heard of the ride of the Five Thousand. She did not stop to think that their operations were long since over—that this message was rather late in coming. She believed, and she tottered backward, with bloodless face.

The farm of Schwartz had, in truth, been scorched by the flying flame of the Five Thousand in its meteor course of destruction; but the message mentioning it had been brought by a carrier-pigeon from his *colombier* many days before to the conspirators at No. 11 Rue Pigalle. They had not so much as taken the pains to mention it to Jeanne until they saw how it might be useful to their ends. The sisters Carhaix were, in fact, permitted to know as little as possible.

" My God ! " gasped Jeanne, with clasped hands. All her hopes at that moment perished. In a few days Agnès would know whether or not she should marry Bach speedily. If she could not marry him, what was easier than the purchase of another husband ?

In a moment or two her pallor vanished. Her face flushed with brutal rage. Revenge, above every other passion, swelled in her—revenge against the hand that had struck her this blow, the hand that had hurled the thunderbolt of the Five Thousand straight at her heart. She had just been about to do this man a service, and all the time he had been crushing her. She had been about to aid France ! And France had been ruining her. What did she care for Vansittart, for France, in comparison with her triumph over Agnès, her laugh of glee.

" Curse them ! Curse them ! " she hissed through her clenched teeth.

She rushed at once toward the room where she had left Folliet, mad with rage. Folliet had crept from his hiding-place meanwhile, and had been busy. He had taken the key from the door between Jeanne's room and the conspirators', then crouched peering through the hole of the lock. The sight that met his eye was, first, a window open, and looking out at the back of the house upon an open space. Then he saw the side walls crowded from top to bottom with square wooden cages, in every cage a bird. The place was squalid, littered with feathers, crumbs, seeds. As he looked, there alighted on the window-sill in winged urgency, glancing in quick query round the room, a feathered messenger. Wrapped round her leg, bound with an elastic thread, was a narrow slip of paper. One of Wilhelm's pigeons. Folliet would have given his left hand to know what was written in that far-borne message. But as he gazed, all his soul in his peering eye, his quick ear heard a hint of Jeanne's returning steps. He slid back behind the curtains.

The woman had lost all control of herself. She deigned no explanation. She simply pounced upon him in intense exasperation with the words :

" Look here, get out of my house, my good man ! You have no right here, you know."

Folliet was not surprised. He was certain beforehand that he was dealing with men of cunning and resource, quite capable of twisting to their own purposes the passions of a woman like Jeanne. He merely said to himself :

" Ah, they have got her out of my hands, then. Well, I 'll be even with them yet."

" I 'll have no prying, peering detectives about my place ; that 's all about it. I tell you to go," repeated Jeanne, " and may the devil take the whole crew of you, French and German together——"

" Softly, softly, ma'mselle," said Folliet. " It was you who brought me here, you know. What is the matter now ? "

" I want you to go away out of my place, I tell you. Will you go ? "

Folliet thought a second. He would go, if Jeanne allowed him to descend the stairs alone ; he wanted to inspect the house. He would not go if she went with him. He made three steps towards the door to try her. Good ; Jeanne sank upon her knees before the bed, hiding away her face like a wretch without hope.

Folliet descended quickly. He touched with his finger the revolver in his pocket. It might be that the horse was guarded. He met no one in his descent. The house was silent, and seemed deserted. The lower he went, the more the sombre obscurity deepened. He knew the way to the room where, on the previous night, he had spoken to the girls. Near it was the improvised stable. But he would have known it, too, by the odour that thickened as he approached it. He came to the door, feeling his way. For a minute he stood listening for the tramp of the restive hoof. But he heard nothing. A vague fear began to fill his mind. He put out his hand, and groped for the handle. To his surprise, he found the door unfastened. It was even a little way open. He intruded his head within the aperture. The reek of the stable greeted his nostrils strongly, but so dark was the apartment, that for the moment he could see nothing. He struck a match. Now he knew the truth. The horse was gone.

At the discovery a pang pierced Folliet's bosom, and at the same time something like a flash of light illuminated his brain. This fact stood out clear and prominent in his consciousness—that the horse, kept cabined in darkness for he knew not how long, had been removed on the same day when Vansittart proposed to leave Paris—or perhaps during the night preceding that day. No clear conception of motive as yet stood defined in his mind, but the coincidence was startling. He rushed from the house and pelted himself into a passing cab, shouting to the driver to fly to the Tuileries. It was already half-past two o'clock. This was the day when Vansittart had *proposed* to leave Paris—" in the afternoon." Folliet blessed himself now for the warning he had given on the previous day to the Queen. In spite of that, would Vansittart, in reality, set out ? He knew that the millionaire intended, whenever he started, to do it in a manner secretly, without pomp or show, thinking that the simple announcement of his departure after he had gone would produce upon the Parisian mind a greater effect of urgency and business promptitude.

Hence it happened that Folliet had no share in the preparations for the departure, no police arrangements to make. Vansittart intended to go in the manner of the simplest private citizen. Folliet had that morning received a budget of instructions from the Tuileries as to his procedure during the next few weeks, which made it rather look as if the departure was, in truth, fixed for that day. But he was uncertain; he had given his warning. Honorine must have mentioned it. Vansittart was not a rash man. He would at least postpone the hour of his setting-out. If there was mischief in the air, he, Folliet, would be in time to avert and frustrate it.

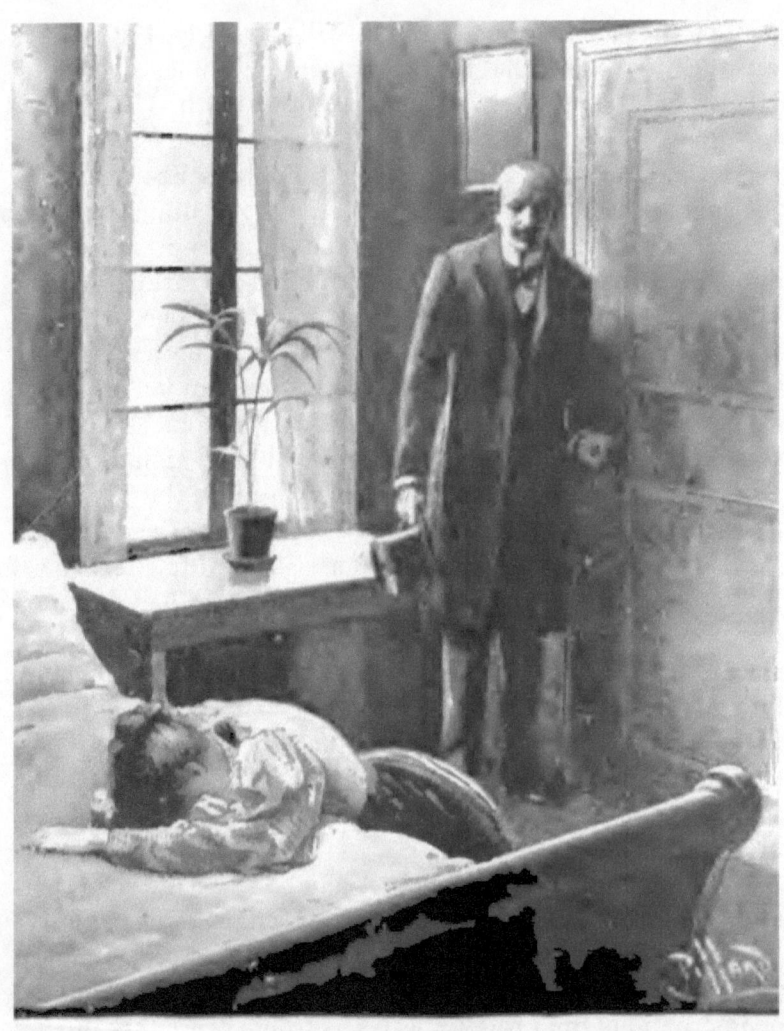

" Jeanne sank upon her knees before the bed, hiding away her face like a wretch without hope."

But what had really happened was this : Honorine had, indeed, found an occasion to repeat Folliet's vague words to Vansittart. But when he had heard them, Vansittart only smiled.

"What can be done?" he said. "One cannot be on
one's guard against the unknown."

"He suggests," announced the Queen, "that you delay
your departure."

But he would not hear of it.

"Impossible !" he said.

"Yet he seemed serious."

"I tell you what may be done," said Vansittart ; "I cannot delay, but I can change the hour. I can go two hours
sooner, if I first fight a battle with my wife—yes, that is
what we shall do."

And so, in fact, it fell out. When Folliet reached the
Tuileries in the cab, Vansittart had already gone. He heard
the news from a footman. On his brow broke out beads of
sweat. A certain definite suspicion of evil was by this time
working within him. He had not deduced, but he had
guessed the truth. He rushed at once round in the direction
of the stables. He thus lost another minute, and Vansittart
had set out fully five minutes before he arrived.

Half-way to the stables he met a jaunty, jockey-like sort
of little man whom he knew.

"Tell me, quick," panted Folliet, " in what did Mr. Vansittart drive away ? "

"A brougham."

"Drawn by what ? "

"The two blood Arabs, Tom and Bess."

"They all right ? "

"So, so. Tom was a bit mad this morning."

"Mad, man ? "

"Pretty mad. Could n't make him out—kept blinking
in the light, his nostrils going—would n't stand the traces
neither. I did n't harness him. It was Karl ; and Karl is
stupid with horses, as all Germans——"

Folliet heard no more. He went bounding across the quadrangle. He looked for a cab. By ill-luck there was none near. He ran farther, shouting : "*fiacre! fiacre!*" Now he was in the open street, still racing, shouting. A cab came galloping towards him. Just then, close by him, a lady passed slowly on a bicycle. In an instant he was after her ; in another he had hustled her roughly from her seat, taken her place, and left her on the ground. He flew. She ran feebly after him, crying: "Stop thief ! Stop thief !"

Through the rather wild traffic of the Parisian streets went Folliet, scorching with all the might of his hurrying legs, his bell tinkling out one high continuous warning, he shouting : "Room ! room ! room !" and cabs, and carts, and carriages scuttling into bewildered jumblement at the street-sides to make way for the frantic cyclist. It was a dry day, and his machine went tailed by a long, cloudy, comet-wake of dust. He found, however, though he was a short man, that there was not sufficient room for his legs to act all his power into the pedals. He would have given ten thousand francs if by some magic the saddle could have raised itself by a single inch. As it was, he felt that he could not be going less than twelve miles an hour. At that rate the Gare de Lyon would not be more than fifteen minutes away, for it was from the southern station that the millionaire must depart. If Vansittart were half-way, even three-quarters of the way, he might catch and save him. His course was direct enough. Straight down the long Rue di Rivoli he went tearing, bawling, tinkling. At one spot a sullen cabman, saying to himself, "Oh, the man 's mad !" drew his *fiacre* right athwart the course of the twinkling wheels.

Folliet shrieked : "In the name of the King ! In the name of France !"

The man at once drew aside, and the travelling streak of dust rushed by. On and on spun the toiling legs with quick piston play in this Gilpin ride.

At last, near the corner of the Boulevard Sebastopol, Folliet noticed something strange in the traffic. His throat redoubled its bawling energy ; but twice, bawl as he might, he found it necessary to slacken speed. The vehicles could not get out of his way in time. Something had happened to throw the traffic into a mere chaos of confusion. What was it ? He knew. Was he too late ? With nicest pilotage he dodged forward amid the disorganised array of wheels, shouting, beseeching, tinkling, with scared, wild eyes, and face of haggard pallor. Suddenly, from the smooth macadamised road on which he had been trailing behind him the wake of dust, he plunged into a stretch of street paved with those large square cobble-stones which make some parts of Paris almost impassable to the cyclist. The machine began to kick with jerky undulations ; he could hardly keep his seat. But it was now or never. He toiled onward.

Now, however, he found himself in a perfect babel of disorder, which thickened with every revolution of his wheel. He was in a region where everyone seemed to have run mad, where every neck was straining in one direction, and every throat was howling. Folliet could no longer make himself heard. His machine ran into the wheels of a backing cart, to be crushed into fragments ; but by an agile leap in time, he saved himself. He dived into the crowd, dashing it aside. He gained the pavement, and recommenced his bawling, shoving, and urging his desperate way among them. The people made way for the distracted man. In less than a minute, a wide, circular space, with a vast columnar monument in the centre, opened before him. It was the Place de la Bastille. Round this circular space he saw, as he looked, two frantic, staring, black horses dashing, and behind them a brougham, and looking from the window of this brougham the astonished face of Vansittart.

Folliet did not now lose his head. His plan of action was already determined upon. Something like what he saw he had expected to see. He had a revolver in his hand. But

7

first he had to discover which of the two was the untamed horse taken from No. 11 Rue Pigalle, and substituted in the stables of the Tuileries for the Arab, Tom. Bess, he knew, was merely following an example, and was harmless. Round flew the racing team like a flash of swiftness. Everyone of the wide-eyed onlookers stood paralysed; they saw that the attempt to stem that avalanche of fury would have been mere simplicity of mind. Folliet stepped out alone.

The substituted horse was on the off-side. But by the time he had determined this fact, so intense was the pace, that they had shot past him before he could fire. He ran the other way to meet them. This was the fifth revolution of the brougham, and with every revolution it had tended nearer, in a narrowing circle, to the central monument. Before it came round again, the carriage bumped. Vansittart, his coachman, and the two horses were sprawling on the ground.

Vansittart lay right in the way of the horses, which at once began to flounder and struggle to their feet. But Folliet lodged a bullet in the brain of the Arab, and the next moment was supporting Vansittart.

" Ah, Monsieur Folliet," said Vansittart, blithely, " you ? Ah, thanks."

He held out his hand to Folliet.

The next moment he fainted. The arm he had held out was dislocated.

Just at the corner of the Rue de Rivoli and the Boulevard Sebastopol, someone, who was not known, had struck fiercely at the plunging and restive Arab stallion. So Folliet heard afterwards.

CHAPTER X

WILHELM'S PIGEONS

THE two sisters, Agnès and Jeanne, were more flurried about the love affair of little Marie than they would have been at the wreckage of all the nations of the earth in mutual war. On the night of its discovery there was a long secret confabulation, wonderment, suggestion, invective, till near morning. Here was an unexpected complication of the marriage problem left them by their uncle. What if *she*, the *p'tite*, the despised, carried off the fortune without knowing it. The idea was too preposterous. But, certainly, there was the possibility; love is a dangerous thing—a thing of whims, and sudden starts, and sudden decisions. And what could they do to avert the tragedy? They could beat her till she sickened : Jeanne actually proposed it. They could lock her in a room, and never let her out till—after things were settled. These were the obvious brute remedies for the situation. But they would not do ; Agnès felt that. The child would be missed from her work ; there would be inquiries. There remained but one thing—to watch her, waiting, hoping in luck, and in what might turn up. Jeanne undertook the charge.

Again on the next night—the night of Vansittart's spill from his brougham—the lovers met at the Buttes-Chaumont, while Jeanne lurked and listened.

Almost immediately after the first rhapsodies, Marie began to question him about " the invention." It had filled her mind all the day. She had a profound faith in its wonder-working powers. What could not her love do? He was the hero of the world, the great magician.

99

"And the model," she said : "have you finished it ?"

"What, the model again ?" said Armand. "Will it keep torturing its little seraph-head about the model, then ?"

"But you promised ! Ah, you promised !"

"Well, I have kept my promise."

"You have been seeing to it ? It is finished ?'

"I have been seeing to it, and it is finished."

"And you yourself think it good ? It will do what you meant it to do ?"

"It will kill something like a thousand men at one attempt."

"How wonderful you are ! And is it big, the model ?"

"Big enough to nearly fill my room."

"One cannot therefore carry it about in one's hand, to show ?"

"No, it is too big."

"What is it made of ?"

"Wood and nails, and nasty chemical things."

"And what will you do now—with it ?"

"Do ? I don't know. Nothing, most likely. I have not thought. It is a bore. I love you !"

"How much ?"

"Right up to the stars."

"And how much do *I* love *you ?*"

"Right round and round the universe."

"Yes—just like that !"

"Sweetest !"

"But what will you do with it ?"

"With what ?"

"The model."

"Oh, the model ! don't think of that. It is of no importance."

"So that we shall always remain poor, and not be married, and be practical ?"

He caught her to him.

"Yes ! soon ! did you say *soon ?*"

" Yes, soon, soon. But—do you know what I shall do? I shall go to the King, or to Mr. Vansittart, and tell him—really."

He laughed. " You ! Why, you silly——"

" You think I do not mean it ? I will ! "

" But Mr. Vansittart—have you not heard ? "

" Heard what ? "

" He had an accident to-day, going to the station to join the army. He is in bed, ill."

Every soul in Paris was full of the strange news. But Marie, all occupied with her divinity, had not even heard of it.

This was a damper to her scheme. She said :

" Then you must write to someone, and tell him about the invention. Promise me. One should be serious, and see to things. Promise."

" For how many kisses ? "

" A thousand."

" One does not know to whom to write."

" But one may discover. Ask a *gens d'armes*, and he will tell you the proper person. To-night, will you ? "

" If I have fifteen centimes to buy a stamp."

" I will give you. Promise."

And so the promise was made.

At about the same time, Folliet was turning a key in the door of Jeanne's room at No. 11 Rue Pigalle. He had been lurking throughout the evening near the gate, and had seen the departure of Marie to meet her lover. Then, crouching behind her, Jeanne ; then, half an hour after, Agnès. The house, he knew, was now empty of its female occupants—his opportunity was come. He entered the courtyard and the house. He had sworn not to sleep until he had in his hands the threads of the conspiracy which menaced the safety of the country.

On the previous day the Prefect had taken careful note of the rather intricate way to Jeanne's triangular room. He was able to reach it in the dark. In his pocket were a number of keys and implements. He entered the room and listened. No sound but the occasional scratching of a pigeon against its cage in the next apartment. All was dark. Folliet, with excruciating slowness, turned the key in the lock which shut him from the pigeon-room. He had provided himself with a duplicate, in case it should be removed, but the original key was there. Then he softly took off his shoes, laid them behind the bed-curtains, and stepped through the open door. He was in the enemy's territory.

The room in which he found himself was small. There, at the one window, was a man, looking out, his elbows leaning on the sill. The faintest sound now would have betrayed Folliet. But he did not make it. No sooner had he discerned the dim and silent figure, than his revolver was in his hand. Then, with eyes that had acquired the faculty of seeing in the dark, he looked about the room. In a corner, a spot of perfect blackness caught his eye ; it was the cupboard in which, on the previous day, the two men had hidden from Jeanne. But it was perilously near the window and the motionless man. It was, however, the only apparent hiding-place.

When a thing had to be done, Folliet was not a man to hesitate. With concentrated alertness, he stepped nearer and nearer to the vague, broad back at the window, ready to shoot if it stirred. Then he touched the open cupboard door ; in an instant he was within the aperture. He drew himself cautiously inward. As he did so, his stockinged toe struck against an old oil-can lying prostrate there, and set it slightly rolling. At the sound, the watchman started into upright alarm, turned, took two steps forward, and looked round the room. Then he resumed his sentry at the window. Folliet waited an hour.

Once, the man at the window lifted himself and paced three or four times round the room, muttering a few inaudible words in his beard. Two of them only could Folliet make

out. The man had said, " No message ! no message ! "
Then he resumed his place at the window, and the dead
silence recommenced.

Half an hour more, and a tramp was heard outside the
room. Then four men entered. All together, in one breath,
they cried out in German :

" News ! is there any news ? "

Folliet held his breath—nothing but a straining ear. The
man at the window turned and said :

" Not a word. Been looking out all the evening. It 's
sure to come, I suppose.",

Someone struck a light, and lit a candle on a table in one
corner. Folliet could hear them, one after another, throw
themselves down wearily on stools and chairs. One of the
pigeons, wakened, sleepily commenced to coo and roll a soft
rotatory lullaby.

For a time there was silence ; the men, it was clear, had
been walking much, or working. They were tired. But
Folliet said to himself : " This is the height of luck. Presently they will start to jabber."

He had not to wait very long. One said :

" Well, Karl, my boy, so far everything has run pretty
well for us, I think."

" Grand, I think ! " came the answer. " We did n't
want to kill the man, after all, but only to keep him a prisoner in Paris for a day or two. And that 's what we 've
done."

" But is that sure ? " said the man at the window.

" Sure enough, Franz. His right arm is dislocated at the
shoulder—or so everyone is saying. If he gets out of bed
before three days, he 'll have the will of a mule, that 's all.
But it is n't likely that the doctors will let him."

" I pity the poor beggar myself."

" Oh, pity! so do we all. But what is one man where the
interests of so many are concerned ? Hurrah for the Fatherland ! "

" Hurrah ! Hurrah ! " said another, with a kind of languid enthusiasm.

A third, a big, red-bearded man, began to hum :

> " Muttersprache Mutterlaut,
>   Wie so wonnesam, so traut ! "

" Poor old Bach ! " said the man at the window, " you mind how he was always at humming the old tune ? "

" Yes, poor old Bach !   Pity he was such a fool."

" Wonderful little fuss the Paris police have made over his death, don't you think ? "

" Good reason why, my boy.   They are so utterly at sea. They are trying to cloak over their own incapacity.   Here is a man who, though found in the river, does n't look as if he was drowned ; and he was n't poisoned : and he was n't struck or stabbed ; what can the poor police think ?   They simply stare, and rub their innocent eyes, and say as little of the matter as possible."

" Still they got pretty near the scent when they came to question this girl Agnès and Jeanne got hold of the detective. As sure as I am a living man that girl would have blabbed if we had n't stopped her."

" Oh, right enough, she would have blabbed.   But she could not have enlightened the dull brains of monsieur *le polisson* very much about Bach, all the same.   Why, she does not even suspect that he is dead, much less the means by which he died, or our motives for killing him."

The conversation by this time had become general among the five.

" I wonder if they genuinely think that he committed suicide."

" Oh, no doubt.   Bach had no enemies, you know.   He was a quiet, easy-going kind of body."

" But, on the other hand, he had strong motives for living. He was going to marry this girl Agnès with her dowry."

" What the deuce can they think of the matter ? Lord ! they must be puzzled."

" But you know, mates, when one comes to think of it, Bach was an honest man. He was a fool, of course. But I say he was an honest man."

" Bah ! so is a tree honest, or a sheep. Every fool is honest enough."

" Oh, yes, we know all that. But just consider : he had always been a struggling man, had Bach, and suddenly this girl with the money takes him up. It was a great thing for him, of course. Just then he comes into contact with the Society. He joins ; he is enthusiastic in the cause of Germany, but when he hears that it is necessary for us to lay hands on Vansittart he draws back, says he is not prepared, as a citizen of France, to go so far ; and, mind you, he was warned—he was warned that death was the penalty which he incurred by drawing suspicion upon himself. But he persisted; he had everything to lose, and he persisted. I say that old Bach was an honest man, mates."

" Well, but so say we all. Where 's the good of wasting sympathy on dead bones ? The thing had to be done ; and the old fool deserved what he got. May he rest in peace ! "

" Who was it suggested chloroform as the means of putting him to sleep—the President, was n't it ? "

" No—it was old Dr. Caspar. And then the vice-chairman of committees said he must go into the river to wash the stuff out. It was neatly done, too."

" Hullo ! Good ! here she comes. Stand by ! "

This from the man at the window, in a regular shout of gratification, and immediately a sound of wings was heard, and there, through the window, with angelic haste from afar, came alighting a white-plumed bearer of tidings, her long embassy accomplished.

She sailed to rest on a cage, her own, and at once was fluttering in the bosom of one of the Germans.

" It 's Beatrix ! " he cried. " She comes from Lorraine—
from Schwartz."

" The very thing we want ! "

They crowded round. The disengaging of the narrow
bandage of paper from the little messenger's leg was the
work of a minute. The man who had sat at the window
held the ribbon stretched between his fingers. There was
a moment's breathless silence. Folliet, in his eagerness to
hear, had almost stretched his head outside the cupboard
door.

Someone read aloud the words :

" Attack on our side put off for a week from now. Meanwhile, nothing likely to happen. Till then, Vansittart to be
kept in Paris at all costs."

" A week ! " exclaimed one.

" A whole week ! " exclaimed another.

" We 'll find it a tight job," said one.

" How will we do it ? " said another.

" He will be out of bed in two days."

" He will be off to-morrow."

" We must summon an extraordinary meeting at once."

" One of us must run to the President instantly."

" This is cursed luck ! "

" It is the devil's business ! "

" But it 's got to be done."

" It has."

" We 'll manage it, boys ! "

" Oh, right enough, we will."

" But what about the pigeon ? "

" Feel her crop."

" She 's famishing."

" She 's travelled two hundred miles."

" She 's dying of thirst."

" Is n't she a beauty ? "

" Just look at her ! "

" Beatrix ! Beatrix ! "

" Groundsel 's best for her empty crop."

" Not it ! Let her have Indian."

" Is there any water in her trough ? "

" Where 's the box with the pigeon-feed ? "

" Look here ! I am going to mix her some fresh."

" There 's the bag of crushed wheat yonder."

" Where ? "

" In the closet."

" Just run and reach it, Fritz."

" Is it hanging up ? "

" Yes—at the back, near the middle."

" Let us have the candle."

" Why ! you don't want a candle. Stop ! I 'll get it myself."

The red beard moved towards the cupboard. Folliet was a bold man, but his heart beat thickly.

What could he do now ? He was full of resource, but what could he possibly do ? The interior of the cupboard was a woefully narrow space. No man could come searching within it and fail, at some point, to touch him. He heard the heavy, approaching step of the German. His knowing and quickly working brain could see only one chance, which might or might not fail. His hand went swiftly groping along the wall behind him where the bag had been described as hanging. He found it. It was of good size. He took it from the nail, stepped quickly backward till he leaned against the wall, and held the bag outwards and upwards before him.

Looking toward the light, Folliet could see someone approaching, while he himself was absolutely in the dark. The door opened somewhat ; a tall man entered—stretched forth his arm. Folliet could faintly see the arm ; he guided the bag towards the out-reaching hand. The German took the bag, thinking he took it from the peg. Folliet almost breathed afresh. Unfortunately, the man did not seize the bag securely ; it slipped from his grasp, and dropped. He stooped to pick it up, and, as he stooped. his head butted against Folliet's stomach.

The German at once uttered an exclamation of astonishment, and, uttering it. tried to straighten himself. The next moment he was flat on his face, his legs sticking out beyond the cupboard. Folliet had thrown him. A loud bellow came from the man's throat. Folliet was running over his prostrate back into the open room, among the others.

" Move, and I fire ! " he shrieked.

He covered one of them with his revolver, stealing rapidly all the time towards Jeanne's room. But so absolute was their astonishment that they stood mere gapers. There was an instant when not a sound was in the room save the fluttering of the pigeons' wings.

Folliet gained the door leading into Jeanne's room ; he pushed it; it opened; and as it opened, they were upon him —the whole five.

The bang of a revolver, once, twice—and a man dropped, wounded. In the next moment Folliet was behind the door. He slammed, and tried to lock it ; but the shoulders of four men were struggling at it on the other side. To continue the attempt he saw to be waste of effort. He took to his agile heels.

Suddenly, as the Chief of Police turned, he saw at the next door through which he had to pass. the apparition of Jeanne, returned to her room, holding a candle in her hand. She stood right in the breadth of the narrow doorway with wide-open eyes. In her bewildered state Folliet saw that she was easy to manage. He simply rushed upon her, dashed the candle from her hand, and slid past, leaving her in comparative darkness. Just near were the stairs, and the next moment he blessed his stars for the unexpected return of Jeanne, for, immediately afterwards, as his pursuers rushed out upon him, they came upon the woman, stumbled over her, and in a moment Folliet, now all the way down, heard above him a confused row of tumbling and bumping bodies, which only ceased when the jumbled mass of rolling men reached the first landing in their fall. Before the Germans could pick themselves up he had gained a good start. He threaded his way with breathless haste through the rather complex house and gained the courtyard before his pursuers had reached the foot of the stairs. He rushed into the open street, bootless, but safe.

Within half an hour No. 11 Rue Pigalle was in the hands of the police, with all its winged inhabitants. But every one of the human birds had flown.

CHAPTER XI

MARIE

MARIE was a sweet child. She had the face of a Madonna, a face pure oval, and stained with the pink of dry roses. But in spite of her pretty face, it was no easy matter for her to see M. Vansittart.

When she went to the palace and said, " I wish to see M. Vansittart," the usher looked at her and smiled. Then he counselled her to go home and be good.

" Be virtuous and good," he said, " and you will be happy."

But Marie was virtuous and good, and yet she was not quite happy. She said :

" May I see the King ? "

The usher said " No," but that good children when they died would stand with a crown upon their forehead, and a harp within their hands. He was an edifying person, but she went away discontented.

Marie returned the next day. Armand had written to " the proper person " about his invention, but had received no reply by return of post. " The proper person " got a score of such letters every day, and never took any notice of them. But Marie dreaded that Vansittart should go away before learning the vast powers of her magician. So, trembling in every limb, she returned the next day, and said :

" May I see the Queen ? "

It was a different usher whom she saw this time ; but he, too, seeing her wan, lovely face, smiled, and counselled her about her morals. The Queen also, it was clear, was far too high up to be " seen " by her.

Yet this time Marie would not go away. Only she got timidly out of sight of the usher, and dawdled about higher up the vestibule. This part of the palace was semi-public ; there were now a good many people hurrying to and fro in it. Marie felt comforted, being lost among the grand folk.

She turned an angle of the vestibule, and came into a fine gallery, open, with Corinthian columns on one side and pictures of battles on the wall of the other. She stood gazing at one of the battles with uplifted eyes, and in this attitude made such a picture that a gorgeously dressed lady, hurrying past, stopped and looked at her. The general public, except those who had business, never intruded so far as the vestibule or gallery; and what Marie's business could be the lady was at a loss to guess. Partly from curiosity, and partly from interest in the upturned face with its air of pretty innocence, she stopped. Then, after a moment's hesitation, she said in a low voice :

" Do you want anything ? "

Marie blushed crimson. Her eyes dropped.

" I want to see M. Vansittart."

The lady, as the usher had done, smiled.

" M. Vansittart ! but——"

She stopped. The proposal was so preposterous, that there was nothing to be said. Words were quite inadequate.

" If not M. Vansittart," hazarded Marie with a still deeper depth of crimson, " then the King."

" The King ! "

" If not the King, then the Queen."

" The Queen ! "

The lady was drowned and lost in notes of exclamation. She was a maid-of-honour, a person starched in etiquette, the prisoner of ceremonial. But when her stays were off, her breast was soft enough. She said quite kindly :

" You cannot see M. Vansittart, for he is not here. You

cannot see the King, for he is overwhelmed with business. You cannot see the Queen, for the hour of her *levée* is long past."

Here was despair for poor Marie. Her head hung in silence. The lady was touched by her air of absolute dejection. She said :

" Will you tell *me* what you wanted to see them about ? "

" It was about an invention," she answered across the lump in her throat.

" An invention to do what ? "

" To kill people."

" Oh ! not invented by yourself ? "

" Oh no, by someone else."

" By whom ? "

" By someone—a great man."

Her head lifted with pride.

" Well—and what do you wish to see them for in regard to this invention ? "

" I wish to tell them about it, and get someone to go and see the model."

" Well, your scheme is rather wild, you know. But stay —perhaps—it is possible—I may do something for you."

Hope leapt in Marie.

" Oh, thank you, mademoiselle ! And shall I see them really ? "

" Not those you wished to see ; but someone—perhaps— whom it will be much better for you to see. Follow me, this way."

The lady led the way into the interior of the palace. How vast a place it was, Marie thought. Then, in an oval saloon, she was bidden to wait, and left alone.

Marie waited half an hour. Then a tall lackey, all lace and gold, was bowing before her ; and in another moment she was following behind him through more corridors and complexities. At last she was ushered into a room, and the door closed behind her.

It was a small room, full of a peculiar atmosphere of home, strange to a French mind. It seemed the sanctuary of a sanctuary. The lace curtains were cheap, and tied with cheap blue ribbon ; but more care and taste had been expended in the tying of those knots than in the furnishing of one of the great *salons* of Versailles. There was a faint odour of cigar smoke about—of cigars smoked in this little den by Vansittart himself. Opposite her, sitting in an arm-chair, Marie saw a lady, whose eyes were rather red, as if with weeping. It was Evelyn.

As soon as she saw the child, she loved her ; as soon as the child saw her, she trusted her. Their hands and eyes met.

" Sit here—near to me, will you ?—and tell me all you have to say. A lady has been telling me about you, and I am glad that you have been enabled to see me, and I am glad to see you, too."

So spake Evelyn. Marie was trembling a little from her previous nervous excitement. But not the least apprehension at speaking with the simple and gentle lady before her now troubled her. She sat, and in a minute was at her ease.

" First, will you tell me what I am to call you ? "

" Marie."

" Very well—Marie. I am Mrs. Vansittart, as I see you guess, and those who like me call me Evelyn. Is it true that you wanted to see my husband ? "

" Yes, madame."

" Well—but that is impossible, you know. He left the Tuileries an hour ago for the Gare de Lyon, and by this time is, I suppose, steaming rapidly southward."

" I did not know that," said Marie ; " they told me his arm was sprained, and that he could not go out."

" Ah, Marie ! " answered Evelyn, her whole full bosom heaving in a sigh, " sprained it is beyond all doubt, but had it been many times broken he would still have gone. Nothing could keep him back. The doctors threatened and commanded ; and I, Marie, tried what many, many tears and prayers would do ; but gone, you see, he is ! ''

" I am very sorry for—for—you, madame," said Marie.

Evelyn's hand fell upon hers.

" Thank you, Marie."

" You would, perhaps, prefer to be alone——"

" No. Tell me—whose is the invention—your father's ? ''

" No, madame."

" A friend's ? ''

Marie crimsoned.

" Ah, I see, Marie—I see ! ''

" He is very, oh, so very clever and great," whispered Marie, in a kind of confidential *entre nous*.

Evelyn bridled, and laughed.

" We all think that of the One, you know, don't we ? ''

" But *he* is, really. Oh, one could not dream——''

" He is at least very lucky, Marie. A Madonna is his devotee."

" Ah, how good it is to be with you ! One feels confident and strong. Are you always so good ? ''

Evelyn stroked her hair :

" We are friends, are we not ? One is naturally kind to one's friends."

" I should like him to know you. He would love you, too."

" There, we shall see. But the invention—are you sure——''

" Oh, yes—quite ! ''

" What is he ? ''

" An artist—a musician."

" Really ? And how comes it, then——''

" He is so clever ! He can do anything. He just dreams of doing a thing, and he goes and does it. A great genius can do what he wills. You doubt, perhaps, because you never saw him. As soon as you saw him, you would know, too. It is all on his great brow, and in his eyes ! ''

" Oh, devotee ! Oh, enthusiast ! "

" I wanted M. Vansittart to see him ! I only wish he had."

Faith begets faith and is as leaven. Evelyn was interested, and Marie, had she known it, had already won her victory.

" But why, " said Evelyn, " did he let you come ; why did he not come himself ? "

" He is strange, you see," the girl answered ; " he does not care about things—only about love, and ideals, and melodies, and all high things. He is like a bird or an angel —I cannot describe him."

Evelyn laughed. A musician who invented destructive engines of war, and was like a bird, or an angel, was certainly not a commonplace person, and could only come from the Latin Quarter. She said :

" And did he take the trouble to make a model of his invention ? "

" Yes, he did. I made him promise to do it, and he did. It is at his rooms."

" And can he bring it here ? "

" Not in his hands ; it is too big."

" Is it dangerous ? Does it go off ? "

" I hope not. I don't think so. Oh! suppose it were to go off, and blow him up ! "

Evelyn smiled. This certainly seemed one of the possibilities of the case. But she said :

" Oh, there is no fear of that. I will tell you now what you must do. You must see him, and tell him to put down in writing an exact description of his model, and send it to me, personally, and then you may depend upon me, Marie, to see that it shall come under the eyes of the King himself, since Mr. Vansittart is away."

Marie, lost in gratitude, turned away her head, and let fall a heavy tear.

" And meantime," went on Evelyn, " just write down in this little book your name and address, and in a few days I shall send you a letter, telling you how the affair is progressing. Write down also in it the address of your friend in case we want him urgently."

Marie took the pocket-book and wrote her own address and Armand's. Then she handed it to Evelyn, who looked at the scribbled words. Even as she looked she started. She saw, " No. 11 Rue Pigalle."

This house three nights before had, she knew, been seized by the police at the bidding of Folliet. The next day Folliet had had a long conference with Vansittart. Evelyn, therefore, now knew of the great German organisation, whose present aim was to keep Vansittart in Paris for at least a week. As she saw this address before her, a dark and sinister suspicion shot, like lightning, through her mind. But one glance at the meek, unconscious, child-face restored her to calm. Marie, though she saw that something unusual was happening at home when she returned from business at night, had no notion of the significance of the strange faces she saw there. The sisters were allowed to continue to live on, as usual, in the house. When Evelyn's eyes rested with keen inquisitiveness on her face, the girl did not even blush. For a minute Evelyn pondered in silence. Then she said :

" Well, Marie—be of good hope. Good-bye. Will you come and see me again ? Can you spare the time from—him ? "

" To see *you*, yes," said Marie ; " I should love to be always near you."

" Ah, Marie, *you* are happy ; you have him always ; but *I!* You must come—will you ?—and comfort me with the story of your happiness."

" I know—I know all that you feel," said Marie, " and I pity you from my heart. If Armand went away I should die, I know. But—perhaps—he will be back sooner than you think. God is kind to——"

Those words of Marie's—" perhaps he will be back sooner

than you think "—were unfortunate. Evelyn remembered them afterwards, and they troubled her. They had hardly been uttered, when the door was flung hurriedly open, and a man stood there in the opening.

" Darling ! "

Evelyn's cry rang through the palace wing. She flew to his bosom.

It was Vansittart. A handkerchief bandaged his forehead, where there was a biggish wound. He only said :

" Well, you see they won't let me go."

His right arm was tightly bound, and his left hand fell in desperate languor to his side. Evelyn was sobbing—sobbing on his shoulder.

As for Marie, she, with wide eyes, slipped away unseen. Outside she met someone who conducted her to an exit from the palace.

What had happened to Vansittart was this : Attended by a goodly guard, who had been warned that there was danger, he reached the station in safety, entered the special train with his retinue and Arizona Jim, and started.

Once clear of Paris the circuit to reach the Eastern line commenced. Whilst waiting momentarily at a junction, the occupants of the train were startled by a vague bang, a sullen roar like distant thunder. What it was no one could guess ; it came muffled, from afar, yet huge. Had the Eiffel Tower, or the Louvre, or Notre Dame been blown to fragments ? All was wonderment, vague surmise. The train proceeded at its former pace.

Two miles beyond Charenton, sweeping round a curve, they came upon a signal of danger—a signal to stop. There, ahead between the metals, was a man shouting and gesticulating, bidding them come no further. The driver at once put on his brake, and cut off steam ; but in another quarter of a minute the train was scurrying at random among hedges, fields, and rustic huts. When the compartment in which was Vansittart toppled on its side and stopped, he pitched forward, bruising his head. Besides, there were a few injuries among the others.

It was found that a vast section of the embankment had been blown up. It was impossible to proceed. On the further side of the disaster there was no train. Two days, Vansittart was told, would be required for the biggest army of workmen he could gather to repair the danger. He returned to Paris in a carriage hired in one of the villages.

Within four days, according to the pigeon message which Folliet had heard, Wilhelm meditated a great attack. And Vansittart could not leave Paris. He uttered not a word till he reached the palace. Rage and fury were boiling in his brain and bosom. His enemies had triumphed over him ; and he must sit still and wait, like an imbecile child.

But there was still a hope, a chance ! Why, he could ride on horseback to the seat of war within four days. He decided, however, that to wait for the repairing of the *chemin de fer* would be the quickest way. The same night a large proportion of the population of Paris—artisans, merchants, priests, confectioners—were toiling far from their beds at the remaking of the shattered line.

All day long arrests of people bearing so much as a German name went on in Paris. Detachments of soldiery from every town on the route of the line were ordered by telegraph to be told off to guard it. In Paris the station became a garrison.

About ten the same night, in spite of all the vigilance of the police, there was a large meeting of men who wore peaked caps with a pigeon's feather for a badge. It was a quiet, yet excited assembly ; it was held in the cellar of a large and lonely house in the seclusion of suburban Passy. The President, on rising, said :

"The work we have done, so far, is good. But it is labour lost, it is a mere frivolity of empty-headed patriotism, if there be not amongst us wit enough to devise some further stoppage, some other delay. Mr. Vansittart has four days.

We are met here to consider what is to be done in that time. Either of the means we have used before is now, of course, out of the question. Repetition here certainly means imbecility. My friends, I implore you, let your words be few. We are desperate men, met to think and act and strike—not to talk. I confess to you that at present I myself stand absolutely hopeless and deviceless before this problem. *What can we do?* Yet we must do something! Our instructions are—' at any cost.' I recommend those words to your remembrance. Let them be our watchword. At any cost—at any cost."

He sat down. There was no cheering, for earnest men have no time for cheers. One after another, the conspirators rose with a few brief words—suggestions. But the word of wisdom was not spoken.

Then a dead silence fell, as in a Quakers' meeting, when men await the Spirit and it tarrieth long.

No word! No counsel! Never men had toiled harder, with more self-sacrifice and devotion to a cause. And it had all been wasted. They had delayed the departure of Vansittart, but they had not delayed it long enough. It was mere childishness—like the charades of little girls.

The red-bearded man whom Folliet had tripped to his face in the cupboard, rose and proposed that they should meet the next night at the same hour, that each might tell what in the meantime he had been able to plan. And this was agreed to.

But all their plans and meetings would certainly have been useless had it not been for Marie, who at the very time of this meeting was with her lover at the Buttes-Chaumont, telling him all about her interview with Evelyn that day. And lurking behind her, listening, was Jeanne.

CHAPTER XII

THE next morning, early, a most singular sight might have been seen in the streets of Paris : crowds upon crowds of people all wending in the same direction, women with spades on their shoulders, young boys with buckets, drapers with pick-axes, music-hall *artistes* mingling with ecclesiastics, pretty young seamstresses with stout restaurant-keepers, and fashionable ladies with newsboys, each bearing some implement of labour, and all trudging, trudging onward with the same will, toward the same point. By noon half Paris had turned out. The whim had caught on, and grown into that special kind of fever which rages nowhere in the world outside the French capital. They were going to make straight Vansittart's way before him—to help with their own hands to repair the ruined *chemin de fer.*

Sometimes the French nation is incomparably sublime. It is a nation of moments. At these moments it stands far, far in the van of man. To the great moments of France the rest of Europe owes the chief part of what is called " modern civilisation."

By three o'clock that day the ruined embankment was perfectly sound and whole. The population of Paris streamed back from their labours into the capital, singing the *Ça Ira*, embracing each other, weeping, dancing, repeating to each other with lingering cadences the name of Vansittart— like sublime children—like heroes drunk with wine.

It only remained for Vansittart to set out.

"Each bearing some implement of labour and all trudging, trudging onward with the same will toward the same point."

On the previous night, Armand, at Marie's imperious command, had written an account of his invention, and sent it by post to Evelyn.

Evelyn received it in the morning, and read it. The description of the contrivance did not convey much meaning to her mind : it might be of importance, it might not. She hesitated as to whether she should show it to Vansittart. She had promised something to the child—but not that. She felt nervous about it, and wondered why. The sweet face of Marie rose before her. Then she thought how singular it was that the child should live at No. 11 Rue Pigalle ; then of the strangeness of the fact that at the moment when Vansittart had appeared at the door the girl should have said, " He may return sooner than you expect." Of course, she argued, it must have been a mere chance. The gentle girl, though she lived in that house, could have had no foreknowledge of the blowing up of the railway. Yet, if the expression was a mere chance, a coincidence, it was a singular one ; so singular that it seemed to her like an omen, a warning. She hesitated.

At ten Mrs. Vansittart decided that she would not show it to her husband that day. She would wait and think—to-morrow would do. About eleven she heard that all Paris had turned out to mend the rails, that they would soon be finished, that Vansittart would be able to set out in the afternoon. This increased her sense of responsibility ; she must show him now, if at all. What did she know? the thing might, in reality, be of the greatest importance to the issues of the war. How she would regret it, if, afterwards, it was proved that her hesitancy had cost to France a single life ! At twelve she showed the letter to Vansittart. They were sitting together in their little sanctum, where Marie had, the day before, been received by Evelyn. As soon as Vansittart began to run his eye over the scribbled leaf, his brows knitted. He read it through ; bent closer over it ; read it again. Then he threw his head backwards, and cried aloud,

" Good heavens, what a brilliant idea ! "

" Is it—is it ? " panted Evelyn.

" The man who wrote this letter is a very great genius, that 's all," he answered confidently.

" And you will see him ? You will see the model ? "

" Oh, rather ! "

" When ? To-day ? "

" This is the only day I 've got."

" Jerome, dear, I have certain fears, half-suspicions—I don't know how to tell you——"

" Come, sit here—no, the other knee is the whole one. Now, out with it."

Then Evelyn told him about Marie and her Madonna face, and how she lived at the wrong house, and how, to the minute, she had prophesied his return.

" But you liked her ? " he said. " You liked her face ? "

" Yes."

" You trusted her ? "

" Yes, wholly."

" Then that is enough. You never yet trusted anything that was base, Evelyn. I can't help thinking that of all the women in the world my darling is the most sensitive and instinctive to the approach of the evil-doer. Oh, I have noticed, you know ! That is so. If you like her, Marie is true to the core."

Still, Evelyn was restless and foreboding.

" Yes. I do not doubt it," she said, " but——"

" But what ? "

" She may be the dupe of others."

" She may."

" And this plot to keep you in Paris ! "

" I do not forget it."

" This may be a ramification, a thread of it."

" It may."

Puff, puff, came the smoke from his lips, he blowing it away from her face.

" Then you will not go ? "

" Yes. I will."

" Ah, obstinate ! "

" No, not that. I reason in this way. Marie is true to the core, for you trusted her till chance circumstance turned you against her. And, let me add, Armand is true to the core ; for no man would reveal to me an idea like this—it is one of the grand inventions of Time, I tell you—if he were at all hostile to me and France. Very well, then—Armand and Marie are true ; that 's settled. Now, suppose I go and visit Armand without any human being but you and the two of them knowing of it ; then I think I shall be in a position to defy their plot—eh ? What do you say now ? "

She had nothing to say. She buried her head on his shoulder, murmuring, " God preserve my dear ! "

Vansittart's reasoning about Marie and Armand was good, and, indeed, infallible. He was not aware, however, of the strange will of M. Carhaix, and the legacy of strife and bitterness which this gentleman had left to his nieces.

By one o'clock Evelyn had written to Marie. The more direct way would have been to write to Armand ; but time pressed, and there was the probability that Armand, a man and a bachelor, would be away from home, without having left behind any indications of his whereabouts. She chose her messenger with great care, a man of prudence whom she knew and trusted. She described Marie minutely to him, and told him on no account to deliver the letter into any hands but her own.

At that time Vansittart did not imagine that the enthusiasm of the Parisians would finish the work on the railway so early as three ; he thought, however, that late at night it would be done. At about ten he might set out for the station with all secrecy, for he had no intention, if he could help it, of being assassinated on the way. Armand's lodging lay in an obscure street not far from his route. So he told Evelyn to make the appointment for half-past ten.

This, then, wrote Evelyn : Marie, on the receipt of the letter, was at once to run and find her lover, tell him, and bind him to absolute secrecy. She—Marie—as soon as she had read the letter, was to tear it up, and scatter the pieces. She was warned that if she mentioned the matter even to her closest relations she might do infinite harm to her friends. The messenger had a hint to wait and see that the letter was destroyed before his eyes. A little after one he reached No. 11 Rue Pigalle. He rang the bell, and the wicket was opened by Jeanne. Evelyn did not know, had not suspected, that Marie went out to any business.

" I want to see Mlle. Marie Carhaix," said the footman. He had no livery ; he was in plain clothes.

Someone wishing to see Marie was a rarity. Jeanne was infinitely surprised at once, spurred to the very acme of curiosity. But she did not show it. She only said :

" She is not at home, monsieur."

" Can you tell me where she is ? "

" Yes, monsieur. She is at her work. I am her sister ; if the matter is not a private one you may tell me what it is, and I will tell her when she returns."

" Perhaps it might be better if I saw her herself," the man said. " Can you tell me where one may find her ? "

" Yes, monsieur ; it is in the Rue du Bac, between the Quai d'Orsay and the Boulevard St. Germain, at No. 26— a *vacherie*."

" Thanks, ma'm'selle."

No more—the man turned away. Jeanne looked through the wicket and saw him step into a *fiacre*. Then she, too, stepped out, got into another *fiacre*, and gave the driver the same address. At the entrance of the Rue du Bac she alighted. The footman by that time had entered the *vacherie* and asked for Marie. Marie was not there. Madame, the proprietress, told him that Marie had asked leave to be out for an hour that day. She might, however, be expected back within five or ten minutes, if he would wait. Jeanne, hanging behind the large column of a house frontage, saw the man come out of the shop and stand waiting at the door.

Marie away from work in the middle of the day ? What, in Heaven's name, could it all mean ? The light of a tiger-cat's eyes gleamed greenish in the woman's intense glances. Her heart beat high with excitement. In five or six minutes Marie came running with hot face towards the door of the *vacherie*. The messenger knew her at once. He stepped towards her.

" Are you Marie Carhaix ? "

She started.

" Yes, sir."

He took the letter from his breast pocket and handed it to her.

A blush of vivid crimson deepened in her flushed face as she ran her eyes over the letter. Here was joy beyond dreams, and communion with the great ones of the earth ! Twice, in a tremor of happiness, she read it. Then Jeanne saw her deliberately take the sheet and tear it into the minutest bits, some of which she cast into a passing hay-cart, and some on the breeze, and some down a grating in the street near by.

The man smiled, and bowed, and turned away.

She called after him.

" Say it will be well—and a thousand, thousand thanks from the grateful heart of Marie."

He bowed again and walked off.

Marie was due in her shop, but the shop to-day was out of the question. Instead of entering it she got into a cab. She had just left Armand. She knew where to find him. In another cab Jeanne followed her.

This, for some reason or other, was a day of festival and large-hearted liberality with Armand. Yonder, at the Res-taurant au Regent, in the Rue Gironflet, red that day flowed the wine. At the back of the house there was a large open yard ; at the back of the yard, an arbour. It was made of rough, upright poles, covered over atop and at the sides with laths. In front it was entered by a little Gothic door ; and over door, and laths, and poles, grew a rank luxuriance of jumbled ivy, and eglantine, and honeysuckle. This arbour had made the fortune of the proprietor of the Café au Regent ; it was a place of wedding-feasts, of lovers' *rendezvous*, of family celebrations. Within there was a dim, religious gloom, and romance, and small round tables spread with spotless naps. To-day it was the very home of riot. As Marie sped down the little lane that led from the wicket beside the restaurant proper, burst upon burst of merriment from within this temple of pleasure greeted her. That morning Armand had scribbled down the score of a song, which was afterwards to be famous all over France, and he had managed to dispose of it to a music-dealer on the Quai St. Michel, for four napoleons. Never millionaire rolled and luxuriated in the consciousness of inexhaustible opulence, as Armand with four napoleons in his pocket. How to dispose of all this excess and superfluity of wealth ? With one half of it he bought a cheap wedding-ring. Then he sat down and commenced writing out fantastic invitations.

They were all here, the rollicking boon companions who lived like the sparrows—the future writers, painters, musicians of France—with their sweethearts, decked out in all the bravery of their cheap best things. Shrill and deep rang the laughter, and red—and white—flowed the wine.

What was the cause of the *fête ?* Perhaps only one of the wild whims of the incalculable Armand. No one knew. Armand guarded it in his bosom, a sacred secret.

Sober-minded Marie had thought of turning back to her work. However, after a short interval, she put her head inside the little Gothic door. There was much shouting and unquenchable laughter—that kind of laughter which has in it the gurgle and *éclat* of bright wines. Everyone now was merry, and the girls had begun to lean their heads on their neighbours' shoulders. Marie entered with a smile of comprehension and indulgence all round, and a bow, and a look of love at Armand. He leapt towards her with flushed face. One of the girls had picked two or three tendrils from the creepers and crowned his head.

She led him at once by the sleeve down to the back of the arbour, where there were no tables. The noise and the laughter of the others went on meanwhile.

She was bursting with the news ; joy danced in her eyes.

" M. Vansittart is coming ! "

" Where to ? "

" To your rooms."

" When ? "

" To-night."

" Now, that is cursed luck, Marie ! He can't, that 's all."

It did not occur to the young man that it was a compliment for the virtual ruler of France to visit his squalid apartments. Armand habitually thought himself—and, no doubt, was—the greatest man in the world.

Marie's eyes opened wide in surprise.

" But—you are *drôle !* " she cried. " Is it not, then, a great thing for us ? "

" It is absurd ! I cannot listen to it. To-night of all nights. It is *bête !* "

They spoke in a somewhat high voice. The noise of the merriment made this necessary. Just near them, outside, hidden by the leafage of the arbour, crouched Jeanne, hearing every word.

" No," said Marie, " you must listen to me, and be practical. Why, he will not stay long ! " she cast her lashes down, with a deep flush. " Will we not have the time after he is gone, whole hours ? "

" Sweet ! "

" Darling ! "

" But it is a bore."

" No—you will be good."

" When is he coming ? "

" At half-past ten."

" It is a bore, a wretched bore. But he is a decent person, Vansittart. Let him come."

He said it with royal condescension. Marie was radiant.

" You will be friends, I know—you and he ! "

" He is coming alone, I hope ? "

" Yes, I think so. Mrs. Vansittart wrote to tell me—with her own hands."

" He will find his way, one hopes, through the dinginess of the Rue Brevet ; he probably never was in it in his life before."

Jeanne, outside, repeated to herself, " Rue Brevet, Rue Brevet."

" But, Marie—you will be there ? "

" Yes—near there."

" Suppose he takes five, say even ten, minutes to see the thing. That will make it ten-forty. You will be with me not later than ten-forty, mind."

" Do I look as if I would be later ? " she said with a sly under-glance. " But I must go back now—or it will be suspicious. Remember you are not to say *anything* to *any-one*."

At this point Jeanne, understanding that they were about to part, began to move rapidly, yet cautiously. When she got beyond the arbour, she started into a run, and was clear of the gate before Marie was out of the arbour door. In the street, she again got into a *fiacre*, and drove rapidly home-ward.

It was now two o'clock. Jeanne's mind was all in a whirl of confusion. Certain turns of expression in the talk be-tween Armand and Marie had filled her with a kind of vague dismay. She had listened to them on the previous night, and nothing that was then said had had upon her this terri-fying effect. Since then, what had happened between them ? Was it possible that—no, it was too much ! Her teeth ground together at the thought. She drove homeward, wanting to sit still and think. What she would do, she did not know yet. What she would do was dim within her, and after a while would work to the surface of her brain. She wanted quiet.

In the first room at No. 11 into which she stepped, she met Agnès, whom she supposed to be out.

Jeanne dropped wearily into a chair, and blurted out :

" We are ruined ! "

" Who is ? " asked Agnès.

" You and I."

It was incredible to Agnès, who, depending upon Folliet's promise to produce Bach in a day or two, was now hourly expecting her lover with keen outlook and hope.

" What do you mean ? " she said.

" Marie is married."

The blood rushed from Agnès's cheek, leaving a face of whitewashed pallor.

" Married ? "

" Yes, married."

" My God—married! "

" Yes, married."

Jeanne repeated the word venomously, as if gloating over the anguish she was inflicting.

" How do you know ? "

" I listened to their talking just now. They spoke like man and wife. There was a wedding lunch."

" I don't believe it ! "

" Why not ? "

" You listened to them last night, and they said nothing about it."

" But her lover is a madman—that is certain. He must have taken a sudden frenzy to be married this morning. Marie asked for leave from the *vacherie*, and was out, I know. They must have gone straight to the Mayor, and been married."

o

This was the real fact of the case ; but Jeanne did not really believe that it was, for she had no knowledge of a character like Armand's—a character impetuous as a torrent, self-conceited, quixotic, sublime. That anyone should marry on the spur of the moment was a thing outside Jeanne's experience. But she was certain from the talk she had heard that something serious had either happened, or was about to happen, between the girl and the boy; and the temptation to be sensational was too strong to be resisted. She said that that had happened which she believed was only about to happen. Human nature is like that.

The blow was even worse for Agnès than for Jeanne, for Agnès was in daily expectation of being married, and Hans Schwartz was still far away in the war-region, with a ruined farm. The two sisters sat silent, looking at the floor.

"That little beast !" said Agnès. "I 'll tear every hair out of her head."

"Her husband is a big, strong man," remarked Jeanne.

"But she need n't get the money—she knows nothing of the will !"

"Other people do, though, and they 'll soon know that she 's married. Don't be a fool, girl !"

"Well, all I can say is, that it is your fault. It was you who undertook to watch them——"

"And did n't I watch them like a cat ? Can I help it if the little frog takes up with a crazy man ?—that is, if they *are* married."

"Ah, now you are changing your tune !" said Agnès.

Jeanne, having enjoyed the misery of the other at the stroke of bad news, now began to discuss the other side of the question—namely, the possibility that Marie was only about to be married.

"I did n't tell you for certain that they were married," she said. "They may be, as they may not. But that 's what it will come to before another twenty-four hours."

"Ah, now you are talking! I knew she could n't be married already."

Hope sprang at once into the virile flower in Agnès's breast. She, she, Agnès, and no other, would yet, after all, carry off the prize! Ah, then would be her hour of triumph!

"But she will soon be, I tell you," said Jeanne.

"If we let them!" cried Agnès.

"What can we do?"

"Marie shall never go outside these doors when once she enters them—till I am married!"

"Oh, I dare say. *You* married!"

"Well, there 's nothing wonderful in that, I hope. It may be you, or it may be me. What is to be will be."

"But there is a better way than that," said Jeanne.

"Than what?"

"Than keeping Marie a prisoner."

The thought which had lurked dim and undefined in Jeanne's brain had now worked itself unconsciously into definiteness. Her plan was formed.

"What other way is there?" asked Agnès.

"We can do for the *man!*" hissed Jeanne.

"The man? How?"

"He has rooms in the Rue Brevet. To-night M. Vansittart is going to them at half-past ten."

"Not the great M. Vansittart!" said Agnès, with opened eyes.

"Yes!"

"What a funny thing!"

"It 's true, though."

"And what can *we* do?"

"It 'll be the death of Marie's lover, that 's all."

Still Agnès did not see.

"How do you mean?" she said.

"Oh, I can't stand a fool, Agnès!"

"Explain yourself, can't you?"

"All we have to do is to run round and tell Heinrich Reutlingen."

"That M. Vansittart is going——"

"Yes!"

"Will he be alone, then?"

"Yes!"

"At half-past ten, in the Rue Brevet. Oh, what a thing!"

"We have got him, my girl!"

"We have—we have!"

"We'll do it!"

"Oh, you are a one, Jeanne!"

"The little beast! To suppose that she could blind *me!* I'll crush him—here—in the hollow of my hand."

"You are a one!"

"They are mad to get hold of Vansittart, those Germans. This will be just what they want."

"It will—what a thing!"

"And it's sure."

"Oh, it's certain."

"And Marie's lover will be there. They will *kill* him. One always kills an eye-witness. And when I tell them the secret I shall make that a condition."

"And you know where to find Reutlingen, and the rest?"

"Yes; he, for instance, is in the Rue des Abbesses, in hiding from the police."

"Then go; why should we be afraid?"

"I am not afraid, if you are."

"I am not either."

"You look it, then. I never could bear a fool."

"It is such a thing! If it should be discovered!"

"Who cares? We shall be safe. Each for one's self, I say."

"Go you, then; I shall be here till you return."

"That is easily done," said Jeanne, as she rose.

And as she passed through the door, Agnès muttered: "Go. Well—it is for me that you go."

It was then nearly half-past two.

CHAPTER XIII

BETWEEN half-past two and three the activity among a large number of Parisian-Germans was simply intense ; there was scurrying, bustling commotion. There was also a meeting in a low corner of Montmartre, to which Jeanne was brought ; and at which she spoke. She was then excluded from the hurried deliberations, but, sitting in a room near, heard them, and ran home to Agnès full of the news of coming events.

Very shortly after five o'clock people in the east end of Paris were startled by some inexplicable events. A prison-van wending its slow way northward up the Boulevard Menilmontant, and making for the Prison des Jeunes Detenus, was shattered by a bomb. All the three policemen in charge of it were severely injured, as well as some of the rather youthful prisoners inside. The incident aroused the tenderest sympathy for the sufferers, not only on account of the age of some of the victims, but chiefly because of the fact that the van was constructed with a number of little cells on each side of a passage running down its length, that each of these little cells contained an inmate, and was locked on the outside ; that the crowds who gathered around the wrecked van were unable to open them, not knowing where the keys were, while the fainting policeman could render no aid. Meanwhile, the cries of the wounded lads were heard. The spectators thrilled with pity. The culprit had not even been seen.

But what was the dismay and excitement of the populace

when, at ten minutes past six, a *second* prison-van—almost
at the same spot—received severe injuries from an exploding
bomb whose thunder filled the street and shook the houses!
No one, *now*, could doubt that this was the work of a maniac
—some mad Nihilist who thus showed his detestation of
punishments and laws. Many of the people, however, believed that the explosive must have been flung from the
window of a house in the Boulevard Menilmontant, and the
report ran like wildfire that it was cast by a hypochondriac
who objected to such things as prison-vans passing beneath
his front windows. This story, in face of the astounding
facts, seemed so plausible that the police searched all the
neighbouring houses, in the actual expectation of gaining
intelligence of such a being as was imagined. But without
success. Again the criminal had got off without leaving
behind him a sign.

However, at eight, a *third* prison-van, crowded with
prisoners in their little cells, coming from another quarter
of Paris was to pass along the Boulevard Menilmontant ;
and, influenced by considerations of pity, the authorities decided not to run the risk of exposing these also to the fury
of the assassin. So that—supposing that there was such a
hypochondriac as had been imagined, determined to force
the police to choose another route than that beneath his
windows—he really succeeded in his object,—for choose another route they did.

But in order to reach the Prison des Jeunes Detenus, there
was only one other possible way by which the van might
pass, and that was along a narrow, dark, and winding alley
called the Rue Lourmel.

The Rue Lourmel is an almost deserted place, owing to
the fact that one side of it is occupied entirely by the dead,
windowless, back walls of two huge warehouses, whose fronts
look over a street which meets the Rue Lourmel at an angle.
The other side of the Rue Lourmel is occupied by dwelling-
houses of a very disreputable kind, half of which are dilapi-

dated and untenanted. At the moment when the prison-van entered the street, there was positively no one abroad in it, except two children playing in the gutter. There was hardly room for the van to go through.

The latter part of the day had been gloomy and just then it began to rain.

When the van approached the centre of the street's length, it was stopped by about twenty masked men, who rushed from the *rez-de-chaussée* of one of the deserted tenements. Three of them were dressed from head to foot in the garb of the Parisian police ; the others wore ordinary clothes.

The guard of the van had been increased by two, and the five made a desperate, but, of course, brief and useless resistance. Two of the assailants were shot, but not fatally. When the guard had been secured, they were borne into the empty house, and chloroform, to a sufficient amount for its effects to last some hours, was administered to them. There, stupefied, they were left. The scuffle, though extremely brief, had not transpired without noise. Some heads, mostly female, had popped from their windows ; but no occupied house was immediately near the scene ; and so dark was the street, and so gloomy the deepening night, that nothing as to the nature of the *mêlée* could be made out from above. When some of the tenants ran down into the street, they were met by the three costumed policemen, who had now removed their masks, and were gruffly ordered to be off. Being of the doubtful or criminal class, they obeyed shamefacedly. In a few minutes the street was empty again.

One of the pretended policemen, who had secured the keys of the van, now entered it, and noiselessly unlocked the two rows of doors behind which the prisoners were confined. In doing so, he took care to leave each door very slightly ajar—so slightly that the fact of its being so had all the look of accident. Then he descended from the van, re-entered the house with the others, and the van was left alone.

From a broken window of the house the men stood looking

out upon the van. So securely had they planned, that they appeared to be in no sort of a hurry. Presently they saw a prisoner appear at the door of the van, descend step by step with gingerly trepidation, leer guiltily and swiftly around, and make off with all the speed of his flying heels. Then another—then another. One by one they came, with gingerly trepidation, with swift and guilty leer, with flying heels.

When they judged that all the prisoners were gone, about seventeen of the assaulting party entered the van and took their seats in the cells. The outer door of the van was re-locked. The three liveried policemen took their stations on the outside. The van drove away. It was now close on nine o'clock.

A few minutes later Folliet received a telegram saying that the 8:45 prison-van had not arrived at the Prison des Jeunes Detenus ; and was there any explanation ?

All day Folliet had been in a state of the keenest unrest. Since noon he had known that Vansittart would be able to set out that day. About one o'clock he sent him a telegram in cipher, asking if he would, indeed, set out. Vansittart replied : " Yes, privately, late in the evening."

At this Folliet lifted his eyebrows. Why in the evening, since he was so anxious to be off? Why not in the afternoon ? And " in the evening " was vague. The message slightly angered him.

The question that filled his mind as time went on was this : What are the Germans thinking ? What doing ?

Something of what they were thinking he was certain of. They were in a state of rancorous desperation. They were thinking that they had toiled and failed. What they were doing he could not guess at all. After racking his brains he concluded that they were doing nothing, for the simple reason that there remained nothing for them to do. And in this conclusion, at the time, he was right. Yet he remained anxious.

At the news of the first bomb explosion he was like an old

lion that had been roused by an arrow wound to pricked
alertness, furious bitterness. At the news of the second he
was overwhelmed by a feeling of impotence and darkness.
What could he do? What did he know? He knew this
much, however—and he was the only man in Paris who had
the shrewdness to know it—that the explosions were not
anarchical, or hypochondriacal, or maniacal, or anything
whatever but German. He knew this by reasonings which,
in reality, were infallible ; reasonings based upon the very
peculiarity of the crimes. There had been anarchists, and
hypochondriacs, and maniacs before ; but their acts had
never borne much resemblance to the acts in question. The
new crime had been committed by new men with new motives. He could not doubt what men. And their general
motive he, of course, knew—the detention of Vansittart in
Paris. But when he came to question in what way Vansittart could be detained in Paris by the blowing up of prison-
vans, his imagination failed him. This thing he could not
fathom. He groaned at his impotence. He felt that between him and light there was fold upon fold of darkness.

But soon after nine, one fold of darkness was removed. The
Prefect of Police heard that the van had not arrived at the
Prison des Jeunes Detenus. A few swift enquiries revealed to
him the fact that the van had been ordered to go by a different
route, in consequence of the previous explosions. This gave
him at once the motive of the explosions ; they had taken
place because the conspirators desired the last van to go by
a different route, and since the van had not arrived, they
had desired it to go by this route in order to prevent its
arrival—in order to seize it. He was minutely acquainted
with the intricacies of Paris ; he knew the low and lonely
character of the Rue Lourmel, by way of which the changed
route of the van must needs pass. It was the very place for
a seizure. If they seized it, he knew that those on the outside would infallibly wear policemen's clothes, and, in this
way, they might probably be able to pass at leisure through

the whole of Paris, under the very eyes of the ordinary *gens d'armes*, without attracting the least notice of any person.

The first thing he did was to circulate a hurried warning of the facts, with the number of the van, through the force. But this took time. He knew well that he was too late. And now Folliet felt not one whit nearer to light. Of what use would a prison-van be to the conspirators with reference to Vansittart ? The obvious guess was that they were going to put Vansittart into it as the only safe, the only possible vehicle in which he could be conveyed from one place to another. But by what means they could hope to get the ruler of France, now safe at the Tuileries, into a prison-van, was a thing beyond his wildest dream. He dismissed his guess as probably wrong—the van assuredly would serve some other purpose. He was at the Prefecture, in a snug room, alone, his head buried in his hands. Having telephoned his orders as to the lost van, and a search for the missing guards, he sat so for nearly an hour, hoping for news, groaning with thoughts, like a man bankrupt of hope, in the last straits. Then power of brain failed him, and for some time he lay, all vacuous and inane, with his head thrown forward on a table between his arms. Suddenly, however, he sprang straight up with an exclamation. A thought, unsought, had passed through his mind. He had remembered that in his hand he held a trump-card—a last chance. His trump-card was Agnès Carhaix.

The first thing that he did was to telegraph to Vansittart : " Be very cautious to-night ; there is extreme danger everywhere ; better, if possible, not set out." But when this message reached the Tuileries, Vansittart had just started.

Having scribbled the telegram, Folliet rushed through the building to his own waiting carriage. He told his coachman to drive at his very highest speed, and gave the address of No. 11 Rue Pigalle. It was now raining in torrents, the night was already black, and gusts of wind were howling through the streets.

He found the sisters, Agnès and Jeanne together. Agnès leapt up to meet him ; Jeanne eyed him with suspicious under-glances.

" I wish to speak to Mlle. Agnès," he said.

" Yes, monsieur," replied Agnès.

" Monsieur may take a seat," said Jeanne ; " if it is necessary, I will retire."

But Folliet had no intention of being listened to by Jeanne through key-holes.

" If Mlle. Agnès will step this way with me—" he said. " Otherwise I must go at once—I am in a great hurry."

" Yes, monsieur—yes ! " answered Agnès, all eagerness to hear about her Bach. " I will come with you at once."

She and Folliet went out together into the courtyard, through the wicket, into the teeming rain of the streets. Then he led her under the shelter of his carriage-hood, and sat beside her on the cushions.

" It was about Bach, you know, that I had to speak to you."

" Yes, monsieur."

" Ah, poor fellow ! "

Agnès turned white.

" Monsieur has not found him ? "

" I have."

" Ah, thank you, sir! "

" Poor Bach ! "

" But, monsieur—— "

" You are prepared for the worst, I hope, my poor girl ? "

" The worst ? "

" Bach is dead."

" Dead ! "

" Murdered."

" Murdered ! "

" Foully, foully, foully murdered."

" It is a lie ! "

" It is the truth."

" Murdered by whom ? "

" By his friends. Ah, foul, foul, foul ! "

" This is some trick—some trick of Jeanne's—to rob me."

" No, no ! If you think that, if you mistrust me in this fashion, I shall simply go away, and leave you to find out what you can in your own way. What do I care about Jeanne, or you either ? I am simply doing my duty in telling you the facts. Bach was foully and brutally murdered by his friends."

" What friends ? "

" His German friends. His body is still at the morgue. You saw it, and did not know it. You should have looked at it well. That cap which he had on you never saw him wear, for the simple reason that he only wore it in attending certain meetings of his fellow-conspirators. There was a conspiracy, you know, directed against M. Vansittart. Well, well, poor Bach ! Because he was an honest man and refused to go beyond his conscience in murdering M. Vansittart— only because of that—they said he was a traitor who was going to betray them to the police. So they chloroformed him and threw him into the river. All that we now know —there is n't the least doubt of it ; I can prove it to you up to the hilt."

He could feel the trembling of the girl beside him. But she said calmly enough :

" Then prove it, monsieur."

He drew from his pocket a piece of paper. It was the bill for beers and spirits found in Bach's cap.

" Look here," he said, holding it toward the light of the carriage-lamp, " is n't that Mr. Bach's handwriting ? It came out of the cap of the drowned man."

Folliet, by the light, scrutinised the girl's face with the intense anxiety of a culprit before the judge who is about to pass sentence of life or death. What was in that face ? If grief, he despaired ; if the rage of a tigress, he had hope.

Jeanne, her sister, when about to reveal to him the plot

of the conspirators, had been stopped by the news of the destruction of her lover's farm. Her predominant instinct had been revenge against the side which had thwarted and injured her. Would it be so with Agnès now? Folliet had not long to wait.

As soon as the girl saw before her the proofs of what her fixity of hope had led her to disbelieve till now, she sank back into the darkness of the carriage as if shot, but there, held out stiffly in the lamplight, was her clenched fist. All was lost to her. In the world there remained but one thing —vengeance.

When she next spoke her face was dark and red with passion.

"May they be burned!" she hissed, "and Jeanne with them. It is her doing!"

"No, it is the Germans. Jeanne has nothing to do with it," said Folliet.

"It is she, too, and they; they are all the same. They are all mixed up together, the whole crew. If it was n't for something I 'd tell——"

"Well," said Folliet, well satisfied, "whatever you have to tell, you must tell quickly. I am in a hurry to-night. If to-morrow will do, and——"

"To-morrow will be too late. What is the time now?"

"Twenty minutes to eleven."

"It 's too late already—curse them!"

"Never mind. Tell me—tell me the whole. Quick, now!"

He patted her hand. She began to speak.

CHAPTER XIV

THE FLIGHT

FROM the route between the Tuileries and the Gare de Lyon, an obscure street leads northward a little way into the Rue Brevet. The Rue Brevet itself is an alley without *trottoirs*, and is not used for carriages on account of its narrowness. Yet the balconied houses that front it are large ; they are occupied by persons of the shady, or shabby, or student classes.

Armand occupied three very poorly furnished apartments on what was in reality the fifth floor, though called the fourth.

Vansittart, having left the main road, stopped at the beginning of the alley, and alighted. He was wrapped in a long waterproof, and had an umbrella. Jim Bates, who preceded him, had by this time almost reached the station. Vansittart told his soaked coachman to wait, and started down the street.

Following behind him was Marie, bent beneath the rain. She had stood beneath a doorway waiting and watching for the coming of the solitary figure, intending to guide him to the house, if need were. But without much difficulty he discovered No. 6, rang, and was conducted by an old woman *concierge* to the stairway. He began the long climb. He was a few minutes late. At this time Folliet was just entering the wicket of the Carhaix family in the Rue Pigalle.

When Marie saw Vansittart within the courtyard, she hurried back to her nook of shelter from the pouring rain, and crouched, waiting for him to reappear.

As for Folliet, he got from Agnes the whole plot in all its details. Then he almost hustled her out of the carriage. But he had so many things to do, and so many places to go to, all at the same time, that he lost a full minute in agonised reflections. Then he called out, " The Tuileries ! "

The first clear necessity was to discover whether Vansittart had received his telegram, and, if so, whether or not he had now actually set out in spite of it.

Not there ! Here was racing at random about the streets of Paris, and wasting of time when moments were of gold ! He hastily scribbled a note on a leaf torn from his pocket-book, and gave it to a warder with instructions to hie on horseback to the Prefecture and deliver it to the officer on duty. It contained an order to despatch instantly a body of armed *gens d'armes* to the Rue Brevet. He himself went tearing at a gallop to the same point. The storm had emptied the streets; there was hardly a stoppage to his swift career. In a few minutes he and Marie, for the first time, were face to face. He was about to rush into the gate of No. 6 Rue Brevet, when, also rushing in, he met Marie, she coming from the direction of the other end of the street.

Folliet glanced at her face, and from the description he had received of her suspected her identity.

" Who are you ? " he asked.

" Marie Carhaix."

" Where is M. Vansittart ? "

She started violently.

" M. Vansittart, monsieur ? I can tell you nothing of him."

" Ah, good girl ! But see, I am a friend—I am the Prefect of Police—my name is Folliet. Tell me quick—quick, now—do ! I am a friend—can't you see ? Look in my face —can't you see ? Do I look like one—ah, tell me, my little friend—do ! "

Marie hesitated ; she had an instinct in his favour—a feeling that he was probably honest. Then she remembered her instructions from Evelyn—never a word must pass her lips. Folliet saw her face harden.

Vansittart had, a minute before, passed her on his way back to his carriage. As soon as she had seen him emerge, she had started to run with glad and eager feet toward the house, knowing her husband was awaiting her. This, poor girl, was her honeymoon—the time of the beginning of the great drama was come. She had made no delay to hie to the arms that awaited her.

So that at this time Vansittart was just getting into his carriage at the street end opposite that at which Folliet had alighted. The Prefect's coachman had made that end of the street his point of arrival, because it was more quickly reached from the Tuileries, by two short-cuts, than the other.

Folliet saw the face of Marie harden against his almost frantic appeal.

" Ah, if you only knew, my child," he cried, and rushed madly from her into the courtyard, without more waste of time.

Up the five flights of stairs he flew, and for a minute crouched, panting, listening, outside Armand's entry-door. He heard nothing but a rather quick tramping to and fro in the room. It was Armand, vexed with Vansittart and all things, throbbing with impatience for the footstep of his bride on the stairs.

Folliet burst into the room.

" Is M. Vansittart gone, then ? " he cried.

Armand stared coolly.

" Who are you, monsieur ? "

" Tell me ! Tell me ! how long ago——"

" It is I who have asked a question, monsieur."

" Oh, this is a mad, mad business ! Can't you see, man —there is no time——"

Without further talk, he rushed successfully past Armand, caught a candle, and before he could be prevented ran with eager eyes through the three rooms. Not there, then ! He threw down the candle, and dashed from the rooms, down the stairs ; Marie, coming up, stood and gazed after the flying man with wonder.

At the gate Folliet stood a second, looking up and down the street. He ran back to his coachman.

" Anyone passed you ? "

" No, sir."

He ran to the other end of the alley, nearly butting upon Vansittart's carriage in the blinding rain and the dark. He examined it ; he peered at the horses. Yes, certainly, this was no other than the millionaire's equipage. But to his call there was no answer.

" They have succeeded," said Folliet—" ah, they have succeeded, then ! "

He stumbled over Vansittart's driver lying stunned or dead near a carriage-wheel. He lifted the heavy hand, and it fell back upon the paving-stones.

" M. Vansittart ! " cried Folliet, lifting up his voice— " M. Vansittart ! "

There was no answer.

The detachment of police which he had ordered to the spot had not yet arrived. Should he await them ? But to what end ? And if not, whither should he go ? He did not know.

Vansittart, meanwhile, locked in one of the little compartments of the prison-van captured that day, was being driven through the nearly deserted streets.

When he returned to his carriage, he had found the van there, and his coachman already laid low. At the same time he was surrounded by men.

They had the insolence to jest. One of the men costumed to personate a policeman said :

" M. Vansittart, I find it my unpleasant duty to arrest you."

Vansittart was a merry wight for bearing the inevitable. When there was nothing to be done, he did not attempt to do anything. A twitch of despair pierced like a sword through his heart, but he said quite blithely :

" For how long, gentlemen ? "

" Four days," said one.

" Well, that is moderation itself. But the night is foul—let us seek shelter. Please do not touch my right shoulder."

They conducted him to a compartment in the van :- the others took their place within. The outer door was locked, the policemen took their stations on the steps, and on the driver's seat ; the van went lumbering off.

En route, Vansittart did what his captors had expected that he would do—he made a noise. He beat upon the thick woodwork of the van, shouting, calling his own name. And he was heard, as was afterwards stated, by several of the scurrying passers along the streets. But the prison-van proved to be a good thought. He was supposed to be some drunken prisoner howling away the riotous mood of his inebriation.

Between the hours of nine o'clock, when the van had been captured, and half-past ten, when it started from its hiding-place to go to the Rue Brevet, the vehicle had lain concealed within the courtyard of a great building shut in by a high wall. It was a depositary for grain, a corn-warehouse, situated in that region of commerce behind the Rue du Faubourg Poisonnière. The distance from there to the Rue Brevet was some five minutes by the prison-van, and the route lay mostly through dark and narrow streets. The warehouse was in the hands of a wealthy German merchant ; and the key of the gate was in possession of the conspirators.

When the van had been got inside the gate, it was drawn up against the wall, the gate was relocked, and Vansittart's cell was opened. They took the van-lamp, and passed through the flag-paved courtyard to the building. It was a dingy-looking, commonplace pile, with small, rudely boarded windows. Within, there was a smell of hay and corn, and fine dust in the air, and worn-down wooden stairs, and pulleys and tackle, and piles upon piles of bags, bags empty and full, yellow, and grey, and brown, and black. Without, two or three cranes projected from windows near the top.

The men with their prisoner ascended four flights of stairs. It was evident that they did not know the place, for, all the while, detachments of them ran opening doors here and there, seeking for a suitable apartment to which to conduct their captive. At last one of them, opening a door, cried aloud :

" In here, then."

They entered. It was an extremely large apartment, heaped in various parts with bags of grain. In one corner, railed off from the rest of the room by an iron railing, was a small, square sort of alcove. Near the centre, was an old deal table with pen and ink on it ; and near this a worm-eaten bench.

The men locked the door of their entrance upon themselves, and gathered round the table. Vansittart shook the wet from his waterproof, and sat among them on the bench. The lamp was placed on the table ; its dim gleam shone on their faces, but left the distances of the room in shadow almost absolute.

Among the men there began at once a guttural discussion in rapid German. It related to what was now to be done with Vansittart. This, the simplest detail of all the plot, had, it was clear, not been yet considered. But the simplest detail, as often happens, called forth by far the greatest wagging of tongues. Jabber, jabber, in mixed, chaotic argument, raced the dissentient tongues.

Putting aside the fact that the warehouse was not exactly a hotel, there had never been any intention that the prisoner should occupy it for any length of time. It had been fixed upon merely as being temporarily convenient, and a good hiding-place for the van. During the daytime, it was surrounded and occupied by swarms of workmen. The majority scouted the idea of making it the four-days' prison-house ; a minority thought that that would be preferable to the risk of another journey, even in the stillest hour of the morning and to the nearest house that was proposed. But there was no agreement ; for ten minutes the confusion of tongues lasted. Vansittart sat listening with his quiet smile.

At length one of them got up, and went whispering round among the others. His idea was that it was not decorous and expedient that their prisoner should sit there listening to their various ideas, and hearing the addresses of the houses which on all sides were being mentioned. Everyone agreed with him, with a nod, and a " quite right."

Until the point in dispute was settled it was agreed that Vansittart should be removed out of immediate hearing. They looked round the room. Yonder, in a corner just visible, was the grating which shut off the alcove from the apartment.

" Kindly come with us this way, M. Vansittart," said one.

Vansittart bowed, rose, and followed three of them.

When they came to the grating they found that it was locked ; but the padlock by which it was secured had in it the rusty key. It turned with a squeak, the grating swung back, and Vansittart stepped into the alcove. As he did so he shivered, and drew his waterproof high up round his chin. The night was cold, and his feet were wet. The men shut the grating upon him and returned to their parley.

Vansittart had not stood there thirty seconds when he felt a hand suddenly clapped over his mouth and deep in his ear heard the snake-hiss of these words :

" Not a syllable ; I am Folliet."

The next moment he felt the flooring gently give way beneath him. In his astonishment and dismay he caught for support at the receding railing ; he was sinking—the railing was rising from him ! His clutching hand, in its passage through the air, struck upon a rope.

He only just succeeded in preventing himself from bursting into loud laughter ; he was in a lift.

The lift was used for the raising and lowering of grain between the upper and lower rooms in this part of the building. Past the third, the second, the first floors, they slowly and noiselessly sank. Then only Folliet spoke.

" Well, sir, I think there may now be a chance———"

" M. Folliet, allow me to compliment you on your ubiquity."

" There 'll be a race, sir, no doubt. Can you climb a gate ? "

" I hope so. But they are engaged in a discussion which may last some time."

" I don't fancy it will, sir. The stillness of the alcove may attract them ; they will go to look. We may not have a moment to lose."

They were in deepest darkness. Folliet struck a match ; they were near the level of the ground-floor ; he touched the rope. They alighted, ran through a store-room, down a passage, came to an outer door, and, passing down the steps, were in the courtyard.

" We can climb on to the van, sir, and so gain the wall : then there is a good high drop on the other side."

They ran forward, flinching and cowering beneath the scourge of the pelting rain, like people toiling on under a burthen. When they came near the gate, in order to climb the van, Folliet, to make sure, groped about the lock on the inside, and, to his surprise, found that the Germans, after turning the key, had left it there.

" Here is luck, sir," he said in a low voice. " We need not climb after all. And I can now offer you a shelter from this rain."

At once he threw the gate wide, seized the languid head of one of the drenched horses, and slowly and cautiously led the van from the yard.

He conducted Vansittart to the steps at the end, reclosed

the gate, and locked it on the outside, mounted to the driver's seat, and started. Inside the van, Vansittart was sitting in the very cell which he had occupied in his journey to the warehouse.

When Folliet thought himself out of hearing of the conspirators, he whipped the horses into a gallop. Once he was hailed by a policeman, who, faithful to his recently received instructions, pursued the van a little way, blowing a whistle of alarm. Folliet, plying his whip continually, took no notice ; he made straight for the Rue Brevet and at one end of it jumped down.

Drawn up along the street, he found the detachment of *gens d'armes* whom he had ordered to be there. He gave the sergeant the key of the warehouse gate, and told him to pack his men in the cells of the van. They were to go to the warehouse, replace the van in its former position, lock the gate on the inside, and remain, all of them hidden, until the conspirators appeared. There was to be no arrest inside the house lest some of them might escape. One of the policemen only he told off to drive Vansittart's carriage back to the Tuileries.

At the other end of the street waited Folliet's own carriage. He and Vansittart ran toward it, entered, and started for the station.

Somewhere about the same time, one of the conspirators, the discussion at the table being ended, walked toward the alcove to fetch Vansittart. He noted as he came near that he did not see the millionaire, but without surprise, for the recess was in a deep shadow, and its inner part in unqualified darkness. He walked to the grating, opened it, and stepped inward, and, without a cry, perished. The drop from the fourth- to the ground-floor was one of some ninety feet.

Then a second, after a minute or two, having seen him go and not return, sauntered listlessly towards the recess, and, without a cry, perished. Then a third.

But now these mysterious disappearances began to be

noted. Cries of "Where are they?" "What the devil—?" "What's the row?" were heard. There was the snatching up of the lamp, the eager tramp, the hurried inspection, the wild discovery! The whole body stared at one another's gaping mouths, then, with a single impulse, started in eager chase through the room, down the stairs, into the courtyard.

There, lying dark and still, beneath the drench of rain, was the van, sinister and deadly as that wooden horse of Troy, whose entrails were treachery and armed men.

"But tell me, M. Folliet," said Vansittart, lying back wearily and painfully in the carriage which bore him at last to the long-waiting train, "tell me, since you are man and not omniscient—how came you there—in that warehouse—in that lift?"

"There is nothing simpler, sir," said Folliet. "Properly speaking, you owe your escape not to me, but to the revenge of a woman."

"Indeed?"

"A woman named Agnès Carhaix, the sister of the Marie whom Mrs. Vansittart knows."

Agnès, in the venom of her hatred, had braved rain and storm to witness the arrest of the Germans in the Rue Brevet. She ran thither immediately after her revelation to Folliet. For half an hour she waited, lurking and spying. Bitter was her disappointment when she saw them accomplish their purpose, and drive off uncaught. But she followed them, saw them enter the warehouse, and returned, breathless, to the Rue Brevet in the hope of meeting Folliet. In the very moment of his acutest despair, she touched him on the arm.

"It so happens, sir," said Folliet, having told the whole story of the sisters Carhaix, "that about five years ago, a workman employed in that very warehouse murdered his sweetheart, and hid himself for quite three weeks in the wilderness of the building. I myself had the task of search-

ing for and finding him ; you will therefore understand how
it is that I know every cranny of the place. From the
courtyard just now, as soon as ever I climbed over the wall,
I could see a glimmer of the light on the fourth floor, and
at once knew quite well how I could get to it. So I went
up the lift and waited for events. You can guess my joy
when I saw them bringing you straight to me. But, sir,
may I ask, are you satisfied with the invention you went to
see ? "

" M. Folliet," replied Vansittart, " the world will yet hear
more of that invention, and of the wonderful man who made
it."

The carriage drew up at the station, and Arizona Jim
sprang forward to meet Jerome, saying, " Well, governor,
this time I thought you were a goner."

Five minutes later, Folliet stood waving his handkerchief
on the platform at the receding train.

" Well, at last," he cried. " Well, thank God—at last ! "

CHAPTER XV

ON THE BANKS OF THE MEUSE

THE Emperor William's soul-consuming impatience to cross the Meuse in force at last received its reward.

Superhuman efforts on the part of his engineers and commissariat repaired, in major part, the damage effected by Le Breton and his Five Thousand. Stores, men, and guns were at hand—nought was wanting save the final order to advance. Officers and men shared the burning desire of their master. To meet the French, to crush them, to pulverise the human barrier that blocked the road to Paris,—that was the supreme object. The proud army of Germany felt that nothing could withstand their iron power. Verdun must be made another Metz, the valley of the Marne a more disastrous Sedan.

On the eve of the attack the Kaiser sat in his headquarters, the château of a small village. Resolve was written on his stern features as he seized a pen wherewith to indite the fateful command. Yet, with unexpected caution, he hesitated.

"Are you assured that no hitch can arise?" he said to his Chief of Staff, Count von Waldersee.

"Quite certain, your Majesty. Reports from the three army corps, from each division, from every brigade, show that all is in readiness."

"Pontoons plentiful and in their allotted stations for rapid transfer to the points selected for crossing?"

"Beyond doubt. My own staff have individually examined them."

" There can be no fear of a failure in supplying reserve ammunition ? "

" None. There is provision for a month if we fought a heavy battle each day."

" Then the word is ' forward.' May the spirit of my grandfather guide my hand." He squared the writing-pad on the desk, but added, as an after-thought, while bending to his task, " Daubisson will not expect an assault to-morrow and Vansittart, I know, is in Paris."

The grave officer standing by the Emperor's side permitted a smile to flit across his stern visage. Not even the ghost of William I. could chase away the vision of Vansittart.

The other wrote with rapid scrawl :

" COMRADES,—The hour is at hand—the period of enforced inaction has passed. To-morrow at dawn, three army corps cross the Meuse. To the 4th, 11th, and 23rd Brigades is given the honour of leading the van. By night we shall have taken a giant stride towards Paris. Let us meanwhile perform a giant's task. WILHELM."

After perusing this forcible order of the day the Emperor added the date. It was not an auspicious one—June 15th, the anniversary of his father's death, that noble prince who hated war as the worst ill known to civilisation.

He scowled as he read it. With angry movement he plucked forth his watch—eight o'clock. Why not issue the order after midnight ? Then do it. But the manuscript would run, " To-day at dawn,"—which was absurd. William II. growled a long German word where an Englishman would have used a short one, whilst he seized another sheet and re-wrote the memorandum in its original form, without the date. Von Waldersee lost no item of this piece of by-play. But the general was also a courtier. Taking the order from the Emperor he remarked :

" Your Majesty's resolve is taken at a fortunate moment."

With a quick and suspicious glance the Kaiser cried,

" How so ? "

" When the history of the war comes to be written, it cannot fail to be noticed that your Majesty formulated this command on the date of your Majesty's accession.''

" Ha ; a good omen, indeed. I had forgotten. Give me the paper.''

The pallid ghost of " Unser Fritz " vanished whilst his wayward son wrote :

" Given at the Imperial Headquarters of the Second Army Corps on the right bank of the Meuse, June 15th.''

Forthwith the field telegraphs clicked the fateful summons north and south. By nine o'clock it was known to half a million of German soldiers, by ten it was flashed to London, and long before midnight its perusal caused General Daubisson's usually complacent face to wrinkle into wrathful fury, as he paced to and fro in a room of the Hôtel de Ville at Bar-le-Dec.

" *Sacré nom de Dieu !* " he yelled, appealing to Le Breton without expecting an answer. " Why does Vansittart tarry in Paris ? ''

The famous cavalry leader's philosophy was crude : " It cannot be a woman, for he loves his wife.''

The French Commander-in-chief might have been sarcastic at such folly on the millionaire's part had not an interruption come from without.

A well-known voice, in barbarous Anglo-Saxon, growled at the sentry at the door : " Put down that skewer, red legs. Don't you know enough ter quit when Monsieur Vansittart turns up ? ''

" *Ventre bleu !* 't is Jeem,'' shrieked Daubisson.

" *Mille tonnerres !* and the Emperor,'' yelled Le Breton.

In the next instant they were gesticulating round Vansittart. Respecting his prejudices no less than his damaged arm, they embraced each other. The delight of these two enthusiasts was a good thing to see.

Whilst they were indulging in a second hug, Jerome turned to Bates.

"Jim," he said, "join the sentry and let no one interrupt us."

Jim swung round and closed the door behind him. He winked at the soldier, jerked his thumb towards the chamber, expressed in pantomime the intention to run anyone through the liver who sought an entrance, and wound up by producing a small flask which he handed to the other.

"Have a nip," he said. "It 's better stuff than *vin ordinary*."

Piou-piou glanced cautiously into the street to see that the officer of the guard was not about, and took a good mouthful,—only to spit the rye whiskey out again with a frightful grimace that his native politeness could not conceal.

Arizona Jim surveyed him with kindly pity, seized the flask, and murmured, after a hearty gulp : "Them chaps make me damp. Switch 'em off from colicky wine, an' they can't drink worth a cent."

Yet, when the sentry got the taste of it, he tried again, with less energy and more success.

Vansittart and his friends hastily exchanged views.

"Why did you not advise us of your departure?" cried Daubisson.

The millionaire smiled as he recalled the fierce whirl of events during the preceding fortnight.

"I was imprisoned in a Bastille of hesitation," he answered. "But I have escaped, and here I am, somewhat bruised, but whole. What is happening at the front?"

"Affairs of outposts up to the present. The German division which managed to reach Montfaucon, has been forced back. Our fortified camp at Verdun, invested at first, is now only threatened from the east. Practically, the enemy occupies the right bank of the Meuse, whilst I control the left. But I have just received some important news. To-morrow the Kaiser will attempt to force the passage of the

Meuse." And the General gave to Jerome a telegraphic "flimsy."

The latter read :

"Intelligence has reached the London *Daily News* that unusual commotion prevails in the German lines. It is believed that the long-delayed advance has been definitely decided upon, and that a few hours hence the first great battle of the Franco-German war will take place."

The sender was the French War Minister. He explained that the information forwarded to the English newspaper had been telephoned to him by the French ambassador at St. James.

Vansittart frowned. "If I had only reached you twenty-four hours earlier!" he exclaimed. "Yet there is time. What have you done?"

Daubisson snatched up a map and showed the disposition of his forces, four hundred thousand picked troops, the vital essence of the French army.

"And you propose?" went on Jerome.

"To remain on the alert and vigorously dispute the crossing of the river at every threatened point."

"Good! Excellent! But we must do more."

The American paced the room with slow strides. Daubisson was too fine a character to snub openly. Nevertheless, another half-day of his inaction would be fatal. Of course the German preparations had already discounted the Frenchman's Staff College tactics. The building of each bridge would be supported by massed artillery, their vastly superior arm, and the attempted resistance would be beaten back in a merciless hail of shrapnel and well-protected infantry fire. If the French troops did nothing before day broke, the Kaiser would sleep in Daubisson's headquarters the same night.

Vansittart halted. "General," he said, "your preparations are superb. Nevertheless we must disconcert the enemy at the very moment when his divisions are ready to march. You have pontoons?"

" Most certainly."

" Where are they ? "

Daubisson flushed slightly as he bent to the table to find the engineer's statement. He had never thought of attacking ; his most sanguine aspirations dreamed of effective resistance. He was clever enough to grasp the situation and accept it without comment. After a brief scrutiny he replied :

" Two complete bridges are here. I regret to say that the bulk of the apparatus is at Chalons."

" At Chalons ! " Jerome could not restrain his amazement. Chalons was forty miles in the rear—on the road to Paris. The French army was apparently prepared for retreat across the Marne rather than advance across the Meuse. Still he forbore to chide uselessly.

" Well, two will suffice. If immediate orders be given, at what hour can they be thrown over the river ? "

Daubisson consulted his watch.

" At 2.30 A.M."

" It is late, but it must serve. Le Breton, where is your cavalry division ? "

" At Pierrefitte. I can reach it by train in twenty minutes. A bugle-call will see the regiments paraded."

" Collect a strong force of horse artillery. Warn a brigade of infantry, march straight to the river and occupy the right bank of the Meuse the moment the bridges are practicable. Drive the German vedettes before you to the east. I understand the German centre is at Troyon ? "

" Yes," said Daubisson.

" Then the Emperor in person will try to cross there or at St. Mihiel, where three roads converge on the river. See that both points are protected by at least one hundred guns and plenty of infantry, entrenched if possible. Telegraph similar instructions to your southern divisional commanders at Commercy, Nancy, and Lunéville. The northern German column will no doubt march due west from Damvillers.

Order the general at Verdun to make a sortie with the whole of his effective troops and to provide plenty of work for the Germans in that locality. In every case add that generals are to hold themselves in readiness to cross the Meuse when they receive orders, probably about midday. Meanwhile the pontoons stored at Chalons must be forwarded by train to the Troyon and St. Mihiel columns. I will personally see to affairs here."

Bar-le-Duc woke into instant life. Staff-officers clattered through the stony streets, drums beat, bugles rang out their imperative notes, streams of men and horses, with all the impedimenta of an army on the march, moved slowly through the night along the country roads.

Daubisson at least possessed the rare virtue of accuracy.

At half-past two precisely Le Breton led the first troop of the 18th Chasseurs across a pontoon that spanned the Meuse between Troyon and St. Mihiel. The engineers were subjected to desultory firing by the German pickets, but they performed their work so smartly that before a brigade could be marched to the place Le Breton was strengthened by twelve guns and three battalions of infantry.

In the dim light the French executed a very pretty manœuvre. Knowing exactly what he wanted to accomplish, their leader sent off two regiments of cavalry on a détour, and the infantry, in skirmishing order, kept up a brisk fire at the rapidly gathering enemy.

Meanwhile the guns got into position, and engaged a German horse battery that had galloped up to the scene of action. A regulation combat, on a small scale, was in process of development when the French cavalry, coming up unperceived, took the German infantry and guns in flank.

Half an hour later, when the dawn of a bright summer's day would render all objects visible, this surprise must have been impossible. But now it was a complete success. Quite disconcerted, and unable to swing round in time, there was nothing for the scattered infantry to do but to bolt, which they did magnificently. The guns, of course, unprotected by cavalry, were captured.

Le Breton ordered Montsaloy, who led this brilliant charge, to follow fast on the heels of the retreating infantry, but not to get himself into difficulties. The General rode back to the pontoons to see how the supporting troops were crossing. He was astonished to meet so many regiments massed in battalions in the fields, and seemingly waiting for orders.

It was simply impossible for nearly fifteen thousand men to have crossed the river in the ordinary way, during the past twenty-five minutes.

But Le Breton had his explanation ready.

"That devil, Vansittart, has been up to some trick," he growled, as he swept along.

Sure enough, when he reached the Meuse, he found the millionaire near the pontoons, surrounded by a number of staff officers, to whom he was explaining the position to be occupied by each brigade in the forthcoming operations.

And now the mystery of the rapid movements of the troops was solved. It was hardly credible, but neither Daubisson nor any of his lieutenants knew that the Meuse above Verdun was fordable in many places.

When Vansittart and Arizona Jim rode up to the military bridges they found a first-rate block in full progress. Even with the utmost patience, in peaceful operations, it is a long and tedious task to transport a large body of men over a narrow pontoon. Here, there were but two for an army corps. A horrible dread seized Vansittart as he looked at the jumble of soldiers, guns, and horses, with ammunition-carts, ambulance and commissariat waggons momentarily arriving to congest the very approaches to the bridges. The firing on the other side warned him that Le Breton was actively engaged. Even if the Germans were repulsed it could only be for an hour, until their supports arrived in overwhelming strength. If the Frenchmen were caught in their present plight they would suffer complete and demoralising disaster.

The millionaire felt bitterly the need of the military training which must have foreseen this error of judgment. He was about to suspend the whole movement and recall Le Breton, when Jim Bates, who had been watching with amusement an altercation between an artillery major and a Zouave colonel turned to his master.

" What 's wrong with the crowd walking across, guv'nor ? "

" Walking across ! Where ? " cried Jerome irritably.

" Why, a'most anywhere," said Jim. By way of example he selected a point a little higher up-stream and rode over, the water scarce reaching his feet.

As he returned, the quick-witted French soldiers cheered him.

" *C'est un lapin !* " shouted an admiring corporal. Bates caught the phrase and it perplexed his slight knowledge of French.

" Boss," he said, when he rejoined Vansittart, " what is a ' lapin ' ? "

At such a moment the question naturally confused the anxious millionaire. He replied shortly, " A rabbit."

" Well, I 'm jiggered," cried Jim. " Some chap called me a rabbit because I showed him the ford."

" Oh, I see. He probably meant to say you were a brick."

" An' if you want to tell a feller he 's a brick in French you chip him about bein' a rabbit ? "

" Jim, I have something else to attend to just now without explaining French idioms to you. Ride fast to Bar-le-Duc, find General Daubisson, and bring me any written message he may give you. Stay a moment. Hand him this."

Vansittart scribbled on a leaf from his note-book :

" Meuse, two miles south-west from Troyon, 3.15 A.M. All well here. Hope to engage enemy in force at 6 A.M.

" I want you to proceed to Verdun, and see that sortie is successful, no matter what the cost.

11

" Leave trustworthy officer at Bar-le-Duc to control and direct rapid movement of all available troops to this point. Full directions will be given to brigadiers as they arrive here.

" Send explicit instructions to commander of troops opposite Troyon to cross at all hazards at 6 A.M., and incline to the south-east, in order to join me about 6.30 A.M.

" I will personally communicate with general at St. Mihiel when I want him.

" Pontoons useful, but not imperatively necessary, as the river can be forded by cavalry and infantry.

" JEROME K. VANSITTART."

Jim did not head straight to Bar-le-Duc, but rode down the river bank. The cracking of whips, the cries of drivers, the fierce yelling of excited staff-officers, told him that the road to headquarters was a raging torrent of maddened horseflesh and cursing men. The ardour of an advance is surpassed only by the panic of a rout.

Le Breton clattered up, tingling with indignation at the latest bungle of the Intelligence Department—in France, too. What would have happened if the affair had taken place in German territory? The military maps would doubtless mark a canal as " a good road, available for siege guns " !

In his excitement he checked his charger so impetuously that he shot onto the animal's neck.

" This is monstrous," he cried, climbing back to the saddle.

Jerome misunderstood him. " It is novel, not to say dangerous," he said, with a laugh. Matters were going well now, and he was confident again.

" I mean," explained the impulsive cavalry leader, " that the absence of pontoons might have caused needless delay."

" That error has been rectified," said the millionaire cheerily. " What have _you_ done ? "

" Driven back the enemy, and sent Montsaloy in pursuit."

" A good commencement. Come with me and organise a general advance." The two rode off to the front, after Jerome had given clear instructions for the disposition of the second division. The first, numbering forty thousand infantry, six thousand cavalry, and seventy guns, was now on the German side of the Meuse.

When they reached the nearest ridge and were well away from the turmoil of the crossing, the sound of heavy firing came from the direction of Verdun. The sortie was already in progress.

.   .   .   .

Fate willed it that at 2.30 A.M. the different sections of the vast German host should begin the movement that was to culminate in the passage of the Meuse at four o'clock. Fifteen minutes later came the first intimation of the unlooked-for French attack.

The Emperor and his staff dismissed the alarm as a trivial matter.

" A too zealous sentry firing at a stray cow," commented Von Waldersee.

" Who commands at that point ? " said the Kaiser.

" Colonel Breitstein, of the 18th Hanoverians. He wants an excuse to enable him to say that he led the first regiment over the Meuse."

" Possibly. What is it now ? "

An aide-de-camp had entered unceremoniously, carrying a telegram.

The Emperor scanned it :

" French attack serious. Have lodged strong force on right bank from Pierrefitte. Breitstein heavily engaged. Am hurrying up supports, with two batteries.   VON HOFER, Major-General."

" This is strange. What can it mean ? " William II. resented any interference with his plans.

" Probably a reconnaissance. Paris is annoyed at Daubisson's inactivity. It is well. Von Hofer can easily hold them. Our attack will develop with the greater ease."

" I hope so. Yet I wish this coincidence were not so marked."

As they conversed, the minutes passed. And each minute was worth an hour, for the German columns were moving with machine-like exactitude in the wrong direction. Like the hands of a clock, they could now go forward, but if called upon to reverse, what would be the result?

Another aide burst into the royal presence, breathless, with a second message from Von Hofer:

"Position desperate. Breitstein and 18th cut up. Twelve guns captured. French division crossing with extraordinary rapidity. Am offering desperate resistance, but hopelessly outnumbered."

And a third, from the chief of the Troyon column:

"Commander of 11th Brigade reports river held by artillery and infantry. Great difficulty and delay will be experienced in building pontoons. Two infantry regiments have forded the Meuse but have been repulsed with much loss. Am about to attack in force."

From the northern army corps, stationed near Verdun:

"Had barely commenced operations for crossing Meuse when delayed by strong assault from Verdun. Compelled to suspend original movement in order to meet this development. Everything points to a serious battle forthwith. KREUZNACH."

"Kreuznach is right, Von Waldersee!" roared the Emperor. "Quick! Recall every division! Suspend the advance! Quick, I tell you, for heaven's sake! Vansittart has left Paris!"

"Impossible, your Majesty!" The chief of the staff knew something of the arrangements made by his imperial master's servants in the French capital.

"Nothing is impossible! This is his doing. Daubisson would never dare attempt it. Oh, hurry, hurry!"

Those few moments had sufficed to change William II.'s mood from dignified generalship into half-hysterical frenzy. He railed at the fate which so cruelly blighted his best-conceived project. He cursed Vansittart and his own staff with admirable impartiality, and finally rushed from the château into the cool morning air without. Above all else he felt the need of motion, the sense of doing something.

He had perforce to wait until a charger was saddled. The whole eastern horizon was now flushed with the delicate pink and green of advancing day. Nature, in sky, field, and wood, wore the colouring of summer. The weather promised to be bright and pleasant—ample sunshine tempered by a cool breeze from the Ardennes. But rude sounds jarred the ear, and gave portent of other and less soothing scenes. Heavy firing at Verdun, in the north-west, betokened the preliminary stage of a serious and extensive battle in that direction. From the whole line of the Meuse came the desultory boom of field ordnance and the crackle of rifle fire, whilst a growing volume of sustained conflict south-west of Troyon, showed that a strong blow was being struck at the very heart of the German position.

An observer in a balloon, were he able to take in details of the range of country extending along thirty miles of the right bank of the Meuse, would at the hour 3.30 A.M. note a curious fact.

Nearly a million of armed men were in motion. The lesser moiety of these, the French, were steadily pushing their way towards the German centre, whilst their opponents, though numerically superior, and fighting hard at the points of contact, were, for the most part, wandering aimlessly about the roads in pursuance of a plan which must be wholly altered when divisional and brigade commanders could be reached by the flying messengers and telegrams now being despatched in hot haste by Count von Waldersee.

The two great personalities in the field, Vansittart and Wilhelm, were distant from each other barely five miles. The man of the nervous and excitable American temperament was quietly smoking a cigar, sipping a cup of hot coffee, and chatting pleasantly with several staff-officers who awaited the arrival of the brigades they would accompany in the subsequent operations. And the Teuton, representative of a race noted for stolidity and sober deportment, was stamping furiously in and out of the château at Troyon, eager to mount and gallop his horse somewhere, but unable to decide in what direction to gallop; irritable, incoherent, and impatient of needful delay, with furious eyes and clammy brow, the picture of helpless annoyance and uncertainty.

Such was the disposition of the forces, the attitude of the leaders, at the outbreak of the battle of Troyon.

CHAPTER XVI

A QUESTION OF GENERALSHIP

I T has been said by a caustic critic of military genius that a battle consists of a series of mistakes on both sides, and that he wins the day who commits the minor errors. This definition is smart, but unsound. It takes note of the salient features of all great struggles—the delays, doubts, cross-purposes, and useless efforts that mark the varying chances of a fight throughout the long hours of agony before victory is assured or defeat unavoidable. But it wholly neglects the underlying principle of masterful purpose—of the dominant will that is content to regard an army as so many human counters, subject to the rigid law regulating so apparently unstable a thing as the tossing of a coin.

The popular voice is in this matter a truer guide than the sneer of a cynic. Wellington won Waterloo, Nelson beat the French at Trafalgar, Grant smashed up the Southern States, say the people, and the people are right.

Waterloo supplies the most telling proof of this singular fact. Nearly all the officers and men who took part on the English side in that Homeric contest were ready to acknowledge subsequently that for many hours they were certain the French were winning. They simply made up their minds to do their duty until they fell, and their resolve happened to be the cardinal condition their great leader required in order to be assured of victory.

Hundreds of experts have since declared that Wellington chose faulty ground, that Napoleon wasted his strength in assaults on Hougoumont and La Haye Sainte, that Grouchy betrayed his master, that this, that, and the other would have been so much better done by the particular expert who was writing the book or essay, but the final summing up of the historian and the man in the street coincides. Waterloo was a personal triumph for the Iron Duke, and a personal defeat for the conqueror who vaingloriously declared that he had six times won the battle.

And it was so in the case of the battle of Troyon. Vansittart set out with the intention of crushing the German centre before the right and left wings could close in and assist the Emperor. He pursued his theory with merciless accuracy.

It has been seen that in the initial stage of events he not only procured a strategic advantage, but that his idea was coherent. It was nearly five o'clock before Count von Waldersee, working with the rapid precision of a well-built machine, was able finally to divert the whole of his troops from the abandoned attack and throw them into something like settled order for defence.

By that time Daubisson's Verdun division was thrust like a wedge between Kreuznach's northern army and the Kaiser's command, whilst the latter's left flank had been turned, thus cutting him off from the southern wing.

Vansittart promptly arranged that the French divisions at Commercy and Nancy should attack the German left in such force as to render it impossible for Duke Albrecht of Prussia to march to the assistance of the hard-pressed Emperor.

Montsaloy, too, had been fortunate in discovering and destroying the field telegraph long before Von Waldersee could adequately devise a combined resistance on all sides. By the time that several aides-de-camp reached Duke Albrecht with peremptory orders at once to move northwards with his army corps, it was quite impossible to obey without converting the march into a rout, so closely was he pressed by the French.

At six o'clock the first French shells fell near the château at Troyon. A thoroughly stiff fight was now in full swing. The German forces were stubbornly contesting each road and wood and stream, only yielding sullenly to superior numbers and gaining more confidence as reserves poured up from the rear.

Nevertheless, the result was apparently a foregone conclusion, were it not that the fortune of war changes with the suddenness of April weather.

So far, the magnitude of the struggle lay with the infantry arm on both sides. Neither of the combatants was able to get his full artillery force into play, for the very good reason that the guns were pounding each other in a useless duel at various points along the banks of the Meuse. The hostile cavalry were massed in the same localities, and when, at six o'clock, the Germans were peremptorily recalled, it took the French some time to cross and take part in the chief theatre of events near Troyon. Vansittart, whose plain civilian attire was oddly at variance with the handsome uniforms worn by his staff, was watching through his glasses a beautiful attack in extended order by a mixed brigade of Zouaves and Chasseurs à *pied*.

As the active and gallant Frenchmen swept an opposing body of Bavarians up the slope and over the crest of a treeless cultivated ridge, Jerome turned with a smile to Le Breton.

" Things are going almost too well," he said.

" When my brave countrymen are well handled, they are incomparable soldiers." Le Breton was already assured of the result.

" All the world knows that. But we must leave nothing to chance. I wonder how Daubisson is progressing."

In rapid answer to his thoughts came an officer spurring for dear life.

" The field telegraph is laid from Bar-le-Duc to the river. This message has just come to hand."

He produced an envelope from the pocket of his sabretache, and Jerome eagerly tore it open. He paled as he read :

"Am caught between Kreuznach and the German main body. Fear that position is untenable. Will hold out until seven o'clock, and then propose falling back on Verdun. Hope this will suit your plans. Cannot communicate direct, so have sent this *via* Verdun and Bar-le-Duc.   DAUBISSON."

"*Nom de Dieu!* What is the matter?" cried Le Breton, astounded by Vansittart's sudden agitation.

The millionaire's pallor was due to hopeless anger. He could not trust himself to speak, but silently handed the slip of paper to Le Breton and averted his stern, set face to watch the devoted troops of France pressing on to needless butchery.

For that was the meaning of Daubisson's short-sighted resolve.

Whatever the cost, it was necessary that the Verdun column should be interposed between the two great sections of the Emperor's army. If a junction were effected all would be lost. The French superiority in the main attack would be converted into hopeless disparity. Their very success in driving the Kaiser's army corps before them towards Fresnes and the frontier would supply the strongest element that made for defeat, as Kreuznach, marching along the line of the Meuse, must take them in flank shortly after eight o'clock.

Nothing could save Vansittart's troops from wholesale disaster. In a couple of hours at the utmost the whole German army would be united and able to sweep away the French right wing at Commercy on the south, leaving Daubisson safely penned up in Verdun until they were inclined to deal with him.

It was a bitter rebuff in the moment of apparent triumph, and it was well that Jerome could not have immediate speech of the pompous but well-meaning little general. His words would have cut Daubisson to the quick.

Le Breton, too, was speechless with anger, and Arizona Jim, cantering leisurely up, after securing a fresh mount, found their attitude so curious that he perforce asked Jerome, " What was the trouble ? "

" Jim, tell me again. You handed my note to General Daubisson personally ? "

" Sure as death, guv'nor."

" And he left Bar-le-Duc at once ? "

" He just said, ' *Sacré*,' kinder pleased like, shouted something to a chap in gold lace, an' quit that fast for Verdun that you could n't see him for dust."

" You are quite certain he read my instructions carefully ? "

" Every word, boss. He did n't skip a line. He said ' All-a-right ' to me twice, an' it was only after he vamoosed that I scratched my head and thought as how he 'd oughter give me somethin' in writin' to bring back."

Le Breton, who guessed the purport of their conversation, broke in :

" It may still be possible to catch him with a message before it is too late."

Vansittart's face did not relax.

" It *is* too late," he said, " but you can go and try." · He mechanically pulled out his watch, and murmured : " Six-thirty. Half an hour for a message to pass through the field telegraph, be transmitted from Bar-le-Duc to Verdun, and thence to Daubisson. It is impossible. Oh, it is hard, hard! " and he clenched his hands together in the impotence of his despair.

Arizona Jim had never before seen his master give way in this manner. Up to the present he knew that all had gone well, and he was quite at a loss to guess the cause of Jerome's self-abandonment. In some way it was connected with Daubisson. If the latter could be reached before seven o'clock the threatened danger might be averted. He realised fully the certainty there was that the complex route of the wires would not meet the difficulty. "Guv'nor," he said in a low voice, for Jim, to use his own phrase, was "skeered" by Vansittart's misery, "I figger it out that General Daubisson is not more 'n five miles from here as the crow flies."

"Well, what of it?"

"I 've just swopped horses, an' I can reach him before seven."

"Impossible, Jim. There are thousands of the enemy between us and him."

"True bill, sir, but they could stop a regiment easier than one man who was in a hurry."

"My friend, do not tempt me. You would lose your life to no purpose."

"Now, look here, boss. Let me run this little show. You are powerful upset, an' you ain't up to your usual form. Scribble out another billy-doo to the old boy, an' I 'll clap it into his fist in twenty-five minutes or know the reason why."

It was a gambler's chance, and the millionaire took it. This is what he wrote :

"You must hold back Kreuznach until the last man has fired the last cartridge. Pay no heed to operations by German main body. In your case they result from chance. If you hold out until ten o'clock, and prevent junction, we will win a great victory. If you do not, the cause of France is lost."

Vansittart gave the precious little missive to his faithful follower with the words—

"Jim, if Daubisson does not get that message the game is ended."

Bates smiled. "Cheer up, guv'nor!" he cried. "This circus ain't done with yet."

Then he galloped down the hill on his northward ride.

No man ever yet undertook more daring mission. Although he skirted the fighting line, he no sooner came within sight of the German position than half a dozen

Uhlans rode out to cut him off. That was exactly what Bates wanted. His chief danger, to his own mind, lay in infantry fire. One well-directed bullet would lay either himself or his charger low, and then farewell to his hopes of success. As it was, when pursued by horsemen, there was less probability of some German officer ordering a volley to be fired at him.

To the intense astonishment of the Uhlans he rode straight towards them. Believing they had to deal with a lunatic, for of course he wore no uniform, they barely trotted on to meet him, and were hugely surprised when he swerved off at twenty paces' distance and shot two of them in passing. His object was to gain a small wood, apparently unoccupied, on the crest of the slope up which he was now travelling, and his four pursuers, enraged at the turn taken by events, pressed bit and spur in a furious chase after him.

With lances at rest, and shouting fierce threats, awe-inspiring by mere reason of their polysyllabic profanity, the troopers thought they could hunt him down within two hundred yards. But he was better mounted than they, and could have distanced them, had not a fanciful notion suddenly seized him. At first he rejected it with a sense of scorn. But the sight, a mile away, of an entire German division, streaming back along the road leading from the Meuse to Troyon, made him sensible of the moral certainty of capture or death should he attempt to ride through its scattered columns in his present guise.

For Bates could fight in no other costume than the flannel shirt, riding breeches, boots, and sombrero of a cowboy, and his strange personality was almost as famous all over the Continent as that of his master. Such a figure could not fail to attract attention, and the success of his mission was the all-important consideration.

So Jim checked his charger's stride, and, being now close to the cover of the trees, turned round in the saddle with the laudable intention of "plugging" his would-be captors.

He performed the operation on three of them. The fourth was not above taking a hint, and tried to escape, but Bates never missed within practicable range.

Jim dismounted, and divested the biggest Uhlan of his jacket and helmet, the man striving to resist the while though his collar-bone was smashed, and rapidly donned both articles, stuffing his wide-awake hat into a holster. Then he took the trooper's overall to throw across his knees, slung the lance over his left arm, and started at a swinging pace towards the German line of march.

" Reckon I lost three minutes by that deal," growled Jim to himself, " but I had no bloomin' cinch on passin' this next crowd without playin' it a bit low down."

His ruse worked admirably. As he neared the retreating Germans he changed direction so as to approach them at a tangent. Few noticed him, and those who did thought him a messenger carrying instructions to some officer in front. He selected a crossing-place in front of a temporary jam of ammunition waggons.

Here he unexpectedly came upon a staff-officer gazing fixedly in the direction of the conflict raging outside Verdun. Fortunately the German was sitting motionless on his horse with his back to Bates. Quick as lightning Jim dropped his lance and gave the animal a sharp prod in the hind quarters. For the next minute the officer had other things to think about than the business and destination of the solitary rider who dashed away into the open.

Bates had now travelled nearly three miles. The pace he had come was telling on his mount, but the charger was a good one, and up to an hour at hunting-pace, carrying his rider's twelve stone. Troops were scattered all over the country, and Jim kept a sharp lookout ahead in order to follow the most open path.

The volume of firing in front momentarily grew more distinct. The most risky, because most indefinite, part of his venture was now at hand.

"Jim dismounted and divested the biggest Uhlan of his jacket and helmet."

Fortune had well aided him up to the present—would she continue to smile to the end ?

Others rode forward like himself. Once, when he had just cleared a small body of infantry marching in the same direction, an officer, flying along with eager haste, inclined towards him, obviously with the intention of questioning him. Jim swore quietly, changed the lance to his right hand, and when the other was near enough hit him such a hearty whack on the back of the head that he tumbled in a heap to the ground.

Some Hamburgers witnessed the act, and gave a great shout of amazement as they ran to pick up the officer. But none of them thought of firing at the supposed Uhlan.

At last Bates neared the fighting-line. He had no trouble in riding through the German artillery, which was in position on a ridge. In front, a large force of infantry was deployed, and a thousand yards away, across some meadows and cornland, he could see the blue frockcoats of the French troops dotted irregularly over an extended front.

When he approached the German infantry an officer roared something at him and waved his sword to the right, seemingly indicating that the commander of the brigade was in that direction. Jim promptly inclined to the right, and he at once resolved to imitate the actions of one whose horse had bolted with him.

Dropping his lance, and spurring the willing steed vigorously, he leaned back in the saddle and feinted to pull hard at the reins.

No one paid heed to him for a few strides until he was clear in front of the extended troops. A German officer gallantly rode after him to help him, but desisted within a couple of hundred yards, trotting back to his own lines considerably puzzled by the tactics of the bolting Uhlan. Bates had but one danger left. In the central zone he might be shot by either side, accidentally or otherwise. To help himself with the French he threw off the helmet, jacket, and cloak, and plucking forth his hat, again resumed the characteristic attire by which he was known to the whole French army.

An absolute yell greeted him as he rode through the first companies of infantry that protected Daubisson's right flank. Heading straight for the colonel of this regiment, the 110th of the line, Jim shouted :

" Where is General Daubisson ? "

The officer addressed fortunately understood him and pointed to a farm-house, nearly a mile away, surrounded by dense masses of troops and a strong division of cavalry.

Something in their disposition told Jim that Daubisson was already preparing for the retreat to Verdun. Glancing at his watch he found that it was three minutes to seven, and he leaned forward in the saddle to press his faithful assistant for the last effort of that memorable ride.

The noble animal stumbled and fell, utterly spent, not by the distance but by the pace, as Jim reached the farm inclosure.

Daubisson was there, surrounded by a number of staff officers, to whom he was giving voluble instructions. Some of them turned to go when Bates ran up, but his stentorian shout caused them to halt for a moment.

" Stop ! " he roared. " I bring orders from M. Vansittart ! "

The name caught every ear, and Daubisson snatched at the note with frantic haste.

As he read, his plethoric face became purple. He crumpled it in his right hand and cried to his staff :

" Gentlemen, the retreat is countermanded. The German centre is crushed and on the point of annihilation. It is our pleasant duty to attack Kreuznach with every available man."

Not even military decorum could repress the cries of delight with which the assembled officers greeted this welcome intelligence. Daubisson, whose volatile temperament soon recovered from the implied rebuke of Vansittart's words, although fully conscious of the grave error from which he had been saved, was about to rush off impetuously to see personally to some detail when Bates caught his horse by the bridle.

" No, you don't, old man," he said. " I want an answer in writing, *roo savvy*, General."

" All-a-right, all-a-right," cried Daubisson, gleefully.

" No, it ain't. It 's all-a-wrong. *Papier, plume.* Why the deuce can't you talk English or Spanish—any blessed lingo but one that you spell one way an' jaw another."

Jim's manner conveyed more than his words, so the General found time to scribble a hasty acknowledgment of the millionaire's message. With this safe in his pocket the gentleman from Arizona went off to look after his horse.

He had given the animal a pail of water and was about to find it some provender when he suddenly burst forth :

" I 've got bats in my belfry. I 'm like a bloomin' bell-punch when the bell don't ring. I 'm clean off my trolley in this sort of business."

Running into the house he found some paper and a pencil, and wrote in a big round hand :

" Telegraphe M. Vansittart que General Daubisson has received his orders and carried them out."

" The kick-off is fine," mused Jim, " but the second half is n't very Frenchy. All the same, they 'll comprenny better that way than if I chin 'em."

He gave the document to the first officer he met. It happened to be one of the Commander-in-chief's aides-de-camp, who spoke English.

" It is well thought of, monsieur," he said. " I will place it on the wire at once."

Bates smiled all over his face. " That 's the ticket," he cried. " When a feller chips in with that sort of song an' dance it takes the blur out of my specs."

12

As the aide hurried off to the field telegraph tent he firmly resolved to renew his English reading ; he found unusual difficulty in understanding the language, though he spoke it quite well.

.   .   .   .

Long before noon Count von Waldersee informed his imperial master that if a wholesale disaster were to be avoided there must be an immediate retreat on Mars la Tour and Gravelotte.

The French infantry had nobly done their work, and the task of hurrying the German rear was committed to cavalry and artillery.

Vansittart did not know he was safe until nearly nine o'clock, so long did it take for Daubisson's answer to reach him. About ten, the right bank of the Meuse was cleared of the German troops, and Arizona Jim had no difficulty in returning. Jerome heartily thanked him for his splendid service, but there was little time for talk just then, his attention being devoted to the final movements of fresh troops, in order to compel the evacuation of Troyon by the Germans.

When the issue of the conflict was beyond the domain of doubt, he wrote a telegram to the King, giving a brief sketch of the day's proceedings, and warmly eulogising the army. A second message to Evelyn asked her to bid the Queen be of good heart. All had gone well so far. If fortune vouchsafed them a few more such victories, there would be an end to German aggressiveness for another generation. Even yet Jerome treated the Queen as the master mind of the royal pair. To Henri he sent the pleasant facts of a victory won, to Honorine he gave the less striking but vastly more important reflections to be drawn from the event. For Vansittart, even in the fierce joy of the moment, harboured no delusions as to the strategic difficulty of his position.

The Germans were but sullenly retiring on their well-equipped base, to form anew upon positions whence the French could scarce hope to drive them. The victors in that day's combat were separated from their supplies by very reason of the obstacles they had already opposed to the invaders' progress. A swift-flowing river cut them off from reserve transport and commissariat, save where precarious pontoons and narrow country roads ill took the place of the solid bridges and railway lines they had destroyed weeks earlier.

A determined rebuff by their opponents might precipitate a catastrophe. Every nerve must be strained to make good a desperate success.

If only this could be achieved, if instead of being driven into the Meuse they could press the Germans back towards Metz, then truly the frenzied jubilation of France at the glad tidings of victory would be justified.

What a sight Paris must present at that moment as the telegrams poured in ! By this time the papers had published his message to the King. The City of Light would be a city of mad rejoicing. And how fondly would Evelyn carry his words to the Queen !

Well, sufficient for the day was the fight thereof.

An aide-de-camp rode up to announce that the Commander-in-chief wished personally to escort him to the château so unexpectedly vacated by the German Emperor. In a moment that worthy officer himself lumbered into sight.

Vansittart reined in his horse as Daubisson approached, and the two heartily shook hands.

" General," said the millionaire, " we have won a great battle."

Tears sprang into the impulsive Frenchman's eyes. He stammered with difficulty, so intense was his emotion, " *You* have, monsieur. But believe me, if I cannot emulate you, I will in future obey orders to the death."

CHAPTER XVII

FOLLIET slept for forty-eight hours after Vansittart quitted Paris.

This was his method of mental recuperation. Physically, he was one of those tense, compact personalities that can outlast time and fatigue until the final moment of complete annihilation. But his brain required periods of torpor. At such periods it refused to act. It gathered renewed force by utter abandonment, and the severe strain of recent events produced such reaction that the Prefect kept to his room for two whole days after the long-delayed train steamed out of the Gare de Lyon.

He ate and drank as usual, but had no mind for affairs. At last, as the second night drew on, he felt a craving for a pipe—the first sign of returning sanity. Half-an-hour's quiet smoke, and he thought a book would be a pleasant thing. Ten minutes of a novel and he required a newspaper.

Folliet was himself again.

He asked his servant to bring him an *Echo de Paris*. A single glance at its staring headlines caused him to spring towards his coat and hat.

" Great Battle—Magnificent French Victory—The Germans Routed after Five Hours' Fighting "—these were the stirring phrases that threw light upon his soul.

" Wake up, you dog ! " he shouted to himself. " Whilst your master works you sleep ! See to it that he sleeps in peace."

As he drove to the Prefecture he bought more papers and

learnt the full significance of the day's doings. A subordinate quickly informed him of the outcome of the raid at the warehouse.

In all, eighty-seven German conspirators were safe in prison, ten were dead, and six severely wounded.

" How ? Ten killed ? Did they fight, then ? "

M. Carot hesitated. " Not exactly, but——"

" Out with it, man. Don't pick your phrases. Say that which first comes to your mind."

" Well, they defended their president, and we had to use force."

" Did he escape, then ? "

" Oh, no ; no one escaped."

" Is he injured ? "

" No. He gave them some order in German and they formed an unbreakable ring round him whilst he ate something—some paper, those of our men believe who were nearest."

" Do you mean that men were killed in order to prevent a document from falling into our hands ? "

" I am sure of it. He chewed the stuff and swallowed it, shouted a command, and in an instant all resistance was at an end."

" It must have been very valuable, this piece of paper ? "

" Yes, sir, of the utmost value. I have searched every house, but have found nothing beyond evidence of this particular conspiracy."

" What ? You suspect something else ? "

" I do. With the president and the leading spirits of the organisation in our hands, I fail to see why such a determined attempt should be made to keep from us any testimony affecting the Pigeon Feather Society."

" Is that their title ? "

" No, sir. It was invented by the *Soir.*"

" Confound it, man ! Has some report of affairs crept into the press ? "

"Yes, a correspondent wheedled it out of Jeanne Carhaix under pretence of marrying her for the dowry."

"A thousand thunders! Every rascal in Paris has been warned by this time. See to it, Carot, that the *Soir* correspondent is compelled to marry Jeanne. He will be more than punished."

"Yes, sir."

Although Folliet's tone was light, his mind trembled with forebodings. It was quite true of this remarkable man, as he had himself told the Queen, that in criminal investigation he was a human barometer, subject to indiscernible pressure of gathering clouds.

He reasoned that the president of the German society, knowing full well the extent of the police capture and their tenancy of No. 11 Rue Pigalle, would credit them with complete knowledge of Hans Schwartz and his pigeon-post to and from the frontier.

Under such conditions it was absurd to think that the destroyed paper had any distinct bearing upon the main objects of the conspiracy. There was a plot within a plot, a hidden scheme in which the common members of the society were not allowed to participate.

What did it forebode? Above all, who were its leaders?

Dismissing his coachman, the Prefect of Police walked through the streets to the palace.

Paris was ablaze with light, tremulous with life. The war, the victory, Vansittart—these filled every breast. Small groups gathered and each person talked to the rest. Total strangers met and shook hands whilst they uttered phrases of encouragement and congratulation. Crowds of urchins marched in military fashion singing war-songs; solitary strollers like himself would quicken their pace and join the chorus; a woman, who was repulsed when she strove to embrace a policeman, embraced a lamp-post.

As Folliet neared the palace he became aware that a grand reception was taking place. He quickly decided to seek the

Queen or Mrs. Vansittart and learn the truth concerning the position on the Meuse. But in his present attire, it was impossible. He must hasten to his residence and don a gorgeous uniform.

Hailing a cab he rattled off towards the Rue de Maubeuge, and, as it chanced, the sartorial peculiarities of court etiquette cost him and France many a troubled hour.

Had he sauntered fifty yards farther he would have seen a private carriage, containing two men in evening dress, stop near the curb.

A blouse-wearing artisan, a tall, truculent fellow, darted from the shade of a column, received some message from one of the carriage folk, and hastened off towards the Seine, whilst the vehicle drove on in the direction of the Rue de la Paix. Not much, this incident, but it would have yielded a whole volume of facts to Folliet.

When at last he entered the brilliant salons of the Tuileries, he quickly found the King.

Henri was intoxicated with the events of the day, but he strove to calm himself as he caught sight of the Prefect.

" Ah, M. Folliet. You must have heard my unspoken thought. Listen carefully, for I have little time to spare. M. Lacontel has been here."

" M. Lacontel ! " Folliet's gasp of amazement was justified. Lacontel was one of the long-since fallen ministers, the most dangerous of the many enemies vanquished by Vansittart in his struggle to found the Empire.

" Yes, Lacontel," laughed the King. " I know what you would say, but years work wonders, and Lacontel is now an ardent supporter of the throne. His very mission here today proves his faith beyond doubt. He came to urge me to reconstitute the National Guard. Paris will soon be denuded of troops to meet the demand at the front. M. Lacontel thinks that the loyal citizens of Paris should be banded together to protect the—er—to protect the public peace."

" May I ask your Majesty if the police are not competent to do this ? "

" Of course, of course. No one spoke of the police. This is a patriotic movement, intended to reinforce the army."

" Surely this is a matter for your Majesty's ministers and not for a discredited trickster like Lacontel ? "

" Why, what a suspicious fellow you are!" laughed the King, uneasily. " Lacontel was an ardent Republican, but he is none the less a true Frenchman."

" Has General Villeneuve approved the proposal, your Majesty ? "

" Oh, yes, I told him, and Lacontel spoke to him, too. He thinks there is something in it. The project will be promulgated by the War Office, and Lacontel offered his services for organisation. He is great in municipal matters, Lacontel."

" And M. Vansittart ? "

" No. I will not have Vansittart worried about such a detail. Why are you so dubious concerning a simple question of self-defence ? "

" Because, your Majesty, there is nothing to defend in Paris. To-day's battle is a far better safeguard for the capital than another line of fortifications. Because Lacontel is a scoundrel. Because the National Guard has too often proved to be anything but a guard for the King."

This time Henri's merriment was unaffected. " Folliet," he cried, " you are incorrigible. You will be dreaming of barricades next. These German pigeons have built a nest in your brain. Eh ? The Duchess of Sainfoin ! I must speak to her."

Folliet sought Villeneuve, the Minister for War. The General was emphatic :

" It is a splendid idea, I tell you. The provincials have no heart for fighting. Prosperity has made them flabby. The cities must supply the troops and Paris must lead. I commence mobilisation to-morrow. It is a splendid idea.

Yes, I will watch Lacontel, but the fellow is cute, all the same. He looks to this move to rehabilitate himself with the King and Vansittart."

Folliet moved away into the throng. "Which is the stronger," he asked himself—"hate or self-love?" Tried by this summary, Lacontel was either a plotter or a patriot. Or was the situation more complex? Might not the fallen minister gratify his self-love by indulging his hate?

What was to be done? Watch Lacontel, naturally, but here there was no solution. Lacontel, dragged into light by his suggestion, would expect this delicate attention from his old-time foe.

The Prefect exchanged a few words with Evelyn, whose joy trembled on the verge of tears. Through all the frenzied jubilance she shivered at the screaming of shells and whistling of bullets which ever thrilled the ears of her soul. These battles meant danger, danger to her husband.

"I would not care," she confessed to the man she regarded as the one friend in that glittering assemblage, "if only I were near him. If I shared the risk I would be happy —I think both of us would be even safer."

Folliet smiled reassuringly. He alone knew the full extent of the peril that environed Vansittart in Paris. The millionaire was a thousandfold more secure in the battlefield than in the Tuileries. So he comforted her and skilfully diverted her thoughts by praising her loved one. Yet her womanly intuition was more accurate than his keen logic. Evelyn was right. Far better would it have been if she rested that night in the château at Troyon than in the seeming security of the royal palace. Folliet remembered her words afterwards.

It was impossible to gain private audience of the Queen.

A bow and a smile were Honorine's recognition of his presence, so, in pursuance of an impulse, he hied him to No. 11 Rue Pigalle. Jeanne had been temporarily dispossessed of her room, which was now tenanted by police. One of these, an intelligent young man, answered Folliet's questions :

"No, sir. No more birds have arrived. It *is* curious, as one fails to see how Schwartz knows that the house has been seized."

Then, with a cautious glance around, and sinking his voice, the policeman continued :

"May I venture to suggest a theory, sir ? "

"Certainly."

"Some of these birds are trained to fly here from Lorraine, but others are trained to fly from Paris to the farm of Hans Schwartz."

"Well ? "

"It seems to me quite evident, sir, that Schwartz can receive messages from other quarters of Paris by the same means. Now, the only way to find out the whole business, is to visit Hans Schwartz's house."

Folliet sprang about the room in a paroxysm of laughter and expletive.

The policeman flushed and trembled.

"I beg your pardon, sir. I only said what was in my mind. I——"

"Oh, shut up ! Your name ? "

"Henri Pigot, sir. But please forgive——"

"Will you shut up ? When the sergeant comes, tell him to convey this note to the Prefecture."

Folliet scribbled, and handed a torn leaf to the quaking officer, saying, "There, read it yourself," and rushed from the room.

The man with some difficulty deciphered the scrawl :

"Henri Pigot is promoted from this date, to be assistant commissary. Place him in sole charge of No. 11 Rue Pigalle.

"FOLLIET."

The Prefect dashed towards his waiting carriage. "To think of it!" he muttered. "The whole business awaiting solution in Lorraine—our troops even now marching on Gravelotte—and *I* in Paris. Confound it! Shall I get there in time?"

Summoning his deputy by telephone to his chambers Folliet gave him instructions as to procedure during his absence. Precious hours had flown, but he caught an early train. The eastward lines were congested. But the officials assured him that by midnight or at daybreak next morning he would reach Bar-le-Duc. Eighteen or twenty-four hours wasted in travelling two hundred miles! It was intolerable. But if it took a week he must visit the farm of Hans Schwartz.

. . . .

With the editions of the morning papers came dramatic news from an unexpected quarter. Since the outbreak of the war the French and German fleets had been chasing each other over the face of the waters. Sanguinary conflicts took place whenever they met. Although the French superiority in numbers of ships and sailors generally brought about but one issue to each engagement, nevertheless the German navy was far from paralysed.

The authorities in Berlin issued stringent orders to their admirals to adopt every device to avoid fighting the French. Their supreme efforts must be devoted to harrying the commerce of France and damaging her colonial empire.

Disastrous blows were struck in this fashion, and the French sailors raged in a fury of disappointment when they failed time after time to bring their enemy to close quarters. In one locality only were they assured of safety for liners and merchantmen. The few German cruisers in the Mediterranean were quickly chased out of it. At last the Minister of Marine in Paris determined to sweep the North Sea and the Baltic with the whole of his available force, and with this object a grand concentration was ordered at Brest.

This was the move that Germany had been waiting for. It was to tempt France into some such exploit that her warships were ostentatiously withdrawn to the neighbourhood of Kiel and Bremenhaven. The Kaiser counted on the strength of his shore defences to safeguard his coasts. On the day that the French fleet, a superb array of fighting material, stood out into the English Channel and headed for the Straits of Dover, all the fast cruisers in the German navy disappeared from the Baltic and North Seas, and were sighted by English fishing-boats making apparently for Iceland.

The French attributed this move to fear; in Whitehall, where naval matters were more clearly understood, its object was read and prepared for. Definite orders were sent to the Admiral commanding the British Mediterranean fleet, with the result that the vessels stationed at Gibraltar and those gathered near Malta suddenly sailed with sealed orders. Thus it came to pass that when the lost German squadron, after sailing round by the Hebrides and down the North Atlantic, suddenly swooped like birds of prey upon the Sahara canal works at Boca Grande and Gabes, the two sections found an overpowering British force calmly awaiting them. Protestation was useless; bluster merely evoked a comparison of the relative weights of ships and guns. The British commanders pointed out that England was greatly interested in the Sahara. She would no sooner permit the destruction of the irrigation methods adopted by Vansittart than witness unmoved the blowing-up of the Suez Canal. She simply forbade any attack. When German ships met French ships let them pursue the quarrel by all means. But in the case of a great colony where British capital was largely invested, it was a matter of " Hands off ! "

More than that, the Admiral would permit no tricks, such as night attacks by torpedoes and the like. If the Germans did not sheer out to sea within an hour of the debate they would not be permitted to depart at all. The alternative was sail or sink. To the intense grief of every man on board the British ships the discomfited raiders chose the safer course.

For once, France was grateful. Albion was no longer
perfidious. Even the *Gil Blas* did not suggest that England
merely safeguarded the Sahara in order that she might
gobble up this delicious mouthful of territory when the war
had developed to the exhaustion stage. Naturally, there
was chagrin at Berlin. The permanent scowl on the Kaiser's
face deepened as he heard the news. But beyond diplomatic
protest no further action was taken. Not even Wilhelm
dared to dream of engaging both France and England in war
at the same time. The incident was soon lost sight of in the
tremendous events that followed. It only proved, beyond
range of argument, that an alliance between England and
France would be the true solution of the Continental puzzle.
If these two led the concert of Europe, all others must pipe
their tune.

CHAPTER XVIII

THE Kaiser awaited the French attack at Gravelotte. The centre of his great army lay across the main road to Metz. Its southern wing filled the defiles that debouch on the village of Mars la Tour, and Kreuznach's force was strongly posted on the famous ridge between Gravelotte and Conflans. This time there was no hope that either of the combatants could be taken by surprise. The nature of the country rendered a night assault by the French a risky and practically impossible proceeding, whilst the Emperor, taught to respect his opponents by the first great battle of the campaign, resolved to calmly await their decision as to time and method of reopening the conflict.

His experienced staff fully agreed with this exhibition of newborn caution. Each hour of delay on the part of the French meant a vastly increased degree of efficiency for the Germans. The splendid organisation of the invaders was most valuable in precisely such a situation as that which now presented itself. With no fear of an unexpected attack on the lines of communication, the magnificent German organisation progressed each moment with the accuracy of a well-regulated engine. Reserve troops and supplies constantly reached the localities where they were most needed ; there was neither hesitancy nor doubt, naught but decision and certainty. The contrast between the two armies was never so marked as at this moment when they were inactive in the field.

True, Vansittart's reforming hand had achieved much

already. It was a bold thing suddenly to remodel the whole system of commissariat and ammunition transport almost under the eyes of the enemy. Few men would dare to undertake such a responsibility. But Jerome dared do anything, and in the result he was justified. A complicated and utterly inefficient method was replaced by one that already gave satisfaction and would surely work with remarkable ease when officers and men were thoroughly accustomed to it. The commanding officer of each regiment was made responsible for his own commissariat and transport; the general of each brigade was responsible for the feeding of the regiments; officers of divisional rank were responsible for the procuring of stores in bulk and their proper distribution.

Yet the advantage in time lay with the Germans, and the dominant intellects of the two armies well knew it. The millionaire did not shirk the issue. William II. must be attacked again and soundly beaten. His strong position must be forced, his north and south army corps driven off into the interior, and his main body compelled to fall back upon the protection of Metz. This was the problem set before the council of war that met in the château at Troyon on the second evening after the fierce combat that lodged the French on the right bank of the Meuse. General Daubisson had recommended a great artillery effort, by every available gun, in order to cut a gap in the German lines across the road to Metz at the point where two main thoroughfares form a junction in the vicinity of Gravelotte.

" To be followed by an infantry attack in the orthodox way?" There was a tinge of sarcasm in Vansittart's good-humoured question.

" Assuredly. We cannot disperse four hundred thousand men with field batteries alone."

" How many guns have we?"

" Two hundred and sixty immediately available."

" And the Germans—how many?"

Daubisson became less confident. "Judging from appearances yesterday," he said, "they must possess nearly double our number."

"Then, General, I fear that the time-honoured artillery duel means, in this case, that an hour's genuine engagement would mean the total loss of every gunner at the front, and the disablement or capture of each gun."

Jerome, with knitted brows and bent head, paced the room slowly, whilst Daubisson stooped over a frontier map to draw further inspiration from the perplexing outlines.

Le Breton thought that this was hardly a case for his cavalry division, so he held his peace, but General Beaumarchais, leader of the Foreign Legion, did not fear to offer a suggestion.

"It will be an affair of infantry, to-morrow's fight," he said, "and I think that to the effective use of infantry we should wholly devote ourselves."

Vansittart suddenly halted. "It is well said, General. What is your scheme?"

"I have hardly formulated a scheme," was the reply, "but it seems to me that whilst a division, consisting, say, of the Foreign Legion and two other brigades, was trying to induce the Germans to believe that we intended to fight in force along the Metz road, two army corps of one hundred thousand men each, largely composed of infantry, should attack the enemy's right and left wings simultaneously, advancing from ridge to ridge and always striving to engage at close quarters."

"Excellent, Beaumarchais, but what of the German guns?"

"There," said the other, "I agree with Daubisson. Whatever be the cost, our artillery should keep them busy."

Vansittart's position in this debate was an exceedingly difficult one. Technically, of couse, he was unable to compete on level terms with his staff. His national characteristic of promptly adapting himself to his surroundings was the sole equipment that rendered him able to convince or over-rule expert military officers who could not help thinking by the book.

In the result he frequently amazed them by jumping to a conclusion that, by their rigid code, savoured of lunacy. So frequently, however, had his seemingly mad proposals been justified by events, that they were one and all very unwilling to commit themselves too strongly to an adverse opinion when he had propounded one of his tactical riddles.

And it happened so in this instance. After another per-ambulation of the room he cried :

" Why should not the German batteries be broken up by infantry ? "

Daubisson valiantly sprang into the breach.

" It is absolutely and utterly impossible," he said.

" Why ? "

" Because the long range of the guns enables them to in-flict immense damage on infantry columns long before the regiments can deploy for attack. Because, even if the men bore the preliminary suffering, they would be mowed down by shrapnel and grape at shorter distances. Because, in this shattered state, they would be an easy prey to the enemy's cavalry. Because the German infantry, advancing to support the guns, would be opposed by exhausted and despairing men. Oh, there are fifty reasons."

This sweeping condemnation did not daunt Jerome. " You will see all fifty yield to one to-morrow," he said, " for I mean to demonstrate that infantry, well handled, have noth-ing to fear from artillery fire. It is a question of quiet de-termination versus noise. In every other affair of life it is any odds on the persistent man getting the better of the blusterer and I fail to perceive why the opposite should prove true here."

Daubisson smiled quite grimly. "Go ahead!" he cried. " Remember my promise: once the game starts I obey orders."

The American proceeded to explain his theory in detail.

There would be no hurry and no confusion. The battle would not commence until after breakfast, and if things eventuated as he desired, it would not assume serious proportions until noon. At first, barely a tenth of the French forces would be engaged, and the whole plan of attack depended upon the weather. If fog or rain obscured the landscape, the fight would either be postponed or carried out on entirely different lines. All indications, however, pointed to a fine, clear day, in which case the commanders of divisions knew exactly what was required of them. It was their first duty to see that each soldier under their control was made fully cognisant of the nature and method of the work entrusted to him.

Vansittart was silent as to the reasons which dominated his resolve.

The French officers, of course, did not lose sight of the fact that the present scene of operations was practically identical with that of the memorable conflicts which determined the fate of France in 1870.

But the millionaire, with his acute knowledge of men and their controlling impulses, was convinced that the Emperor William would insensibly follow the tactics which brought such conspicuous success to his grandfather and Von Moltke. In other words, if tempted sufficiently, he would throw forward his troops to attack the French instead of holding the impregnable position he now occupied. If the Emperor only possessed sufficient self-restraint to await and repel all assaults made upon him, Vansittart felt that the gallant Frenchmen would be unable to drive their foes from the fastnesses they held.

But this shrewd empire-builder believed more in human nature than in tactics. How far he was justified in his confidence the impending battle would reveal.

At eight o'clock on the morning of June 18th, the Foreign Legion of the French army quitted the village of Fresnes to a lively accompaniment of bugles and drums.

This crack brigade, eight thousand strong, is the last representative in European armies of the mercenaries of the fifteenth and sixteenth centuries. Hope and fear have long deserted each man in that contingent. To forget the past and to die fighting, is his creed. He is an outcast of society. In the ranks of the Foreign Legion are to be found Englishmen, Americans, Italians, Spaniards, Danes, Russians, men from nearly every civilised nation, and, in the majority of cases, men who have fallen from the upper walks of life by reason of folly or misfortune. Princes and peers march shoulder to shoulder with social outlaws who, if they were recognised, would keep the extradition courts busy. But they can fight. In man's last resource they are pre-eminent. It was no faint-hearted mob of criminals that General Beaumarchais led so confidently along the high road to Mars la Tour by way of Horville, but eight regiments of stern soldiers, bound by an iron discipline, and more joyous in the forgetfulness of battle than in the thought-laden hours of barrack-room existence. They were followed, in quick succession, by three brigades of infantry. Once clear of Fresnes the music stopped and the leading regiment advanced in extended order, covering the fields on both sides of the road for a considerable distance.

The small hamlet of Horville was held by a strong German picket, which the French drove off with small loss.

By nine o'clock, however, the growing density of the German skirmishers and the presence of numerous small bodies of cavalry demonstrated to Beaumarchais that his further progress would soon be seriously disputed.

He forthwith adopted the specific method of fighting recommended by Vansittart and practically threw the whole of the Foreign Legion into extended order. The movement took some time to execute, as the front thus covered was of tremendous extent, embracing, from flank to flank, fully two miles. Beaumarchais could not, of course, exercise personal command over a brigade split up into sectional units of ten men each.

But each unit had its definite instructions. It must on no account retire or incline right or left. Taking every advantage of cover, and never wasting a shot which had not a target selected by the section commander, it was, if possible, to advance in line with its neighbouring units, and fire long-range volleys at every visible body of the enemy in the direct front.

When the German massed batteries were sighted the skirmishers were advised to gain the best shelter obtainable within fifteen hundred to two thousand yards, and then settle down to deliberate volley-firing at the guns.

In a phrase, the opening stage of the battle would be a duel between the long-range rifle and the long-range cannon, between the tiny bullet and the screaming shell. Which would win ?

The question had been asked and answered once before. During the Transvaal War the desperate issue was tried, and the bullet conquered. Out of eighteen men of the British field artillery who strove to bring one gun into effective action against the Boers, seventeen were struck by Martini projectiles within a few minutes. Not a shot was fired at a less range than one thousand yards, at that time the maximum distance for anything like effective shooting. But the Frenchmen were now armed with weapons sighted up to two thousand five hundred yards—capable, too, of throwing their silent and deadly missiles nearly twice the distance—and calculated to inflict far more loss than shells aimed at a practically invisible enemy.

Cavalry availed naught against these scattered assailants. Well handled, under skilful fire-control, the Foreign Legion easily bent back such small bodies of horse as rode against them.

The only practicable method of grappling with and repelling a persistent and invertebrate attack of this nature was to oppose infantry to infantry. But the Germans had no troops immediately available for the purpose. Beyond a few isolated battalions to supply guards and pickets at the front the great mass of the Kaiser's soldiers lay behind the guns at Gravelotte or in the defiles to the north and south of that town.

Beautiful positions had been selected by the Prussian artillerists. Five hundred modern guns, of the latest type and flattest trajectory, were so disposed as to make a holocaust of any army corps that strove to force a passage along the Metz road. According to the drill-book the position was impregnable, and in the German army the drill-book's authority cannot be gainsaid. The Kaiser's staff relied on the machine; Vansittart relied on the man who directed the machine.

At ten o'clock the heavy staccato notes of the field ordnance mingled with the incessant crackle of rifle firing, and Beaumarchais at once strengthened his irregular but unbroken fighting-line by the extension of another brigade. The commander of the 3d Brigade received orders to lodge his men in half-battalions at various points in the rear of the extended troops, leaving to the discretion of the colonels and majors the exact time and direction of any decisive movement in support of the skirmishers. The General himself, stationed with the fourth and last brigade on a cross-road between Mars la Tour and Conflans, occupied the centre of the base of the triangle formed by those two villages with Gravelotte at the apex. From that base the French attack advanced in a convex crescent, whilst the German guns, roughly speaking, followed the same semi-circular line at a distance of about a mile.

No less than sixteen thousand French troops were dotted singly and in small groups behind every tree, house, and mound, over an area of nearly three miles. The 3d Brigade, in compact bodies, supplied supports at different centres, and the 4th Brigade, a dense mass of eight thousand men, formed the hub whence radiated the different lines of the attack.

The German centre, consisting of two hundred and fifty thousand troops, lay at Gravelotte, three miles in the direct front, whilst the north and south wings, of seventy thousand men each, were posted on the flanks of the attacking troops.

The French main body, numbering two hundred and fifty thousand all told, were now advancing in three well-defined army corps, marching parallel to each other, some four miles in the rear of General Beaumarchais's division. Midway between lay the French guns and cavalry.

It will thus be seen that, so far, the fight savoured of an affair of outposts rather than a general engagement, and at 10 A.M. the Kaiser gleefully exclaimed :

" This Yankee adventurer is a greater charlatan than the third Napoleon. He is marching into the trap. By one o'clock I shall have crushed both him and France."

Von Waldersee nodded assent. This time there was no mistake. The German position was indeed a trap, with its steel jaws gaping to enclose the hazardous Frenchmen, whilst from its throat five hundred guns were already beginning to spit death and disaster.

Count Holbach, the commander of the German artillery division, and his subordinates, actively engaged in directing the gun practice, were not so sure of the excellence of existing arrangements.

These experienced officers well knew the folly of assuming that all the loss is on the other side. The well-placed German shells must have wrought havoc in the now clearly discerned French fighting-line. Yet the percentage of loss among the gunners was growing more serious minute by minute. Slight leaden gusts swept through the batteries, and a steadily increasing train of ambulance-bearers showed already a heavy list of casualties.

Eagerly did the German leaders look for signs of development in the attack. They came not, save perhaps a slight increase in the frequency and severity of those terrible gusts, that sighed and hummed and whistled amidst the intermittent booming of the guns.

Holbach at last shut his field-glasses with an impatient snap and a still more impatient exclamation.

" The devil take them ! " he cried. " Where are their guns ? "

A phlegmatic officer by his side answered : " There are no guns. It is a stroke of genius, this unsupported infantry attack. We must either hurry up our own battalions or fall back upon them. There is no alternative. We are firing at thin air."

The General turned angrily upon him. " You had better take that message to the Emperor."

" With pleasure." The other turned his horse to ride off.

" No, no, not yet. I did not resent your words. We cannot retreat, and the Kaiser is firmly resolved to wait the French attack in his present position."

The officer made no reply, and they both, for a little space, watched the progress of events. In a battery beneath them on the right fully half of the officers and men were disabled. Two guns were silent for the want of people to work them. As they looked, a leaden shower of extra severity fell against the hillside. Five soldiers dropped, three from one gun, two from another. The survivors, quite coolly, reapportioned their duties. Three guns out of six were out of action in a single battery !

The object-lesson was not lost. Count Holbach's face was set firmly as he said :

" Telegraph the Emperor, Colonel Holtz, and say that I *demand* the immediate support of one, if not two, infantry divisions. If not supplied within half an hour I will retire every gun."

The Kaiser's face flushed when he read the message. But he was slowly learning self-control, and he said little beyond giving the necessary instructions for the dispatch of the much-needed relief. When it came, the *rôles* quickly changed. The French infantry had been allowed a good innings—it was their turn to endure a bad quarter of an hour.

The German attack would not be denied.

" No matter what your loss," wrote Count Holbach to the commander of the Hanoverian division placed at his service, " you must crumple up the centre of the French crescent and strive to take the outer horns in flank after you have broken the line."

But the Foreign Legion, which throughout had borne the brunt of the shell-fire, was not made of the stuff from which retreats are manufactured.

There was now every prospect of a sanguinary encounter, were it not that Beaumarchais had his imperative orders, based solely on the clock, and at present justified almost to the second. A few minutes before eleven he threw forward the 4th Brigade to check the rapid onslaught of the Hanoverians, and at the same time sent out several aides with emphatic instructions for a gradual but definite falling back upon Horville.

Each quarter of an hour since 8 A.M. a mounted messenger brought to Vansittart a written report from Beaumarchais.

When Jerome received that dated 11 A.M. he smiled appreciatively and handed it to Daubisson, saying :

" Instruct the artillery to take up position, and send a warning for immediate readiness to the commanders of the three army corps."

By 11.30 the German infantry came within the fire-zone of the French artillery, and halted for supports. Count Holbach, on his own responsibility, threw forward one battery after another to help the Hanoverians, but kept the Emperor constantly apprised of his actions. The excitement of the situation was rapidly working the Emperor up to the boiling-point; and, truth to tell, each member of his staff, every officer and man in the German host, was chafing under the compulsory inaction.

A considerable battle was in progress in the front, under ill-understood and indefinite conditions. Half of the long summer's day had sped whilst the superb German army waited for the general attack which never came. Nay, it even seemed that a solitary division was now driving the French back upon Troyon and the line of the Meuse. The temptation was too great to be resisted. Shortly before twelve, William II. issued orders for a combined advance from flanks and centre in overwhelming force. His command put the position pithily : " Fight your way straight through the French lines to the river, and then converge on Verdun," he said. By 12.30 his object became clear, and Vansittart consulted his watch. In rare conceit with himself he cried exultantly to Daubisson :

" The Kaiser fights on our ground after all. He is only half an hour late."

CHAPTER XIX

THE COTTAGE OF HANS SCHWARTZ

THE Graemes of Netherby never mounted their willing
steeds with greater alacrity than was displayed by the
aides-de-camp whose duty it was to carry to generals
of divisions Vansittart's orders for a general attack. Now
that the gage of battle was fairly thrown down, the millionaire experienced a strange buoyancy of spirit. The very
dash and *élan* of the staff-officers as they rode off with his
message were pleasing to him. They were typical of the
high hopes he himself built upon the issue of the day. If
Bellona withheld her favour from the French troops it would
not be the fault of leader or men. Their powerful opponents
had been tempted to abandon an impregnable position, and
not in vain. Whilst the French had quietly and without
fatigue taken up an excellent line of country for rapid
manœuvring and quick concentration, the Germans were
suffering from precisely contrary conditions.

Yet he would be a bold man who decried the mettle of the
invaders, and if Providence be indeed on the side of the big
battalions the great preponderance in numbers of the Kaiser's army must determine the fortunes of the field.

It was a considerable factor in the situation that the
French troops did not enter the fray beaten before a shot
was fired. This has too often been their lot. Men win
battles quite as much by good food and serviceable clothing
as by cannon and small arms. For once the gallant sons of
France were not weighed down by wretched commissariat
and inefficient handling.

Vansittart was about to move to a slight hill on the left of the Metz road when his watchful eye chanced upon Folliet. At first he almost refused to believe his senses. But there could not be the slightest doubt that the famous Prefect of Police was standing near a cavalry escort stationed on the road, and that he had just ridden up on the small pony whose bridle hung over his arm. Even in the fierce excitement of the moment Jerome felt such keen curiosity to learn the cause of Folliet's wholly unexpected appearance that he checked his horse.

"Jim," he said, "go and ask M. Folliet to come here a moment."

Bates was an interested spectator of the events in front when his master's words caused him to wheel in the saddle. When he saw Folliet's diminutive form behind the stalwart cavalry soldiers of the escort he exclaimed :

"Wall, goldarn me, if he ain't a reg'lar Jim Dandy. Is it you, or your sperrit?" he cried, as he pulled up alongside the Prefect.

Folliet smiled, shook hands with him, and, still dragging his pony, ran to Vansittart.

"Have you brought a regiment of police, monsieur?" inquired Jerome.

"No, oh no. Just myself."

"But tell me—I have a moment to spare—surely some extraordinary event has dragged you thus far from Paris and into our biggest battle?"

"Yes, monsieur. The farm of Hans Schwartz is beyond Gravelotte, by the side of the Metz road. I want to inspect that farm to-night."

"Ha! Then you think we will help you to get there?"

"I am sure of it."

"There are four hundred thousand Germans in the way. I wish I were assured of it myself, though I believe we will get the best of the struggle."

"Yes, four hundred thousand Germans ; but they have

the Kaiser to direct them. I know him well. He plays the conqueror on parade. He cannot smile. He poses. To-day's events will overpower him. He will see his mistakes to-morrow. If I am told aright he has already allowed his impatience to master his reason."

Jerome smiled at this caustic summary. " Well, we shall see. I hope to meet you near the house of Hans Schwartz."

Beaumarchais's division, the Foreign Legion in particular, was suffering severely during an orderly retreat. Sullenly, desperately, steadily, the Frenchmen retired before the crushing onslaught of the Hanoverians, now strongly reinforced.

At last the check came. The French guns, admirably screened and disposed, suddenly rained shrapnel upon the advancing Germans. The enemy flinched, halted, and reeled back beneath this infliction, and their guns rapidly unlimbered to engage the French batteries. Soon the in-fantry combat died into nothingness beside the thunder of the giant encounter that ensued forthwith between the op-posing artillerists. Battery after battery galloped up on both sides, and the superior numbers of the German guns would have quickly decided this phase of the struggle were it not that the French had the tremendous advantage of selection of ground. The nature of the country precluded long-range firing as gunners understand it. Barely a mile separated the most distant batteries, and, here again, in view of the appalling accuracy and effect of the missiles, the Ger-mans laboured under a drawback. Their exposed positions rendered the French practice more deadly, and it was clear to the experienced officers on Vansittart's staff that the French guns were able to hold their own against the assailants.

Daubisson rocked in the saddle with admiration.

" There !" he gasped. " I told you so. The artillery duel ! It is superb. *Voilà la guerre !* "

Vansittart heard him and answered not. He simply

looked at his watch. But Daubisson fully understood. Five hours in time and three miles in space made a vast difference between his ideal of war and the millionaire's.

Suddenly a sharp-sighted young aide, eagerly scanning the opposite heights with his glasses, shouted vehemently, " The Kaiser ! "

Every man followed his direction. On the verge of a wood, a little over a mile away, to the extreme right of the German batteries, stood a small group of horsemen. One figure, conspicuously clothed in a scarlet tunic and red-plumed, gilded helmet, sat motionless on a fine bay horse, some twenty yards in front of the others. It was undoubtedly the Emperor, and it seemed that he, too, had discovered their presence, for his right hand never moved his field-glasses from the direct range of vision.

Whilst the Frenchmen looked at this magnetic personality whose uniform rendered him so plainly visible in that clear air and bright sunlight, a French shell burst a little to the left of him. Others had observed him, and some enterprising gunner hoped to bring matters to a crisis by a well-directed shot.

" Go," cried Vansittart, angrily, " tell them to stop that. Our guns have enough to do with their opponents. The enemy's batteries supply their only target."

As a rider raced off to convey his wishes Jerome turned from the statuesque form of the Kaiser, who had not paid the slightest heed to the obvious danger that threatened him.

Column after column of the German infantry put in an appearance, and the leading division of the French central army corps was deploying for the attack. Soon the bellowing of the cannon failed to drown the continuous roar of the magazine-rifles. Gallopers came from both flanks to announce a definite engagement with the enemy. At 1.30 P.M. the battle became general, and the tide of conflict surged in red waves over a front extending nearly five miles. This was a small area for the number of men on the field, and the fight, thus condensed, raged with the greater ferocity. On neither side were there signs of yielding. Regiments took up position and simply fought to a stand-still. The two great armies might have been duellists, firing at measured distance until one or both fell.

During this period of the battle Folliet betrayed his nervous tension in a strange manner. He was a human electric machine. His mind swayed with each trivial feature of the fray. He found relief in strange murmurings, whilst his eyes devoured the road to Metz. Did a French infantry line advance he gave a subdued yelp : " One hundred yards nearer." Did it retire to form behind its supports he growled : " *Sacré bleu!* Too bad ! That good distance lost."

To him there was a single object in the tactics of the troops. He approached, or was driven away from, the house of Hans Schwartz.

French excitability nearly drove Vansittart mad.

So far, it will be seen, the host of cavalry with either army had been inactive, invisible to each other, massed close to the scene of action, but unemployed and chafing at the re-straint. Daubisson recollected the fact during a lucid interval.

He roared to Vansittart amidst the din :

" A cavalry brigade could sweep that hollow clear."

And again, in more passionate tone :

" A strong cavalry charge now, and we can order a general advance."

Finally he shrieked :

" *Mon Dieu!* What fatality is this ? Why not send for Le Breton ? The Germans will crush us by sheer weight."

Vansittart, with wonderful self-command, merely said :

" Remember your promise, General Daubisson ! "

Then came hysterical appeals from the wings. The com-manders, of course, had some mounted troops with them, but not sufficient. He on the right promised a successful flanking movement if only he had ten thousand additional sabres. He on the left reported a fierce attack by Kreuznach, which *must* be repelled by cavalry and guns. Jerome's senses were beginning to swim before this ceaseless iteration, for many of his senior staff-officers joined in the demand, whilst Daubisson, mute indeed, watched him with eyes from which the tears flowed down his fat cheeks.

To the right wing Vansittart sent the imperative order : "Upon no account attempt to outflank the enemy. Hold your ground against all attacks."

To the left : "Stand fast. Fight in square if necessary."

With his glasses glued to the centre of the German line he watched and watched and watched, with the air of a man who expects something which comes not. Four hundred yards in the rear, Le Breton, who could see naught of the fight, watched Vansittart.

At last, in the rage of the hour, men swore at Jerome and even threatened him. They importuned Daubisson to use his prerogative as nominal Commander-in-chief and give orders for the cavalry to be employed. Daubisson wrung his hands in the impotence of abject despair, but he uttered no word. At last Vansittart lost his temper. Beckoning Arizona Jim he told him to shoot the first officer who rode away without his instructions, and Jim's attitude as he faced round, revolver in hand, was more eloquent than a long speech.

The exceeding ferocity of the battle had now reached its height. The din assumed the sustained note of a tempest—the outlines of the opposing forces became blurred, uncertain, merged in a sea of horror.

On the Metz road the bodies of the slain lay so thickly that it was difficult to cross the dividing belt.

From out the turmoil stood one patent fact. Although the Kaiser had launched the full power of the mighty thunderbolt he controlled, the German infantry had not gained a foot of French ground. With splendid heroism his famous troops hurled themselves on the defenders, and the gunners sacrificed themselves to the French batteries by turning their fire upon the French infantry.

It was no use. If the Germans were brave, so were the French. They could die, not unavenged, but they could not break through the living barrier that resisted them.

Many a time did the thought possess Jerome that perhaps he was wrong, perhaps the cavalry were needed, perhaps he was sacrificing victory to stubbornness.

But still he remained steadfast in his resolve, and the comforting reflection came to his aid that if the French horsemen were in reserve so were the Germans. If his attitude concealed a purpose what did the Kaiser's betoken? And he was right. At a quarter to three o'clock he discerned the fluttering lance pennants of a vast body of mounted troops gathered in the rear of the German guns.

Wilhelm was emulating Von Moltke. Mars la Tour was again to have its Death Ride. A second time the flower of the German cavalry was to crash resistless through French guns and lines of infantry, turning possible defeat into certain victory, breaking up the French centre, and rolling back their opponents to be outflanked and vanquished in detail.

Vansittart's face flushed with triumph when he saw the rapid preparations in progress behind the batteries.

Turning to the staff he said, " Tell Le Breton to advance at the trot."

Four officers raced off. Jim Bates returned his revolver, and an alert air of jubilation swept away the frenzy of the others. But Daubisson gazed at the millionaire, awestricken. Now he understood.

He approached Vansittart closely, so that he might be heard. " I deal with manœuvres, monsieur," he said; " you deal with men."

Even in the anxiety of this supreme moment, for the next ten minutes would irrevocably determine the result of the fight, Jerome was able to reply smilingly :

" It is my only accomplishment, General, but it suffices."

Not until the German horse were fairly launched down the opposite slope did the startled gunners and perplexed colonels of infantry perceive the full extent of the storm about to burst upon them. Brigade succeeded brigade across the ridge and down the hill, riding in beautiful lines, and pouring on over a wide front until thirty thousand troopers were in motion, gathering pace as they came. The guns tore gaps in them, hundreds fell before showers of bullets, but the glittering rank swept on and the earth thundered with the myriad beats of iron-shod hoofs. A cavalry charge on such a colossal scale is the most awesome thing in war. Men will face death in any form rather than be trodden into a shapeless mass beneath the feet of infuriated horses.

The Germans were still a quarter of a mile from the advanced line of French skirmishers and men were running back to their regiments for dear life, when a great roar of delight went up from the French army. Le Breton, leading the 18th Chasseurs, followed by the Cuirassiers of the Guard and many another crack cavalry corps, rode grandly across the ridge and onwards to meet the German onslaught. Owing to Vansittart's foresight the French troops were fully equal in strength to their opponents, and they now had the inestimable aid of the down gradient in their favour. What this means the cavalry officer alone can tell. In mere dynamic computation it counts hugely in the scale of weight.

The Kaiser saw the advance of Le Breton long before the majority of the French army were aware of it. Thus far throughout the day he had been rigid, inscrutable, Napoleonic. But now he abandoned himself to white rage. He knew that he had failed, that his theatrical blow would recoil upon himself, that a quicker intelligence than his had read his plans, and simply awaited his move to checkmate him with conscious ease. A German Emperor in a passion is a terrifying spectacle. His language helps him. A man cannot rave in French. He perforce remains polite. In Eng-

lish he can be forcible, but in German he possesses ready to
his hand a tongue that clanks and bangs like a steam engine.
It is furious in the utterance, it snorts with power, it thunders
with compound and triply expanded meaning.

Wilhelm's staff forcibly restrained him from joining in the
fray. Not his worst enemy could call the Kaiser a coward,
and he panted to strive singly to redeem the tottering balance. It was now too late for any human intermediary to
stop the magnificent cavalry combat that forthwith took
place.

By common consent artillery and infantry alike were silent,
and the two great bodies of horse closed together with a great
thud that was distinctly audible above the cries of men, the
neighing of animals, and the clash of weapons.

It was not soon ended. Sixty thousand troops cannot get
at one another so quickly. Charge after charge took place,
and the ensuing *mêlée* revealed a gigantic and disorganised
mob. The Germans at first withstood the French, but it
was absolutely impossible to make headway, and a time came
when Vansittart could discern a definite movement backwards into the dip between the hills. Instantly he launched
forward two big cavalry brigades, Montsaloy in command.
They swerved off as they rode, and avoided the struggling
hosts in the valley. Up the hill they went, and in a few
strides were among the German gunners. Regiment after
regiment followed, until practically the whole of the French
mounted arm was in motion. The American had also read
the records of Mars la Tour. It was his turn to try the
value of Von Moltke's strategy.

The issue was never in doubt for a moment. By 3.15 the
German centre was crushed, by four o'clock the village of
Mars la Tour was occupied, and the French soldiers were
frantically cheering at the base of the statue that looks so
piteously towards the lost province of Lorraine, by five they
were in Gravelotte, and were only withheld by sheer force
of discipline from pursuing their routed foes to the very walls

" The two great bodies of horse closed together with a great thud that was distinctly audible above the cries of men, the neighing of animals, and the clash of weapons."

of Metz. Simultaneously with the central advance, the French right and left wings respectively attacked Kreuznach and the Grand Duke Albrecht. The one was driven off towards Diedenhofen and the other into the Vosges.

Wilhelm's defeat was complete and utterly disastrous. If the mobilisation of France were only on a level with that of her hereditary enemy, there was a splendid opportunity for the investment of Metz and an advance to the left bank of the Rhine. Some enthusiasts did urge Vansittart to press forward beyond Metz with two strong columns, but Jerome quietly repressed them. In the moment of victory the born tactician knows the value of restraint. Notwithstanding her boasted number of troops France was practically fighting with her entire available army on the frontier, whilst Germany could place eight such cohorts in the field as that overthrown at Mars la Tour.

Now that the battle was won the millionaire's anxiety redoubled. There was little fear of an effective rally in the vicinity of Metz for some days at least, but it was a ticklish question to decide how best to follow up the advantage already gained. Was it possible to invest the great frontier fortress with troops at his disposal and at the same time ward off the attacks which would surely be made from Strasburg and Diedenhofen?

He must take thought. In a multitude of counsellors might be found wisdom. So he summoned an assembly of divisional commanders and the general staff at the small inn in the centre of Gravelotte, the house in which Napoleon III. and the Prince Imperial slept on the night before the battle of Vionville.

Meanwhile, where was Folliet? Weak from the fierce exhaustion of the fight, hoarse with the involuntary cries he uttered as he followed up the French advance, yet professional zeal came to his aid. The abandonment of the conqueror yielded to the pertinacity of the sleuth-hound. Even as he partook of some slight refreshment he plied his quest among the dazed villagers. He could not get them to collect their scattered wits until a postman, an old soldier, put in an appearance. On him the detective fastened eagerly.

" Where is the house of Hans Schwartz, friend ? "

" Hans Schwartz, the farmer ? Why, close to the Bois des Ognons. I know it too well, confound the place and Hans Schwartz, too."

" So. 'T is a long walk, then ? "

" A good mile from the village, and he had more letters than ever man needed who only went to Metz for the weekly market."

" Say'st so ? Whence came these letters ? "

" Some from Metz, but most from Paris and Berlin."

" Have you long served in this district, postman ? "

" Ever since the war."

" A lifetime. And not a postmaster yet ? "

" Ha, ha ! Postmaster ! That 's good. Who am I, to be made a postmaster ? Not that I am unable for the work, but I have no influence."

Folliet bent his piercing eyes upon the intelligent face that smiled so broadly at the preposterous suggestion.

" Listen, postman," said the Prefect of Police. " Answer me fully and carefully and you become a postmaster within a week. Take this as earnest of my words. Men do not give away hundred-franc notes for a jest."

The simple-minded villager gazed with wonder upon the crumpled piece of paper in his hand.

" *Bonne vierge !* " he murmured. " No wonder men oft say that a war does good."

" Take time to reply," went on Folliet, motioning the man closer and dropping his voice. " How long has Hans Schwartz lived on the farm near the wood ? "

" Not long. Eighteen months, perhaps."

" Whence came he ? "

" From Strasburg, they said. He was no farmer, as any man could see. How he made a living I cannot tell, as he only scratched his land. Perhaps he sold some of his birds."

" Birds. What birds ? "

" Pigeons. He was a great pigeon-flyer, was Schwartz. He was constantly sending them off in crates, and they told me at the station they were addressed to Chalons or Verdun or Nancy, sometimes to Paris."

Folliet knitted his brows for a moment. Then he laughed drily. Of course it would arouse suspicion if the pigeons were invariably consigned to Paris. So they were met at the other places and taken to the capital.

" Your name, postman ? "

" François Noir."

" François, that post-office of yours is built. Proceed."

" Well, let me see. It was only of late that he had so many letters. They came in different handwriting from Paris, but always the same writing from Berlin—a square hand, official I called it."

" I call you a gem. Were there any printed addresses or seals on the envelopes ? "

" Only once, a long time ago, four months at least. Some crack-jaw German on a Berlin letter. Schwartz frowned and swore when he saw it. I was sure it was a police summons."

Folliet laughed again. He scribbled in his note-book the German for " Police Headquarters," and showed it to Noir, saying,

" Anything like that ? "

" *De Dieu en Dieu !* the very words. You are a wizard."

" Nay, François. I but conjure with thy wits. Were you friendly with Hans Schwartz ? "

" Not I. He was a surly brute, and I hated the hill to his house."

" Where is he now ? "

" Well, his place was terribly damaged by Colonel Mont-saloy during the great ride, but he still lives there, unless he was driven out by the battle to-day. For two hours some German guns were posted near the Bois des Ognons."

" Will you guide me thither ? "

" With pleasure. But is it really true, what you say about the post-office ? "

" Would you were as certain of going to heaven ! But come ! "

The oddly assorted pair walked off down the street. They passed the village inn as Vansittart stood at the open window to draw a quiet breath of air before the council of war set to its deliberations. Something in Folliet's manner impressed him and he sent hurriedly for Arizona Jim.

" Jim," he said, pointing to the fast-walking couple, " Folliet is on the trail. This locality is dangerous just now, and I cannot spare him. Follow him unobtrusively and take care of him."

Bates grinned delightedly.

" Bully for me!" he cried. " Take care of Folliet ! I 'll look after him all right, guv'nor. If he was n't around I 'd feel kinder skeered, sometimes."

CHAPTER XX

PIGEONS, SOME HAWKS, AND A TELEGRAM

THE house to which François Noir led the Prefect stood near the crest of a hill crowned by a thick clump of trees. They followed the bridle-path from Gravelotte to Arssur-Moselle for a short distance and then turned off through some ploughed land. Bates kept them well in sight, but the prairie instinct, imbibed during an infancy spent among Indians, told him that they were going to the ruined farm near the trees and caused him to remain a little while in the road hidden by the willows lining the tiny tributary of the Moselle that runs near Gravelotte to the river. There might be others interested in their movements.

Although the hour was late, the midsummer twilight rendered all things visible. Through the quiet air came the hum of thousands of voices from the French camps dotted along the Metz road through Mars la Tour, Vionville, Rezonville, and Gravelotte, whilst fitful sounds of distant firing showed that the last remnants of the pursuit were dying away towards Metz and St. Privat.

But Arizona Jim was a remarkably single-minded individual. Folliet and his companion filled his thoughts, whilst his eyes roamed restlessly over the hillside and among the trees.

Steadily upwards pressed Folliet and the postman, the latter inclined to be talkative.

" It was a great fight to-day, sir," he said, when Folliet's questions had momentarily ceased.

" Magnificent."

"And it covered just the same ground as the battles in September, 1870. It seems like yesterday since I saw the Emperor and the young Prince——"

"How long is it since you saw Schwartz, François?"

"Oh, it may have been last evening, or perhaps the day before. To-day's battle has almost dazed me."

"Where was he?"

"In the village, drinking at the Estaminet of the Black Dog."

"Alone?"

"Oh dear, no. He was talking quite a long while with two men, one an officer, and the other an older chap in plain clothes."

"What was he like, the man in plain clothes?"

"Well now, I don't know. Just a sharp-looking fellow like yourself, if you will pardon me."

"François, you must leave the post-office."

"Now I have offended you. Believe me, sir——"

"No offence. But anyone who can come to the point as you do, deserves a higher position than that of a village postmaster."

Folliet naturally puzzled the straightforward letter-carrier. They approached the dismantled farmhouse in silence, Noir covertly glancing at the other and wondering what was the hidden meaning of his words and actions.

The place was dreary enough in ordinary times and now looked positively woe-begone. French shells had torn gaps in the roof and walls. The place looked deserted and forbidding, whilst several dark objects huddled up near the verge of the wood gave ghastly evidence of the loss sustained by the Saxon battery which had temporarily held the position.

Folliet was about to enter the main room when the soft cooing of pigeons fell upon his ear. Following the sound, he reached a sheltered loft in the rear of the premises, climbed to a small window by means of a ladder, and found three birds pecking at the remains of the last supply of grain given by their attendant.

He quickly examined them. One bore a small quill, securely fastened. With this treasure-trove he descended the ladder and opened the rolled-up scroll. It read :

"P 18, 6, 2 p. Soon, perhaps to-night. No fear of failure.

"R."

If, as he believed, the opening letter and figures meant, " Paris, June 18th, 2 P.M.," the fleet messenger had but recently arrived. Further, it had not come from No. 11 Rue Pigalle, as this was impossible, the house being in possession of Pigot and the other police agents.

Here was proof positive that there were others in Paris who communicated with Schwartz. Who were they ? Who was "R." ? What would happen soon—or to-night—which could not fail ?

Folliet was viciously vituperative for a moment. Why could he not drive from Gravelotte to the Prefecture of the Seine ? If only some inventor could equal the pigeon as a flying-machine !

François Noir watched him. " This rascal Schwartz gives information to the Prussians, then ? " he said.

" Yes, and to me also."

" But, monsieur——"

Folliet cut him short by darting towards the house. The interior was dark, and the Prefect stumbled over a corpse at the threshold. Producing a small electric lantern, he switched on the battery and examined the prostrate body, thinking that it might be the proprietor of the farm. But it was a German infantry officer, who had been shot through the forehead with a shrapnell bullet and now lay on his back in the smiling unconsciousness of one who dreams pleasantly.

The chamber was long and low. It had a fireplace in the farther wall opposite the door—two windows, the panes shattered to atoms, on the left—and an open door, communicating with another room, on the right. A long table ran down the centre of the apartment.

Folliet made the tour of the house, but the dead soldier was its only occupant.

The place was so bare that a rapid scrutiny revealed the poor chance there was of finding aught likely to prove valuable. Returning to the large room, the Prefect examined the table. In the table drawer near the fireplace was a bulky volume and some loose sheets of thin paper. Folliet could not resist a cry of surprise when he discovered that the book was a telegraph code in German.

The user was a careful man. To make sure of the code words exactly conveying his meaning he had ticked off each one, and the detective promised himself an interesting hunt through the maze of phrases. On the title-page was the significant legend : " Strictly confidential. For State purposes only."

François Noir broke in upon Folliet's tumultuous thoughts.

" That little machine of yours only lights up one spot, and this room is getting confoundedly dim. Shall I put a match to my postman's lamp which I always carry ? "

" By all means. The more light the better."

Noir ignited the wick of a small globular lantern he brought from his coat pocket, and when the oil burned up it cast a dull gleam upon the bare walls and blackened rafters overhead.

Folliet examined the grate—the substitute for a waste-paper basket in many households. Some charred bits of paper were rescued, but they bore no writing. A larger piece of wholly consumed paper lay near the lowest bar, and Folliet stooped low with his electric ray to look at it minutely.

If he touched it the black tissue would surely crumble to atoms. Nevertheless he could see quite plainly, showing white in the scratches of a pen, the single letter " R."

" Now who the deuce is ' R ' ? " cried Folliet aloud, and François Noir bent down that he also might see.

" You had better ask those who know," came a deep voice from behind them.

Both men sprang up and turned. A tall, rough-looking man, carrying a double-barrelled gun, was standing within the doorway, astride of the German officer's body. His eyes blazed at them with malignant pleasure, and he lovingly clutched his weapon as he poised it in the manner of one on the alert for a covey.

" Hans Schwartz ! " cried the postman. " Good evening, Hans ; this gentleman wished to see you, so I——"

" Are you Folliet, the Prefect of Police at Paris ? " asked the newcomer, paying no heed to Noir's stuttered explanation.

" That is my name."

" I thought so. I was told you had left Paris, and I partly expected you."

" Well, I am here, Hans Schwartz. Your game is up, so you had better save your own skin by making a clean breast of the shady business you are engaged in."

Folliet spoke coolly enough, but he knew that he was in a desperate position. He felt certain that Schwartz would murder him and the unfortunate François in cold blood. For this man, with his excellent French and his calm, self-contained manner, was no bungling clodhopper, but an experienced and able member of the German secret police.

" The game is up, is it ? " Schwartz showed his teeth in a ghastly smile. " Well, Folliet, you are right. It is ended, and the loser pays. No. Keep your hands quite still. Otherwise I must shoot you at once. Perhaps—I say perhaps—if you answer my questions I may spare your life, and conduct you to Metz as a prisoner. After all, you are a professional like myself—a devilish clever one, too—and I should be sorry to be compelled to injure you."

François Noir, after the first shock of surprise, regained his nerve ; the ex-soldier was plucky enough.

" Look here, Schwartz——" he began.

" Peace, fool. Another word from you, and you die." The German spoke to Noir, but his eyes never quitted Folliet.

" Don't interfere, my poor friend," said Folliet, sadly. " This quarrel does not affect you, and, however it ends, I hope Monsieur Schwartz will let you go unharmed."

Schwartz scowled in another smile. " We shall see. Now, Folliet, tell me what was the message you took from my pigeon ? *Please* don't move. You can remember quite well."

Folliet told him, wondering the while how this grim farce would end. Personally, he was quite sure that Schwartz would kill him.

" Soon, perhaps to-night, eh ? " repeated the German. " Good. If our arms cannot prevail against your mighty Vansittart, we will see what our wits can accomplish during his absence. Indeed, I may say during *your* absence, colleague. It would be most awkward for certain people were you in Paris just now."

" Something is going to happen there, then ? "

" Oh, yes. Something far better for us than a mere battle, even if we had been victorious to-day."

" Really, you interest me."

" I am sure of it. I have interested you for weeks, confound you."

" It is true. You are a clever man. And I hope you are a wise one. Monsieur Vansittart is rich. He will reward you beyond your dreams if you help us instead of plotting against us."

" Ah, you would bribe me. I have taken care of that for myself. Your millionaire will pay me more in a week to tell him something he wants to know than he would now give me to rescue France."

It was a new *rôle* for Folliet to be played with in this fashion. His pride was wrestling with his reason. Soon he would rush at this taunting spy and spend his life in the effort to reach him, for he was unarmed, though Schwartz thought otherwise. In the madness of the battle he had wildly and uselessly emptied his revolver.

But he bottled up his wrath for a moment.

" You take every trick, monsieur. But tell me, as a mere matter of curiosity, who is ' R ' ? "

The other hesitated a moment. Then he laughed scornfully.

" There is no reason why you should not know. Your old friend, Ribou, aided by another old friend, Lacontel, is leading the new Commune. Paris is about denuded of troops. To-night, or within twenty-four hours, the revolution breaks out and your King and Queen will be captured if they are unable to fly. It is going on now, Folliet. Whilst Paris rejoices at the downfall of the Kaiser's troops her own downfall is being arranged. You, yourself, have told me, and you, the Prefect of Police, are here in my power, wholly at my mercy. Strange, is n't it.

Folliet was a small man physically, but he could have swollen with rage to gigantic proportions. He felt that what this man said was true, and he knew criminal Paris too well to doubt that a large measure of success would be achieved by the Communists. It was now or never for them. The very victory of the French troops only hastened their resolve. A few more such and the opportunity would have passed. Fool that he was to leave Paris without placing every suspect safely in jail ! His burning thoughts must have leaped from his eyes, for Schwartz half raised his gun.

" Steady, Folliet, steady. You must keep still, else——"

A tongue of flame hissed through the window, accompanied by a sharp report. Schwartz dropped his gun and faced round with a roar of pain, for a bullet had smashed the thumb-joint of his right hand, just where it closed round the stock.   In turning he stumbled and fell over the corpse.

Arizona Jim, bringing revolver and head into sight between the shattered framework of the first window, said :

" The confab was gittin' warm, Folliet, so I just thought I 'd chip in."

Even as he spoke, Folliet darted forward to seize the gun, which had fallen on the table, shouting the while,—

" Quick, François, a rope ! "

Schwartz rose to his knees and gazed at Bates with the glare of a wounded tiger.

" *Herr liebe Gott !* " he cried; " who is this ? "

Though the words were German, Jim grasped their meaning.

" You talk too much, mister.   You 'll find out who I am, for you 've got my trademark on you."

François returned with a rope.

" Schwartz," said Folliet, " it 's my turn now.   Place your hands behind your back until Noir ties them.   Don't hesitate.   I have no time to lose, and I will blow your brains out to avoid delay.   You have told me all I wish to know."

The German obeyed.   His swarthy face was pallid with pain and desperation, but he managed to screw his features into one of his terrible smiles.

" Not all, Folliet, not all.   I still have my revenge left."

" Pooh, a telegram to Paris will clap your precious fellow-conspirators in prison."

" Ah, yes !   Ribou and Lacontel.   They will be shot. But ask Vansittart to-morrow.   He will explain."

The man perplexed Folliet, but the urgent need of haste prevented further questioning.   With a warm word of thanks to Jim, he asked him to help Noir in escorting the prisoner to the village.   Then he tore off rapidly to Gravelotte, for it was 10.30 P.M., and the Paris authorities must be warned of the Communist plot, if it were not already too late.

At the council of war, discussion waxed hot as to the next move to be made. The advocates of a forward policy were numerous, but divided among themselves.

One section, headed by General Daubisson, counselled the immediate investment of Metz, with the possible chance of isolating the Kaiser from his people. Another, with Le Breton as spokesman, urged the need of penetrating into Lorraine and thus emphasising the nature and extent of that day's victory.

Vansittart, tired and worn after the fearful strain of the afternoon, superadded to the physical weariness of continuous riding for nearly fifteen hours in his crippled condition, did not at first interfere in the argument, until, in more than one instance, it threatened to culminate in a duel.

Then he quieted Daubisson by a few tactful questions.

" Have you seen Metz since the war, General ? "

" No, but I am well acquainted with the situation of the town."

" Yet you have surely forgotten that the Prussians could not properly invest the French fortress with an army of two hundred thousand men. How much less can we hope to do so with even twice the number when the Germans have converted it into a fortified camp ten times the size. The very positions from which Prince Friedrich Charles menaced Bazaine are now important portions of the defences."

" Exactly," broke in Le Breton. " That is my contention. March into the interior, I say, leaving a sufficiently large corps of observation to hold the Germans in Metz until our supports arrive and enable us to reduce the place."

" Your plan is bold, Le Breton, but, I fear, impracticable," said Jerome. " The enemy will allow us no more surprises. Though we have won to-day it would be the wildest folly to underrate their resources, and if we were defeated somewhere near the Vosges we should meet with irreparable disaster."

" We must either advance or retreat," cried Daubisson.

" Hardly." Vansittart rose and bent wearily over a map.
" What I recommend is that whilst an army corps of fifty
thousand men remains here, strongly entrenched, the remainder of our force should line the left bank of the Moselle,
from Nancy to Bigny, and thence inland to join the troops
at Gravelotte. Meanwhile, powerful columns should immediately advance from Verdun and Montmédy towards
Diedenhofen, and complete the seizure of the Moselle. In
other words, Metz will be partly invested on the French
side, whilst we will be in a favourable position for advance
in any direction when our lines of communication are complete and our supports arrive."

As usual, his words carried conviction. More than that,
he conveyed by his manner to both Daubisson and Le Breton
the pleasant assurance that he had combined both their projects to the best effect.

There were other members of the staff present who recalled his attitude during the crucial period of the day's
fighting, when he told Jim Bates how to emphasise his opinions if necessary. But that incident might reasonably be
forgotten as quickly as possible.

Once the main question of tactics was settled, the council
devoted itself amicably to details. Vansittart had, with his
left hand, drafted a long telegram to the Minister of War,
urging him to forward another quarter of a million of troops
to the front without any delay, when a field-telegraph
orderly entered with a message.

Jerome had communicated with Evelyn and the King
about six o'clock. Henri V. had long since sent his congratulations, but there was no response from Evelyn, a fact
that the millionaire attributed to the vagaries of the over-
crowded telegraph service.

A glance showed him that this message was from Evelyn,
but his wearied brain did not for a moment grasp its full
significance.

It ran :

" I am more than terrified, yet I rejoice that I shall soon be with you. Bear up for my sake. I come with the utmost speed."

When Vansittart awoke to the actualities of the case he forgot the weariness, the anxieties of the day, no less than the physical agony of his slowly recovering disabled arm. He almost yielded to the hopeless agony of the moment. To his quick intelligence no protracted thought was needed to extract the terrible meaning of poor Evelyn's distracted message.

Someone, a bitter and malignant enemy, had cleverly managed to send her a bogus message telling her that he was wounded. It was this false alarm that had disturbed the troops hours before, and now his wife had heard of it. She had left Paris to seek him. It was a decoy. Evelyn would be captured, perhaps wounded, in order to shake his set resolve to free France from her open foes.

At that moment if the American's uninjured hand could have closed on the throat of the sender of that message he would have throttled the man without mercy. His pale face, with its tense expression and wildly staring eyes, alarmed the officers present. Eager questions broke from them, but he murmured incoherently that his news in no way concerned the army. Then he burst from the room, to encounter Folliet in the passage, just returned from the farm.

" We must be alone ! " he hissed.

One glance at Vansittart's face told the Prefect that there was no time for ceremony. He rushed into the inn kitchen, roaring to the occupants, " Outside, quick."

It was war-time and they required no second telling.

" Now ? " he said.

" Read that."

The Chief of Police rapidly devoured the words, and like a lightning-flash came the memory of Hans Schwartz's sneer.

15

'' Wait ! '' he cried. '' I will bring definite news.''

He disappeared, to return instantly with Arizona Jim, François Noir, and their captive.

Face to face with the great Vansittart, the man at whom all the world marvelled, the German's self-assurance forsook him. His wound had weakened him, his puny strategies had failed, his intelligence had been dwarfed to the level of his own pigeons.

But Folliet gave him no time to recover.

Producing a revolver, and speaking with the air of a dignified judge sentencing a prisoner to death, he said :

'' Hans Schwartz, if you fail to answer my questions fully and truthfully, I swear that I will in the next moment send you to answer for your crimes before the last tribunal. Who sent a telegram to Mrs. Vansittart, announcing that her husband was wounded and required her presence ? ''

'' Herr von Ritterburg, the chief of the Berlin secret police.''

'' At what hour ? ''

'' When our troops retired—about five o'clock.''

'' From where ? ''

'' Some place behind the French lines. He managed to get through in the disguise of a French soldier.''

'' What was in the telegram ? ''

The prisoner, livid with pain and terror, hesitated, and the revolver clicked. '' I am not sure,'' he faltered. '' I did not see it.''

'' But you know what was intended to be said ? ''

'' Y—yes. The Herr told me he would word it so that the lady would tell no one—to avoid panic in Paris.''

'' My poor girl ! '' broke in Vansittart. '' She would obey too well. It is devilish. You hound—to fight with a woman ! ''

He strode forward, and the stalwart German cowered before the blaze of his eyes, but Folliet restrained him.

'' Who devised this infernal plot ? ''

"I cannot tell. It was an order from high quarters—a last attempt to drive *him* away from the front—to leave the French troops leaderless."

"You dog ; you dogs !" cried Folliet, and he turned from Schwartz.

"Take comfort !" he said to Vansittart. "Your authority will clear the wires. She will be traced and pursued within the hour."

Then to Noir : "Lead your prisoner to the guard and let him be taken to the village lockup."

He went out, followed by the postman and Schwartz.

Vansittart sat down near the table and buried his face in his arms in utter despair.

Arizona Jim picked up the telegram and read it. With this testimony he grasped the meaning of much of the scene which had so rapidly transpired.

Tears sprang to his eyes and he tenderly placed a hand on his master's shoulder.

"It hurts, guv'nor," he whispered. "I know it hurts. But cheer up. God can fix things when a man feels that he wants to quit."

Jerome raised his wistful eyes to those of his faithful follower.

"Go, Jim," he said, "go to Folliet and tell him to bring her back to me."

CHAPTER XXI

THE STAB IN THE BACK

TO Evelyn, sitting quietly and alone in a private apartment at the Tuileries, was handed a telegram. It was addressed from Troyon ; it implied that Vansittart was gravely wounded, and in urgent need of her care ; it purported to come from him, and urged her to keep its details a secret to avoid exciting the public.

In reality, it came from one Carl Gottlieb Ritterburg, a man who was to the secret police of Berlin pretty much what Folliet was to the secret police of Paris ; the same man whom the postman of Gravelotte had, as he told Folliet, seen conversing with his pigeon-training associate, Schwartz.

The scheme had arisen in the brain of Ritterburg ; but it was a thing so bold, so novel, so atrocious, that the man did not dare to put it in execution solely on his own responsibility. He went whispering ; he gave out his meanings in hints and darkly worded adumbrations ; he approached the leaders of German policy with suppositions of cases, with innuendoes of what one might do, if one would. And if the truth must be told, they listened to him ! they understood him ; they gave him to know that, as for them, he had a free hand—he might do his will. They did not say it in so many words ; but there are more ways of committing or countenancing a crime than one—a smile may kill, the pressure of a hand may destroy. Ritterburg understood, and was satisfied. He went away from his whisperings and negotiations, saying : " How shrewd a dog am I ! and a man likely to stand high in the estimation of the great ! "

The object of the scheme was this; to paralyse utterly, at one blow, the mind which was winning the battles of France; once and for all to strike Vansittart low, beyond hope or help, to the earth.

It was well understood by everybody in Europe that the marriage between the millionaire and Evelyn was no common match. To win her he had forfeited a throne—he would have forfeited a thousand thrones. And it was easily conceived by his enemies that to touch *her* would be to destroy him as a general of armies quite as effectively as he could be destroyed by the drugs or dirks of the assassin.

Only, let this one fact be understood, that of this dastardly stab in the back Wilhelm himself had, at first, absolutely no sort of knowledge or hint.

But imagine the effect upon Evelyn, sitting there, all her thoughts bent upon the perils which lay thick about her other life, when this inoffensive-looking message was placed in her hands. She leapt up, staring a moment with scared and blanched face about her. Then the instinct of woman for the help and sympathy of man in the hour of her extremity arose at once within her. She ran from the room, making her way towards her brother's apartments near.

Dick had just finished his *déjeûner* and lay back luxuriously in an arm-chair, thinking of nothing but the smoke-rings from his cigar. She handed him the telegram. He bent with knit brows over it. Then he said:

" Oh, I say ! "

Evelyn's head fell upon his shoulder.

" Well, by Jove ! " said Dick.

" How soon—can we go ? " she murmured faintly.

" Poor old girl ! "

He smoothed her hair with one hand. She was sobbing now a little ; but her eyes were dry and red.

" How soon ? "

" It seems a strange thing, too ! It is quite possible, you know, that the thing may be a hoax."

" No, no."

" I don't say it is. But such things have been. It is quite possible."

" No, no. I feel—How soon ? "

" I don't know, dear. We shall have to get a special train, I suppose. It may take an hour, or two, or three."

" Oh, not so long ! I can't—I can't——"

" Poor old Evie ! Try and bear up, won't you ? "

" Send a telegram—at once. Then the train——"

Gathering strength, she raised her head, went to an *escritoire*, and wrote with fluttering hand the message which Vansittart had showed to Folliet.

Dick took the telegram, and summoned his valet. Then he dispatched another messenger for Honorine, and bore Evelyn to a couch. By the time the Queen arrived, he had already set out.

No one else seemed to share his suspicion that the telegram might be a hoax ; even in his own mind there was no real distrust of its genuineness. The telegram was conceived quite in the style of Vansittart, making light of a wound, the seriousness of which he tried in vain to hide. Although the secret was kept in the palace it leaked out elsewhere. By two o'clock it was bruited all over Paris that Vansittart had been wounded at the battle of Gravelotte. At half-past four Dick and Evelyn steamed away from the Gare de l'Est. They continued their journey safely until near nine o'clock. Night was then falling, and they had reached the little station of Vimes, a mere village. Here the railway officials had arranged to change engines, and Harland, in order to rest his sister, and procure her food somewhat more sustaining than any they could carry, settled by telegram to break the journey, and rest an hour in the local inn. All these facts were published that afternoon in Paris, both in *La Presse* and *La Patrie*. Everyone knew that the travelling pair, " upon whom the sympathies of all France were turned," would stop a little while at Vimes.

The station consists of a mere platform without any building. Ten minutes' walk from it is the inn at the bottom of the steep street, which is paved with large square, slippery stones, grass-grown in the crevices, old and slanting. The inn bears on its ancient sign, in faded red letters, the words, "*Le Dragon Dormant.*" It is of large size, rambling, and decayed. There is a tradition that down a secret stairway at the back, Louis XI. escaped in the fifteenth century, when pursued by the Duke of Burgundy, his enemy.

At the time when Dick and Evelyn arrived at the station there were four guests at the Dragon Dormant. They had arrived there an hour before. While the brother and sister walked down the village street, two of these guests paid their bill, and took their departure. They drove away in their own carriage, in which they had come, and which was waiting ready for them in the stables. The other two remained in an upper front room, watching through the leaves of the jalousies the arrival in the courtyard of the pair.

No one was abroad in the dull and ancient village street. The night was sombre and heavy with clouds, and unusally dark for the hour and time of year.

Mine host received them in the courtyard with many a bow and the opening arms of invitation. On the first floor he introduced them into a large and faded old parlour, lit by two candles, and grey with the tatters of ancient arras and furniture. Here he left them, to serve a hasty meal.

Evelyn was in a very uncertain and hysterical state of health. She fell with a deathly sigh from her brother's arm upon a couch. Her eyes closed, and she complained against the delay.

"I think, dear, it would be a good thing if you would lie down a bit in bed," said Dick, "and have some real sleep."

"No, no, I will stay here," she moaned. "Tell them to be quick, Dick—oh, tell them to be quick for me——"

"But you must listen to me, Evie. You don't know how

dreadfully ill you look. I am going to make you have a little sleep, just to please me, now.''

He touched a bell-pull of colourless old worsted. The landlord appeared.

'' Just show us to your best bedroom,'' said Dick.

And as the man preceded them, Dick went, bearing the languid and lingering steps of Evelyn, up a short flight of stairs to a room containing a broad Louis Quatorze bedstead —an apartment roomy and heavy-timbered, with slanting roof, and narrow mullioned windows with tiny panes. She, beyond doubt, was desperately drowsy, overcome by the long tension of her woe. As he laid her on the bed, her lips parted in a fluttering sigh of sleepy peace.

Dick and the landlord descended again to the first-floor parlour together. As they passed from the bedroom, the two other guests, watching from behind the shadow of a door on the other side of the stairs, saw them.

In a quarter of an hour Dick was eating a solitary and hearty meal in the parlour. This over, he rose and threw himself upon the couch, waiting. The house was absolutely still ; not a sound in the drowsy village. The silence made itself heard, and oppressed him. Ever and anon he glanced at his watch. Once, from the station, sounded faintly the whistle of the waiting train ; he seemed to hear it strangely, as in a dream. Then, again, all was sleep and silence. He rose and began to pace the room.

After half an hour he again glanced at his watch, and started toward the bedroom to rouse Evelyn. He tapped at the door and received no answer. Then he entered.

A candle had been left burning on the old mantle-shelf, but there was no light there now. It struck him with a vague surprise. He stepped toward the bed, saying, '' Evie, dear, it is time——''

The room was now almost totally dark. He put out his hand over the bed, groping to touch her. His fingers met nothing but the ruffled bed-covering. He said :

" Evie, dear—Evie ! where are you——"

At the same time a blow, like the blow of a club, or the butt-end of a pistol, fell upon the back of his head. He dropped stunned, to his knees at once, his arms spread out over the coverlet.

In a quarter of an hour a man came running from the train, asking when the travellers might be expected to continue their journey. The landlord took the message up to the parlour, and not finding Dick there, proceeded to the bedroom. There on his knees he saw him, with his arms spread out over the coverlet. But of Evelyn there was no sign. Then the alarm was raised and spread through the village. By the time the apothecary had arrived, it was discovered that the other two guests of the inn had also mysteriously disappeared.

What was now to be done ? Dick remained unconscious. The apothecary, at his wits' end, hearing that the gentleman had come in a special train, advised that he should be put to bed in his saloon-carriage, and taken back to the nearest large town. So he was carried on a stretcher to the train.

The train-men, on their side, were of opinion that their right destination now was Paris ; and when, after a time, Dick opened his eyes, he was asked whether they should not return to their starting-point. He moaned a dull and half-unconscious assent ; and some time after two o'clock in the morning, was borne up the great staircase of the Tuileries palace.

About nine the next morning Folliet arrived at the Gare de l'Est. He had telegraphed that his carriage should await him at the station ; he had some rapid travelling to do that day. As he leapt from the train, he ran to the telegraph office, and sent a message to the management directing the retention of a special train at his disposal ; then another to Vansittart, containing this falsehood : " I find already that much is in our favour. Absolutely no ground for despair. Please hope." Then he pelted himself into his carriage, and went at a gallop across the breadth of Paris towards the Tuileries.

In half an hour he was sitting by the side of Dick Harland's bed, holding and patting Dick's hand. But Dick's hand was not easily held that morning. Honorine's fingers were seeking to lull and soothe the flushed forehead ; but Dick did not like that either. He was tossing with fever, and he was delirious. To Folliet's questions he answered with mere ravings.

" Not much good to be got out of *you !* " muttered Folliet.

But he got from the Queen a good description of Dick's wound, and decided that it had been inflicted by the butt-end of a revolver ; and he got this further light from Dick himself—the oft-repeated name of Vimes.

" Vimes, your Majesty," he said, " is where the event happened, I suppose ? "

" Yes, monsieur. The addresses of the train officials are here, and their detailed statements, also, sent from the Prefecture. All that could be done has already been done in the way of telegraphing to the police all over the country."

But Folliet wished to see the train officials himself. They were off duty and at home. This was his next journey. From them he got no guidance, except the details as to the length of time they waited, and the like. He galloped then to the Prefecture, had some hurried interviews, wrote some hurried instructions, re-entered his carriage, and started back for the Gare de l'Est. But half way he looked at his watch, and pulled the check-rein. He was not far from the Rue Brevet. He told the driver to hasten to the Rue Brevet. At the end of the narrow street he got out, and walked to No. 6. He had there a message to deliver, and some instinct told him that in delivering it he was very far from losing time. Of the *concierge* he inquired if M. Armand Duprès was at home.

No—Armand had flown to higher atmospheres. Armand had migrated to No. 147 Boulevard Malesherbes. Armand was rich. Armand was luxuriating in the fortune which Marie derived from her uncle's will. Armand was living in a grand house, if you please, with a fashionable *entourage*. Armand had a silk hat, and Armand was wearing a frock-coat, and patent-leather boots, and an orchid in his button-hole.

Never, surely, did fortune vanish so swiftly as, at that very time, was vanishing the fortune of Marie's uncle.

Armand was cutting a dash.

"Then we shall be poor again, and return to No. 6, and no longer be respectable like those of joyous life?" said Marie, when she saw him scattering the francs about with royal largesse and nonchalance.

"My dear," replied Armand, "lay not up for thyself treasures upon earth, where moth and rust do corrupt. You think it was not a great man who said that? It was! I, who am also a great man, tell you so. And the words of great men remain true everywhere and forever. Let us spend, spend, spend, and be happy. What was the good of your uncle's scrapings if we do not pay him the compliment of spending them?"

In two days the fortune was reduced by one half: in a week it had dwindled to its final francs. Marie shed a private tear or two, but in her perfect trust of his wisdom and luck, was not unhappy. Armand began to feel the pinch of inconvenience; but he only laughed. He could suffer as greatly as he could enjoy.

No. 147 Boulevard Malesherbes! Folliet hesitated. Could he go? Had he time? He decided quickly. It was not far—he would lose only a few minutes.

Armand occupied a *troisième*, the whole of it, with half a dozen unnecessary apartments, all splendidly furnished. When Folliet was shown in he could hardly believe his eyes.

"Ah, Monsieur Duprès," he said, holding out his hand, "you have seen me, yet, I fancy, you do not know me. I am M. Folliet, the Prefect of Police. I have only a few minutes before setting out from Paris. Yet you see, I come to you. I have a message for you from Mr. Vansittart."

" Pray be seated, monsieur," said Armand.

" No ; this is what I have to tell you—and it is soon said : Mr. Vansittart spoke to me of you at a time when he was in a great hurry, and his words were not many. You have invented something ?"

" Quite so, monsieur."

" What is it ?"

" Oh, it is nothing ! something for killing Germans."

" Mr. Vansittart certainly does not think it nothing, sir. Pray tell me what it is. I have reasons for asking."

" In its present state," said Armand, " it is a contrivance for expelling from a generator a quantity of hydrogen every five minutes sufficient to cover the space occupied by about a thousand men. The hydrogen is mixed with oxygen, and also with carbonic anhydride—the anhydride adding weight to the flying mixture, so that it travels along the ground. The mixed oxygen and hydrogen, ignited by intense friction with the air, explodes at from nine to twelve hundred yards from the source of expulsion : and you get a wide area of flying flame, burning to cinders all it meets in the most intense heat known to man. It is, you see, only an application of the well-known oxy-hydrogen fire. So now, monsieur, you know. Instead of shooting your enemy dead, you burn him dead. A flame darts along the ground, and, in an instant, he is not. It is a living cremation. It is a plague of fire. If the sun shoot forth his flames through the universe, who can resist him ? The rain of fire and brimstone from Sodom and Gomorrah you might escape, but he who is caught by this fury shrivels, and, like a vapour, he passes away."

Folliet smiled at this grandiloquence. Was he dealing, then, with a mere wind-bag ? He did not yet know that with his high-flown manner Armand united the hard practicality of the acutest mathematician.

" Ah, but monsieur," said the detective, " what I specially

wished to know on the part of Mr. Vansittart is this : Is your contrivance *simply* made—can it be manufactured by practical workmen without delay ?"

" Oh, quite so," answered Armand. " You know that nothing is simpler than the preparation of the gases in question ; and as to the expulsion of gases through a narrow aperture at an intense rate, with that method I suppose you are already familiar. I have, by the way, a model of the thing somewhere about. I make it a present to Mr. Vansittart on the sole condition that he gives me no more bother in the matter——"

" But stay, monsieur," interposed Folliet ; " I am commissioned by Mr. Vansittart to ask you, firstly, if you will undertake to have at least one hundred of your engines of destruction made in Paris so as to be available for the defence of the city if it be attacked ? And secondly whether you can do this or not, I am commissioned to offer you three million francs at once for the invention, the sole rights to all European patents, etc., to remain vested in Mr. Vansittart personally."

Just for one instant, at these tremendous figures, Armand's face paled. Then he was himself again.

" I say, Marie," he called through a door ; " come here, will you ? Here are superfluities, and the arrogance of wealth, if you like——"

Marie had been listening behind the key-hole. She stepped blushing into the room, her eyes alight.

" Well, you accept, I suppose ?" said Folliet, with a smile.

" We are told, M. Folliet," answered Armand, " to lay not up for ourselves treasures upon the earth where moth and rust do corrupt——"

" Ah, that was in the old days," observed Folliet ; " when you are as old a man as I am you will begin to understand that that won't do for modern Europe. But come—I must be going. If you will undertake to have the hundred machines ready, you will find no difficulty as to money-arrangements at Kasine & Lafitte's, to which firm I was to recommend you. Do you undertake it?"

"Yes, monsieur," Armand answered; "as far as I am concerned——"

"Good. Then I 'm off."

"Where to, monsieur, if I may ask?"

"To Vimes."

"I thought so. To hunt for Mrs. Vansittart?"

By this time all Paris was discussing the news of the atrocity at Vimes. Armand had heard it with a flush of indignation, and then forgotten it.

"Yes, monsieur," answered Folliet; "just that—to hunt for Mrs. Vansittart."

"Are you likely to find her?"

"Ah, would to God I could say yes. The truth is, I don't know at all."

"Will you be at Vimes to-night, monsieur, at say nine o'clock?"

"Very probably. Why do you ask?"

"Oh, nothing. I will not keep you. By the way, can you lend me a hundred francs. Thank you. So much obliged. Good-bye."

"Good-bye, monsieur."

As Folliet passed out of the room, Armand turned to Marie; and with strong emphasis, with flushed face, and with knit brow, he said:

"This man Vansittart is a confoundedly decent person! There is no doubt of it! Just pack your trunk and mine. We are off to Vimes this afternoon to find his wife for him."

CHAPTER XXII

A T about the time when the news of the abduction of Evelyn reached Paris, it reached also the German corps at Metz. The great men laid their heads together, and whispered and smiled. But there was one man who heard nothing of it—the Emperor Wilhelm. When he did hear, as undoubtedly he must, what would he say? That became the question. And also this; who should undertake to tell him?

One thing was certain ; an eye like Wilhelm's would not fail to see the really, the directly, strategic importance of the coup. Already there were rumours in the town that Vansittart was no longer *compos mentis*. Men began to envy Carl Gottlieb Ritterburg as a man whom the king would surely delight to honour. And the next best thing to being Carl himself, seemed to be the one who should first announce to the Emperor the feat of Carl. A deep, secret eagerness to be first with the announcement throbbed in the bosom of many a young hauptmann, greedy of pre-eminence, of many an oberstlieutenant pining for a smile, and of many, too, both older and higher in the hierarchy of the approved.

Yet some shook their heads, and were for hesitation and delay. There was an uncertainty as to *how Wilhelm would take it;* Wilhelm was a queer card, not " of the centre," not always seeing eye to eye with the ordinary practical human animal. There was never any telling on what particular occasion his freakish point of view might manifest itself. And then there was that flash of wrath which all dreaded, the explosion, and, following swift upon the lightning, the thunder-clap and roar.

To-day he was intensely practical, a man of the world, hard as nails : to-morrow you might find him composing operas, spouting magnificencies, half Réné, half Cagliostro. He had in him the stockbroker, and hero, and the charlatan ; something of the seer, and something of Cæsar, and something of the harlequin. Through which of his hundred-hued spectacles he would view this affair of the abduction of Evelyn, and what would be his line of conduct thereupon, no one was certain. Many guesses were formed : but all the guesses were wrong.

What really happened was this : William suddenly found himself the object of a steady persecution of all the men around him who could by any means get at his ear.

To exclude one's self from the atmosphere is not easy. And his persecutors pressed upon him with the pertinacity and the omnipresence of the atmosphere.

He became suspicious of every presence, of every turn of every conversation ; ten times a day he grew red with rage ; he stamped with bitterness at the violation of the sacredness of his jealously guarded ears.

It began in this way.

About the same hour of the evening as that when the event happened at the inn of Vimes, but on the following night, Von Gossler was alone with Wilhelm. It was in an apartment of the Hotel de Ville at Metz. Wilhelm curled the uptending arc of his aggressive moustache, and then pointed to a spot on the map which lay open on the long baize-covered table in the room.

" You understand, then," he said, " it is here—here about three miles east of Conflans, where the hills open. What the American's plans may be——"

Now was von Gossler's chance.

" The truth is, sire, that, at the moment, if rumour be correct, the American has *no* plans ! "

Wilhelm glanced quickly up.

" What do you mean ? "

" I mean, sire, that something has happened to him which unfits him to manage any affair which even a child might direct."

The General sought to read keenly the face of the Emperor. Wilhelm's eyes were cast down, and hidden. For ten seconds there was silence.

" What something ? "

" His wife, sire—his wife has been kidnapped."

The Emperor knew and felt that the eyes of the General was rivetted upon his face : and felt, too, that from it every sign of colour had faded. But he did not speak. The clock ticked sixty seconds, and sixty more, filling a perfect silence ; and during that silence the devils were busy in the room.

When Wilhelm raised his head, he was still very pale. He said :

" You understand, then ; it is here, here about three miles east of Conflans, where the hills open——"

" Yes, sire," returned von Gossler ; " that is quite plain. The idea arose in the brain——"

" What idea, sir ? "

" The idea of kidnapping Mrs. Vansittart, sire. It arose in the brain——"

" It has nothing to do with me, General."

" It seems to me a piece of superb strategy, sire. The man who conceived it——"

" Deserves to be hanged, sir ! However, it was no one in the pay of Germany. It has nothing whatever to do with me."

" But, sire, I was going to tell you, the man in whose brain the scheme originated, *is*, as a matter of fact——"

" Not what he ought to be, General von Gossler. Pray let the subject drop. I desire now to discuss with you the relative importance of these two hills here——"

16

The two heads went together over the map in a long colloquy. After an hour Von Gossler rose. In the very act of his final bow he said, as a man who bursts with words and *cannot* be silent :

" I may whisper—in your Majesty's ears—that he is said to be utterly prostrated."

" ' He '—who, General ? "

" Mr. Vansittart."

" What about ? "

" Well, your Majesty, about the disappearance of his wife."

Now Wilhelm lost his temper.

" God in Heaven, General ! " he cried; " can't you let me alone with this man and his wife ? Is it *my* fault if this man's wife is stolen, or hanged, or quartered, or the deuce knows what ? Where is your tact, your penetration ? Why should I be compelled against my will ? Confound you, man ! is it *my* fault ? "

Wilhelm stamped with his foot. Von Gossler cowered backward and was silent. With bowed head he walked from the room. At last, he understood Wilhelm ; not fully, for the man's nature was not cast in so good a mould as that of his master ; yet, dimly, he understood that here was a noble soul in the throes of a struggle with a huge temptation ; and it was clear that the soul had succumbed.

But this was only the beginning of Wilhelm's troubles.

Von Gossler, piqued at the snubbing he had received, took care to make no boast of his announcement to the Emperor of the event at Vimes ; and each of the other busy-bodies, anxious to break the news, still believed that the task yet remained to be accomplished.

Wilhelm found himself in the midst of a nest of stinging ants. In his inmost heart there was the recurrent whisper that only by one of his own men could this deed have been done ; but the whisper was a still, small voice which he could stifle, provided only that its message was not confirmed by

actual information forced upon his outer ear.   How good if
he could destroy his enemy, and yet keep his own hands
clean !   But his hands would be stained the moment he knew
for certain that it was one of his own agents who had accomplished the act, if he did nothing to remedy the wrong.   He
did not wish to know ; his friends, in their eager self-adver-
tisement, insisted that he should know.   For the next few
days he lived in perpetual prickly-heat ; continually inter-
rupting, with stamp and hard words, the information which
was coming to his ears, crushing hauptmann after hauptmann, and general after general, into abashed bewilder-
ment ; and, so corrupting is the beginning of sin, resorting
to meaner and meaner dodges, lower hypocrisies, to avoid
the knowledge he dreaded, and feeling more and more the
growing taint of his guilt in his own secret consciousness.
Every hour he became fiercer.   To judge by the frequency
of his stamps, it looked, in truth, as if he was treading out
a nest of ants.

At last, on the second day, the situation became intolerable, and Wilhelm was compelled to acknowledge to himself
the inner motive of his constant interruptions.

He was then, early in the morning, riding down the Rue
des Clercs towards the outworks in company with a bevy of
officers.   The mass of horses came with a slow clatter behind ; he himself rode somewhat in advance, in company
with a Teilungs-major.

The two had been discussing for some minutes Vansittart's
device of presenting infantry before artillery.

" It has only one element to recommend it, sire," the
major had said, " and that is its success."

" But we are engaged in a regular war, Major," Wilhelm
answered.   " The tricks of an upstart are one thing, and
the rules of tactics are another.   The upstart may succeed
once, twice, thrice ; but tactics will tell in the end."

" He is said to be very low, sire."

Here was Wilhelm's sore point.   He flushed.

" Who, sir ? " he asked, with averted head.

" Mr. Vansittart, sire."

Wilhelm did not reply. There was a minute's silence. Then the Teilungs-major cleared his throat. He said :

" We need have little fear, sire, of further novelties proceeding from that head."

" Which head ? "

" Mr. Vansittart's, sire."

Would the man keep on repeating the same thing in infinite iteration ? Wilhelm wondered.

" I care nothing about his head, Major," said Wilhelm.

There was a pause ; there was embarrassment.

Then the Major said,—

" No doubt you have heard, sire—— ? "

Wilhelm had heard ; Wilhelm objected to hear again. He turned sharply in his saddle like a horse pricked by a sudden spur, saying loudly,—

" Heard what, Major ? "

" That Mrs. Vansittart—— "

" What about her ? "

" Has been—— "

" You lie, sir ! " he shouted, all encrimsoned with sudden rage, brandishing his fist. At once he stopped his horse, turned round, and pranced into the midst of the bevy of oncoming horses. Then he lifted his voice, and a torrent of invective came from him.

" Once and for all this shall be put a stop to ! " he cried. " Are you officers of the German army, or babbling fishwives met in conclave to whisper putrid gossipings? *Gott im Himmel!* am I, then, the keeper of Mr. Vansittart's wife, that I cannot have an hour's peace from the private affairs of these people ? Understand it, all of you ! and let every man in the army know it ! Woe to the man who comes with any more whisperings about this, that, and the other which does not concern him ! Why, the meanest of my subjects has a right to refuse to hear what—God in

Heaven ! let this be the last of it, I tell you, or, by the bones of my grandfather, some of you shall tremble beneath the terror of my frown.   I—— "

The officers round hung their heads in half-bewildered awe at this wholly unexpected outbreak.   As Wilhelm once more turned his horse's head, and the procession moved on, the guilty major slunk quietly behind.

Thus did Wilhelm securely seal his ears against the truth. Later in the day it became widely known that no whisper of the facts was to be permitted to reach the monarch.   Wilhelm had crushed his nest of ants.

But, in doing so, he had definitely admitted to himself that he had a motive for this imposition of silence ; and that the motive was not a good one.   Within his bosom there began to swarm and sting *another* nest of ants—eternal ones, heavenly in origin—not easy to be crushed.

CHAPTER XXIII

MONSIEUR FOLLIET, Prefect of Police, was busily eating a long-deferred meal in the immemorial old inn at Vimes at nine o'clock in the evening, when there reached him the sounds of voices from the courtyard below, and presently there was a sound of feet on the stairs, and now the landlord entered backward, bowing, ushering in two new guests with hospitable amplitude. Folliet stared, almost starting to his feet.

There was Armand, and there, bonneted and begloved, was Marie.

That morning Folliet had left Armand in Paris with no apparent intention of coming hither. But now, with sudden remembrance, he recollected Armand's question whether or no he, Folliet, would be found at Vimes that night, and he recalled the fact that Armand had asked it just after the detective's expression of uncertainty as to whether he would be able to find Mrs. Vansittart. In a moment the incomparable self-assurance of the young man dawned upon him, and, in spite of himself, he broke into a laugh. He understood the other's whole motive ; stirred by some whim of gratitude toward Vansittart, the Conservatoire freshling had come to help the old ferret in his chase !

" Well, I 'm very glad to see you, sir," said Folliet, " and you, madame," extending his hand. " This is very unexpected. Are you passing through ? "

" No, not exactly that, monsieur," answered Armand. " I always make it a point to be surprising ; and Paris is getting insufferably dull just now. So I thought I would give you a shock. To be startling is my vocation ; omnipresence is with me merely an instinct. I see that the village is quite a charming bit of quaint antiquity. Are the wines drinkable ? "

Armand, within the last few days of wealth, had become a fastidious connoisseur of wines, though his extra travelling expenses to this place had only been obtained by two journeys of Marie to the Mont de Piété.

" So so," said Folliet ; " but about the machines? I thought——"

" Oh, quite so, monsieur. Those have been attended to. I had plenty of time for that matter. I have left my instructions with the firm you mentioned, and the things will no doubt be ready within the specified time. But—Mrs. Vausittart ! Is there any hope, monsieur, if one might ask ? "

Now that Folliet's laugh was over at the whimsical apparition of the pair, he was rather vexed at the intrusion. He wanted to be alone, to think.

" Well, I suppose we must not despair," he said dryly.

By this time Marie had taken off her things, and sat at the table. The landlord's daughter entered with a roast capon and a grimy bottle of wine. Armand began to eat, and also to drink.

" Here," he said, " is to her speedy rescue," and drained his glass twice in succession.

" But if you drink much wine," whispered Marie, " how is M. Folliet to find her then ? "

The relation between the amount imbibed by Armand and Folliet's powers of discovery, though vague, seemed quite clear to Marie. Folliet, had he heard, would not have been greatly flattered, perhaps.

Armand grew rosy and jovial, filling himself with good capon and contentment. He said :

" I have been reading the Paris papers, Folliet. Of

course, they are full of nothing but the story of the abduction, as much of it as our host here could supply to reporters. And I have been making a theory of the event. I am a theorist, sir—a born theorist. The difference, M. Folliet, between the theorist and the practical man you will find to lie in this, that the practical man is always wrongly theoretical, and the theorist is, in general, rightly practical. If you tell me, sir, that I am a dreamer, I reply that to dream well is to hit straight on the head that central, inner nail which rivets the universe. Except the dreamer, M. Folliet, believe me, there is nobody worth mentioning. I find this wine good, sir."

"It is not bad wine," said Folliet, meekly; "one has only to keep on drinking it, in order to arrive at a stage of absolute self-satisfaction."

"Good; then we will keep on drinking it. In *vino veritas*—in wine is Truth. And it is Truth that we are now pursuing, monsieur. Puzzle—to find Mrs. Vansittart. Answer—drink till you get at Truth."

"Oh, Armand! you *are* a one!" said Marie, her eyes full of loving, humourous worship.

"Well, he is perfectly consistent, madame," the detective observed; "for, according to his view, it is the dreamer who hits the truth; and we need only keep on drinking to become dreamers with a vengeance. I, however, cannot join in the experiment to-night, as I have to make——"

He half rose as he spoke.

"Stay, monsieur—pray stay!" cried Armand with a downward wave of the hand—a rather excited, impassioned movement; "stay, I implore! Give me leave to drink one—only *one* more—half-glass of the wine, and I think I may then be able to tell you exactly where the lady we seek now is. Do you doubt, monsieur—do you *doubt* the truth of the adage that in wine is Truth?"

Folliet looked at the young man with wide, astonished eyes. Was he *really* a little crazy? Even Marie glanced at him with surprise. His brows were knit above eyes that had in them a strange look of fixed introspection ; his face was slightly flushed. In spite of himself Folliet sat still.

There was silence for a full minute. During this period Armand had poured out another glassful of wine and borne it to his lips. But this time he took only the tiniest sip ; and he did not swallow even this sip ; he kept it on his tongue, opening and shutting his lips with a quick little sound, in an almost comic effort to get the exact flavour of the wine. At last he swallowed it, and then he spoke.

" Yes," he said, " it is—it *is* Argonne wine. Monsieur, Mrs. Vansittart is at Argonne."

The first thought of Folliet was that the fellow *was* crazy, or an idiot, and he smiled. But in another instant the swift-reasoning mind of the detective swung round upon itself. " No, no," he said inwardly, " the man who invented that for which M. Vansittart is willing to pay three million francs can't be such a fool as all this." He looked up and met Armand's eyes. They were the eyes of a man elevated, but not drunk. Folliet was confused ; he could find no words to say ; his lids drooped ; Marie broke the silence.

" Oh, I am so glad you 've found out, dear, dear, dear Armand ! " she cried, with hands clasped like a worshipper before a saint.

It has been said that Armand during his fortnight of reck-less luxury had become quite a connoisseur of wines—more, he had become an authority, a theorist, a canonist on the subject. By means of his wonderful quickness of acquisi-tion, he, who at the beginning of this period was accustomed only to the cheap grape-juice and water of the restaurants of the Latin Quarter, was able in a few days to discuss the subtleties of distinction between sherry and Amontillado, and to apprise with nice exactitude the relative bouquets of Setian, Chian, Samian. He " went in for wines " with all the sudden flighty enthusiasm of his disposition. He ordered a dozen dozens of bottles of the wine of Mount

Vesuvius; but sent them back to the dealer with his compliments, and a message to the effect that, at his time of life, he very well knew the difference between Lachryma Christi and Spendi. As to the wines of France he became recondite, a storehouse of lore, a palate of encyclpædic nicety. He was taken by an actual minister of state, the uncle of one of his student friends, to test the genuineness of a sample of l'Hermitage '94. Armand denied that it was l'Hermitage '94; he said it was La Nerte of some later and unimportant date.

Even a dealer, so rapidly had his new fame spread among the Bohemians, had coaxed him to give the testimonial of his taste to a sample; and Armand had gone, and tested; then, shaking his head mournfully, had said, "This is not wine, monsieur; it is cider made of grapes." He was, for the moment, or the week, rather proud of this newly acquired science; so that now, when he said, "It is the wine of Argonne; Mrs. Vansittart is at Argonne," he was far more self-conscious of the cleverness of the first half of the discovery than of the deductive wisdom which enabled him to utter the second half.

Folliet cast down his eyes. He decided that the young man must have some sort of meaning, not being a fool. All that remained to be said was this, which he now quietly and deliberately said:

"What *do* you mean, monsieur?"

"That in wine is Truth, monsieur—sometimes quite unexpected. Truth, as now. I presume you are able to see some sort of relation between the fact that this wine is Argonne and the disappearance of Mrs. Vansittart?"

Folliet winked a little—meditatively,—then he lifted his head and looked round the room. No, certainly, here the chain of inference was too long for his ken; and he had been able to see much in his time, too.

"I do not see any relation, monsieur," he said simply.

"No," replied Armand; "perhaps it is unfair to expect

that you should. The fact is, I believe that I have a far more intimate knowledge of French wines than you, monsieur. Let me, however, tell you two facts, and then, I think, you will be able to comprehend : first, that when I entered this inn I ordered our host, with threats which he could see I meant, to place before me the very best wine in his house ; and secondly, that, in spite of these threats, I never for a moment supposed that he would give me Argonne, inasmuch as Argonne has lately become the rarest, as it is one of the most exquisite wines on earth."

" And why did you not suppose that he would give it to you when you asked for his best ? " said Folliet.

" Because I felt sure, monsieur, that such a wine could not possibly be found in such an inn."

" Yet here, you see, it is."

" Yes, here it is, monsieur. But I am willing to wager you a thousand francs that if you offer our host a million louis for a dozen similar bottles he will be unable to produce them."

Saying so, he rose, and tugged the bell-rope. The old man came shambling into the room.

" Monsieur," said Armand carelessly, " this is excellent beverage you give me. I compliment you."

" I am pleased you like it, sir," said the old man, bowing.

" So well, monsieur, that I have determined to offer you four hundred francs per bottle for six bottles to-morrow when I continue my journey."

" Four hundred francs ! " echoed the old man, in a kind of glee.

" Four hundred francs."

" But, sir, I have only four bottles left ! "

" That is a pity," said Armand ; " four will be useless to me." He glanced at Folliet.

" I am sure, sir—it is very unfortunate," said the old man, confused ; " you have one, the gentleman near you another —there are but four left."

" What ! you gave monsieur a bottle, too, without his asking for it ? You are generous, landlord."

" It is, then, very excellent wine, monsieur ? "

" What ! do you not know its name even ? "

" No, monsieur, no—I forget its name. But I am aware that it is the best I have—for I tasted it."

" So ? when ? "

" A short time since, monsieur."

" That is not telling me when, however."

The old man hesitated.

" When do you say ? " persisted Armand.

" Yesterday, monsieur."

" You only bought them yesterday, then ? "

" That is all, sir."

" How I should like to buy some ! Pray tell me, whom did you buy them from ? "

Again the old man hesitated. Folliet's eyes, fixed on his face, saw it pale a little, though, so far, the detective knew not in the least whither this dialogue tended.

" Ah ! you are unwilling to tell me whom you bought them from," said Armand. " It is a trade secret, perhaps. Yet I know. Let me tell you—you bought them from the two guests who drove away from your inn last night at eight o'clock ! "

The old man's eyes opened in some alarm. Suspicion, he knew, had turned upon these two as being connected with the two who had remained behind, and had presumably committed the outrage. The old man begun to perceive clearly that these were none other than detectives from Paris before whom he stood. What if he, too, were implicated, and his neck endangered ? He shuffled, and stammered.

" No, monsieur," he said ; " I swear——"

" Do not swear," interrupted Armand, " for there is no necessity : merely assert. You did not *buy* the wine, then ? These gentlemen *gave* it to you ? "

" Sir, neither the one nor the other," cried the land-

lord, resolving now to tell the history of the six bottles of
Argonne ; " yestere'en, near six, there arrived at the inn
yard four gentlemen ; two of them in a *carrosse* and pair, and
about ten minutes later two others on foot. The first two
did n't know the second two, or did n't seem to. But they
all had dinner together in the parlour : and during the meal
one of the carriage two sent my daughter down to the carriage in the stables, telling her to look inside, and she would
see a basket of ten bottles of wine in the squares, of which
she was to bring four—which she did ; and all four drank of
it, friendly like, though there was hardly a word spoken
among them. Well, messieurs, about eight or thereabouts,
the carriage two went off in their carriage, leaving the
others ; and with them, of course, they took their basket of
bottles. *I* did n't care about their wine ! *I* did n't want
their wine ! But what was my surprise this morning, on
going to the bottom of the garden, to find there the basket
with the six bottles in it right enough, and the squares, half
choked with mud and the rain which had fallen during the
night. There 's all my fault, messieurs—a poor man who
finds a windfall of wine ; what would you have ? "

" Why did n't you tell me all that before, when I was
questioning you ? " asked Folliet.

" I thought it of no moment, sir—a poor man who finds a
windfall of wine—where 's the harm ? "

" No harm whatever," said Armand ; " on the contrary,
to find a basket of Argonne at the bottom of one's garden is
the eighth and greatest of the virtues. You may retire,
monsieur."

The old man bowed himself out.

" And am I to understand, sir," said Folliet, " that you
divined, or deduced, this tale which we have just heard
from observation of your own ? "

" Something of that sort," replied Armand, still sipping
at the wine with evident gusto. " Nor must you think me
omniscient as well as omnipotent, monsieur. There is abso-

lutely no mystery or magic about the matter. You are perhaps not so *exquisitely* familiar with the aspect of bottles that
have long lain in old cellars as I ; and here is the key to my
present penetration. The first thing, of course, a connoisseur
looks at on the presentation before him of his wine, is the
grime-stains on the outside. I, looking at this bottle to-
night, determined first of all that it had never, even for a
day, lain in a cellar at all. It was grimy ; yet, with absolute certainty, I knew that here was not the grime of the
cellar. We now know that it was the grime left by soil and
rain-water when dried, and this, as a matter of fact, I guessed.
I expected, on pouring it out, to taste the wretchedest dregs ;
guess my delight at finding delicious Argonne."

Folliet was listening with as much wonder as interest. If
he could get this man to join the Prefecture as a permanent
official ! He had the thought that you might as easily
get the winged horse of fable to join a brewer's cart. He
said aloud :

" Pray go on, monsieur ; I am all ears."

Marie snuggled closer to Armand. He presented half a
glass of wine to her lips, and drank the drainings which she
left. Meanwhile, he was saying :

" But, monsieur, it is impossible to express my perfectly
immeasurable surprise when no doubt any longer remained
in my mind that this was really Argonne which I tasted
under these conditions—Argonne that had never lain in a
cellar—Argonne begrimed with rain—Argonne, above all,
whose bottle had no label on it, and whose cork had not been
sealed with resin. I think *now*, monsieur, that I need go no
further. You draw your own conclusions ? "

" I do ! I do ! " cried Folliet, with some excitement.
" Yet let me hear yours. I know quite well that they are
worth hearing, Monsieur Armand."

" The first conclusion, at least," said Armand, " was at
once obvious ; namely, that the landlord had, from whatever
source, only just acquired the wine—it had never been in

his cellar. But the Paris papers assert that he declares that for some days he has had no visitors whatever except the four who interest us. I say the *four*, for Mrs. Vansittart and the two men who carried her off must have used some conveyance, and since none was hired in the neighbourhood, it can only be that the two in the *carrosse* having gone away, returned and waited for their confederates in the dark at the bottom of the garden. You have seen this garden, monsieur, and I have not ; my conjecture is that at the end of it runs a path large enough to admit a *carrosse*. Is that so ? "

" It is, monsieur. Pray go on."

" Then in that path the *carrosse* waited. We have therefore to do with four, and not two. And you see how it was impossible for me to doubt that, somehow, by means of the four, our host had obtained his Argonne. But Argonne ! Really, M. Folliet, one cannot think of the superb goodness of this liquor, even if one knows nothing of the methods of wine-distribution, without knowing by instinct that it is *never* sent out without being sealed and labelled. As a matter of fact, believe me, it *never* is. Liquid light and joy is a precious thing. No one would dream of distributing it in that slipshod manner. In the district of Argonne itself, however, you will find many bottles without labels or seals. A wine, you perceive, is like a prophet—without honour in its own country. The *vignerons* of Argonne drink their wine as the peasants of Normandy drink their cider, or as the people of cities drink beer. If you see a company of four people going about with an indefinite number of bottles of Argonne without labels, drinking it prodigally at their ordinary meals, and casually leaving the rest of it behind at the bottom of a garden as soon as it becomes inconvenient to them, you may be quite certain that at least *one* of them is a denizen of Argonne, probably a wine-grower, accustomed to think as lightly of his Argonne as a peasant of Normandy of his cider ; and you may be sure that it is this *one*, who, having plenty of Argonne habitually in his possession, brought with him, for the pleasure of the rest, these odd, unlabelled bottles.''

Folliet's eyes were rivetted on the young man's face. He did not speak ; he murmured and nodded assent.

'' I do not know, M. Folliet,'' proceeded Armand, '' I do not know if there now remains any sort of doubt in your mind that at least *one* of the four confederates is a *resident* at Argonne ; as for me, certainly, there is no such doubt. But have you considered the enormous difficulties as to the placing and keeping of his captive with which the man had to contend in whose brain the idea of capture first arose ? He had to hide away for an indefinite period a loving woman in a country which, he knew, would at once turn itself through all its length and breadth into a lynx, myriad-eyed and alert, to re-discover her ; to hide her away here, in France, at a spot not very remote from that at which the capture takes place—a spot which can be reached for certain in the interval between night and morning, and reached in a *carrosse*, for the railway is out of the question. We thus see that the area of choice as to where Mrs. Vansittart should be taken was bounded by many, many limitations ; but it was bounded, above all, by *this* limitation—that the first mover, or movers, in this villainy was undoubtedly German. This we can say without any sort of proof ; every-one at once says it—and the plotter knew that everyone would at once say it.

'' He knew, moreover, that there must be no hiring of a house, no sign of preparation, no purchase or hire of a conveyance, within many miles of the abduction as to space, within many days of it as to time. But, being German, he would not be likely to have these necessary things in France, or, at least, to have them conveniently where they were wanted ; and, being German, would draw upon himself doubt and remark if he attempted to procure them. I can almost fancy him in despair. There was, however, *one* obvious way out of the difficulty ; supposing he knew a fellow-countryman willing to fall in with his plans, who possessed things of the sort he desired, and near the locality. He could then proceed with absolute secrecy. A whiff of chloroform delivered to Mrs. Vansittart previous to her journey through the night would be all the precaution he need take."

" Such a friend, monsieur," said Folliet, " *was* actually found ; for the landlord tells me that three of the four spoke with marked German accents, whereas the fourth spoke quite good French, but was fair-haired. He probably was a German, too, you see, but spoke good French, for the simple reason that he has lived a long time in France."

" And if in France, monsieur," replied Armand, " then in Argonne. That one of them came from there I have proved. To be certain that they returned there, one need only remember that Argonne at least fulfils the conditions as to remoteness, a friend, a house, and so on, and to remember the extreme rarity of the chances that any other place would fulfil all the conditions necessary to the accomplishment of the design. *Two* friends, conveniently circumstanced for this design, our German plotter almost certainly did not have ; he had one at Argonne, as we know. I was able, therefore, to say, monsieur, that Mrs. Vansittart is at Argonne."

Marie's head, leaning on his shoulder, suddenly nodded with a jerk. She was asleep.

Folliet rose.

" It is well reasoned," he said. " Through your acumen, monsieur, perhaps by this hour to-morrow night we may have——"

" Discovered their motive for leaving their wine behind, monsieur," said Armand, with a rather strange laugh.

CHAPTER XXIV

THE RACE

HOW they came to leave their wine behind seemed to Folliet as simply-guessed as possible. With Mrs. Vansittart, there were five people to be squeezed somehow into the *carrosse*, and, when it came to the point, they must have found that there simply was not room enough for the basket to be wedged among their feet. Whereupon they had dropped it over the hedge into the garden. It seemed to him, too, that, even supposing there *was* room, they would be anxious to get rid of every ounce of additional weight, in their frantic haste, with a long journey before them. All this, lying on his bed, tired after the previous sleepless night, he was thinking. Armand fell slightly in his estimation for his failure to see this simple explanation of the discarded basket.

"Never mind ; he 's a wise fellow—a wise man. If only the lad's opinion of himself was a little more modest !" he said, and fell asleep.

Armand, too, not so tired, was lying awake thinking. Near him lay Marie, one arm across his chest, her lips parted like a half-opened flower close to his cheek. Armand, too, had thought of the explanation of the discarded wine which had occurred to Folliet, but this explanation did not quite satisfy him. They had apparently brought to the inn ten bottles, of which they had drunk four ; there remained six, and the whole of these six they had left behind. But if the carriage was not large enough to contain them and the basket, too, could they not have smuggled away at least one of the six bottles somewhere—into some pocket, into some nook, under the seat?

How good would one such bottle be to them toward morning, before they reached the end of their headlong, dusty journey! It must be, he thought, that their discarding of the whole six was an idea, a design, some trick. But what? He lay thinking.

The course which the landlord had actually pursued with respect to the treasure-trove of wine could not, he thought, have been calculated upon by the Germans. The old man had cunningly concealed the matter till forced to disclose the facts. But the Germans must have expected him to find the basket and declare publicly the fact of his finding it. That was the natural course, the thing which most men, under the circumstances of alarm and commotion, would do. Hence they had taken the trouble to bear the basket from the carriage to the garden and lay it there, where the landlord would be certain to see it.

And the only possible motive at which Armand could guess, was this : that they wished to create an impression of careless opulence ; that, supposing they were seen and traced upon the road in the direction of Argonne, then the crudely-reasoning police might say, "They are people of position and wealth ; they have left behind them six bottles of Argonne ; they have borne Mrs. Vansittart to a palace or a castle, and in a palace or a castle we must seek her."

"As for me," said Armand, "if I had to seek her, I should seek her in a hovel." And then he, too, fell asleep.

At about four in the morning, Folliet knocked at his door, and roused him.

"Monsieur," said the detective, "I am about to breakfast, and set out upon my search ; I need not say that I shall be delighted if you will share my investigations."

"Certainly, monsieur," Armand replied ; "I, too, shall be delighted. Can you lend me a hundred francs?"

Folliet smiled in the half-darkness.

" By all means, monsieur ! here is a note."

Armand turned to dress ; when the process was completed he bent over drowsy Marie and kissed her. She put an instinctive arm about him, murmuring sleepy contentment. He said,

" I am going away."

" No ! "

She leaped up at once.

" I am."

" Armand ! what for ? "

" To find Mrs. Vansittart."

" And you are going to leave *me* ? "

" I must, darling."

" How wretched you will be, and I also ! Ah, cruel ! "

" I can't help it ; one must be practical and good. I don't quite know where I may have to go to, or I could take you. It won't be for long, our parting. Here are a hundred francs which M. Folliet has given me. With these you will pay your expenses at this inn ; and from Gravelotte I shall telegraph to you, telling you where to come to me. There are some novels in the trunks which you can read ; good-bye, sweet—ah, sweet ! "

He undid her arms from his neck and ran away from her half-vexed, half-tender tears. In half an hour he was with Folliet in a train.

As the engine began to puff and move, Armand said :

" And now, monsieur, your plans ? "

" They are simple," replied Folliet. " The distance between Vimes, which we are now leaving, and Argonne, to which we are finally going, is about eighty miles. Just about midway between the two is a little station called Renne. I intend to stop at Renne."

It was just possible that Armand was somewhat piqued by this hard-and-fast decision of Folliet without having consulted one whom he had taken into collaboration, and who was putting himself to a great deal of gratuitous inconvenience—rare for him ; for the young man said, with marked coldness,

" What for, monsieur ? "

" You will immediately agree with me when you hear," said Folliet. " This distance of eighty miles it was evidently the intention of the kidnappers to traverse during the hours of darkness. Morning, of course, would be extremely dangerous to them. But their horses had already done some travelling when they arrived at Vîmes, and the rest there was short. It is certain, then, that, by some contrivance or other, they managed to change horses during the night, and the place most advantageous to them for the change would be somewhere not far from the middle point between Vîmes and Argonne, somewhere not far from Renne. Within a radius of twenty miles round Renne I intend, therefore, to make personal, well-directed inquiries. The descriptions given by our old host at Vîmes of the horses, the carriage, the men, are as vague as they can be. All he can remember of the man who spoke good French is that he was fair ; that is no good to us, you know. But men changing horses in the small hours of the night leave a deeper impression. We may even get a sight of one of those horses still remaining in some stolid peasant's stall thereabouts, and that would be almost as good as having the name and address of the man who owned him. Renne is the place for us, then."

" Excellent, monsieur ! " said Armand, " if we had only a year to spare."

At these words the countenance of Folliet flushed to a deep and angry red.

" Pray explain your meaning," he said, curtly.

" I suppose that M. Vansittart is anxious for the recovery of his wife as soon as possible, monsieur ? "

" I suppose so, sir. That is why I propose the very speediest means of recovering her."

Armand bowed.

"I differ from you, monsieur, that is all. I think we should go on straight to Argonne at once."

"Very well ; then we must agree to differ, monsieur."

"Very well, monsieur."

Armand at once turned to the book he was reading ; Folliet to his memoranda. Till the train drew up at Renne, neither spoke a word.

Folliet rose, collected his stick, mackintosh, and papers, and stepped toward the door. To his surprise, he noticed when he reached it that Armand had not moved.

"This is the station, monsieur," said Folliet.

"Which station, monsieur?" answered Armand.

"Renne."

"I know."

"Are n't you coming out?"

"No—I am going on to Argonne."

"Oh, very good. Good-morning."

"Good-morning, monsieur. I shall find Mrs. Vansittart before you."

Folliet flushed.

"That time alone can show, sir."

"Before you, monsieur!"

Folliet had put out his foot on the step-board by this time. He half turned to answer :

"Happy season of youth!"

His foot touched the platform.

"Before you, monsieur!" cried Armand.

"Blessed innocence of childhood!" sneered Folliet.

"Oh, but M. Folliet!" called Armand, "will you lend me a hundred francs? I have no money."

Folliet put his hand in his pocket, and, without a word, handed the other a note. As he was about to pass through a doorway of the station, he heard the unrelenting voice crying after him :

"Before you, monsieur!"

"Well, we will see about *that!*" muttered Folliet, with

tight-pressed lips. A moment afterwards the moving train whirled Armand away ; but Folliet, glancing round, could see a head popped from a window still bawling something at him.

If ever he was on his acme of effort to do a thing well and swiftly he was so now. He had been challenged by a child.

Armand,. too, as soon as he found himself alone in the train, knit his brows.

" Come now," he said aloud, " suppose we teach M. Folliet, the Prefect of Police, a lesson in modesty."

Beneath this youth's froth was the elemental rock itself.

By Epernay, by St. Hilaire, by St. Menhould, passed Armand. The railway is circuitous—the train was slow. Not till ten o'clock did he get out at Clermont-en-Argonne.

The district of Argonne is scattered and ill-defined, and it is not, properly speaking, recognised at all as one of the great wine centres, owing to the extreme uncertainty of its yields. A plot here, another far yonder, yet another over the hill—such is Argonne. One year the yield, all told, was ten barrels, another it may swell to hundreds—it is never much. Hence its fame hides modestly from the world beneath the august shadow of Epernay and Rheims. But its grapes are far smaller and more exquisitely sweet than those of its louder rivals; and, to the connoisseur, Argonne is elect.

Its cellars are goodly excavations cut far into cliffs of chalk formation. M. Moet's, at Epernay, extend some nine miles. Two at Argonne are over three miles in extent.

At the station Armand drank a large tumbler of genuine Argonne, for which he paid only about fourpence. He walked twenty yards down the street, stopped at an unpretentious hotel, and drank another, preparatory to *déjeûner*. Here was Paradise to the light of heart, and the quaffing of goblets in Valhalla ! His eyes began to sparkle, and his feet to tread on air.

His problem was not merely to find Mrs. Vansittart ; but to souse himself with Argonne wine and find Mrs. Vansittart as well. The thing was not easy; but with every additional glass his hopes grew rosier-hued.

"Do you know a German named—I forget his name—but a wine-grower about here?" he asked a patron of his hotel.

"A German, sir? No."

"Just think, now."

"I know none such, monsieur. But I have been here only six months ; you would be more likely to find what you want by inquiring in the villages."

"Ah, well, it is all one," said Armand to himself. "Folliet can't be here before night, and I shall know by then. Another glass of '90, monsieur."

He went presently, after breakfast, sauntering through the town, whistling loudly for the benefit of passers-by, his hat thrown far back on his head. Armand, as Mr. Arnold says of Heine, was so essentially "disrespectable!" Just now he was being violently torn two ways. The sun was bright, the wine ran vividly in his veins ; he wanted to make a day of it, here, in this land beyond Jordan, flowing with milk and honey. In his pocket was a hundred francs crying, "Spend us ! spend us !" On the other hand, there was his boast to Folliet. He felt sure that he was at least a step nearer the truth than Folliet ; it would be too hard, too poor, if he threw away his advantage.

And Folliet all the time was probably working hard, straining every nerve. Every time Armand thought of this he quickened his steps ; every time he heard the cry of the hundred francs in his pocket he struck up a song and entered a drinking-house. He was not, in reality, a person of weak will, but he had two wills in him, both strong, equal, and opposite. This rendered his equilibrium unstable. He was "unsteady." But through all the ferment of his brain he did not for a moment entirely lose sight of the end in view, and his fine faculty of thought remained pretty intact, like a glowing coal under heaps of fluff and ashes. He stopped a passer-by, and said :

" What is the nearest village ? "

" Rouflet."

" How far ? "

" Four kilometres."

" Is it a decent place ?   Any fine houses in it ? "

" It is rather a poor place."

" Any vineyards near it ? "

" Two or three round it."

" Can one get good Argonne wine there ? "

" Oh, certainly. It possesses the best vines in the district."

" Thank you, monsieur."

He set off. He had already decided to seek what he wanted in a poor rather than a rich locality, and in a village rather than the town.

Rouflet he found to consist of a steep street, flag-paved. He passed through it singing, and near the further end entered a diminutive *cabaret*.

On each side of the door two men were leaning, talking. One was the proprietor, a burly figure with a thick black mane of hair ; the other was tall, wore rings and a heavy watch-chain, and had a nose with a distinct dent in the centre of the ridge. The proprietor of the *brasserie* spoke to him with a certain deference which Armand, as he entered, noted. He could hear that they were talking about the war, and the rumoured probability of another great battle taking place on the following day.

As Armand entered, the landlord left the door to serve him. The other man, who seemed to be merely lounging away a morning's hour at the inn-door, followed ; and, as he did so, said with a yawn :

" Well, gossip Pierre, it is long since I have bought a glass of my own wine from you. I, too, will have a sip for good luck."

" Ah, that 's talking," answered Pierre ; " we must mark it up with chalk."

Yet the tip of the wine-grower's broken nose was of so

vivid a scarlet that it was certain the drinking of his own wine was not such a rarity with him as Pierre implied.

"Now, here's a spark from Paris," said the wine-grower; "you can see it from the very cut of his clothes, and the way he sips his wine, as if it were dangerous. Is n't that so, neighbour?"

With this playful sally he addressed Armand. They were standing side by side, shoulder to shoulder.

"You are right," said Armand; "I am from Paris."

"And what are you doing our way—touring?"

"No; they sent me down here—doctor-people. Left lung. Argonne air, Argonne wine—and plenty of it."

"You are quite a stranger here, then?"

"I don't know a soul."

"What do you think of the chances of a battle to-morrow?"

"I don't care a curse about the chances of a battle to-morrow. What does it matter to such as you and me? I am come down here to drink wine—and get health. My left lung is ba-a-d."

"Well, I would n't have thought that to look at you. Do you play chess?"

"Rather. Do you?"

"Hear him, Pierre! He asks if I can play chess! Why, man, of course I can."

"Oh, that 's all right, then. Only—don't play with *me*. I shall certainly beat you."

"You? Just hear him! Well, it 's wonderful what these Paris chaps think of themselves!"

"Oh, it is n't that," said Armand; "*I* learned to play at Heidelberg, which is the very best place to learn."

"What! You have been in Germany?"

"Rather. My mother was a German."

"Damn it! Well, so was mine; and I 'm not ashamed to own it!"

"Good! I don't mind taking you at a game, then. But

chess playing is n't what I devote myself mostly to. I have another hobby."

" And what 's that ? "

" Stamp collecting."

Armand had seen a pocket-book end sticking from the breast of the stranger, such a one as is used for the temporary home of stamps, and, standing a little out, the serrated edges of some specimen sheets.

The man was surprised.

" No ! " he said ; " why, it 's wonderful ! It 's the very thing I do myself ! "

" I 've got a fine example of the suppressed Nevis '84," remarked Armand.

" No! Well, that 's a treasure ? Will you show it me ? "

" With pleasure. My stamp-book is in Clermont. Some day during the week, if you will pay me a visit."

At this point the landlord presented to them the chess-board and the box containing the pieces. They proceeded to a little room back of the bar, and sat with the board between them. Armand ordered a bottle of '90. At the end of three hours they still sat there. Of five games Armand won three ; and with every game he ordered a bottle of '90. The talk was all of stamps.

At four o'clock, in a little village twelve miles from Renne, Folliet, on his side, was deep in talk with a small *vigneron* of the district.

He had been hearing a tale about a carriage from which the horses had been taken at midnight in order to put in their places two of the *vigneron's* own which had been bought from him during the day for ready-money down.

" How many people were there ? " asked Folliet.

" Four, I fancy, monsieur, but I only saw one of them well."

" A German ? "

" No—French."

" How do you know ? "

" He spoke French quite well."

" What sort of looking man ? "

" Tall, with fair hair and moustache."

" Go on."

" That 's about all I remember. He was a pleasant kind of man to talk to, too. Oh, stop ! There was something wrong with his nose. It had a dent in the middle of the bridge."

" Why did n't you give information of all this to the police instead of giving me this trouble ? "

Folliet, as he said it, glanced anxiously at his watch, with an exclamation of impatience.

" I had no idea that there was anything wrong," answered the man. " All was square and above-board."

" Well, here 's a louis. I may want you again."

He jumped into a fly at once, and went galloping through the lanes towards Renne. Here he sent a telegram to the Bureau of Police at Clermont :

" Find out at once address of man, fair, tall, broken nose, probably German, probably vintner, in district of Argonne. Promptitude of supreme importance. Will arrive next train.

" FOLLIET, Prefect."

Then he went to the station, and, chafing with nervous impatience, walked up and down the platform, waiting.

CHAPTER XXV

TO GRAVELOTTE

FOLLIET did not arrive at Clermont till after seven that night. But he arrived full of hope.

Momentous as the matter at issue was, his human nature could not resist a sardonic grin at the thought of Armand and his boast. If someone had told him (what was the truth) that Armand at that moment was snoring off the effects of a long day's debauch, he would have roared with victorious laughter.

When Folliet got the faintest clue of a mystery into his head, few things could balk the shrewd and practised scent with which he tracked it to its ultimate convolution. And this day he had been even luckier and swifter than he had expected. He had not a doubt that at the *bureau* at Clermont-en-Argonne the address and name of the man he wanted were waiting for him.

And there, in fact, they were. The detective who made inquiries was in attendance, and handed him a slip on his entry into the *bureau des renseignements*. There was a man who almost entirely answered to the description, and there was only one in the district. His name was Henri Reichenberg, and he was the owner of the vineyard called La Piblouette, about two kilometres north-east of Rouflet, which in turn was a village four kilometres north of Clermont.

Folliet sent an officer for a cup of coffee, swallowed it in big gulps, and ran out into the street alone. He had to spy —to make sure—and then——

With joy he saw that there was no moon, and that the sky

was covered over with black clouds. He took a cab to Rouflet, dismissing it just outside the village. The night was then confirmed and dark. He drew the collar of his mackintosh high over his ears and chin, and passed quickly down the street. Then he struck north-east over the open country. He met no one anywhere. In three quarters of an hour, following a winding road, he came upon a chalk cliff which stretched right across his path. Its bare white cragginess just loomed upon him in the darkness before he butted upon it. The edge of the cliff ran about fifteen feet above his head.

Folliet had received a description sufficiently minute of the place. He turned to the left along a footpath which ran along the base of the rock. In his course he passed by a square spot of deeper blackness in the rock-face. He tapped it ; it was wooden. It was a door, the entrance to the cellars of Henri Reichenberg. He walked on, and in three minutes came to a break in the continuity of the cliff ; it was a narrow, steep flight of stone steps cut out of the rock to the upper level of the cliff. He ascended. At the top he found the entrance of an extremely long avenue of lindens which met overhead. Here it was very dark. He proceeded up the avenue with intense caution, though in reality there was little need for it, for not a sound broke the silence of the world, and the moss underfoot was deep and continuous, rendering the footfall noiseless. Presently, at the far end of the avenue, where the trees almost met in perspective remoteness, he saw the glimmer of a light. But it vanished almost at once.

He went on. " That light," he said, " is a light in the house of Henri Reichenberg. Someone has opened and shut a door or a window—hence its appearance and disappearance. Is Mrs. Vansittart really and truly behind those shuttered apertures ? I wonder—I wonder. The mere shuttering of them is suspicious. I shall know, Henri Reichenberg, within fifteen minutes."

But he knew sooner; he knew within five minutes. Suddenly, as he walked through the now dense darkness on the absolutely soundless moss, he came into sharp collision with someone coming in the opposite direction down the avenue. It was a man bigger than himself and heavier. Folliet nearly fell backward.

"Pardon, m'sieur," said a rather thick and drowsy voice. "Collisions are natural to Erebus and modern civilisation alike."

The remark was quite in the tone of the Latin quarter. Folliet, with a start as violent as though he had heard the Devil speak, recognised Armand.

"Ah, M. Armand—you——" he gasped.

"What, you, M. Folliet?"

"It is I," admitted Folliet.

Armand's hand went out and hit upon Folliet's in the dark. He gave the detective a hearty grip.

"M. Folliet," he said, "allow me to congratulate you. You are a great man!"

"How!" exclaimed Folliet. "It is *you!* You were here first!"

"That is true, monsieur. But, then, I did the right thing. You did the wrong—and get here all the same. That is what I call greatness."

"Well, if this fellow is n't a gentleman to his marrow!" said Folliet to himself. He added aloud: "But, monsieur, this is the mere sophistry of generosity. Don't you see that it is you this time at least who are the great man."

"Monsieur, we are both great men," said Armand with large sententiousness.

"But—but—how long have you been here?"

"About two hours."

"Good Lord! not in the house?"

"Yes, in the house. I have just left it."

"And is Mrs. Vansittart there?"

"For the last hour and a half I have been sleeping in the room adjoining hers."

"*Sleeping!* Oh, this is incredible."

"Only at first, monsieur. Not when you know the facts. The truth is, monsieur, I have been—drunk on Argonne wine. Or if drunk is too coarse a word to apply to the effects of Argonne, say transfigurated. It is not an intoxication—it is a sublimation. Nectar is not a wine—it is an essence. I doubt, monsieur, if I am sober now."

"Yes, you are. I believe you are soberest when you are drunk. Pray tell me—how did you manage?"

"There is a man, monsieur, who, according to my present recollection, is called Henri Reichenberg. This man, almost as soon as I saw him, and as soon as I heard him, I knew to be one of the four. It is not true that he speaks perfect French, though his French is near perfection. He has, in fact, lived half his life in Munich. Having understood this, I persuaded him to get drunk in my company. When I am transfigurated, monsieur, I do not fail to retain a certain empire of my soul, a little light amid the gloom ; but in the case of Henri Reichenberg, if that is his right name, you get a gloom which is the primeval gloom itself. I played chess with Reichenberg and beat him only sufficiently to induce him to keep on playing. Finally, as we are both ardent philatelists, he took me home to see his collection of postage stamps, and while he was showing me we both fell asleep. Reichenberg, believe me, still slumbers."

"But—Mrs. Vansittart! You saw her?"

"I saw her, monsieur. She will die soon if not rescued."

He said it in an awed whisper. And in an awed whisper Folliet answered :

"How! die, you say? How do you mean?"

"I only caught one glimpse of her face. The house, I may tell you, is a small, mean one—two stories, built of white freestone—not more than eight rooms. But six of these rooms are crowded with men, armed, soldier-like people,

Germans. The seventh room, on the first floor, is Reichenberg's, who has her under his immediate surveillance; the eighth is Mrs. Vansittart's. As I passed into Reichenberg's room I saw through a slightly open door a woman. She appeared to be slowly walking to and fro; it was evident at once that she was harassed to the point of lunacy. But her face, monsieur! Anything as wan, and drawn, and pity-kindling you can hardly imagine. If this lasts——"

He stopped.

"Ah, but it won't last!" cried Folliet, with clenched fists. "It is you who have found her. What do you advise?"

"I don't advise anything, M. Folliet," said Armand; "a practical point like that I leave to you. But I have one warning to give—*don't* make an attack upon the house unless you are quite sure that your force of gendarmes very largely preponderates over the force of armed men within it. Bring a merely equal force against the place, and we lose Mrs. Vansittart."

"Ah, that's the point," said Folliet—"*can* I bring a sufficient force? Look here, this is a matter which no man but one should take into his hands, and that man M. Vansittart."

"I entirely agree with you, monsieur."

"Then let us go to him and consult him."

"By all means, and at once."

"Can you ride?"

"Is there no train?"

"Not for some time. Two swift and strong horses—that's what we want. Twenty miles or so—the distance is nothing. Let us go back to Clermont; I can get two of the *gendarmerie* mounts."

They at once set out at a rapid walk. On the road near Rouflet they met an empty cart, and offered the driver a louis to take them at a gallop to Clermont. In twenty minutes they arrived in the town.

As they went toward the *bureau de police*, they passed a

post-office.   Armand entered, and dispatched a telegram
to Marie at Vimes :

" Take the first train to Gravelotte.   I shall be there looking out
for you."

Then he joined Folliet at the *bureau* over the way.

In ten minutes they were mounted on two stout coursers,
and clattering through the town.

Twice only they drew rein to knock at cottage doors and
make themselves certain of the route.   The rest of the
journey was one long, silent, intense gallop.   They passed
through the French army, and about midnight dashed into
Gravelotte on horses panting and wet with foam.

Vansittart was staying at the inn called Cheval d'Or,
He had retired to bed, but a chambermaid was able to give
the positive assurance that he was not asleep.   He could be
heard walking still in his room.   She took up a message,
and returned with the command that Folliet should wait in
the *salon*.   Armand had not sent up his name.

Presently Vansittart entered, wrapped in a dressing-gown
of crimson silk, with a gold-wrought *ceinture*.

" Ah, M. Folliet," he said, " this is a surprise.   And do
my eyes deceive me ?—surely here is M. Duprés."

He spoke quite heartily.   But his pretence of nonchalance was as hollow and shallow as possible, making
him still more an object of pity.   He could not hide the
haggard glare of his eye, or the care which sat on his faded
cheek.

" We are now arrived post haste from the neighbourhood
of a small town called Clermont, in Argonne, M. Vansittart," said Folliet.   I may tell you at once that we have
found Mrs. Vansittart—or rather, to be exact, this gentleman here has found her."

" M. Duprés ? "

" Yes, sir."

" *Seen* her ? "

His face was screwed into an expression of gaunt, distorted inquisitiveness.

"Yes, I have seen her," said Armand.

"Really? You have? My God! you have *seen* her, then?"

His knees gave, and he sank backward upon a couch.

"I merely caught a glimpse of her face in passing," said Armand.

"And she is—well? Did she seem—well? To think that you have seen her!"

Armand, in pity, said:

"Oh, she is well enough—a little pale, perhaps—no more than is natural under the circumstances."

"A little pale, perhaps," Vansittart repeated, mechanically.

"She is in a healthy locality," ventured Folliet.

"But where—where?"

"At a house surrounded by vineyards in the Argonne district."

"But, M. Folliet, you have *left* her there?"

"The place is full of armed men, monsieur. I did not at the moment feel myself in a safe position to attempt a rescue without consulting you. An attempt which failed would make matters only worse."

"How many men?"

"I should say between thirty and forty," replied Armand.

"How far away?"

"About twenty miles."

"Then—we will go at once!"

He staggered to his feet.

"M. Vansittart, this is a matter for coolness and deliberation. There are extensive wine-cellars beneath the house, a labyrinth of hiding-places, doubtless in direct communication by stairs with the building. During an attack which is not also a complete surprise, your wife could be——"

"Ah, I see! Taken down into the cellars, eh? An excellent plan! Is your object, then, to drive me mad, monsieur?"

" No, no. It is merely a suggestion which I make. Find me the men and I will undertake the rest. You must not come. You must see that you are not in the right frame of mind for such an enterprise. And the army here cannot spare you."

Vansittart's head was bowed down to his knees. For some time he sat so. Then he said :

" Leave me, M. Folliet, for half an hour—an hour—leave me. I must think. Monsieur, pray leave me "—to Armand —" I—I must think of this matter."

But as Armand passed by him he put out his arm and gave a momentary pressure to the hand of the young man.

" Ah, thanks ! " he said.

CHAPTER XXVI

VANSITTART'S TEMPTATION

THE reason why Vansittart wanted time to think was this : that it was confidently believed in both armies that at the next dawn an attack would be made by the Germans. If he was at Clermont he could not be at Gravelotte ; and if he was not at Gravelotte, he would be away from the army in its hour of need and conflict. He would have deserted his post.

He lay half-stretched on the couch, and one side of his face lay flat on the dark velvet of the couch-head. Anyone looking at him would have seen him writhe, and would have seen the pain upon his face, and his closed lashes moist and clotted, and would have heard the groans that broke from him.

Whether it was a foreboding of what really was to happen, or whether he had some extraordinary insight into the facts of the situation, he felt not the least doubt that whoever he might send to recover her would somehow fail, if he himself were absent—that he would lose her again, this time perhaps forever.

" No, I can't bear that," he moaned ; " Oh God !—I cannot."

And as he writhed, on his face was the stamp of keen physical pain, and his eyes were closed.

After all, what was France—or the world—to him compared to her ? A man has one little life which, to him, is more important than the ruin of all the remaining universe. There are times when it is the duty of a man to be selfish, surely. Every fibre within him, every instinct of his humanity—impelled him towards her ; a thousand voices shouted to him to fly, only to fly, to the luxury involved in one renewed sight of her face, one kiss of her lips. But he did not move. He lay there crouching, half on his knees, his distorted face against the couch-end.

He mechanically repeated several times Armand's words : " A little pale, perhaps—a little pale, perhaps."

He easily divined that this was a confession compelled only by the force of a truth far more emphatic than stated. " A little pale, perhaps," meant, probably, that she was dying.

Vansittart started up. Suddenly hesitation seemed to him absurd. He rang the bell violently. But when a man entered the room, he had again flung himself upon the couch. He waved the man away backwards. He had changed his mind.

Was it to be France or Evelyn ?

The momentary thought flashed through his mind that, by means of extraordinary dash and enterprise, it might be both. But the notion soon vanished. It was going on to two o'clock. To set out for Clermont, reach it, remain there engaged for even one hour, and return to Gravelotte could not be accomplished before seven or eight in the morning. The attack was expected two or three hours earlier.

It could not be both, then ; it must be one or the other.

That he could save Evelyn he felt confident : he, with his own hand, felt the prowess and the might to fight and beat down in her defence a score of men ; he felt that, for her, at the critical moment, his brain would have the clearness of an angel's to think and contrive. If he went, he could save her. If he stayed, could he save France ?

No one else, certainly, believed that he could. More and more, for the last two days, had he become incompetent to direct, a sorry general of armies. Was it likely that on the morrow, while he still hung in uncertainty as to the fate of his wife, he would be able to interest himself capably in the direction of great schemes of generalship ?

This thought decided him. He jumped up again. He had found an excuse, with the same readiness that a mass of rushing water finds a channel down a hill. His heart and brain were at that moment as unreliable as quicksilver. His whole nature was tending in a strong current toward Clermont ; even his reason tricked him, and, when he attempted to use it, slipped back at once into the general trend of the rest of his being.

He stood upright, his eyebrows lifted in eager outlook ; and he said decisively :

" I will go ! I will go ! "

Again he rang the bell. As he did so, his eye happened to fall upon the mantelpiece near, and there caught sight of a tiny watch set in a long handle of filigreed ivory. It was a watch which he had brought with him, and which, when he was at home, usually lay on his dressing-table. He wished to know the exact time, and took it up. In the handle was a miniature photograph of Evelyn. For the moment, all his mind turned in another direction. He had forgotten the fact that in lifting the watch he would see the photograph ; and its sudden apparition before his sight produced upon him a startling effect. He bent looking upon the mild lineaments of his wife with eyes wide with interest.

At that moment a servant entered in answer to his summons.

" Never mind," said Vansittart ; " I will ring again when I want you."

He bent once more over the photograph ; and so bending, for five minutes stood. Then, with the reverence of a neophyte kissing the cross, he kissed it, and laid it down. The effect of this pure woman's pictured face upon her husband had proved the very opposite of what might have been expected. Instead of wildly moving him to rush to her, it had said to him in words which he could almost hear, and with the mildness of an angel's reproof, " I expect of my hero that he act heroically."

The consideration of what *she* would wish him to do threw a new and a sudden light over the whole question. For the first time, the magnitude of the impersonal claims upon his presence here grew clear to him ; a nation had trusted him —though his heart broke, it must break at his post.

Once more he was down on the couch, on his face, fighting it out in his torn brain. If he should lose her? If they should kill her slowly? If he never saw her again, at all, forever? This was the contingency, on the one side ; on the other was poor, perishing France, and his honour, and the upward-pointing finger of Evelyn reminding him of the old hero-souls, and of the unseen eyes that regard the brave in their struggles and secret triumphs, and of that fulness of reward which, beyond doubt, Nature keeps in store for them who love not their own lives. Lying there, he gave one deep groan, as though in it he would deliver up his spirit. Thus a minute passed. Then he rose, a peaceful smile curving his lips.

Vansittart, as was the way with him, had emerged from the fire purified and strengthened.

He ran hurriedly up some stairs, entered his room, threw off his dressing-gown, and put on some clothes ; all this, very rapidly, yet with perfect calm. Then he ran down to the room where he thought Armand and Folliet were probably awaiting him, and found them there. They had been wondering what he could possibly be doing. Now, looking at his face, they wondered still more. He seemed a new man to the distracted person they had lately left ; he was more than calm—he was genial.

" Well, M. Folliet," he said, " if you will come with me, I think I can put at your disposal at once whatever force we may think necessary for a rescue. As for myself, I am sorry I cannot accompany you ; things here, you see, will probably require my presence."

The three left the inn together, and proceeded down the street to a private house where Colonel Montsaloy, a man whose activity and resource Vansittart had observed, was now lying asleep. They roused the house, and in a few minutes the four men were in deep colloquy.

Vansittart recommended a contingent of sixty *chasseurs* as a suitable escort, insisting upon the necessity of secrecy, and reminding them of the wine-cellars beneath the house. In case of need, the local *gendarmerie* might be called into requisition.

" If I have the happiness to see you here by nine o'clock to-morrow morning, monsieur," he said to Montsaloy, " you will possess my lifelong gratitude."

They walked toward the west end of the village. Within twenty minutes Armand and Vansittart stood listening to the hoof-beats of the troop lessening in the distance and darkness.

CHAPTER XXVII

MARIE ACTS

AS early as four o'clock, after a brisk sleep, Vansittart was awake and up. Thenceforward, as the hours passed, he was all anxiety, awaiting two things : first, news from the front of movements on the German side preparatory to the anticipated attack ; and second, the return of the *chasseurs* from Clermont.

But the hours of suspense passed. Six o'clock came—seven—and nothing happened.

At seven Marie was in the arms of Armand, having travelled the greater part of the night. From the station he took her to the Cheval d'Or.

Her first exclamation was this :

" But, oh Armand, is she here ? Have you got her ? "

" Mrs. Vansittart ? "

" Yes."

" We have found out where she is, but we have not got her."

" Not ! Oh, Armand, the pity of it ! And where is she ? "

" At a vineyard near a place called Clermont."

" How do you know ? You have not seen her ? "

" Yes, Marie, I have seen her."

" Poor thing ! She is so awfully ill. One saw it already weeks ago. Does she bear it well ? Is she well, Armand ? "

" To me her face seemed almost like the face of a dying woman, Marie."

" Oh!" shrieked Marie, burying her face, pierced with

pity. " How gentle, how good she is ! And to be treated so ! "

" It 's hard on poor Vansittart, certainly. He was a pitiable object last night, I can tell you."

" I pity *her*. Who is it, *really*, who has done it, Armand ? "

" Oh, the Emperor Wilhelm, no doubt."

" Well—I can't, I can't think that ! " she said, frowning with thought.

" Why not, Birdie ? "

" Could any gentleman do such a thing ? "

" No—but then he is not a gentleman."

" What ! are n't all kings gentlemen ? "

" Not by any manner of means."

" Well, I can't understand it."

" That is the fact, pretty."

" He has such a noble face ! "

" Who, Wilhelm ? "

" Yes."

" He did not do this wickedness with his face, he did it with his merciless heart and brain."

" Suppose—I only say *suppose*, Armand—that all the time he knows not one word of the matter ! "

" Oh, Birdie, that is impossible, you know."

" It may not be."

" But it is."

Armand was seeing with his eye, which is reason ; Marie, with that deep, inner eye, which is instinct. The wisest man is foolish in comparison with a woman who sees with her soul.

" Suppose," she said, after a silence, " that you went to him and told him the whole truth ? "

" That who went to whom ? "

" That you went to Wilhelm."

" All right, I can see that you are tired of me. You want me to go and get hanged."

" Oh ! would he hang you, then ? "

"He would."

"What a wretch!"

"But there is no need. In an hour's time you will see Mrs. Vansittart here. Vansittart has sent a troop of *chasseurs* to fetch her."

So Marie was comforted, and waited. But in an hour's time Evelyn did not come, and the troop of *chasseurs* did not come.

At ten o'clock they had not arrived.

For Vansittart the waiting was killing; he hid himself away where no eye could watch his now craven and demoralised despair. As he ran up the stairs, Armand pointed him out to Marie, and she saw the abject woe of his working face. Arizona Jim, miserably distressed, did not even dare to question his master.

At half-past eleven, half a dozen of the *chasseurs* of the expedition, with Folliet and Montsaloy among them, arrived with blackened clothes and scorched faces. They had a tale of piteous defeat to tell. While it was yet dark they had surrounded the farmhouse, secretly as they thought. Then, finding every aperture closed, they had set to work to pick the lock of the front door. The operation, however, was neither noiseless nor very speedy; and while it was in progress they must have been heard from within. Finally they broke in a body into the house, only six or seven of the troop remaining without as guard. When they entered the house, they found within it not a single living being.

As they searched round in wonder, the building, and they with it, went skyward in a fearful explosion. The occupants of the place, before descending into the cellar, had lighted a slow-match communicating with a heap of powder. Most of the *chasseurs* inside and surrounding the house had been scorched, and two killed. Folliet had then posted to Clermont for the *gendarmerie*, with the idea of bombarding the cellars; and it was the bombardment of the cellars which had retarded the return of the remaining *chasseurs* to Gravelotte. But they found the cellars empty. The Germans had escaped under cover of the dense darkness, presumably by distant egresses, taking their prisoner with them.

Such was the tale of defeat and disaster which Folliet had to tell. He had come in person to tell it, undertaking the bitter task as a self-imposed punishment for his failure.

Where now was hope? Evelyn had vanished as utterly as she had vanished before.

The truth was that there was no hope—if it was not to be found in the head and heart of Marie.

She lost half an hour in useless weeping; then when she understood definitely that everybody, even her god-like Armand, was at a loss what next to do, she slipped away from him, ascended to her room, put on a dainty little Parisian bonnet, and her gloves, and by a back stair, stealthily went down into the garden of the inn; thence into the village street; and at the end of it, asked someone this strange query : what was the way to Metz?

The way was pointed out to her, and she took it, without any idea of the difficulties and dangers she would have to surmount that day before reaching her destination. There were the French lines—there were the German lines; these had to be passed. At the first she met with jests, but escaped contact. At the second she was roughly kissed several times on the mouth by a sentinel, and then ordered back on the road she had come.

But with every defeat the wild fluttering at her heart with which she had set out lessened. Her will congealed within her. She escaped from the kisses of the sentinel, weeping no longer with fear, but with rage. At every step she grew bolder.

She made a wide détour, and crossed the Moselle. By the eastward gate, through which the market-people of Lorraine streamed to bring their produce to the citadel, she entered Metz. But instead of the five miles from Gravelotte which she had thought to travel, she had travelled fifteen.

She was faint now, and pale, and very weary. It was late in the afternoon. Her eyes had in them the wistfulness of the pilgrim.

Her object was to speak personally, face to face, with the Emperor of the Germans. Several times, now, she stopped dead, appalled by the bigness of the enterprise. She remembered the difficulties she had encountered once, when she wished to speak to Mr. Vansittart. And this was an Emperor ! If she had run with the footmen and they had wearied her, how could she contend with the horses ?

To her immense surprise and joy, destiny so ordered it that she found not the least difficulty in speaking with Wilhelm. She had asked the way to the Hôtel de Ville, and as she came to it there was Wilhelm, just descending the marble stairway outside the entrance portal, surrounded by officers. A moment, and Marie's heart gave one transcendent bound ; the next she had darted agilely up two steps, pressed through the throng of men, and, hardly recognising her own voice, was speaking :

" I wish to speak to your Majesty—Pray ! Pray ! "

She fell on her knees before Wilhelm.

At once a favourable omen came from the Emperor—he answered her in French.

" Well, now, what is all this, ma'm'selle ? " he said.

" I want to speak to you, sir ! "

" Well, you have invaded my presence, willy-nilly. Speak on, ma'm'selle."

" Your Majesty, Mrs. Vansittart is dying ! She is very ill ! "

Wilhelm turned as white as a corpse.

Then, flushing into scarlet wrath :

" Here, drag this wench from my presence, you men ! How dare you let her come here to annoy me ! "

Marie sprang upright. Several hands caught at her shoulders, pulling her backward.

" She was roughly kissed several times on the mouth by a sentinel."

" I *will* speak," she cried. " Oh, it is a shame—Mrs. Vansittart——"

" Be silent, you ! " exclaimed Wilhelm.

" I am not *going* to be ! " shrieked Marie, at the same time throwing herself bodily down on the steps like an obstinate child. " I thought you did not know about it. I took you for a gentleman—and I came to tell you that it was *your* man—a man called Ritterburg, M. Folliet says—who carried her off—oh ! oh ! let me go, will you ! "

Now, it was out—Wilhelm had heard it, chapter and verse. He had been able to guard his ears from an army, but not from the shrillness of a woman's tongue. His right hand dropped with a gesture of abandonment.

" Unhand her ! " he cried out. " Leave the wench alone with me. Now, woman, speak your full."

Marie, speaking in sobs from behind her handkerchief, began to pour out her tale.

" I thought—your Majesty did n't know—because my husband says no gentleman would—have done it. And I thought—I 'd come and tell you—it was a man called Ritterburg—so M. Folliet, the detective, says. And she is dying ! she is very ill ! and she is my friend—so good—and sweet. And I—don't think your Majesty knows, to judge from your face. And the men M. Vansittart sent to get her last night have been blown up—and there is n't any hope at all—and Mrs. Vansittart will die—except your Majesty——"

She stopped, choked with sobs : and Wilhelm stood, looking at her, and said nothing. The next day, for certain, there was to be a battle ; if only for that day the mind of Vansittart could have been kept in a state of paralysis : the fool of a girl should have waited at least a day.

This was not quite what Wilhelm was thinking, but it was not remotely dissimilar from what he was feeling.

" Where are you from ? " he asked suddenly.

" From Gravelotte, sir."

" Then you had better get back to Gravelotte as quickly as you can."

" And will your Majesty——? "

" Be silent ! Here, some of you see this young woman taken safely through the lines on the road to Gravelotte. You, Schlegel, find out at once where a man named Ritterburg is now, and let me know by sundown."

CHAPTER XXVIII

IN THE EMPEROR'S CARRIAGE

NOT a word did Marie speak of her expedition at Grave-lotte ; on her arrival there she fell a-faint into her husband's arms, but he thought her overcome by the ill-fate of Evelyn, as before. Only, late at night, she wept out the facts to him.

" Ah, I thought there was something," he said—" these expeditions of yours, Marie——"

" I did it for the best, Armand."

" I know, Birdie. But the very worst might have come of it. As it is, nothing at all will come. I told you the man was a ruffian."

" Well, I suppose," said Marie ; " though it is very strange—I don't know—he was not altogether unkind to me. At first he broke into a terrible rage. But afterwards —and Armand !—I saw him give such a sidelong look into my eyes, and then at my lips ; it made me blush."

" Hm ! he does n't know who it is you belong to, evi-dently."

" I told him my husband said no gentleman would have done it ; so that was one for *him* to swallow ! "

" But the ruffian ! Did n't he say anything ? Did n't he even attempt to excuse himself in any way ? make any sort of promise ? "

" No. Not a word. When I was going to ask him he said: ' Be silent ! ' with such a frown. He can frown, I can tell you. And such a mustache, with hard tags at the end ! it is not a mustache, it is a weapon."

So, babbling together, they at last fell asleep, and Marie's last murmur was, " Poor Mrs. Vansittart ! "

It was the intention of Armand to take her out of the neighbourhood by early morning ; for there was no doubt that either at dawn or sunrise some hostile movements would begin, and that long before midday the whole locality would be rolled in war.

But he had an intense curiosity to see at least the beginning of actual fighting, and hung on in Gravelotte till the sun was high, and the clocks pointed to eight. At that late hour there was still, however, no sign of anything in the way of blows.

Vansittart was riding slowly across a meadow about half a mile out of Gravelotte in company with some eight or ten persons. His eyes were hollow, and his careworn face all faded ; but with a certain toughness, characteristic of him, he had stuck to his guns. In his heart, however, as he rode, there was nothing less than black and blank despair. Defeat or victory now—he did not greatly care. He was merely doing his duty. His life was in ruins about him.

Armand, wandering and loitering here with Marie before their departure, saw and approached him.

" What ! " said Vansittart, assuming a woeful blitheness ; " is this good-by, then ? And Mistress Marie is running from the fire and smoke ? Well, good voyage ! And thanks, thanks, endless thanks, for your presence here. Are you off to Paris ? "

" I am going to join M. Folliet at Clermont," said Armand.

" Ah ! " sighed Vansittart, and turned his face away.

At this point they heard an unexpected sound behind them, a trundling sound, and looking round, they saw near to them, coming from the direction of Gravelotte, a gun-carriage drawn by two horses, but without any gun on it. Instead, there was a massive cubical box—a strange object to the conservative eyes of the old campaigners.

" Stay ! " said Vansittart, " is not this—yes, it is—your engine of flame. I ordered one to be sent for experimental use. By nightfall, monsieur, all Europe will know that the victory of this day was due to the genius of Armand Duprés."

He said it with a visible touch of enthusiasm, and even Armand's eyes glistened.

" If it does its work, M. Vansittart," he said.

" It will do its work, monsieur. It has been tested, and I have telegrams confirming its absolute efficiency from the manufacturing firms and the War Office. If I have not discussed the matter with you since you have been here—if I have seemed ungrateful—you must put it down to my—my trouble." His voice broke, and he added, " I—I am not fit for anything."

" ' *Wir heissen euch hoffen,*' " said Armand. " So says the German poet."

" Well, then, I will ' hope,' if I can. But—what is that ? " He pointed across the field.

" That " was a body of horsemen, some thirty Germans, coming toward him from the direction of Metz. Uplifted in their midst there fluttered on the morning breeze a white flag of truce. They were escorted by a French officer.

They came forward at a rather slow pace, for the reason that one of their number—a short, squat man, with a fat neck—was on foot. He was in front of all, and his dress was peculiar. It was a black robe reaching to his feet ; and on his head was a skull-cap.

Then, after a minute's breathless surprise, Vansittart, rising in his stirrup, could see that in the midst of the horsemen was an open carriage, and that leaning back in the carriage was a woman.

" In the name of God, what is it ? " he cried, his face lighted with wildly inquisitive scrutiny.

His heart was thumping against his ribs as though he would die.

The troop approached, approached, in a silence which was

absolute. A minute—two! Vansittart's field-glass was at his eyes. Suddenly, with a cry, he dropped it and at the same instant had leaped to the ground. As though the avenger of blood was after him, he flew to meet the advancing body.

In another minute, Evelyn was sobbing on his shoulder.

Her new hiding-place on the German side of the Moselle was known to some men high in the German councils. During the night, Wilhelm had discovered it, and sent a messenger ordering her immediate conveyance to Metz.

The whole party, Marie holding Evelyn's thin hand in the carriage, proceeded to the Cheval d'Or. The carriage was blazoned with the royal arms of Hohenzollern—it was Wilhelm's own private landau.

The man dressed in the long black robe was Carl Gottlieb Ritterburg. When Vansittart had come near him, he had seen that around the man's neck was a rope; and on the black skull-cap, which was of the shape worn by condemned criminals in Saxony, had been fastened a band of white paper bearing these words in red ink :

" To M. Vansittart, with the Emperor Wilhelm's compliments."

" But observe—observe, M. Armand," said Vansittart, hardly able to get out his words in the wildness of his transport—" only observe the time which this man selects to make me this present—it is just before a great battle ! When he has everything to lose and nothing to gain from his act ! Was there ever such generosity in this world before ? Oh, what return can one make to a man for largeness of heart such as this ! "

" We will give him back one of the Lost Provinces when we have won them from him," said Armand ; " and Marie and Mrs. Vansittart shall go and spend a fortnight at the imperial palace ! "

" He *shall* have a return ! " said Vansittart, musingly. " He shall ! Do not imagine that I shall lie under this burden of debt—and, stay—it shall be done at once ; but at your expense, monsieur ! ''

An hour later, after Wilhelm's messengers had been feasted, they returned. They took with them Ritterburg, and a letter from Vansittart—and a specimen of Armand's engine of fire. Vansittart, in the letter, declined to hang Ritterburg, though he admitted that he should be glad to hear that he had been shot by the proper German military authorities. As for the machine which he sent, it was the invention of a great genius, never before used in war, and certain to effect a revolution therein. Mr. Vansittart, in his unbounded gratitude to the Emperor Wilhelm, sent it with a view to its impartial use in both armies, or, if the Emperor preferred, to its abandonment on both sides during the remainder of the present war. An explanation of the method of making and using the contrivance was enclosed therewith.

But toward noon Wilhelm returned the specimen, with a letter written by himself. He appreciated the extraordinary character of the contrivance, and its value; also, he appreciated to the full the great-mindedness of the gift ; but he preferred to avail himself of Mr. Vansittart's second alternative—that during the present war the engine should not be employed by either party.

Whilst these mad pranks were being indulged in by the leaders, General Kreuznach was leading a host of two hundred thousand men from Diedenhofen across the Moselle. Within three hours the left flank of the French army was turned, and men were murmuring that Vansittart had betrayed France in order to secure the release of his wife.

CHAPTER XXIX

A REVERSE

WHEN the Kaiser struck, he struck " with mailed fist." The physical and mental collapse of his powerful rival gave him time to formulate his plans and opportunity for their development.

During Vansittart's period of weakness it was General Daubisson's duty to attend to the needs and disposition of the army, and Daubisson's essential principle of strategy was to await the enemy's attack, according to accepted theories of warfare.

But the German Emperor had learned something of the *Kriegspiel* (war game) as played by his opponent, so the flanking movement carried out in force by Kreuznach was only intended to blind Daubisson's eyes to its real intent.

It succeeded perfectly.

Early in the afternoon Daubisson and his staff hurried northwards to the village of La Chapelle. In their eagerness to drive back the unexpected intruder, they placed far more men in motion than was absolutely necessary. The whole French army buzzed with excitement and conflicting rumour.

About four o'clock Arizona Jim perpetrated a colossal mistake in the French language, a mistake the consequences of which went farther than a mere outrage on French grammar and pronunciation.

Jim had made some slight progress in the diplomatic tongue under the tuition of a red-cheeked and black-eyed waitress employed at the hotel.

When Jerome and his wife had poured forth tumultuous narratives of their sufferings and fears, they changed *rôles* and Evelyn became the nurse.

Vansittart expressed a desire for a hearty meal, but this she would not hear of.

"What you want, dear," she said, "is sleep, much more than food. Take a little wine and some biscuits, go straight to bed, and sleep until you wake of your own accord. Then you will be yourself again. I will lie down in Marie's bed, and I challenge you to eat more than I do at supper-time."

He smiled acquiescence, but first went to the door of the little sitting-room and called Bates.

"Jim," he cried, "go outside and see if anything is stirring. Ask if there is any news? I want to rest for some hours."

Jim soon came back.

"There 's nothing fresh, guv'nor. All the talk in camp is that General Daubisson has lost his hat."

"Lost his hat !"

"Yes, an' a rare fuss they 're makin' about it—chaps gallopin' like mad. I should n't have thought they 'd kick up such a shindy if it had bin his head."

The millionaire looked puzzled, but he was already nodding with sleepiness. He lay down without undressing, and was soon as one dead, so utter his fatigue, so overpowering the exhaustion of reaction.

What Jim had heard was that Daubisson had lost La Chapelle, but the difference between "chapelle" and "chapeau" was far too minute for the unpractised ear of the Texan.

Meanwhile, as the day wore on, some desperate fighting took place in the north. Kreuznach's strong and determined force was not to be denied. Careless of all odds, the Germans carried position after position, until, when night fell, they were wholly surrounded by the huge masses set in motion against them by General Daubisson.

At last it seemed that the invaders must be annihilated, and the stout little Frenchman was congratulating himself on having won a notable victory. Kreuznach was fairly caught in a trap. Let the bluebottle struggle ever so fiercely, he must be crushed in this all-pervading web of men and guns with the first beams of returning day, as the staff reported that the Germans apparently intended to hold La Chapelle during the night.

A brilliant idea then occurred to Daubisson.

His own men, no less than the Germans, were spent with the fight. Why not, during the few hours of darkness, assemble a fresh force of forty thousand troops and carry La Chapelle by a superb assault at dawn? Such a body, eager, high-mettled, anxious to show their comrades why they had been kept in reserve, would simply sweep the invaders into nothingness. Such a glorious achievement would be the chief event of the war. True, he would be compelled to weaken the French front, but what did that matter? The Kaiser had evidently played Kreuznach as his trump card. He, Daubisson, would now show that he held the ace.

So the aides rode forth, and the German Emperor's plan was made more easy than he had ventured to hope. For Wilhelm, at that moment, was attending to the final disposition of eight strong columns, which, marching by parallel roads, and acting quite independently of each other, were destined to cross the Moselle, fall upon the French lines at midnight, throw the whole French army into disorder, and make clear the path for two army corps to advance from Metz at day-break. Kreuznach was instructed to maintain his dogged hold on La Chapelle, and the Emperor believed that if the combined scheme was even partially successful, he would be able to throw back the shattered and dismembered French army across the Meuse.

The hours passed and men marched through the darkness, yet Vansittart slept.

Arizona Jim kept anxious vigil at the door of the Cheval

d'Or. He well knew that an action of some magnitude was in progress on the left flank, as the incessant cannonade and roar of magazine rifles betokened the numbers of men engaged.

So he bethought him to take counsel with the aforesaid serving-maid as to the exact facts bearing upon General Daubisson's hat.

Then he quickly discovered that it was a large village, and not his headgear, that had been taken from the worthy commander-in-chief, and with the knowledge came the reflection that his master's slumbers, excellent though the purpose they served, might not be the best thing that could happen in the interests of France.

Should he awaken him to allow the indomitable spirit to force the weakened body into the saddle, and snatch the army from peril or possible disaster? Jim was well aware of the powerful reasons that obtained on both sides of the torturing question, so he turned for guidance to Armand.

Marie had constituted herself maid to Mrs. Vansittart, and positively refused to leave Gravelotte without her mistress, so the pair still tarried in the village.

Armand was quite fluent in the English tongue, and expressed his opinions with an air of conviction that satisfied Bates.

"Wake Mr. Vansittart? Not for worlds. He is a great man. His rest is more important than other men's actions."

"But things seem kinder unsettled," urged Jim. "Everybody is dancin' about like a turkey on a hot plate."

"That is a national characteristic, my friend. Excitability is the fundamental cause of French genius. It is the same with the Americans."

Armand's philosophy was lost on Jim.

"I guess nit," was the rapid answer. "If this crowd hailed from the States it is the Germans that would be doin' the quickstep."

The war correspondent of the *Gaulois* rode into the village en route to the telegraph office. He drew rein in front of the inn.

" Where is M. Vansittart ? " he cried.

" Within," answered Armand.

" What is he doing ? "

" He sleeps."

" Sleeps, when such a battle is in progress ? "

" A battle can take place any day. Vansittart has not slept for a week."

The correspondent laughed.

" Well, it is all right, I suppose, as Daubisson has got the Germans in a tight corner."

He went on to despatch his message, and did not forget to add to the gossip of the past few days about the millionaire that during the long-deferred action he slumbered peacefully in the Gravelotte inn.

A staff-officer clattered up in furious haste. " Where is M. Vansittart ? " he demanded.

" Monsieur," cried Duprés, " the question becomes monotonous."

The officer, believing that Armand's civilian attire betokened a secretary, roared at him, " Confound you, where is he ? "

Armand's steel-blue eyes sparkled. He took a cigarette from a case, moistened it with his lips, and answered with a jerk of his thumb, " Within."

" Then take him this despatch from General Daubisson," and the newcomer tossed a folded paper to the other.

" I thought as much," observed Armand, speaking to himself, as he struck a match, applied it to the paper, and lit his cigarette.

" *Mille tonnerres !* " shrieked the aide-de-camp. He leaped from his horse too late, for the charred remains of the document were fluttering to the ground.

" What have you done, you rascal ! " he hissed, as something in Armand's face restrained him from the physical violence he contemplated.

" Saved your General from an indiscretion."

" How, miserable one ? "

" Daubisson blunders when he speaks ; he commits a crime when he places his thoughts in writing."

" The General, in that despatch, announces a great victory."

" Impossible, unless the Germans have evolved another Daubisson," and Armand turned on his heel as though the matter were worth no further discussion.

When, late at night, Jerome awoke to find Evelyn bending over him, it was with difficulty he realised his surroundings. He thought at first they were back in their summer home in the Adirondacks, and gazed with wonder at the queer, old-fashioned furniture of this village public-house.

But Evelyn's sweet voice restored his wandering senses, and he sprang up to clasp her in his arms with an alertness that showed the efficacy of Nature's only restorer. Though pale and attenuated from the strain of recent events, his mind had regained its normal balance.

Could the French troops have seen him at that moment they would have shouted, " Vive l'Empereur ! " with all the old vigour. As it was, they believed him to be broken down and half demented. They were forgetting the wonders of the past in the delays, the uncertainties, the weaknesses of a few doubtful hours.

And, whilst the army of France swayed in its allegiance to the one man capable of leading it to victory, the Kaiser was silently preparing the most terrible and effective blow yet struck in fair fight during the campaign. Of both these elements of disaster Jerome was happily unconscious. He only knew that Evelyn, whom he thought dead, was alive, nay more, tremulous with joy in his arms.

Mrs. Vansittart and Marie had long been superintending the preparation of a meal to which Jerome and Armand were now ready to do full justice.

Another messenger had arrived from Daubisson, and this time the General's missive reached the right person.

It read :

"As announced at 3 P.M., I have surrounded Kreuznach's corps at La Chapelle. At this hour, 9 P.M., a complete cordon is established, whilst the 7th, 8th, 13th, and 17th divisions will march forthwith to take up positions for an early assault.

"I have made full arrangements, and these cannot be altered in any way, but I will keep you informed of events, so that you may understand movements of troops which might otherwise seem inexplicable to you."

Jerome read the second paragraph twice and smiled contemptuously. It was his first conscious intimation of the new aspect of affairs.

"Daubisson speaks of a German force surrounded at La Chapelle," he said to Armand. "Have you heard anything of this?"

"Yes," said Duprés. "I lit a cigarette with his announcement of the fact."

"Indeed." Jerome lifted his eyebrows in mild surprise. "But how comes it that the Germans are established in that village, the very heart of our left flank?"

"Exactly because they desired to get there. Daubisson thinks they have lodged themselves there to enable him to smash them with ease at daybreak. That is just what Daubisson would think, and what they know he would think."

"Then this successful attack by Kreuznach is simply a prelude to a larger effort elsewhere?"

"That is how I regard it."

Jerome started to his feet. "It must come direct from Metz. Where are these corps stationed that Daubisson speaks of moving to-night? Surely not at the front?"

He hastily searched among his papers for the daily parade state of the army. The last supplied to him was three days old.

Evelyn, watching her husband, saw his lips tighten and his brows knit.

"What is it, dear?" she cried, coming to him.

" Only this, my sweet, that the worst curs are those most ready to bite the hand that feeds them. I am going to teach them the art of fawning to-night."

" But what has happened ? "

" Simply this : that a few days of neglect on my part has made my staff forget their duty. By Heaven, it will not occur again ! "

Strange things happened at that period. Jerome, after regaining his senses, had lost his temper.

He went outside. In the next building, where his personal staff were wont to assemble, there was a forgotten sentry on duty.

The man was a *chasseur* of the 18th, our old friend Pierre Laronde, whose promised promotion had been forgotten in the rush of events since the memorable ride of the Five Thousand. He presented arms when he recognised Vansittart in the gloom.

" Where are all the officers of the staff, soldier ? " said the millionaire.

" Gone off to the picnic at La Chapelle, your Excellency."

" Have they *all* gone ? "

" Well, your Excellency, General le Breton was here until half an hour ago. I reminded him of my promised commission, and he went too."

" Why was your commission promised ? "

" Because I cut the wires that night at Longuyon."

" Is your name Pierre Laronde ? "

" It is, your Excellency."

" I remember now. Bring General le Breton to me within ten minutes, and I will introduce you to him as a captain on my staff."

The *chasseur* rushed to the nearest stable for a horse, and clattered along the Metz road, in which direction Le Breton had departed. Jerome listened to the hoof-beats dying away in the distance. There were fitful sounds of firing towards the north, but in the direction of Metz all was quiet.

He returned to the inn after a few minutes of deep thought, having evidently made up his mind to a definite course of action. His own spacious travelling-carriage stood in the yard of the Cheval d'Or, and he gave orders that it should be prepared for a journey forthwith.

And now a bustle in the village street showed that some-one had arrived. Laronde had returned, bringing with him General le Breton, Montsaloy, and several officers of the brigade stationed on the main road to Metz.

They were surprised to receive the trooper's message, and Le Breton essayed to explain his absence :

" We thought, monsieur, that you were indisposed."

" I was," said Vansittart.

" So on hearing General Daubisson's orders we went to visit the outposts."

" Excellent ! Where is the parade statement showing the disposition of the army ? "

After a pause, Montsaloy answered :

" It has been sent to General Daubisson during several days past."

" Why ? "

" Because, monsieur, when it was placed before you, you paid no heed to it. Someone must command. Bad orders are better than none with an active enemy in front."

The blunt cavalry leader stated in plain language what Jerome knew to be the fact. However unpleasant the truth might be, it was useless to disguise it, but there was a tinge of irony in his tone as he went on :

" I have quite recovered, Colonel Montsaloy, and if the gentlemen present think I am capable of resuming control, I will do so, as there is little time to be lost."

" *Ma foi !* " roared Montsaloy, " I am glad of it. Now we sha'n't be long ! "

A chorus of acclamation gave undoubted proof of the general opinion — the dazed army was simply hungering for Vansittart's leadership.

" Then tell me," said the millionaire, " where are these corps stationed ? " and he read aloud the note sent by Daubisson.

" They command the left front and centre," exclaimed Le Breton.

" I feared as much. Ride, some of you, quickly, and countermand their orders. If they have moved, bring them back. Stay, I will give you written instructions." He dashed into the house and hastily scribbled imperative commands to the respective brigadiers.

When these were despatched, he bethought himself of Daubisson, and he wrote the following note :

" HEADQUARTERS, GRAVELOTTE, 10 P.M.

" Delighted to hear of your success, but have good reason to believe that Kreuznach's march is a feint. The Emperor will probably attack our front in force to-night. Come to me here with whole staff at once, but first send out orders for immediate concentration of all available troops on Mars-la-Tour. Leave corps of observation only to look after Kreuznach. Guns and cavalry must be massed in rear of infantry, ready to move with daybreak. I have already dealt with brigades mentioned in your second despatch. I look to you for implicit obedience, irrespective of any conditions that may have arisen since your last communication with me.

" JEROME K. VANSITTART."

He read the document to Le Breton, who rubbed his hands, crying :

" That 's the style ! No humbug about that ! "

" Who will carry it to Daubisson ? " said Jerome.

They looked through the doorway, and saw Laronde standing there, saluting, with a grin on his face.

He had been forgotten again.

" If I were only an officer——" he began.

" You are ! " cried Vansittart. " Here is your first mission. See that it is well performed. Le Breton, place his name in orders as a captain on my staff, and provide him with an outfit at my expense."

Pierre Laronde required no second bidding. Daubisson

was six miles away, with difficult country intervening, but within thirty minutes he was in possession of Vansittart's message.

" Ha ! " he yelled to those near him. " The madness has left our chief. Hurry now ; he means what he says this time. All the same I should like to have a smack at Kreuznach in the morning. Here, soldier——"

" Captain, my General ! " interrupted Pierre.

" Oh, Major, if you like."

" Certainly, General—Major by all means ! "

" Confound you, shut up! Take my answer to M. Vansittart. Say to him, ' I come.' "

" He will know that when he sees me, General."

" Tell him that General Daubisson said ' I come,' blockhead ! "

" Major ! " growled Pierre, as he swung himself back into the saddle. " By gad," he went on, as his charger broke into a gallop, " my luck has turned. I shall be a colonel before daybreak. Get up, mare ! "

In the meantime Jerome had accomplished a difficult task. He had persuaded Evelyn, with Armand and Marie, to drive off to Bar-le-Duc in his travelling-carriage.

He explained the need for this journey by telling Evelyn that it was more than probable the Germans would occupy Gravelotte within a few hours. Most certainly they would make the effort, and he would feel so much more at ease if assured of her safety. Jim Bates, with half a troop of *chasseurs*, would provide an escort.

And so, after a too brief reunion, they parted, but only on Jerome's solemn assurance that he would see his wife again next day, when the present dangerous situation had been dealt with satisfactorily.

Shortly before midnight Daubisson arrived. His unfeigned joy at Vansittart's reappearance on the active list dispelled the last shade of resentment in Jerome's mind at the apparent neglect shown to him by his associates.

Daubisson eagerly detailed the steps he had taken to fulfil Vansittart's orders, and concluded by saying :

" Perhaps we may have to attack Kreuznach to-morrow, after all."

Before the other could answer, a sudden roar of musketry came through the still night air from the direction of Metz. It was sharp and continuous, betokening a very lively affray at the French outposts. Even as they listened the fighting area widened until the crackle of small-arms spread through an extended section of the front.

Daubisson was as impulsive as he was brave. Tears came to his eyes as he realised the frightful nature of the error in which he nearly involved the whole of the magnificent army under his command. He came near to Jerome and said, in a voice deep with emotion :

" Monsieur, if you retain my services I shall perhaps learn something of generalship by the close of the war."

" General," cried Vansittart, " one cannot have all the virtues. Believe me, I depend wholly upon your splendid co-operation."

But if Daubisson's mistake had been seen in time, it still required to be rectified. At several points the French front was rapidly driven in before reinforcements could arrive. Le Breton's brigade, strengthened by two others hurried up from the rear, was able to hold back the assault delivered from Metz along the main road. But it was a fierce and uncertain combat, in which small knots of men sought out their enemies in the darkness, and fought with equal ferocity and determination.

Three quarters of a mile farther north, where the French line was weaker, the German advance was rapid and un-checked.

The watchers in Gravelotte were able to discern the progress of this attack by the gradual approach of the sounds of combat. Although several staff-officers had been sent flying to bring up regiments from the rear, there was no appreciable pause in the enemy's advance.

Matters began to look serious about one o'clock.

At this moment Pierre Laronde growled to himself:

" I must back my luck, even if I get snubbed." He came to Vansittart and said :

" I think, sir, I could lead a couple of squadrons of *chasseurs* across country and take the Germans in flank if you will permit it."

" Very well. Try it, Captain."

" Major, sir, if you please. General Daubisson gave me a step for bringing your despatch."

" Did he ? I agree with him. If you dispel that column you return a colonel."

Montsaloy found the troops for Laronde, and they clanked off along a lane. But they soon quitted the high-road and made for a tree-crowned hill beyond which the conflict raged. Laronde knew quite well that with two hundred sabres he could do little against a compact German division of eight or ten thousand infantry. He counted wholly upon surprising the enemy and creating a panic, thus giving the French infantry a chance to rush the Germans at the point of the bayonet. Pierre's lucky star was certainly in the ascendant that night. He and his comrades came upon the second German brigade at the moment it was deploying to support the fighting line. Some farm buildings gave the *chasseurs* splendid cover until they were right in the midst of the Prussian regiment, and in a few seconds the orderly and compact mass became a torrent of disorganised humanity, fleeing in abject terror before the furious charge made by the *chasseurs*.

Fighting by night is an eerie and ticklish business at the best. The awesome effect of the mounted arm is magnified tenfold when maddened horses thunder from out the darkness. Nor had Laronde forgotten to send a trooper to the commander of the French infantry to inform him of the expected charge, so that he might take advantage of it if successful. In fifteen minutes one at least of the German columns was shattered into atoms, its officers and men hurled into hopeless rout, its leaders stampeded by their own troops, and its fragments rushing wildly to Metz for safety. So Pierre got his colonelcy with comparative ease, though none marvelled at his good fortune more than he did himself.

CHAPTER XXX

WHAT HAPPENED IN PARIS

THE struggle went on through the night with no very certain results. Three of the eight columns launched by the Kaiser made good their lodgment on the left bank of the Moselle—those operating on the north, where they were supported by Kreuznach's strong corps.

When day broke, the French left and centre had been swung back, with the result that the French line now formed a crescent, of which the left rested near Verdun on the Meuse, the centre lay at Gravelotte, and the right touched the Moselle six miles south of Metz.

So great was the confusion in both armies that it was absolutely impossible for either the Kaiser or Vansittart to attempt an extensive battle.

In this uncertainty, commanders of divisions simply held their respective positions until further orders were issued. Wilhelm seized the opportunity to hurry up reinforcements to his new centre by way of Diedenhofen, and Vansittart consolidated his own array by bringing all the available troops from Nancy and Bar-le-Duc. All this took time. Though both men chafed under the delay, it would have been folly and useless loss to undertake a number of small, isolated engagements over a wide expanse of country. So the armies halted within striking distance of each other during the whole day, and not one man among the million of Frenchmen and Germans gathered in that fertile province dreamed of the tremendous events that were then shaping themselves at Paris. For the Soldiers' Battle, as the previous engagement came to be called, had its issue in the metropolis rather than amidst the low hills of Gravelotte and Conflans.

If the Queen was distracted at the loss of Evelyn, the King and Liancourt were more concerned with the lethargy displayed by Vansittart at the crucial period of the campaign.

Everything depended on those few days. France will suffer grievously and cheerfully if her troops march to victory. So far the successes of the war lay with the French arms, but everyone was now anxiously awaiting the decision of the momentous question: Would the Kaiser burst through the bonds that confined him within the walls of Metz, or would the American lead the French across the Rhine?

But the period of inaction, of depression, of vague rumour and mysterious inference, was rapidly undermining public confidence in Paris.

" It 's always a woman that ruins France," exclaimed the peripatetic philosopher of the boulevards.

" Our heroes' strides are hindered by petticoats," wrote the moralist of the *Figaro*, and he cited apt historic parallels to lend weight to his already heavy epigram.

The people's gratitude was still too keenly alive to the value of Vansittart's services to render possible an open howl for his suppression. So, in default of attacking him, the newspapers fell foul of the King and his advisers.

In a word, Paris was fermenting, and in such a city the process is a dangerous one.

When Folliet reached the metropolis, after a naturally fruitless search at Clermont, he received the first news of Evelyn's safety and restoration. It came in a characteristic telegram from Duprés:

"Wilhelm has sent back Madame Vansittart with compliments. The situation appealed to his dramatic instincts. There is hope for the man yet.   ARMAND."

It was some minutes before the Prefect of Police fully

realised the import of this message. Not until he had read a brief account in *Le Soir* of Evelyn's arrival at Gravelotte did he clearly grasp the situation. Then he drove to the palace. He was promptly accorded an audience with the King.

" We have missed you, monsieur, " said Henri. " There are troublous movements on foot in ill-defined quarters. Some powerful force is controlling a certain section of the press. M. Vansittart's indisposition has resulted in a bitter attack upon me personally and the chief members of the government. It was deemed inadvisable to accentuate the position of affairs by authoritative action, so I need hardly say that we will await your early investigations with anxiety tempered by confidence."

" Your Majesty may rely upon me fully. May I ask if events indicate any marked channel of hostility ? What, for instance, is the most definite incident that has led to your Majesty taking note of the temper displayed by the newspapers ? "

The King paused a moment. He frowned as though he disliked the question. Then, with the air of one who has resolved to make a clean breast of an avowal, he answered :

" I fear, M. Folliet, that I erred greatly in not listening to your advice concerning M. Ribou's proposal to form a National Guard. We hastily jumped at the idea. Once it received official sanction it developed with amazing rapidity. Men were enrolled, clothed, and armed at the rate of many thousands daily, and ere we well knew what was happening, we had gathered in Paris some sixty thousand armed citizens, who are under very lax military discipline."

" Why not start a patriotic expedition to the front ? "

" Liancourt has tried, and got laughed at for his pains. They declare that they were constituted to defend the metropolis."

" Defend the metropolis ! From whom ? "

" That is what we are all asking each other now. I tell

you, monsieur, that I would be glad if these too willing
levies were disbanded and their arms safely stowed away in
the arsenals."

Folliet's face clouded at the news. "Sixty thousand," he
muttered. "Probably the scum of Paris. What madness!"

The King heard him, but paid little heed to this outspoken
criticism. What he keenly watched for, and in vain, was
some gleam of confidence in the Prefect's troubled features.

"And Ribou, your Majesty, where is the apostle of loyalty
at this time?"

"There, again, we are at fault. No sooner were these
haphazard battalions created than he disappeared. No one
has seen him for some days. Your subordinates believe
that he has left Paris."

"And who commands the new regiments?"

"Reserve officers were selected by the Minister for War.
But they are useless. They report that their control is
nominal, that the men have elected leaders of their own
whose names are not known save in isolated cases. Your
question, monsieur, reaches the very vitals of the affair. It
was by reason of this fact coming to our knowledge that we
first realised the gravity of an action taken by us solely in
the interests of the country."

"By your Majesty's leave I will hurry off to the Prefecture."

Folliet was now genuinely alarmed. He had not the
slightest doubt that a most formidable organisation had
been called into life during his absence in Auvergne. Never
had dragon's teeth produced more certain crop of armed
men. His only hope was to strike rapidly and effectually at
the leaders. Not a moment was to be lost. Those sixty
thousand vagabonds were a greater menace to France than
the German legions.

On his way to the Prefecture he noticed great excitement
in the streets, people eagerly buying the newspapers and de-
vouring their contents.

At last he stopped his carriage, and secured a copy of *L'Echo de Paris*. It announced the flank march of the Germans across the Moselle, and gave some details of Daubisson's magnificent victory over Kreuznach at La Chapelle. Sneering allusions were not wanting at Vansittart's exchange of courtesies with the German Emperor.

Arrived at his office, he was received by Carot, the official next to himself in rank.

"Well, M. Carot, what's the news?"

"It is hard to say, sir. I wish there was some news of some sort. This is the sort of thing that is going on, and I don't like it."

Carot displayed before the eyes of his amazed chief a placard, printed in glaring letters, containing the words: "Treason! Vansittart has sold to the Kaiser the invention of a patriot which would have destroyed the Germans. Citizens, the story will be printed and given to you to-day. We must save France!"

When Folliet had read the poster, Carot produced a small leaflet.

"Here is the story alluded to," he said.

The sheet gave a sensational and distorted account of Armand's machine and Jerome's action in forwarding it to the Emperor Wilhelm. From beginning to end the narration read very convincingly, even Folliet's visit to Armand being cleverly distorted into an alleged co-operation with the millionaire's attempt to betray the national cause.

The Prefect himself was not yet aware of the negotiations between the two leaders on the frontier.

"This is a farrago of nonsense," he cried. "M. Vansittart has not, to my knowledge, seen the invention in its completed form."

Carot scratched his head. "Perhaps so, sir, but if you are right all the newspapers have been terribly misled."

He searched through several files of papers and produced a number containing varied accounts of the incident from their war correspondents. They were guarded in tone, and mostly inaccurate in detail, but they all united in deprecation of the millionaire's unheard-of act of generosity to an armed foe in the field.

Folliet was quickly assured of the truthfulness of the main facts recorded. He knew how Vansittart had suffered ; he knew how a man like Vansittart could reward. But, in view of the excited condition of the fickle Paris mob, the damaging nature of the transaction could not be disputed.

If Folliet had been inclined to swear at Armand in Auvergne he now bitterly reviled him as the unconscious cause of a possible calamity.

" Whence come these precious productions ? " he said at last, turning fiercely upon Carot.

" They sprang into existence all over Paris an hour ago. The police have seized them in thousands, yet they appear to be in everybody's hands."

" What have you been doing, you imbecile, to allow such things to happen during my absence ? "

An angry gleam shot from the other's eyes.

" I have done my best, sir, to look after affairs, but I neither knew where you were nor the extent of my responsibility."

The answer was so absolutely justified by circumstances that it mollified Folliet's wrath.

" Well, well," he exclaimed testily, " I am here now. Where is Ribou ? Let us find Ribou ! "

But this was not an easy task, as he soon learned by his deputy's statement. Ribou seemed to have been swallowed up bodily. He might have passed off into an astral existence, so utterly had he vanished.

As the day merged into night Folliet became convinced of one thing—he felt, rather by intuition than by reason, that a Commune was brewing.

When France trembles on the brink of downfall Paris always changes her political faith. Republic succeeds monarchy, and monarchy republic with monotonous regularity in the face of national disaster.

But events on the frontier had not yet reached the stage when the government could be justly charged with failure. Indeed, a decided victory for French arms must mean the utter collapse of the revolutionary spirit. But it was useless to deny the existence of such a spirit, and Folliet was not one of those *laissez-faire* individuals who believe that a thing will not happen because they hope it will not.

Shortly after ten o'clock he was summoned in hot haste to the Tuileries. Sensational news had come from the front. Daubisson had defeated Kreuznach whilst Vansittart slept in the inn at Gravelotte.

The sharp-tongued French correspondents made much of the millionaire's prolonged rest. It was the outward and visible token of the utter prostration that had lately seized upon him. The representative of *La Soir* went so far as to say that Jerome's brain had given way before the rush of domestic trouble so unexpectedly added to the cares of the campaign. "I fear more for him awake than asleep," was this writer's caustic comment, and the phrase was a disastrous one. No sooner had it sunk into the public mind, to take root there and blossom forth in the rank maturity of malicious rumour and careless falsehood, than there came the startling intelligence that Vansittart's first waking act was to upset the whole of General Daubisson's masterly plan of campaign, and withdraw the troops intended to crush Kreuznach at daylight.

No wonder that the King frowned and the Queen marvelled, whilst on the faces of the courtiers settled an expression of anxious doubt.

As Folliet was the last official in Paris who had seen and talked with Vansittart, Liancourt urged Henri to take counsel with him before sending a long telegram to Jerome asking for some explanation of the extraordinary news that was flying about Paris.

But Folliet was hardly the best witness possible. " I cannot deny," he said, " that M. Vansittart was quite unable to attend to the details of the campaign when I last saw him. But he has marvellous powers of recuperation. His wife is restored to him, and the absence of anxiety on her behalf has induced physical exhaustion. He has slept long, say the papers, and is now awake and directing events. Trust him, sire ; his is a noble nature. He would not seek to control were he unfitted for the task."

" But," urged the distracted King, " these later telegrams presage ruin. They indicate an absurd interference with Daubisson's arrangements. If aught goes wrong with the army as the result of Vansittart's fresh dispositions, the effect in Paris will be incalculable."

" Hardly that, your Majesty," said Liancourt, quietly.

" What then ? "

" There will be a popular outbreak, a revolution, possibly an attack on this palace, and a demand for the establishment of a republic."

" Yet you stand there telling me these things and in the same breath implore me to leave unlimited power in the hands of Vansittart ! "

" Yes," said Liancourt firmly. " My confidence in him is unshaken."

" And mine ! " chimed in Folliet.

" Then Heaven help us, for I know not what to do ! "

The distracted monarch was on the verge of tears in his misery, but he allowed himself to be constrained by his advisers, and sent no word to Vansittart of events in Paris. What no one thought of doing was to advise the millionaire of the ticklish state of affairs in the metropolis whilst expressing the fullest approval of his arrangements in face of the enemy.

This, the middle course, was the safe one, but it was not thought of until too late.

Leaving the King and Liancourt to devise some means of

checking the turbulent and unruly National Guard, Folliet set out again in his search for Ribou. The first thought that occurred to him after perusing the latest report of his unsuccessful myrmidons was, "Now I wonder what Armand Duprès would do in this case."

.   .   .   .

Clanking to and fro over the stone floor of a room in the Hôtel de Ville at Metz, the Emperor of Germany listened attentively to the statements made to him by various members of his staff.

The dogged persistence of Kreuznach's division in reaching and holding La Chapelle, followed by the rapid march of the German columns to the new front on the Meuse, constituted the first real German success of the war. It did not mean much. It was chiefly a tactical advantage, and it was hard to see how best to utilise it. The Kaiser's heart had been set upon driving the leaderless French army before him into the Meuse, and he would have accomplished his desire had not Vansittart so suddenly and effectually checked him.

Without being quite sure of the fact, Wilhelm felt that his redoubtable opponent had again resumed control of the French, and in his rage at the failure of his pet scheme he railed at himself for his absurd generosity in endowing his enemy with fresh life.

So the imperial staff was more elated with the present phase of the struggle than the Emperor himself, and it was with clouded brow—though intently enough—that the chief heard the lucid reports of his splendid Intelligence Department.

Suddenly an aide-de-camp entered.

"A man without, your Majesty, who says his name is Hans Schwartz, asks audience of your Majesty. He says he is in possession of most important intelligence affecting your Majesty's interests vitally."

The Emperor paused in his walk. "Show him in," he said.

In a moment, Hans Schwartz, pallid, unkempt, but confident as ever in demeanour, entered.

"Well, you rascal, what is it?" The Emperor's tone was such that few men would have cared to face him boldly. But Hans Schwartz, what between the pain of his shattered wrist and the collapse of his projects, was in desperate plight.

"I have news for your Majesty's ear alone," he said, glancing defiantly around at the officers scattered through the apartment.

"Of what nature?"

"I am Hans Schwartz, who helped Ritterburg to capture Madame Vansittart. I——"

"You villain! Seize him, someone, and have him shot at daybreak with his associate."

Several officers sprang forward, but Schwartz stood his ground.

"I tell you," he shouted, "that I can enable you to conquer France fairly in the open field within a week. Can you not listen to me? You can always have me shot at your pleasure."

The man's determined attitude, his contempt for danger, and the earnestness of his tone impressed the Kaiser if they did not convince him.

"Quite true," he said, with a sarcastic smile. "Leave me with this fellow, gentlemen, and have a guard in readiness to march him off."

General von Gossler protested. There might be danger to the imperial person. Though the Emperor laughed at the idea, the Chief of Staff carefully searched Schwartz for concealed weapons before he was satisfied. Then he left the two alone.

"Well?" said the Emperor, seating himself on the edge of the table.

"In the first place, I must state my terms."

"Of course. I expected that."

"I demand freedom for my friend Ritterburg to leave the

country within reasonable time. I know that in honour you cannot grant more than this for him."

" 'T is a sturdy scoundrel!" thought the Kaiser. "He first asks a favour for his companion in villainy."

" For myself," went on Schwartz, " I ask a substantial pension, as I can no longer work," and he held up his maimed hand in explanation.

" Go on ! "

" I will not say another word until your Majesty assures me that if my information be really of the utmost value, you will grant both my requests."

The Kaiser reflected for a moment. " I will give you the pension," he said finally, " but Ritterburg must be shot."

" Then call your guard. I will be shot with him."

Wilhelm could not help being impressed by this dog-like fidelity. And the thought came, too, that these men had been trying to help him by their machinations. Perhaps some lingering memory of his own doubts and temptations came to his aid, for he quietly agreed to the other's stipulations.

" I have kept up communication with Paris by means of my pigeons," said Schwartz, " and even when the French police seized the house where some German friends were established, they did not discover that my birds were trained in two sections, to fly to and from two places in Paris to my house near Gravelotte."

" Yes," growled the Emperor.

" I was wounded in a scuffle at my house, captured, held prisoner for some days, and escaped during the excitement following Madame Vansittart's arrival at Gravelotte, and the attack by your Majesty's troops. I hid all night and to-day in the wood on my farm, and to-night visited my forgotten birds. One of them had just arrived from Paris, and it bore a message written in a cipher which I alone understand."

" Ha ! " Wilhelm was obviously interested.

" It contains news which all the world will know in three days, but which may be worth much more to your Majesty at this moment than I have asked."

" Let us have it, then."

" An absolutely overwhelming Communist movement has been organised. Within three days, perhaps sooner, there will be a general rising ; the city will be sacked, the King and Queen driven from Paris, if not killed, and a republican government proclaimed, with leaders anxious and ready to make peace with you on very favourable terms."

" *Gott im Himmel !* " roared the Kaiser. " Can you prove this ? "

" Beyond a shadow of doubt. Here is the cipher. I will explain it to you."

Schwartz produced a scrap of flimsy paper and read a message, of which his explanation to the Emperor was an accurate summary.

" But how am I to know that this is reliable ? Who are your authorities for the statements made ? They are almost incredible without substantiation."

" I am faint," said Schwartz, sinking into a chair. " Give me some wine and a morsel of food, and I will tell you everything. My wound has weakened me, and the difficulty of crossing the French lines has quite exhausted me."

So within a few minutes of ordering him to be shot, the Emperor was waiting on Schwartz, and helping him to such eatables as were in the room. Whilst the spy ate and drank he talked, and the Emperor listened.

Half an hour did the wondering staff remain in the ante-room before the Kaiser called them, and there was an eager-ness in his manner, a settled purpose in his words, that had long been absent from the imperial methods and utterances.

" With our present troops between here and Verdun we can keep the French fast in their new position ? " he asked of Von Gossler.

" I think so, sire."

" Zounds, man, *can* we do it ? "

" Yes ! "

" Then why qualify your answer ? "

The General was nettled at this rating before the other officers, so he answered warmly : " Because I never know what we can do with such a firebrand as Vansittart in front of us, and people say he is all right again now."

" Well, well. Surely it is impossible for the French to dislodge us if we simply resolve to stand fast and intrench ourselves."

" Oh, yes, I am sure of that."

" Good. We have one hundred and fifty thousand reservists gathering at Diedenhofen ? "

" Yes."

" They are now all mobilised, and completely equipped for the field ? "

" Fully. They are under orders to march to-morrow at daybreak."

" Then send additional instructions that they are to take the shortest route to Paris."

" To Paris, your Majesty ! "

" Yes, I said Paris, not Berlin."

" Who will lead them ? "

" I, myself. I will issue a proclamation from the French capital within a fortnight, as my march will be positively unopposed. But above all else, you and Kreuznach must hold Vansittart fast on this bank of the Meuse. If he retreat, attack him. Do not leave him night or day. It is matterless what happens so long as he is unable to bring a large body of troops to Paris before I do."

Wilhelm had his opportunity, and he was not slow to take it.

"The Emperor was waiting on Schwartz and helping him to such eatables
as were in the room."

CHAPTER XXXI

THE REVOLUTION

FOLLIET could not lay hands on Ribou. But he felt quite certain that the republican ex-minister was in Paris, and actively engaged in controlling the somewhat feverish energies of the National Guard. The aspect of affairs was now so threatening that attempts to conceal the alarm felt by all responsible persons were abandoned as useless. There were less than ten thousand regular troops in Paris, and of these two thirds were required for the mere duty of guarding the extensive line of forts that girdle the city. As a precautionary measure the Minister for War ordered two regiments to encamp beneath the trees of the Champs Élysées, but the appearance of the soldiers in that unusual locality almost precipitated an outburst.

Even in the Chamber of Deputies there were not wanting expressions of resentment at this exhibition of monarchical distrust of the people.

Several advisers besought the distracted King to temporarily withdraw a considerable portion of the garrison of Chalons, and, by adopting a bold front, put an end to disaffection by disarming and disbanding the precious National Guard, which had been the cause of so much trouble. Perhaps, had Henri acted with firmness and rapidity, this drastic step might have resulted in success. But he hesitated, hoping for some thrilling news from the frontier to give another bent to the easily diverted sympathies of the Paris mob. The news came, but it was appalling. Not only were the French close pressed by a superior German force, but the

Kaiser had crossed the Meuse at the head of a gigantic and well-equipped army, and was marching at all speed by way of Damvillers and Montfaucon towards the capital. A telegram from Vansittart to Liancourt gave the first intelligence of this tremendous development.

It read :

" Strong German force of four divisions, estimated numbers between 150,000 and 200,000 of all arms, commanded by Kaiser in person, has crossed the Meuse above Verdun. Let Chalons troops move out to meet and delay German advance. There must be no general engagement until further orders from me. Utmost pains should be taken to note exact direction taken by enemy, and, if possible, to ascertain his object. No cause for alarm."

Vansittart himself, together with every officer on his staff, imagined that the German Emperor's *coup* was a bold attempt at a flanking movement, intended to cut off the French main body from its reserves and base of supplies.

But the consternation caused in the Tuileries by this message was greater than would have resulted from the explosion of a mine beneath the royal palace. Madness and chaos for a while reigned supreme. Liancourt alone preserved his senses. He persuaded the King and the Minister for War to obey at once Vansittart's instructions so far as the Chalons force was concerned. They then drew up the following answer :

" Chalons force despatched as requested. Regret to inform you of serious state of affairs here. Revolutionary movement hourly gaining strength. Unfortunate circumstances have led to arming of overwhelming numbers of citizens, whose intentions we now know to be hostile to government and monarchy. Can you advise us?"

This astounding communication reached Vansittart about midday at Verdun, whither he had gone as the most central point between the new and the old spheres of operations.

It must be remembered that he knew nothing of the formation of the National Guard, of the political unrest of the capital, of the doubts and fears that had perplexed the King and the responsible ministers for days past. To his mind the people of Paris, and of all France for that matter, had abundant reasons for self-elation at the progress of the campaign. Up to the present, from the cool, common-sense point of view, the invaders had been soundly beaten. Their splendid organisation was seriously damaged at the very outset of hostilities. They had sustained crushing loss in two engagements of the first magnitude. They had been driven back across the frontier, and the major part of the French forces were actually lodged in Lorraine. Against these achievements—marvellous when the unprepared state of France at the declaration of war was taken into account— the trifling offset was the turning movement resulting from Daubisson's blunder and the theatrical march of the Kaiser.

No wonder that Vansittart became scarlet with indignation when he realised the purport of Liancourt's telegram, nor was it surprising that he sent the emphatic reply :

" Crush this nest of traitors with a strong hand. Proclaim martial law, demand immediate disarming of suspects, and let available troops shoot down all unauthorised persons found with arms in their hands."

This explicit counsel was placed before Henri V. about two o'clock in the afternoon, and a majority of the councillors called to consider the situation advocated its immediate adoption. But the Bourbon monarch sprang from stubborn if not stiff-necked stock.

" We are asked to deluge Paris with blood," he cried, " simply because M. Vansittart himself has bungled in the conduct of affairs at the front. I will not be a party to it. Rather would I proclaim myself the undeviating leader of the people in their legitimate aspirations to drive the invader from our soil."

Liancourt, white with anger, sprang from his chair at these words.

" I will not remain silent," he said, " in face of such un-warranted statements. Your Majesty must well know that were it not for M. Vansittart's foresight and splendid quali-ties France would now be suing for mercy beneath the iron heel of a conqueror, whilst another French king would, if he escaped with his life, be seeking a dishonoured safety in England, that asylum for distressed monarchs."

Henri also sprang to his feet.

" You forget that you speak to your King !" he shrieked.

" Not I! I speak to no king ; I speak to a weak puppet, who in the hour of danger whines like a frightened child, and strikes at those who would protect him."

" I have still sufficient kingship left to protect my dignity. I demand your immediate resignation, sir."

" You have it, and God help France !"

During this furious scene the other members of the Cabinet sat with blanched faces. None of them dared to speak. The rage of the King and the impassioned avowals of Liancourt, by far the ablest man in the room, rendered them dumb spectators of this unheralded quarrel.

Liancourt was about to withdraw, when Henri flung him-self into a chair, threw his head and arms on the table, and burst into tears.

The action softened Liancourt as naught else would have done. He hesitated a moment, and then walked to the stricken monarch, to place his hand kindly on his shoulder and say :

" We both spoke in anger, sire. I beg you to forgive me. My only excuse is the distress of France. I could not bear to think that the King was disloyal to himself by reviling the only man who can save the country."

The King, too, sobbed his regret, and peace was restored. But the fateful hours were slipping by, and nothing was done.

Meanwhile scenes of violence were enacted in the Chamber of Deputies, and all Paris was electrified by the news that the German Emperor was marching straight on the capital.

Whence came the tidings, or who was responsible for their authenticity, no one knew. The fact suddenly thundered into existence and was shouted by a million voices. The city forthwith went mad. It was seized with alternate fits of wild movement and complete paralysis. Men and women gathered in crowds or went whooping through the streets. Trains and omnibuses stopped running, shops were closed, even government departments ceased work. The Chamber of Deputies adjourned amidst uproar and disorder.

In the frenzy of the hour it was stated and believed that the Germans were already in possession of Versailles, though the nearest German troops were actually two hundred miles distant as the crow flies, and a strong fortress, with a large army corps, barred the way to Paris.

Folliet, who had lived in the city through the Commune, recognised the signs of the coming storm. He rushed to the Tuileries and broke in unannounced upon the assembled council.

" Within an hour," he cried, " the Palace will be sacked. Your Majesty must fly with the Queen at once. It is a question of minutes, if you would save your lives."

Though impulsive and excitable to the degree of folly, the King was no coward.

" What do you mean, M. Folliet ? " he said coolly enough. " What has happened to so upset your reason ? "

" Your Majesty has not heard that the people believe the Germans to be already within a day's march of Paris. They have been told that the government has purposely deceived them, that our army on the frontier is annihilated, and Vansittart a captive. To try to persuade them would be to dam a torrent with a pebble. Let me implore you to leave the city at once, if it be still possible. Even now the streets of Montmartre and the Faubourg St. Martin are crowded with armed hordes intent on mischief."

" But we have troops. We can crush these reptiles."

" Impossible ! It would need an army and you have but

two regiments. In an hour, or less, you will not have these, as the men will believe the popular cry and probably join the revolutionaries."

Folliet's earnestness was convincing, yet the King hesitated. "How can I leave Paris to the mercy of its criminal classes? Surely I must remain, whatever be the consequences to myself. Let some of you safeguard the Queen. My place is here; I cannot desert it."

The Prefect of Police wrung his hands with impotence. "Let me beseech your Majesty to do as I ask. I have devised means to stamp out this outbreak, but I need time. Of what avail will it be for your life to be uselessly sacrificed?"

Liancourt now joined his powerful voice to that of Folliet: "If things have reached this desperate stage, it is certainly advisable for your Majesty to leave the city. Why should you not join the army in Lorraine? I think the Cabinet should insist upon this course being taken."

Every minister present echoed this view and the King yielded.

Folliet had not exaggerated the condition of affairs. When, half an hour later, the royal carriages dashed through the gates leading towards the Champs Élysées, where a strong escort of dragoons awaited them, a horde of the so-called National Guards were beating in the doors on the Louvre side.

Without much difficulty the fugitives gained the open country by way of the Bois de Boulogne, and a circuitous route brought them to a wayside station of the Chemin de Fer de l'Est. They had to wait here over an hour for a train to be brought from the nearest junction, the Paris terminus being already in the hands of the mob.

Through the gloom of advancing night a great glare suddenly suffused the sky over Paris, and when the King asked Liancourt what it meant, the statesman sadly replied:

"I fear, your Majesty, that the palace of the Tuileries has a second time provided a national bonfire!"

The King was so downcast that he uttered no word, but Honorine, who had comforted herself with splendid *sang-froid* throughout the harassing anxieties of these last miserable days, looked proudly around as she smilingly said : " It is well. Let us regard it as a torch of defiance, not as an emblem of despair ! "

The Queen's hopeful utterance was worthy of her, yet the position was desperate enough in all conscience. With the quickness of a tropical tornado the revolutionary blast had struck the royal house of France. For over a century every ruler of that remarkable country has had to fly from the clutches of an enraged people. Few of them had the chance of escaping with such dignity as was possible in the case of Henri ; one lost his head as a sequel to the attempt. Truly the throne of the powerful monarch is built on no more stable foundation than the hut of the poorest peasant.

When the telegraph flashed throughout Europe the news of the Communistic outbreak, and the flight of the King and Queen, it created a fierce sensation. The sweet unreasonableness of the whole business was the most puzzling part of it. Already the Conservative English press—which early in the fray had predicted the immediate successes of the highly trained German army—was beginning to find some saving virtues in the French nation. Russia had serious thoughts of making a cautious move towards renewing the Franco-Russian *entente* which had proved such a lucrative investment for Muscovite politicians and bondholders. Italy and Austria were openly felicitating each other on having broken loose from the entanglements of the Triple Alliance. Yet in view of this roseate aspect of affairs, here was Paris in flames, the Tuileries sacked by a mob, and the Court flying, panic-stricken, to the protection of the troops on the frontier.

Everything happens in France, indeed, but occurrences are strictly governed by historical precedent. That wonderful nation can never fight a war without kicking out a king. That is why there are no campaigns under republican government; they could not be conducted with the requisite scenic accessories.

Three men in Paris kept their heads cool and their intellects on sharp edge during the troubled hours that succeeded the departure of the royal party.

Pompier, who, it will be remembered, was placed by Vansittart in charge of the stores and arsenals, doubled his trusty guard of sailors and awaited events.

Ribou, the arch-plotter, directed everything from his secret abode and awaited the arrival of the German Emperor.

Folliet, disguised so as to be unknown to his own subordinates, awaited the appearance of Ribou.

The Prefect of Police, though he mixed freely with the mob and even attended a sitting of the bogus revolutionary Tribunal that met in the Grand Hotel, was unable to find out the whereabouts of the man whom he believed to be the prime mover, both in brains and money, in the uprisal.

The visible leaders were noted criminals; the only genuine motive of the common horde of patriots was lost. The few troops in the city having been withdrawn to the outlying forts, all authority was, of course, at an end. Anyone in the uniform of a policeman was at once bludgeoned to death, and the rioters amused themselves by indiscriminate firing at shop windows, at public monuments, and, when sufficiently drunk, at one another.

Late at night, when the streets were crammed with tumultuous mobs intent only upon robbery, an idea came to Folliet, and he acted upon it without a moment's needless delay. Making his way to the chief commissariat stores on the south bank of the Seine, he reached a quieter area than the disorderly thoroughfares across the river. The reason for this change was obvious, as the pavements were strewed with corpses wearing the uniform of the National Guard.

Pompier and his sailors had got the better of a slight argument that took place earlier in the evening as to the possession of the government stores.

Folliet had not gone twenty yards long the Quai before he was gruffly ordered to halt.

He obeyed, calling out :

" I am M. Folliet, Prefect of Police, and I want to see Admiral Pompier."

" Very well," came the answer. " Wait till the officer of the watch comes. If you move either way I will shoot you."

After a delay an officer arrived. He surveyed the diminutive Prefect in his artisan's blouse, and said kindly enough :

" Look here, my good man, you are not built for barricades. Be off, before ill happens to you."

Folliet repeated his request.

" Don't you understand ? " said the officer. " If you are an impostor the Admiral will have you shot forthwith."

" Lead on ! " was the dry response.

Without further parley the Prefect was marched off between a couple of men-of-war's men, and the officer's surprise was unfeigned when he saw the warm greeting extended to the suspect by his chief.

" This is a nasty business," said Pompier, when they were alone.

" Yes, and a perplexing one."

" I agree with you. Even Communists must have a method in their madness. That is, I mean, the leaders. The rank and file, of course, care only for plunder, but what the people meant who planned this outrage I cannot, for the life of me, imagine."

" Pray proceed. I want to see if our independent views are identical."

" In my opinion, the thing can be stated very simply. Elaborate skill and preparation were necessary to foist this National Guard on the government. Then money must have been spent wholesale. But to what end ? Even a Socialist dupe must see that the revolutionaries will be wiped out of existence when the royal troops come to sweep the streets clear of them."

" Then what do you assume ? "

" That someone at the head of affairs believes that the regular army will be unable to re-occupy Paris, because the Germans will keep them busy until, by a forced march, one of the enemy's army corps arrives within striking distance of the city."

" Precisely. The rumour was even spread to-day that the Kaiser and his men had reached Versailles—by telephone, I suppose."

" Well ? "

Both men looked at each other. Pompier knew the question uppermost in Folliet's mind. After a pause it came : " We will assume, as the only possible hypothesis, that Vansittart can upset the German Emperor's plans. This gang of ruffians in Paris will soon run short of ammunition. How long can you keep their hands off the stores you have here ? "

Pompier looked around to make sure that they were not overheard. " I have only one hundred and fifty men on guard here ! " he said. " We employ two thousand men and women filling cartridges, and fortunately I emptied the stores yesterday in making up a very heavy consignment to complete the reserves at the front. But there is nearly a hundred tons of gunpowder on hand, and the work-people can soon supply deficiencies. We had a skirmish with a number of the National Guards this evening, but if they attack in force by daylight, well—you know my numbers."

" Briefly put, Admiral, early to-morrow all your stores will fall into the hands of the Communists."

" I fear so. Indeed, I can see no other result."

" Then they are already lost to the government. Being lost, they may as well be destroyed. Let us waken up Paris."

The project was a diverting one. Both men laughed with schoolboy glee at the sensation such an explosion would create. It would establish a record. But they quickly realised that it would probably bring down in ruins Notre Dame and the Louvre, and every other large building within a mile's radius.

So they adopted the safer expedient of opening every case of powder and playing upon the contents with a hose. The sailors made short work of this task, and long before day-break the whole party marched off towards the Porte d'Orléans and reached the fort at Montrouge without meeting with any striking adventure.

Folliet telegraphed full details of his achievement to Van-sittart, and the latter promptly ordered several train-loads of reserve troops to be concentrated on Paris from the west and south during the early hours of the following day.

The rioters were so much taken by the attractions of shop-pilfering, and carousing on the well-stocked cellars of the wine-merchants, that they paid little heed to the lack of ammunition.

It was not until the regulars commenced to converge to-ward the centre of the city that they realised their desperate position. At first there was some hard fighting, but such scanty supply of cartridges as was available soon gave out, and the rest of the business became mere slaughter ; for the royal troops, mostly steady-going provincials, had no sym-pathy with the miscreants who had laid bare the most pros-perous streets of the beautiful capital, defaced many of the public buildings and memorials, burned the Tuileries, and murdered many inoffensive people. They were shot down in hundreds and hunted like rats. In ten minutes the in-surgents were beaten; in two hours annihilated.

Folliet, as he watched the sport, was gleeful.

" When the war is over," he said, " the Prefecture will be a sinecure, as every gaol-bird in Paris will be dead."

But his joy at the thought was chastened by one damping fact—he had not found Ribou.

CHAPTER XXXII

STRAINED RELATIONS

A S the King of France steamed slowly eastwards, along lines congested with traffic—reservists and munitions of war going to the front, and thousands of wounded coming west to the great hospitals of the interior—he resolved, when he met Vansittart, to give him what is vulgarly known as a piece of his mind.

" It is intolerable," thought the diminutive monarch, " that I should be driven from my capital, and the fortunes of France imperilled, simply because the Germans chose to run off with Madame Vansittart. Why should the kidnapping of his wife affect his reason ? Does an American think more of his family circle than a Frenchman ? Anyhow, I will take care that the weight of blame is removed, in public estimation, from my shoulders to his."

Few people will doubt that this line of reasoning was absurd and dangerous. Had it been suggested to Honorine or Liancourt they would have strongly condemned it. They were fully conscious that the self-important Henri V. was a mere puppet dangling at the end of a chain of circumstances —that the future of France lay in the hands of two men, Vansittart and the German Emperor—that the war had resolved itself into a simple duel between them—and that anything the hot-headed, passionate King might do would not affect the situation in the slightest degree.

But of this possible explanation of events Henri was sublimely unconscious. He nursed his wrath and formulated cutting speeches until he reached the station at Verdun.

Here a somewhat unfortunate incident added to his ill-humour.

Evelyn was present to meet the Queen, and General le Breton was the official head of the troops that lined the platform.

"Where is M. Vansittart?" growled the King after a cursory inspection of a somewhat ragged guard of honour, obviously composed of second-class reservists.

"He awaits your Majesty at the Hotel de Ville."

"Oh, does he? And were there no more presentable soldiers of *my* army available than these scarecrows to greet my arrival?"

General le Breton, profoundly surprised at the King's manner, answered pithily :

"M. Vansittart has taken every trained man from the garrison of Verdun, among others, to constitute a corps for special service this afternoon."

"Oh, indeed! I want you, General le Breton, to countermand all orders until I have personally examined into affairs. I am here, and I will command."

The General saluted, but said stiffly :

"Your Majesty, I beg of you to convey such instruction to me through the Commander-in-chief, General Daubisson. I have not the authority necessary to give effect to your Majesty's orders."

"Oh, bosh!" cried Henri, walking rapidly towards a carriage in which the Queen was already seated with Madame Vansittart.

Addressing the latter, he said, with a wintry smile :

"Your husband was too busy to spare a moment to greet us, madame."

"Yes, indeed. He has been at work since before daybreak. Some great movement is on foot which requires a tremendous lot of careful organisation, and he is superintending every detail himself. I have not seen him. He sent me a verbal message telling me ot your arrival, and I came to the station of my own accord."

"So thoughtful of you, dear," interposed Honorine tenderly, in blissful ignorance of the storm brewing.

"What does he think of this frightful outbreak in Paris?" went on Henri.

"The news reached us about seven o'clock last night. At first Jerome was greatly concerned, but when he was assured of your safety he laughed. He said it was sensational, but unimportant—thoroughly Parisian, in fact." And Evelyn's pleasant face dimpled into a smile at her little joke.

"Unimportant, eh, that the King and Queen should be expelled from their capital by the bludgeons of a mob? We shall see!" Henri's tone was so fierce that the two ladies gazed at him in wonder, and a sudden turn seized the Queen lest perhaps her headstrong consort should commit some foolish act at this crisis in the national history.

But it was too late now to reason with or repress him; they had reached the Hotel de Ville. Not quite, though. In the bustling activity that presently possessed that pretentious building, no thought was given to royal personages or the ceremonial attending their movements. The pavements were crowded with soldiers, through whom mounted orderlies or bicyclists continually pushed their way; and in the main thoroughfare was drawn up, surrounded by a curious and surging crowd of officers and men, a couple of strong-looking vehicles—roomy, quaint, warlike structures on wheels—whilst to the pair was harnessed a gigantic motor-car.

The block in the main street was so complete that the equipages from the station could not get through, and the occupants had to force a passage through the crowd as best they could until a couple of staff-officers cleared a little space for the party by vociferating : "Room for their Majesties! Back there, you rascals!"

In a boiling ferment, breathless with spleen and exertion, the King gained the entrance to the Town Hall, and was at once conducted to the apartments prepared for his reception.

But he needed neither rest nor refreshment in his present temper.

"Tell M. Vansittart," he shouted to the officer in attendance, "that I require his presence at a council of war in ten minutes. Also warn M. Liancourt, General Daubisson, and the other ministers who accompanied me to attend."

"Why this haste, Henri?" said the Queen anxiously.

"There is much to be determined at once. Now that I am with my troops they must learn of my presence. The idea that we should be hustled through the streets like tradespeople!"

"Henri," said the Queen, and there was an ominous tightening of her firm lips, "this is no time for etiquette. There was even less display last night when the mob was thundering at the gates of the Tuileries."

The King flung himself off on the pretence of searching for some papers. When he returned, an official announced that the council had gathered.

Henri followed the man, but stopped when he saw the Queen coming close behind.

"What do you want, madame?" he said.

"I want to attend this council, and hear what is said."

"But——"

"There are no buts; I am coming."

When they entered the spacious apartment in which the chief officers of state were gathered, Vansittart was not there.

The King placed Honorine in a chair, seated himself at the head of the table, consulted some memoranda without acknowledging Daubisson's greeting, and at last pettishly inquired:

"How is it that M. Vansittart is not here, although I expressly requested his presence within ten minutes?"

"Here I am," came a cheery voice behind him, for Jerome had entered at the moment by a side door. "I heartily bid your Majesties welcome, and hope that the disagreeable incidents of yesterday have in no way distressed you."

The Queen rose and cordially shook hands with the millionaire. Henri, somewhat taken aback by Jerome's sudden appearance, welcomed him with less effusion, and pointed to a chair.

" I have convened this council," he said with as much dignity as he could summon to his aid, " to discuss the exceedingly grave situation which presents itself."

Jerome, affecting unconsciousness of the King's distant manner, which he put down to the turmoil of events in Paris and the fatigues of his journey, said briskly :

" I hope your Majesty will either postpone it or excuse my non-attendance. It is no exaggeration to say that I cannot spare a second of my time to-day, beyond telling you the latest developments at Paris."

He half rose, but Henri said coldly :

" Pray be seated, sir. We know them too well."

" But let me assure you that I cannot pretend at this moment to enter into any full discussion. If you will come with me and sit by my side for half an hour I will in the intervals of receiving and answering telegrams, and other messages, explain to you the reasons for my extreme pressure just now."

The King's tone gave serious emphasis to his words : " I insist, M. Vansittart, that you remain."

Jerome could no longer maintain the pretence that the King's attitude was due to weariness. He hesitated a moment, with a slight flush on his face, whilst Liancourt looked imploringly at the Queen, as if to say : " Can't you restrain him ? "

Honorine placed her hand on the King's arm, but Henri quietly removed it.

" The fact is, M. Vansittart," he resumed, " I have much to say that you should listen to, and it will, perhaps, be better if the preparations you have in charge—presumably affecting the future movements of the army—be left until they have been approved of by myself and my advisers."

The millionaire now saw that a quarrel was imminent. He sat down, pulled out his watch, and said calmly :

" I will listen to your Majesty for five minutes."

This was very unlike the opening the King had privately rehearsed, but the exceeding tension of the assembly, the strained expression on every other face in the room nerved him to desperate coolness.

" I meet you here, M. Vansittart," he said, " virtually a dethroned monarch, solely by reason of your acts."

He paused, expecting some outburst on Jerome's part, but the other merely toyed with his watch-chain.

Henri was about to state his case, elaborating it by quotations from the Paris press and other such reputable authorities, when some final glimmer of reason saved him from adopting this ludicrous course, so he contented himself with the straightforward question :

" It must now be settled once and for all whether you or I rule France. Which is it, M. Vansittart ? "

The reply came with stinging quickness : " I have never disputed the point since I chose your Majesty to reign in my place."

" It is a sample of your good taste, monsieur, to remind me that I occupy the throne by your favour. It cannot be disputed. But since I do happen to be King I am surely not straining my prerogatives by seeking to restrain you from not only ruining the country, but plunging this unhappy land once more into the vortex of revolution, republics, and bad government."

" Henri ! "—the Queen's tone was one of agonised entreaty.

" Your Majesty," said Liancourt, " will you then repeat the folly of yesterday ? "

" Of yesterday ? " said Vansittart. " Am I given to understand that the King held these views before even a possible justification for his words was provided by the Paris tempest in a teapot ? "

" Yes, I did. Your meddling interference and ridiculous

dealings with the German Emperor had already precipitated the crisis of which the *émeute* in the capital was the first and most serious outward sign." The King was now helplessly committed to hostilities, and in his wonted pig-headed way, adhered steadfastly to his programme.

"Oh, M. Vansittart," smiled the Queen, "for the sake of France, for my sake, do not heed him. He only means well for all of us, and has taken this course absolutely without the knowledge of those who would advise him differently, myself included."

Honorine's appeal obviously checked the bitter retort which trembled on Jerome's lips. By a powerful effort he restrained himself.

"Listen to me," he cried, his vehement voice ringing through the room. "Were I not wholly devoted to the cause of France, I would gladly leave you, King Henry V., to work out your own salvation. As it is, I have no choice. To desert the army now would be a grievous error, to leave it to your direction would be a crime. If all goes well, within forty-eight hours the war will be ended. How, is my affair, and I will not be questioned, or hindered, or restrained. He who attempts it will have to abide by the wish of the gallant troops now gathered in this city, for, by Heaven, he will either lead them or be imprisoned by them. Do you understand me?"

"You threaten me?" shrieked Henri.

"Call it what you will—my meaning shall be made clear to you."

"So I am not only to be driven from my capital, but disgraced in the eyes of my own army as well."

The King groaned the words out with difficulty, as even in his supreme excitement he could see that the Queen and the members of the council were opposed to him.

"Nonsense! You can, if you wish, return to Paris today. Telegrams I have received from Folliet and Pompier show conclusively that the troops I have ordered to proceed there will clear the streets of every Communist before night-fall. I would have told you this sooner had you even permitted me to welcome you as the King of France, come to see his troops annihilate their enemies. For the rest, it lies in your own hands to undo your folly by striving to help rather than cripple those who are working might and main to preserve your kingdom."

"Monsieur!" broke in the Queen, "I beg you to leave us and attend to affairs. Let us forget this wretched wrangle, and remember only the great cause committed to our, to your, care, for I, the Queen of France, by whose existence and your generosity my husband solely derives his position, solemnly declare my unabated, unshaken, undeviating trust in you."

Honorine's pathetic and heart-broken words evoked a deep murmur of assent from the others, and the King fiercely bit his lips to restrain the tumultuous thoughts that surged within him.

Jerome was visibly touched. "I am keenly conscious of your Majesty's confidence," he said, "and I will add that in the many difficulties we have faced together it has never, in my humble judgment, been more justified by circumstances than in this trying hour. I repeat my prophecy, that in forty-eight hours this unjust and iniquitous war will have closed, most favourably so far as France is concerned. I must now leave you with the hope that the King will, after reflection, see fit to modify his harsh views in regard to events for which my own private affairs may have been, in some sense, responsible."

He bowed and walked to the door, where he turned to ask General Daubisson to accompany him and Liancourt to come to him at the earliest moment.

A deep silence fell on the council when Jerome and the Commander-in-chief had quitted the room. The Queen was sobbing quietly, and Henri sat with elbows resting on the table and his head propped up between clenched fists.

At last he spoke, querulously and complaining :

" Am I to remain dumb, then ? Can I not even ask a question concerning events in the theatre of war ? "

Liancourt, rapidly interpreting the King's mood as one of submission, turned to the Chief of Staff and adroitly led him on to a general statement of affairs, and, in particular, to a detailed history of recent operations.

The officer naturally expatiated on the highly dangerous situation from which Vansittart's re-awakened genius had extricated the French army. He showed that the German successes, of which so much had been made by the disreputable Paris press, were in reality mere changes of location, and in no wise denoted a tactical triumph for the enemy. The Kaiser's march, too, whilst disconcerting enough at the first blush of the intelligence, was now regarded as a grave blunder, especially since the staff had learned the means whereby Vansittart hoped to deal with it.

As the King listened he felt his house of cards crumbling away before the officer's simple and explicit analysis. Poor Henri was rash enough in all conscience, but he was as prone to fits of extravagant humility as to the other extreme. The final blow came when Vansittart forwarded for his information a telegram from Pompier detailing fully the steps taken to annihilate the insurgents. Seizing a pen and some paper he dashed off a few hurried words and handed the document to the Queen, saying :

" There, Honorine, I mean all that I say this time, so, with unusual wisdom, you will think, I have been brief."

This is what she read :

" MY DEAR VANSITTART,—It is useless to apologise. I have been a fool. My only excuse is that I arrived at conclusions on faulty information. Forgive me, and find me work. Surely I can do something to help you.

" HENRI."

The Queen sprang up and kissed him before them all.

" That is like my own dear," she said. " Let M. Liancourt take this message of conciliation."

" Assuredly," he cried, with some of his wonted enthusiastic animation. " But first let me make my *amende* complete." And he gravely read the note to the council, pausing melodramatically at the end of the second sentence.

The council hummed with admiration. It must not be forgotten that they were all French.

Vansittart, on his side, exhibited equal magnanimity. Soon came the reply :

"Your Majesty's co-operation will be invaluable. Pray join me at a stand-up lunch whilst I explain matters."

The King hurried off, whilst Honorine went to sob out her thankfulness on Evelyn's shoulder.

CHAPTER XXXIII

THE MARCH OF THE MOTOR-CARS

WHEN the German Emperor crossed the Meuse near Damvillers, he headed a superb army of one hundred thousand veteran infantry, thirty thousand cavalry mounted on hardy and powerful Westphalian horses, and three hundred guns. In physique, equipment, and stamina, in every soldierly quality to endure and to accomplish, it would be difficult, if not impossible, to surpass throughout the world this splendid expeditionary force. The men, like their leader, were imbued with the spirit of daring which recks not of defeat. Too long had the great armies of Germany been pent up in the narrow valleys or arid plains of Lorraine. From causes almost wholly unavoidable, the German advance had been delayed far beyond the period assigned to it by military experts at the outbreak of hostilities.

The Germans believed, as did the Kaiser, that the reverses they had sustained at the hands of the French arose from accidental circumstances which favoured the latter. At Troyon Vansittart's "luck" in attacking the enemy's columns at night whilst they were taking up positions for an assault at daybreak, at Mars-la-Tour the success of his "trick" in fighting shells with bullets—these were explanations at least of the failure of the Teutonic spider to entrap the French moth.

But now the coast was clear. Vansittart, even if he were restored to health, was hopelessly blockaded to the north and east by Kreuznach and the army of Metz. If he attempted to fall back towards Paris he laid bare his extended flank and line of march to disastrous attack. If he marched southward he would be hard pressed in pursuit, and could do nothing to resist the Kaiser. In a word, the road to Paris lay open, defended only by the garrison of Chalons, which Wilhelm could swallow during the course of the ordinary day's routine. The distance to be traversed was one hundred and thirty miles, and the Emperor told his troops that he expected them to bivouac in the Forest of Bondy, on the outskirts of Paris, at the end of the sixth day.

In mere statement this task, to the trained military mind, seems almost impossible. The movement of an army numbering one hundred and fifty thousand fighting men, with a vast army of commissariat, medical, and other subsidiary services, at the rate of nearly twenty-two miles each day, has never yet been effected over anything like the distance stated. But the clockwork accuracy of the German machine manifests itself with telling force precisely in such a stupendous undertaking. Every man, from the general officer commanding a division down to the humblest driver of a commissariat cart, knew exactly what his personal share was of the many duties which resulted in the satisfactory completion of each day's march. Every animal had been carefully selected to withstand the severe strain entailed by the operation. Every nut and bolt and screw, every button and every shoe-lace, had been tested to insure good order and serviceableness when the final tussle came at Paris. Nothing is forgotten in the German army, nothing left to chance. The only thing the wonderful German staff cannot do is to make quite sure of the intentions of their adversary. Could they achieve this they would indeed be irresistible. During the war of 1870–71 they came very near to perfection. Their famous cavalry screen, always pushed out between twenty and fifty miles' distance from the main body, not only shut off the French from all knowledge of the German movements, but kept Von Moltke and Prince Frederick

Charles accurately informed of every change of direction and attempted combination of the French troops. So Wilhelm did not forget his cloud of Uhlan vedettes— hence the great proportion of the mounted arm in his expedition.

But the great *coup* that the German Emperor evolved in the Hotel de Ville at Metz, when he heard of the incipient Paris Commune, had, strangely enough, been foreseen and discounted by Vansittart before he left New York. It will be remembered that Jerome had set in motion an expenditure of nearly twenty millions sterling before he sailed in the *Seafarer*. Much of this vast sum had gone in the immediate purchase of a great variety of stores and animals, in which he knew the French defences to be seriously deficient ; but a huge sum was devoted towards the construction and equipment of motor-cars solely designed for the rapid transport of troops across country by means of ordinary roads. In the United States a tremendous development had been given to internal traffic of a heavy nature by the adoption of motor traction. The quick-witted American manufacturers soon saw that the horse would never be displaced as a means of conveyance by the pleasure-loving public. It was quite a different thing where the haulage of goods was concerned. Here was the true future of the horseless carriage, and the result of a general activity in this direction enabled the millionaire readily and promptly to secure the multitude of motors he required.

So secretly and efficiently had his agents worked, that large consignments of the road-engines were shipped from the States and landed at Toulon without public notice being directed to the event.

Meanwhile the artificers of Lyons and other metallurgical centres in the south of France were busily engaged in constructing the carriages intended to be used in conjunction with the motors.

As these vehicles will figure largely in the history of the

forthcoming operations, it will serve to elucidate matters if they are described with some degree of minuteness.

The engines were compact, extremely powerful, and so simply and strongly designed as to be capable of withstanding rough usage. Small, broad-tired running wheels, with seven clear feet of axle width, gave ample margin for security in rapid running over roads of steep gradient. They were capable of drawing a load of forty tons at an average rate of twelve miles an hour, whilst on level, straight roads, and for short distances, this rate of progress could be greatly exceeded. They were protected by plates of tough steel fixed at reclining angles, and it was estimated that even artillery fire, unless exceptionally accurate, would fail to do them material damage by isolated hits. Against musketry they were practically impregnable. The motive power was petroleum, fused to a high explosive temperature by intermixture with a small jet of steam generated by a tiny subsidiary boiler, and it was possible to carry sufficient fuel to last for a run of one hundred and fifty miles without replenishment.

Each engine drew two cars, similarly armoured and running on bogies, whilst a marvellously effective set of spiral buffers gave cohesion and fairly comfortable resilience to the whole turn-out, even when travelling very rapidly. Each of these cars accommodated, at a squeeze, thirty men or eight horses, besides carrying rations and forage, whilst one in every set of ten was fitted for the conveyance of two guns without limbers, the recoil being absorbed on the quick-firing principle.

At the very moment when Vansittart received ample assurance from the Lyons arsenal authorities that motor-car carriage for one hundred thousand men was available for immediate delivery, he received the news of the German Emperor's march on Paris.

He did not then know the real object of the German movement, but this catastrophe in the metropolis revealed to him the full extent of the plot. Instantly he jumped to the conclusion that the Kaiser was hurrying to the assistance of his confederates, for such, he was convinced, was the true description of those who inspired the revolutionaries.

The German army had set out on its six days' race before the situation was fully revealed, and the paramount question now was—Could they be intercepted and beaten en route?

Acting with his accustomed rapid and final decisiveness, Vansittart ordered the mobilisation of the motor-car army at Vitry. He chose this town as being south of the German line of march and consequently less liable to sudden attack.

He ordered the general commanding at Chalons to throw his whole force in the way of the Emperor and to delay him as much as possible, but on no account to destroy bridges or tear up roads, even if retreat became thereby imperative.

Above and beyond every other consideration the French cavalry must keep the Germans from scouting to the south of Chalons, else they would infallibly discover the preparations being made at Vitry.

Vansittart, in his own mind, fixed upon Rheims as the probable scene of conflict between himself and the Kaiser, and, as a matter of fact, the subsequent battle centred round Verzy, a village only ten miles to the south-east of that historic city. This plan of action once settled, he threw himself into the mass of details necessary for the mobilisation at Vitry, at twenty-four hours' notice, of the one hundred thousand troops selected for the enterprise and the strange means of locomotion which they were to use for the first time in warfare.

It is not to be wondered at, then, that he resented the waste of time caused by the King's stupid attempt to interfere in the direction of affairs, or that he thought more of a loss of five minutes in the work of organisation than of Henri's unwarranted and childish outburst of temper.

When the King came to him he was holding a glass of wine between the thumb and forefinger of one hand, a sandwich similarly in the other, and between the remaining fingers were stuck telegrams or memoranda which he was dealing in rapid monosyllabic words to staff-officers and short-hand writers. The floor was littered with paper ; telegraph instruments clicked incessantly from tables ranged along two walls ; and the place rang with the clatter of spurred boots as men came and went in a constant stream.

Henri gazed round at this scene of activity with a kind of dismay.

" I shall be worse than useless here," he said plaintively.

" Not a bit," cried Jerome, after bolting a large mouthful. " Sit down there. Read that " (indicating a type-written document), " as it gives all the details of the men selected to go from Verdun, and then go off with Beaumarchais to inspect them. They entrain at four o'clock, and I cannot possibly get away. Tell them that you and I follow to-night, and that we will beat the Prussians the day after to-morrow. And, by the way, have a look at the specimen motor in the street, so that you can give me your opinion of it when you return."

The King looked at his watch. It was 2.30.

" When do the troops parade ? " he said.

" Sharp at three."

" Then, please, let me share your plate of sandwiches. I am famished."

The unfortunate little monarch had not tasted food since he left Paris on the previous evening. Misery oft takes the place of a good dinner.

" Jim," shouted Vansittart, " more sandwiches and wine, and see that a charger is provided for his Majesty."

Bates left the doorway on his errand, and all the employees in the room looked up. It was the first intimation they had received of the King's presence.

The incident was not lost on Henri. When men are working for their country and obeying the orders of a man whom they believe to be the saviour of their country, a king is an insignificant item. The lesson did him good ; it was a fitting sequel to the trials and cross-purposes of the past few hours.

Henri rode off with Beaumarchais to inspect the Verdun contingent, some twenty thousand of all ranks, the picked men of the army. The right of the line was taken by the Foreign Legion, and the bosom of the brave soldier who rode at the King's side swelled with honest pride as he gazed at his gallant regiments.

The King passed down the long ranks in silence. The troops were drawn up in half-battalions—the largest tactical units which, in the opinions of Vansittart and his staff, could be effectively controlled under the peculiar conditions evolved by the presence of the motors.

He addressed a few inspiring words to the men each time he halted, but otherwise was unusually silent and pre-occupied.

Not until the end of the tour of inspection did he turn to Beaumarchais with the question :

" General, whence do we get all these veterans ? "

" Your Majesty, they are not old soldiers. They are picked men, but, beyond the Foreign Legion, few of them exceed three years' service."

" Am I to understand, then, that a month's experience of war has developed my army from striplings into seasoned veterans ? "

" Well, your Majesty, a few stiff fights have a remarkable effect in turning boys into men."

" I wish I had joined you earlier. It might have had a similar effect on me."

The remark nonplussed the other. The best thing he could think of to say was :

" If your Majesty accompanies this expedition, I think you will see plenty of fighting."

" You think so ? Do you believe these motor-cars will be effective ? "

" They are new-fangled notions, your Majesty, but what

M. Vansittart approves of turns out all right as a rule. We, of the older school, have ceased argument, and simply obey him."

" That saves a lot of trouble, I should imagine."

" It does, your Majesty."

Henri could not tear himself away from the troops. When, with colours flying and bands playing, they marched off to the station, he placed himself at the head of the leading regiment and rode with them. He saw each train start, passed along every carriage, had a pleasant word and smile for everyone, and generally succeeded in leaving a very good impression with the men.

When the last train-load had left, joyous and cheering, he returned to the Town Hall, there to find Vansittart still dealing with the clicking telegraphs and the stream of messengers.

The millionaire naturally looked pale and worn. The effects of his recent indisposition were still visible ; he could not yet use his right arm freely for a long period without feeling pain in the shoulder ; and the strain of the terrific work he was now engaged upon was sufficient in itself to upset a man of less heroic mould.

" When will you be able to take some rest ? " said the King. He already found himself marvelling how Jerome could undergo so uncomplainingly the trials of his position. What would he have thought had he seen him during that awful night in the inn at Gravelotte ?

" In an hour," said Vansittart. " Even at this moment I can light a cigar." And he suited the action to the words.

" Do you hope to have everything in readiness to make a start to-morrow ? "

" Without doubt. Every car and engine, with complete equipment, is already packed at Vitry. I do not think anything has been forgotten. I had provided for ropes to drag them out of the way if disabled, when it occurred to me that should any of them be captured by the enemy, they might be used against us with disastrous effect, so now steps are being taken to place a dynamite charge in such a position in each vehicle, that when exploded by a fulminate the car or engine will be destroyed. All the stores are at Vitry, and are now being loaded into the cars. You have seen a fifth of the expeditionary troops start from this station. Three-fifths are drafted from the main body, and travel to Vitry via Bar-le-Duc, and the final contingent is drawn from Nancy."

"Have you no fear of failure through the inexperience of drivers or the unaccustomed nature of the contrivance to the men who will use it?"

"None whatever," said Vansittart, with a smile at the King's evident hesitancy to accept all he heard without reservation. "Any man who can drive a horse can drive this motor, as it is guided by steel reins precisely as the animal is by leather ones. As for the men, they are saved all fatigue, and, if only the officers obey me implicitly, they will fight nearly all the time under shelter, protected by these small movable forts."

"It will be the most wonderful event of your wonderful life, if this battle really comes off, as you believe."

Jerome now laughed outright. "Oh," he cried, "I cannot have your Majesty dubious on that point. I can spare a little breathing space. Come, you shall drive a car yourself."

When Henri had with his own hands—guided only by the simple instructions of an officer who stood beside him—navigated a motor and two cars, laden with four field-pieces and a full complement of gunners, at a high rate of speed through the streets, and found he was able to turn corners with as much ease as though he were handling a coach and four, he was converted.

He returned with Jerome to the Hotel de Ville. A messenger handed a telegram to the millionaire, who read it with a gesture of annoyance.

"What is the matter?" cried Henri, anxiously. He

feared lest the Vitry mobilisation had collapsed, or Pompier
had failed to recapture Paris.

" It is too bad," said Vansittart.   " I cannot get any cigars
and cigarettes, not even tobacco."

" Is that all ?   I have a supply.   Pray use——"

" Not for myself.   I wanted some for the troops during
the march and afterwards.   Everything smokable has been
cleared out of Verdun, and there is none available from the
military stores.   Supplies were requisitioned from Paris, but
Pompier has been too busy with recent events to forward
them.   It is disgusting.   I *did* hope every possible item was
in readiness this time."

" Tell me," said the King with much gravity ; " have the
men got matches ? "

" Oh yes !   Let me see ! "   Vansittart consulted a note-
book.   " They are stored in cars No. 18, 110, and 187."

" And pipes ? "

" Pipes we were compelled to omit because they occupied
too much room.   Cigarette-papers are in the same cars as
the matches."

" But, supposing the men had tobacco, how would they
know where to obtain it, as I have been working out in my
own mind that you require at least nine hundred engines and
eighteen hundred cars to convey the expedition."

" That is simplicity itself.   Every officer to-morrow morning will be given printed lists containing all articles carried,
arranged in alphabetical order, with the numbers of the cars
opposite."

" Then," said Henri tragically, " since you have done so
much, I will complete the task.   *I* will procure that tobacco."

Jerome could not help laughing at him.   " How ? " he
cried.   But the King had gone.   He had found something
to do, something which he could honestly say was his own
definite task.

Late at night he reappeared, dishevelled, covered with oil
and soot, but triumphant.

"I have done it," he shouted delightedly when he met Vansittart. "I went on an engine to a tobacco manufactory at Troyes, and at Ravigny Junction I detached a truck-load of tobacco, cigars, and cigarettes for Vitry, whilst I telegraphed instructions to the Commissariat officers at Vitry to allocate the proper cars for them so that they may figure in the printed lists. That is all right, I think?"

"Excellent. And now we must start to join the troops. I can only give you half an hour. Everything waits us in a special at the station. We will sup en route."

There was not much time for leave-taking. Honorine and Evelyn would possibly have borne the separation unflinchingly had they been alone. But the knowledge of each other's misery rendered their efforts at stoicism unavailing, and they unfeignedly broke down when they were called for the farewell embrace.

"Dearie," said Evelyn to her husband, "come back to me! The parting will not be for long in any case. If any evil befall you, I cannot live without you."

"Eh, what is this? My brave girl full of forebodings? Surely you do not fear now at the very eve of success?"

"No, no, not that. If I could only come with you I would be sure that all was well."

"My darling, that is impossible. Come, let me kiss away your tears. We will meet the day after to-morrow."

Evelyn did not tell him the cause of her terror. The very aspect of the murderous-looking motors in the street had frightened her more than all the warlike paraphernalia she saw around.

But the Queen of France smiled even in her grief. She rejoiced at the fact that Henri had made peace with Vansittart, and was now so ready to work loyally with him.

After a brief rest in the train, Vansittart and the King rose at dawn and rode off to see the troops start. Early the previous evening a strong force of cavalry had marched along the road to Chalons. Telegrams from that city showed that a determined attack by the Germans was expected during the day at Valmy, where the Chalons Army Corps held a strong position.

Vansittart's final orders were that the expedition should move at a regular pace not exceeding eight miles an hour, that ten cars should constitute half a battalion, with an eleventh carrying the officers' horses and some machine guns, and that intervals of not less than fifty yards should separate each set of vehicles, thus minimising the risk of collision in case of a break-down.

All the available country roads were utilised, and a large plain in the west of Chalons was fixed on as the halting-place.

At the outset the motors were grouped on an open space, and it was now patent to any observer that for concentration of a vast force of fighting material this arrangement could not be surpassed. The motors and cars were about the same size as an ordinary railroad-goods waggon, and three thousand of these, when arranged in long parallel lines, stood upon a comparatively limited area.

Each officer in charge of a car had a sketch-map, showing the road he was to follow, irrespective of all eventualities save an absolute break-down. In the latter event the car was to be at once hauled on one side, and if the damage was irreparable, destroyed if in the enemy's vicinity.

This preliminary march to Chalons was really in the nature of a day's field exercise. Actual contact with the Germans was not expected until the following morning.

But in war, as in all else, it is the unexpected that happens. When Beaumarchais, who commanded the advance brigade, gave the order to march, the cars moved off with beautiful precision. When stationary they looked so cumbrous that the military critic might be inclined to scoff at them ; in motion they suggested a deadly facility of movement that evoked unanimous praise.

" When my *chasseurs* become used to those chargers on

23

wheels," cried Le Breton, "they will take them across country."

To test the leading battalion, Vansittart and the King, surrounded by a numerous staff, galloped to the front and suddenly asked Beaumarchais to halt. A bugle rang out, and within ten yards every vehicle was motionless, though they were previously travelling at the prescribed pace. The enthusiasm of the rank and file was unbounded and gratifying to witness. Whatever others might think, the men thoroughly believed in these new engines of warfare.

Chalons was reached in three hours by the first brigade. By midday all the motors had arrived without a single accident, save delay caused by the partial collapse of a weak bridge at the prolonged strain of such heavy weights.

The discovery was a fortunate one, and the Intelligence Department forthwith set to work to strike out of the maps such unfrequented country roads as might contain uncertain structures.

News now came of the issue of events at Valmy. During the morning the sounds of sustained conflict announced a serious engagement in that direction. By three o'clock Vansittart learned that the French were in full retreat, closely pressed by an overwhelming force of Prussians.

For a few minutes he was on the horns of a dilemma. He did not know whether to offer battle to the Emperor that night or not.

Several officers urged him to employ a few of the motors and thus test them in active service. The proposal served to put matters in their true light.

" No," he said, in answer to this suggestion ; " whilst the exercise might be useful to us, it would be of the utmost value to the enemy. The quick-witted German staff would soon grasp the significance of this new device, and we should find every road they governed quite impassable. No ; they must be held back to-night and fought to-morrow."

To the utter dismay of the soldiers they were ordered to

fall in without the cars. They feared so greatly that some unexpected collapse had happened, that Vansittart told the officers to explain matters to the men. By pushing forward a division, supported by cavalry and guns, the German pursuit was checked, and after some sharp fighting, completely stopped.

The Emperor imagined that the defenders of Chalons had rallied, so he detailed his left wing to hold them tight during the night, and carry the town by assault next day, whilst his cavalry scouts pushed ahead to reconnoitre the country between Rheims and Chalons. They found it well patrolled by French horsemen, but otherwise untenanted, and the Kaiser, eager to continue his race to Paris, decided to march at daybreak, leaving two divisions to complete the capture of Chalons.

Thus the two armies rested during the night, in close juxtaposition at their extremities, but so disposed that the German Emperor was happily oblivious of the possibilities of the following day. This time the Uhlan cavalry screen had not been extended quite far enough.

CHAPTER XXXIV

THE MOTOR-CAR BATTLE

THE Chalons garrison had been driven from the hilly country in the neighbourhood of the two villages, Le Grand and Le Petit Mourmelon, situate midway between Rheims and Chalons.

A glance at the map of this part of France will show that the hamlet of Verzy lies eight miles due west of Little Mourmelon, on the slopes of the famous champagne country, and in direct line between the German bivouac and Paris.

Late into the night did Vansittart and his principal officers examine every topographical detail of the locality, falling back upon the personal knowledge of residents in Chalons where the excellent maps in their possession seemed in any degree vague or misleading.

This fertile and well-cultivated province did not favour military operations on a very extensive scale, except in the immediate neighbourhood of Verzy. Hedges and orchards were plentiful, whilst farmhouses or the tiny villas of *vignerons* dotted the landscape in all directions.

These elements made in favour of the invaders, who, taken probably by surprise, would be able to convert every piece of leafy cover into an ambuscade, and each building into a fort.

However, this feature of the affair could not be helped, and Jerome trusted to the exceeding rapidity and remarkable nature of the French attack so to demoralise their opponents that a dogged and stubbornly fought battle would be out of the question.

It was proposed that the struggle should be postponed until the Germans reached the plains of the Tardenois district, but Vansittart would not listen to the suggestion. He well knew that each hour brought greater danger of notoriety for his new motor-cars. Notwithstanding a strict censorship of press telegrams, the remarkable nature of the French equipment must soon leak out, and then he might say " good-bye " to an attempt to surprise the Kaiser.

The forthcoming battle must either bring the war to a catastrophic conclusion for the Germans, or plunge both countries into a protracted campaign of waiting behind fortified camps. It would then become a mere question of endurance, the severest of all tests, whether for an individual or for a nation.

The most pressing immediate difficulty was to contrive to hold back the expected German assault upon Chalons, whilst not forcing matters so seriously as to compel the Kaiser's main body to turn from its obvious route next morning.

Vansittart entrusted this task to the engineers. Before midnight he received the assurance that field-works were in course of construction to an extent that would easily enable the Chalons garrison to beat off their assailants until late next day, by which time the millionaire promised them active help.

The motor-car army was divided into ten strong brigades of one hundred cars each, thus constituting six thousand men per brigade. With these there were no field-pieces, and but few Maxims. It was purely an infantry force, and each brigade had its line of operation strictly marked out, beyond which it was not to deviate a yard.

The artillery was massed in two divisions, which, with motor-car infantry escort and a considerable force of cavalry, were intended to be used principally along the crests of two small ridges that ran north and south through the position which, it was expected, the Kaiser's army would occupy about ten o'clock.

Every possible detail having been repeatedly checked, the King and Vansittart were about to seek a few hours' well-earned rest, when a telegraphic despatch from Daubisson arrived.

Its intelligence was serious, though not unexpected.

"Kreuznach attacked in force this afternoon," he wrote, "marching by four strong divisions against right and left centre, Gravelotte, and three miles west of Verdun. Fighting was thus spread over an area of nearly thirty miles. Am glad to be able to report that each attack was repulsed with severe losses to the enemy, but regret that our estimated killed and wounded amount to over 3000 of all ranks. Returns not yet complete. From nature of German movements I have reason to believe that each separate column was intended as a reconnaissance in force."

"What do you make of it?" said the King, when Vansittart had twice read the message aloud.

"I think that Daubisson has hit upon the right solution in his last sentence. I have no doubt that Kreuznach was beaten back fairly enough, but the real object of the day's fighting was to ascertain our strength so that he might inform the Kaiser whether or not to expect any considerable army in pursuit."

"Ah! Then I take it that Kreuznach's report will be favourable to us," said the King, after a pause.

"Entirely so. Daubisson's vigorous resistance has convinced him that our whole available force, save Chalons and other isolated garrisons, is still east of the Meuse."

"Daubisson has done well, to all appearance?"

"Admirably. He is a splendid general for conducting a defence. As soon as he enters the enemy's territory he goes wrong. Nevertheless I will enable him to do something noteworthy to-morrow."

Jerome sat at a table in the wine-grower's small abode he tenanted for the night, and wrote:

"Your despatch received, and its contents noted by his Majesty and myself with utmost gratification. Whilst not materially weakening present lines, I desire you to gather strong column in vicinity of Gravelotte to-morrow, and precisely at two o'clock march to Metz, and endeavour to carry the fortress by assault. You will probably succeed, as such a *coup de main* will be the last thing expected by the enemy, and the garrison of Metz has in all likelihood been depleted dangerously to strengthen Kreuznach's right wing. If you fail do not fear censure : if you are established in Metz by nightfall, the King empowers me to state that your future title shall be—— "

" What ? " said Vansittart, when he had read the document thus far to Henri.

" Oh, let us say Marquis—Marquis de Metz ! "

" Marquis de Metz, by all means."

Vansittart handed the message to an officer, asking that the chief telegraphists only at both ends of the wire should be cognisant of its contents.

Within two minutes he was asleep, to dream that Evelyn and his eldest son were flying before a furious motor-car, which he was driving and powerless to control.

Soon after dawn some intermittent firing to the north announced that the Uhlan scouters were endeavouring to drive in the French cavalry outposts. They did not accomplish their object, but the French horsemen were handled so carefully that they gave no sign of the presence of an army in their rear. Soon, too, these minor conflicts were drowned in the sustained roar of the expected German assault on the outskirts of Chalons, towards the north-east.

By seven o'clock the French pickets brought definite news of the German advance guard being in possession of the heights beyond Verzy to the west.

At eight o'clock Montsaloy led a cavalry reconnaissance in that direction, and distinctly saw the Germans, in dense columns, filing down the slopes leading to the village.

But the alert German staff noted the unwonted assiduity of the French mounted patrols, and the appearance of Montsaloy and his troops led to a counter-reconnaissance by a field battery and two regiments of Uhlans.

This compact little body rode forward so gallantly that it was necessary to stop them by some display of force. They would not retire before several guns opened fire on them, and a French cavalry brigade galloped out in the hope of cutting them off.

The Kaiser would not believe that any notable opposition could be expected from this quarter, but the symptoms were so dangerous that he unwillingly ordered a general halt, whilst two brigades of infantry, supported by four batteries and three thousand sabres, marched south to dispel the mystery that hung about the proceedings on the German left flank. It took a good hour for this opening phase of the battle to develop itself. The Hanoverian infantry, beautifully handled, and manœuvring with faultless efficiency, pressed the attack right up to the banks of the Marne, and did not retire until crushed by a vastly superior French force.

At the first sign of yielding on their part Vansittart said to the King :

" The battle has now fairly commenced, and the Kaiser has at last learned his mistake."

No answer came, and Jerome dropped his glasses to turn in the saddle and look at the King, who was slightly in the rear. Then he smiled, for he realised what had happened.

Henri's eyes were glazed and fixed. On his drawn face was an expression of unutterable awe. He gazed at the dread drama being enacted across the river with the fascination of one who has seen a ghost.

It was his first battle. For the first time he looked upon the stern realities of war. Over the face of the smiling landscape, lit by the vivid midsummer sun, he saw men riding, or moving, or marching with the mad indefiniteness that marks the opening movements of a conflict, whilst, with ever-increasing rapidity, the green fields became dotted with little dark motionless specks and small parties of bearers hurrying off to the rear. Each of these specks he knew to be a dead man ; each party, he knew, was carrying a

wounded one. Death was all around him. It whistled
through the air in invisible flight, it left its testimony in the
crumpled-up bits of humanity that lay so still on the grassy
terraces or in the country lanes.

It mesmerised his sight and hearing ; with dry mouth
gaping wide he could utter no sound ; had his horse moved
he would have fallen from the saddle.

" Here," shouted Vansittart, " you are thirsty. Take a
long drink of this," and he handed a flask to the King, thus
momentarily arousing him from his stupor.

Henri mechanically obeyed him, and a mouthful of strong
cognac made him cough.

Calling a staff-officer, Vansittart said, with slightly elevated voice : " Kindly accompany his Majesty to General
Beaumarchais's brigade. Tell the General to march at once,
as directed, by way of Oiry and Avenay. His Majesty will
assist the General in the flanking movement."

Still nearly unconscious, Henri rode off with the aide-de-
camp, who took in the situation at a glance. Within five
minutes, restored to animation by the rapid pace of his horse,
he was discussing the German attack with the aplomb and
self-possession of an old soldier. He had received his bap-
tism of fire.

Vansittart's remark anent the Kaiser was fully borne out
by events. The undeniable repulse offered to the recon-
noitring brigade showed Wilhelm that some new and determined foe was in dangerous proximity. There was
nothing for it but to offer battle with his whole force at
once, and this he did, cursing his Intelligence Department
and Kreuznach with the utmost impartiality at the same
time.

The Emperor was under no delusion as to what had happened. None but Vansittart could have so neatly stolen a
march on him, and befooled his ablest general.

" Confound everybody ! " roared the vexed Kaiser. " I
shall lose a whole day in the march to Paris."

Nevertheless, this display of temper did not prevent him from issuing orders for a general advance, pioneered by clouds of skirmishers, to ascertain the exact nature and strength of the French position.

So far the Germans had been held back by the reserve infantry, dismounted from their motor-cars for that explicit purpose.

Already Beaumarchais and the King were tearing off along the roads to the north-west in order to fall upon the German right flank about 10.30 A.M.

At 9.45 the country in front of Vansittart was alive with the Kaiser's troops. Batteries of artillery were taking up position at the verge of a plateau beyond the Marne, and shells were screaming through the air in every direction where a body of infantry or cavalry could be discerned by the German guards.

The supreme moment of action had arrived. Vansittart simply waved his hand to Le Breton, who commanded the leading brigade, drawn up in the street of the small hamlet ensconced in the leafy hollow close to the French centre. Le Breton signalled a response, nodded to the driver of the first car, and the vehicle moved slowly to the front. Quickly getting pace, it dashed across a bridge over the river, nearly coming to grief in the eagerness of the driver to turn a rather sharp corner.

Five other brigades stationed across the Marne, but near to Chalons, started almost simultaneously, and within ten minutes from the time of Vansittart's quiet signal six hundred motors, containing thirty-six thousand soldiers, were rushing towards the German columns at a pace exceeding twelve miles an hour, or more rapidly than a similarly large force of cavalry could possibly get over the ground.

The Kaiser and his staff had ridden to the crest of the ridge where the German guns were at work, and were momentarily expecting the bold stand so far made by the French to wither before the vigorous assault now in progress, when the first of the motors, with its two attached carriages, dashed into sight across the Marne.

" What on earth is that ? " cried Wilhelm, with field-glasses glued to his eyes.

" A running steam-engine ! " laughed an aide.

" A charge by the commissariat ! "

" Perhaps a new sort of military steam-roller ! "

" Whatever it is, it is full of soldiers ! "

" With a machine gun ! "

" Another of Vansittart's dodges, eh ? "

The concluding comment drew the Emperor.

" If it be one of Vansittart's dodges, gentlemen, it will need all of our skill to counteract it."

In silence the distinguished officers present steadily watched the progress of the motor. With even keener interest Vansittart and those near him also watched it, for they alone knew what was expected of this new and terrible engine of warfare.

Conscious that the eyes of both armies were upon him, Le Breton implored the driver to pay heed to naught but the safe guidance of the motor along the straight road, which now ran at easy gradients through the centre of the German attack. Almost before a shot was fired at it the motor was within two hundred yards of the advanced firing line. The officer in command of a scattered company, seeing this strange object darting rapidly towards him from the French position, realised that, whatever its powers, it must have hostile intent. So he ordered his men to fire a volley at it. Several bullets struck the motor and the cars with resounding clang, but the angle of impact was so acute that the missiles glanced off harmlessly. And now the Frenchmen commenced firing in return, wildly, it is true, owing to the impossibility of taking accurate aim, but several Germans dropped. It was different when, with tremendous clatter, and amidst clouds of whirling dust, the motor swept through the fighting line and supports, to come within short range of a couple of battalions drawn up in close order. Here the French fire began to tell with awful effect. The machine gun, mounted on the left front of the leading car, poured a torrent of projectiles into the German ranks, and, as it passed them on the flank, had a destructive influence which could never be obtained under ordinary conditions. The leaden shower beat upon the masses of soldiers with the directness of a rainstorm on a field of corn. Whole sections of companies were crushed to the ground—a half-battalion was demoralised in a few seconds.

A company of infantry stood on the roadway itself. The men bravely emptied their magazines at the steel-clad monster rushing towards them with the speed of a train. Then they realised that in another instant the thundering, crashing motor would be upon them. Human nature could not withstand this modern car of Juggernaut. Officers and men rushed dismayed to the hedges and sought to save their lives by flight. One after another of these fearsome structures came panting up the slope, each spitting fire and smoke and deadly bullets, each crammed with frantic, cheering, intoxicated French soldiers, half frenzied with the consciousness of irresistible force given to them by the motor, and barely able to obey the impassioned appeals of their officers to steady themselves and fire with anything like self-control into the ranks of their opponents.

The first man to comprehend the full scope of the motors in such a battle as that they were now engaged in was Vansittart. He turned to his staff and said :

"Go, some of you, and warn the reserves to be in immediate readiness. Also send the 7th and 8th motor brigades to the assistance of Chalons. The rest is mere sla..ghter."

The second to grasp the situation was the German Emperor. With a cry of fierce rage he drove his spurs into his horse, and wheeled the startled animal into a gallop towards the nearest batteries.

" The Machine gun, mounted on the left front of the leading car, poured
a torrent of projectiles into the German ranks."

" Stop them," he roared to the artillery officers. " Stop them, or the army will become a mob."

With the utmost rapidity half a dozen guns were swung round to the new front and fired at the line of motors, for although the incidents described took little more than two minutes in transaction, already some forty of Le Breton's moving forts were inside the German position.

But it is not an easy thing to train a field-piece and fire it with precision at even a large object travelling along a road at a high rate of speed.

Some dozen rounds were fired before one of the cars was struck. Even then the shell only succeeded in tearing away a portion of the upper screen, and killing a few of the occupants. The car swerved badly from the shock, but did not overturn, and its forward progress was in no way affected.

" Idiots ! " shrieked the Kaiser ; " select a definite point, aim low, and fire salvoes by word of command."

The artillerists quickly grasped his meaning. The first volley was not successful because the officer in charge of the operations gave the word too soon. But, at the second attempt, four shells hit one of the motors vitally, smashing it bodily from the bogey truck, and bringing its two cars to hopeless ruin.

" Ha ! that is better. Now we have them."

The Emperor was so excited that he leaped from his charger, and himself assisted in laying one of the guns upon the next car, the whole line being brought to a standstill whilst the French troops rushed to the task of clearing the stricken motor from the roadway.

Wilhelm did not know that Vansittart was fully prepared for this emergency.

With wild scream and demoniac energy the shells from eighteen French guns, stationed on the opposing slope, tore through the German battery, now thoroughly enfiladed. Two guns were wrenched from their carriages, gunners were crushed into shapeless atoms on all sides, and the Emperor himself had a miraculous escape, his *pickelhaube* being knocked off by the wind from a passing shell.

Undaunted, he cried out : " Never mind, my lads, we will soon silence them," and he yelled instructions for every available gun to open fire on the French batteries, whilst additional artillery was to be hurried to the front.

At the time he, of course, believed that Le Breton's motor-car brigade was the only one in the field ; that Vansittart hoped to demoralise the Germans by this weirdly unexpected method of attack before he delivered an orthodox assault ; and that the effectual stoppage of the motors would upset Vansittart's theories, whilst it enabled the superior German force to get the better of the fray.

As for Paris, it was becoming dim in the distance. A victory would be but a shade removed from a defeat, for Wilhelm knew that, at the best, a hard-fought and dearly won battle lay before him. Had he been told at that moment that Le Breton's brigade was one of six then tearing wildly through the German position from the south and west, whilst Beaumarchais had completed his flank march and was on the point of driving the Uhlan pickets in dismay before him from the west, it is possible that this latest scion of the line of Hohenzollern would have sought immediate death on the battle-field. As it was, the whirl and confusion of events, the eager haste of expedients to combat the present danger, shut out from him all knowledge of proceedings elsewhere.

The Frenchmen worked like fiends to remove the *débris* of the smashed motor. In this task they were practically unhindered, as the nearest German infantry had been brushed far from the place by the passage of the preceding cars.

Soon they had the road sufficiently cleared, the two cars were shoved off into the field, and the line of motors again resumed progress, for the German guns were so hampered by the French artillery that it was impossible to secure efficient fire for the main purpose in hand—namely, the stoppage of the French advance.

In a fury of despair the Kaiser felt that his guns, devotedly served though they were, could not perform the task he required of them. The arrival of a small regiment of staff-officers from all parts of the German position, reporting disaster after disaster, revealed to him the full extent of the fearful conflict raging around Verzy between the German main body and the bulk of the French forces.

Up to this time, so awfully sudden had been the development of events, he had heard nothing of the main attack. Riding back to the reverse side of the plateau, Wilhelm at last became aware of the magnitude of the disaster which had befallen him. Along every highway darted the huge motors, paralysing all opposition, crumpling up brigades and divisions into terrified hordes, smiting with unfettered violence their helpless opponents, and utterly dislocating the whole army, for artillery, cavalry, infantry, and commissariat were piled together in shapeless masses. As he galloped on like one in a dream he suddenly saw ten of the French motors halt, and commence firing shells at a body of German troops drawn up near a plantation, at too great a distance from the roadway for practical rifle-fire.

" My God ! " groaned the stricken Kaiser, reining in his charger and covering his face with his left hand. " They even carry cannon. Is he man or fiend ? "

General von Gossler, who rode near him, now dared to say what every man on the staff thought when they first learned the true position of affairs.

" There is nothing for it, your Majesty, but a rapid retreat to the north. We can still save many of our men by blocking the roads and blowing up bridges, where these devices of the devil cannot follow us."

His broken-hearted chief murmured: " Tear up the roads ! Destroy the bridges ! Yes ! Now we know why the French did nothing to hinder our march. Yet how could I have foreseen all that has happened ? "

" Your Majesty," urged Von Gossler, " may I give orders for a general retreat ? "

His persistence stirred Wilhelm from his stupor of grief.

" Retreat ! " he cried. " Orders ! Look, man ! What orders are necessary ? Who will listen ? Who will obey ? "

In very truth, the frightful state of confusion into which the erstwhile magnificent German army was thrown was heartrending. All over the field small knots of men who scorned to fly were savagely if vainly trying to retaliate upon their armour-clad assailants ; but the rest of the force was utterly panic-stricken.

The sight so unnerved the Emperor that he bowed his head and cried repeatedly : " My poor lads ! my poor lads ! " whilst unchecked tears streamed from his eyes.

" Yet, your Majesty," persisted the other, " we may do something. Let us at least try."

As if in answer to this despairing utterance came the sound of sustained firing from the north and west. Beaumarchais's division was speeding along the only possible lines of retreat, King Henri leading one attack and the General the other as they closed in upon the hapless foe. The Kaiser saw them, and made no reply to Von Gossler. He looked behind, to see a French cavalry division ride furiously into the valley from the south, intent upon completing the ruthless work so fearfully cut out for them by the motors, from which, too, long lines of infantry, fresh as though drawn up for parade inspection, were beginning to emerge.

Then he answered.

Forcing out the words with desperate calmness, he said : " Yes, Von Gossler, we can do something. We can stop useless butchery. Go with a flag of truce to Vansittart. Tell him I will meet him in the village here ! "

CHAPTER XXXV

JEROME AND WILHELM

THE German Chief of the Staff was far too good a soldier not to know when the game was up. He bowed in silent acceptance of the Kaiser's command, and at once sought the means to execute it. But a flag of truce is not usually carried as part of the equipment of an imperial army corps. From a farmhouse on the road he obtained a small white table-cloth. He was about to run his sword through the end when his nerve forsook him. With a cry of bitter rage he dashed the weapon to the ground. Then he snatched a lance from a Uhlan orderly, and rode off with his significant banneret.

He did not go straight along the ridge, the most direct way to the French centre, but cut across country diagonally into the valley. By this means he hoped to stop the advancing French cavalry and prevent the horrible massacre, for it could be naught else, which must ensue if once the horsemen got mixed up with the stricken German troops. Fortunately he was in time.

Montsaloy, riding at the head of the leading regiment, the 18th Chasseurs, caught sight of the solitary officer dashing down the hillside, and checked the order trembling on his lips which would convert a steady gallop into a charge. As the courier of peace drew near, Montsaloy recognised him. The mere fact that General von Gossler himself carried the merciful signal showed the gravity of his errand, and the French cavalry leader brought his brigade to a halt, the rest

24

of the division pulling up in rotation as the loud command passed from squadron to squadron.

When the two officers met, Von Gossler begged the other to conduct him at once to Vansittart, and to delay the advance of the French cavalry until the *pour-parlers* had taken place. Montsaloy felt that he assumed a grave responsibility, but he was assured that the kindly hearted American would sanction a proposal intended to prevent useless bloodshed. Leaving instructions with his second in command to forthwith resume the charge if any manifestly hostile move were made by the enemy, he accompanied Von Gossler towards the place where he had last seen the millionaire.

But Vansittart, too, had noticed the flag of truce and the sudden halt of the French cavalry. Before the envoy had travelled a hundred yards with his escort, Jerome rode up, followed by every officer who could invent the slightest pretext for accompanying him.

They galloped on amidst the wild cheers of the cavalry division, for the news travelled like lightning through the ranks that the Kaiser had capitulated. It was barely eleven o'clock, on a bright, cloudless day of late summer, and the magnificence of the spectacle afforded by the glittering staff and the thousands of mounted soldiers on the field formed a picture which impressed itself vividly on the memory of all who were privileged to witness it.

The most notable figure of all was that of Vansittart himself.

Attired in a simple tweed coat, riding-breeches, and boots, with a broad-brimmed felt hat to shield his eyes from the sun, and carrying no more offensive weapon than a riding-whip, he sat gracefully the powerful charger that bore him on this short but eventful journey, quietly acknowledging the vociferous plaudits of his gallant troops as he passed.

"I am commissioned by his Majesty, the German Emperor, to ask you to meet him in the village of Verzy, and arrange terms of surrender," said Von Gossler, when he drew near to the spot where Vansittart halted.

Jerome bowed, but before he could reply the German officer continued :

" In view of an immediate and peaceful settlement, I ventured to ask General Montsaloy to defer the cavalry charge he was conducting, and which could only achieve the useless butchery of our demoralised men."

" General Montsaloy did well to accede to your humane wishes," said Vansittart. " But I cannot meet the German Emperor immediately. You must acknowledge, General, that you are utterly defeated. It would be needless cruelty to prolong the conflict."

" Certainly, monsieur. That is why I am deputed by his Majesty, my master, to arrange an immediate meeting."

" Ah! Permit me to conclude. The only possible preliminary to negotiations is the instant surrender of your whole force. No ! Pray do not argue. Every moment is of importance. I quite understand that you personally cannot accept my proposal. General Montsaloy and the members of my staff will ride with you to the Emperor, learn his decision, and act in accordance with it. If he is agreeable to my suggestion these officers will convey to every French division my orders to cease hostilities, whilst commanders will individually receive the submission and carry out the disarmament of those German corps nearest to them. This part you must see to on your side. If the Emperor declines the battle must proceed."

Jerome's determined words showed to Von Gossler the futility of further discussion. The millionaire repeated his explicit instructions to his staff, and the party rode off rapidly towards Verzy.

On the return journey Von Gossler had further evidence of the German collapse. All the disintegrated divisions were now gathering pell-mell on that centre. A few officers had collected some of their men, and were hastily striving to put the place in some sort of condition for defence. A bridge or two had been blown up to obstruct the motors, and other preparations made for a final stand.

They were worse than useless.

Verzy was commanded on every side by artillery fire, and long-range musketry would render the place an absolute inferno if once the Germans showed fight against the iron ring that encompassed them.

"A Prussian Sedan!" muttered the veteran to himself as he rode at the head of the French officers, still carrying the white flag in order to shield himself and his companions from possible attack by his own troops.

Vansittart watched the small body of horsemen until they disappeared among the trees of the village. He eagerly listened to the ceaseless crackle of small-arms and the roar of the opposing batteries, hoping against hope that each minute would work a diminution of the firing, for he loathed the unnecessary loss of life that must now be taking place. At last it came. The French guns to the west went out of action, and even as the lull deepened Montsaloy spurred back down the valley waving his helmet.

The Emperor had yielded after a bitter struggle. It was one thing to come to terms with the enemy whilst leading a powerful though defeated force; it was another to surrender unconditionally, and learn the victor's demands without ability to deny or abate them. But Vansittart had resolved that the war should cease that day, if it cost the life of the Kaiser himself and of every man in his army who faced the French with armed hands.

This struggle of peaceful peoples had gone far enough. It was a combat founded on the boastful arrogance of one individual. The masses in France and Germany required nothing more than good government, security of life, and liberty to follow their homely and commercial pursuits. The militarism of the Continent, he well knew, arose from the necessities of dynasties, and not from the antagonism of races.

This monster of civilisation must have its neck broken, and he would not flinch from the task, no matter what the cost. His emotions may well be understood, therefore, when he at least felt certain that the Kaiser had adopted the wise and more humane course. He listened in silence to Mont-saloy's enthusiastic account of the proceedings in the village, where Wilhelm, surrounded by his principal officers, met Von Gossler and heard the ultimatum.

Then he bent in the saddle, and scribbled a telegram to Evelyn announcing the victory.

"Here," he said to Arizona Jim, who had never left Jerome's side since they departed from Verdun; "take this to the field-telegraph. Let it have precedence of all other messages."

Soon the King came speeding up.

"It is glorious," he shrieked in a falsetto due to excitement; "France will again have her boundary on the Rhine!"

Vansittart smiled and acknowledged Henri's congratulations, but did not discuss matters beyond their general aspect; he waited until the King had calmed somewhat.

After a hasty luncheon Jerome attended to the details of the surrender, which was proceeding without undue difficulty. Von Gossler was again announced, to prefer a simple request that Vansittart should name the earliest hour at which it would suit his convenience to meet the Emperor.

Jerome fixed upon six o'clock, sending a short note to the Kaiser, asking him, as a favour, to summon the chief officers of the German force to the conclave.

Then he drew the King aside.

"I want to ask your Majesty," he said, "what, in your opinion, would have been the fate of France had I not taken control of affairs at the moment and in the manner I did."

Henri opened his eyes in wide astonishment.

"Surely that is an extraordinary question!" he cried.

"Not in the least. Pray tell me without reservation."

" Why, no one in his senses can doubt that the country would have been utterly subjugated and ruined, whilst the Germans would long since have occupied Paris. I was once idiot enough——"

" Thank you," interrupted Jerome. " Then I take it I may ask a reward ? "

Henri was so obviously mystified by his words that he continued : " I will at once explain. If France and yourself are so indebted to me, I may at least stipulate that the settlement of the terms of peace shall be left unreservedly in my hands."

" Surely, Vansittart, they can be entrusted to none so competent."

" Is that a bargain, then ? "

" On my life and honour as a king."

They heartily shook hands on the compact, but Henri was puzzled at the millionaire's earnestness. He understood later.

At the appointed hour Vansittart and the King, attended by a brilliant suite and an escort of the 18th Chasseurs—if any other corps had accompanied Jerome there would have been a mutiny—approached the small chateau which served as the German headquarters.

They were received by Von Gossler, who forthwith conducted them to a room on the ground floor ; for the first time, Vansittart and Wilhelm were face to face.

The Emperor stood in the centre of the apartment, dignified and impassive, with his hands behind his back. His face was rigid, and although tanned by exposure, its dull pallor betrayed the agonised hours he had endured since the morning. Behind him, in compliance with Vansittart's request, were ranged the divisional officers of his army, and the heads of military departments. His sword and sabretache rested obtrusively against a chair.

For an awkward moment there was silence.

Then Von Gossler spoke. " This is M. Vansittart, your

" Then he bent in the saddle and scribbled a telegram to Evelyn announcing the victory."

Majesty," he said. As an afterthought he added : " Permit me also to announce the King of France."

The Kaiser inclined his head. " I am at a loss," he said, with even, metallic accents, " to know whether to present my sword to the King or to the man who makes and unmakes kings."

" To the King ! " said Vansittart, whereupon Wilhelm handed his sword to Henri, who gravely received it.

" And now tell me your resolves, monsieur." The Kaiser turned and looked Vansittart square in the eyes.

" I am here for that purpose. They are brief and to the point. I require the prompt capitulation of the German forces now stationed west of the Rhine, when, after the requisite formalities, all officers and men will be at once free to return to their homes. I also require you to sign a treaty of peace, leaving the delimitation of the frontier between France and Germany to the mayors of twelve French and German towns, six to be nominated by you and six by me. These gentlemen will be asked, in addition, to devise such means as they think fit to prevent further trouble in regard to frontier affairs, both countries binding themselves to accept such recommendations without cavil or complaint."

An absolute buzz of amazement ran through the room at this extraordinary proposal. Men looked at each other in wonder when Vansittart ceased speaking. Henri was as much astonished as anyone, whilst Wilhelm, flushing red with angry surprise, at last blurted out :

" Do I understand, monsieur, that you ask me to leave the dismemberment of my Empire to the vagaries of a parcel of municipal councillors ? "

" Yes, your description will serve."

" And if I refuse ? "

" I will no longer leave the question to you, but to your people and Parliament."

The reply staggered the Emperor. Such a course of procedure meant the disappearance of the House of Hohenzollern. The pallor returned to his cheeks as he said :

"In the name of the saints, why mayors?"

"Because it may be fairly assumed that they represent the mass of the people, without whose taxes and military service it would be impossible for such as you to plunge peacefully disposed nations into the horrors of war."

The Kaiser swept aside this all-sufficing answer. With intense bitterness of tone he said, turning to his staff : "You hear, gentlemen. This is the first instalment. The second will doubtless deal with indemnity."

Vansittart produced a cigar-case, cut the end off a cigar, and lit it, before he said, with the utmost coolness :

"There will be no indemnity. God forbid that I should fine your unfortunate people because of your blunders."

Such an announcement was the last thing that Wilhelm expected from his noteworthy antagonist's lips. During the long torture of suspense since the surrender, he had estimated the French demands to be assuredly even greater than the two hundred millions sterling his grandfather had wrung from suffering France in 1871. It was such a payment that he feared most. Already Germany was resentful of military imposts. What would his people say, what would they do, when they learnt that his folly had robbed them of a colossal sum?

Yet this American calmly told him that no indemnity would be demanded. Involuntarily he murmured :

"You are a marvellous man, M. Vansittart."

Jerome, irritated slightly by the Kaiser's fitfulness, merely nodded his appreciation of the compliment.

Wilhelm had perforce to continue the conversation.

"Notwithstanding your last remarkable concession, M. Vansittart, I cannot accept your terms. It is impossible that the Emperor of Germany should consent to expose any part of his dominions to the bartering of a set of provincial mayors, excellent though these gentlemen may be."

"You forget that France likewise submits to their arbitrament. I should have the utmost faith in their collective good sense."

" Pooh, it is out of the question."

The millionaire picked up his hat and riding-whip, which he had placed on a chair.

"Then further discussion is unnecessary," he said. "Have I your Majesty's word that neither you nor the members of your staff present will attempt to escape ? Or must I place you under restraint ? "

The Kaiser flared out again into animation :

" It is matterless to me what you do. My unbeaten troops still hold the field, in French territory, too. I will pay the full price of my transgressions. I abdicate in favour of my son. My brother, Prince Henry of Prussia, will carry on the campaign, and mayhap yet crush your *protégés* and disappoint your magniloquent theories."

The King of France stamped impatiently on the floor. He would have retorted angrily had not Vansittart's restraining look plainly said :

" Remember your promise."

From the German officers came murmurs of indignation showing how they chafed at the situation.

Jerome directly addressed them.

" So," he said, " you share your headstrong leader's view. You still hold your opponents in such feeble esteem that you believe your armies in Lorraine to be superior to circumstances. Let me undeceive you. To-day your expedition, consisting presumably of your picked troops, was beaten by less than half its numbers. Only one-third of my men were in the field when you were hopelessly crippled. You have seen the value of the motors in action, and I tell you emphatically that if my demands are not acceded to fully within the hour, all my available force will march to-night for the frontier. To-morrow General Kreuznach will be asked to defeat the same combination that you have already found irresistible. What will be the result ? "

The Emperor broke in. " I have abdicated," he cried. " A German Emperor in the clutches of the enemy can at least refuse to betray his country."

" What care I for your abdication?" was the scornful retort. " An Emperor is no more to me than the driver of a baggage mule. It is of Germany I am thinking, not of her puppet ruler. Beware, sir, lest the German people lose a dynasty as well as a province."

The two men were but a couple of paces apart during this impassioned dialogue. The stubborn Saxon nature in each shone from their resolute blue eyes. Wilhelm's attitude showed that if the vital issues before them could be determined by strangling his opponent he would gladly make the attempt—Vansittart's, that he entertained profound contempt for a monarch who cared little if he brought his country to degradation in order to gratify his personal pride.

How the meeting would have terminated had it gone on unchecked in this fashion no man in the room was afterwards able to say. The effect of another angry phrase or biting retort might have shaken Europe to its foundations.

But a dramatic *finale* was at hand.

A sudden commotion drew all eyes to the door, which was violently flung open, revealing a German aide-de-camp, struggling ineffectually beneath the giant grip of Arizona Jim.

" Come off, you sausage-eatin' shrimp," yelled Bates. " When I wants ter see my boss every Dutchman in the Fatherland hez got ter quit. See, sauerkraut?" and he threw the officer in a heap into the passage.

" Why, what 's the matter, Jim?" cried Vansittart.

" A telegram fur you, guv'nor. An' when General le Breton says quick he means quick. So here it is, if there was forty bloomin' Emperors in the room." Jim glanced with fiery disdain from his fallen adversary to the Kaiser.

Wilhelm had already heard a good deal of Arizona Jim, whose fame was great throughout the Continent, particularly since his ride through the German lines at Troyon. He surveyed him for a moment before he said to Vansittart :

" Your servants adopt the masterful methods of their employer, it appears."

" Emperors are of small consequence to an American, anyway. Leave us, Jim. Wait for me outside."

Jerome handed the telegram to the Kaiser, continuing : " Possibly this may influence your decision."

The Emperor disdainfully took the little bit of flimsy paper. He read its contents twice before he seemed to fully comprehend their purport. Then his customary pallid complexion assumed an ashen hue. He visibly trembled. Even his voice shook as he murmured : " Can this be true ? "

" On my honour," said Vansittart, " it is sent for my information, and I have no reason to doubt its accuracy. Indeed, it only obeys my order and fulfils my expectation."

Wilhelm dropped listlessly into a chair, to bury his face in his hands ; the slanting rays of the sinking sun, striking in patches through the low diamond-framed windows of the room, showed great drops of perspiration glistening on his forehead.

All else wondered what the fateful intelligence could be that had such potent effect, for even Vansittart, notwithstanding his powers of self-control, betrayed unusual emotion.

The square-shouldered, plank-like Germans stood in rivetted attention, whilst the King of France almost whispered : " What is it ? "

The little King's eager curiosity brought a smile to Jerome's grave lips. He stooped to pick up the telegram from the floor, where it had fallen from the Emperor's nerveless fingers.

" I will read it aloud," he said.

And this is what he read :

" Metz is ours ; the tricolour floats again above its walls. Whilst our attack on Kreuznach was developing, I formed strong column for the assault of Metz, and carried position after position with astounding ease. The gallant troops of France would not be gainsaid. Fighting in outskirts still proceeding; but we are firmly established in the town itself, and in the forts to west and south. Kreuznach will probably make desperate efforts to recapture Metz; but I am confident of ability to hold him off pending further orders. Have just heard of your great victory. Most hearty congratulations.

"DAUBISSON."

Not even German military decorum could withstand this momentous news. The staff-officers broke out into strong guttural ejaculations, but Vansittart stayed them by a wave of his hand.

"Now, your Majesty, which is it to be? Am I to march to complete Daubisson's *coup*, or do you accept my terms, frankly and fully?"

"I have abdicated," groaned Wilhelm, without rising.

"Nonsense. Withdraw your hasty words. You are far too great a man, far too brave to desert your post when the clouds have gathered over your country. Come, you have lost the game. Make the best of it. If I know aught of your character you will be more truly a monarch in adversity than when you were free to follow your own unhindered impulse. But you must decide at once. The time for parley has passed. One or other of us must act."

Wilhelm dropped his hands and looked around.

"Very well. Be it so," he said; "but soldiers, not mayors, shall utter the first word. Gentlemen, you are cognisant of all that has happened. Am I to answer 'Yes' or 'No' to M. Vansittart?"

No member of his staff took the initiative.

"Nay," cried the Emperor, "out with it. I yield to the majority. Which is it to be, Von Gossler?"

"Yes," came the firm answer.

"And you, Grüdenau?"

"Yes."

He named them all individually. Each man agreed, though some of the voices were tremulous with grief. It was a bitter sequel to the war of '70–'71 for the veterans of Mars-la-Tour and Sedan.

" Good," said the Emperor, rising from his chair. " I will make the best of it, M. Vansittart. There is my hand on it."

" And with the King of France ! " said Jerome, accepting the proffered handshake.

" With the King of France, by all means."

But they were continental monarchs, so Wilhelm and Henri embraced.

" Now," cried Wilhelm, from whom a great depression had seemingly passed in an instant, " what is the best way to set about it ? "

" After your Majesty has signed a document briefly reciting our agreement, I will have much pleasure in giving you and these other gentlemen every facility for rejoining your army on the frontier. You can, like me, telegraph orders to suspend hostilities until your arrival."

" But what if I fail ? What if my men refuse to obey me ? "

" That will mean your abdication in grim earnest. I do not, however, anticipate your failure. It was in order to strengthen your hands that I desired your staff to be present at this interview."

After a moment's thought Wilhelm said : " You are a generous man, M. Vansittart."

" Not so generous as your Majesty has been to an adversary who hit harder than is possible in the battle-field."

This was the first allusion by either to the Emperor's action with regard to Evelyn. Those simple words did much to make smooth the future way.

" And these mayors ? When do they meet ? " The Kaiser did not yet take kindly to the stipulation. It still rankled.

" The day after to-morrow, at Metz."

" So soon ! We meet there to ratify their—their verdict ? "

" Assuredly. You will think better of mayoral intelligence when they have ended their sitting."

" Then I am ready to start forthwith."

Some writing materials were produced, the preliminary treaty drawn up and signed, and some telegrams despatched. As he laid down his pen the Kaiser said :

" I would ask one small favour. Let me see one of your infernal motor-cars."

In the growing twilight the whole party trooped out together, to find the French soldiers in Verzy cheerfully preparing rations for themselves and their captives.

The vanquished at least realised the superiority of the victors in one respect : they did not dream of disputing their pre-eminence as cooks.

CHAPTER XXXVI

WHEN the bells of Paris clanged out the joyful news that the war was over their cheerful peal did not lift the gloom from Folliet's soul. He could not find Ribou.

Paris, that huge barometer where humanity provides a more suitable element than mercury, was now "set fair." The Communists had been shovelled into pits, for the most part, and the only visible records of the revolution were the gaunt walls of the Tuileries, some few wrecked buildings, and a large number of new mortar patches, breast-high, showing the bullet marks in the stucco in those streets where the fighting had taken place.

Beyond these trivial disfigurements, soon to be remedied by the builder and Time, the City of Light wore her wonted aspect when her lively inhabitants declare themselves *en fête*.

When Folliet had assured himself that the news in the papers was true—that the Germans had really capitulated at Verzy, and Metz was occupied—he gave no further heed to affairs of state. These he knew to be quite safe in Vansittart's hands ; the paramount question with him was the hiding-place of Ribou, that arch-plotter, that repository of intrigue.

He guessed, and rightly, as it transpired, that the ex-minister was still in Paris. The retreat which had been proved so reliable would not be readily given up. If the man attempted to leave France he would try to slip the hounds when the chase had cooled, and not at a moment when each post, each frontier train, was carefully searched by detectives well acquainted with his identity.

Every artifice known to the Prefecture was tried in vain to discover his hidden abode.

Theoretically, the Paris police can at once lay hands upon any person they want. The residents of every house in the city, their occupations, names, ages, and habits, are supposed to be known to the officers of the law. But it is precisely in the exception to an otherwise admirable system that the real difficulty lies. There are nearly three hundred thousand houses in Paris. By the theory, they were all incapable of shielding Ribou from police scrutiny ; in practice, he might be in any of them.

Such of his accomplices as had escaped being shot were in custody, but the offers of rewards and pardons were unavailing to attain the desired object. Ribou had as sedulously concealed his temporary dwelling-place from his associates as from the police. Many had seen him before and during the *émeute*, all testified to his direction and control, but none knew where he lived.

Folliet had to confess himself baffled, and with the unpleasant admission came the still less consoling thought that very probably Armand Duprés would lay hands on Ribou in a day if he were so minded.

" Now how would Armand set to work ? " said Folliet to himself. " Let me try to be *en rapport* with his methods. Let me see. He would surely start by consuming quantities of Argonne."

So Folliet purchased a dozen of superb Argonne, made himself very ill, and got no nearer truth. Finally he pocketed his pride and sent the following telegram to Armand at Verdun :

" I want you to come and help me to find Ribou. He is hidden in Paris. Wire me when to expect you."

In due course came the reply :

"Leaving Verdun this afternoon. Will reach Prefecture to-morrow evening at seven, for dinner. See that the '73 champagne is in ice for forty minutes. It gives wings to the soul."

"The rascal has changed his wine," grumbled Folliet. "And why does he require thirty hours for the journey if he departs from Verdun at once? Ah, if I could only catch Ribou before he arrives!"

But Armand came, and there was no news of Ribou.

With Armand was Marie, for Dick Harland, now recovered from the blow he received in the inn, had brought his sister's retinue to Verdun, so Marie's services were no longer required. Besides, Marie was now the wife of a rich man.

At the Prefecture they were conducted by Folliet to his private apartments. The manager of the Café Riche had charge of the dinner—his standing with the police depended upon the excellence of the wine—so even Armand's exquisite taste was satisfied.

"You find it good?" said Folliet, more hopefully than he had spoken for days, when Armand set down his glass with an approving smile.

"Superb. Mere wealth should not be able to purchase the like. It should be reserved for men of undoubted genius."

"And you think——"

"I think Marie should drink it more heartily. You are weary, my sweet. Drink, and fear not."

"I passed a restless night," murmured Marie. "I hate to be left alone."

"Monsieur Duprés quitted Verdun before you, then?" said Folliet, who could never resist the chance of putting a leading question.

"Yes! He went off like a rocket after receiving your message. We met at Chalons to-day en route."

" And may I ask where you went, monsieur ? "

" Certainly. To Metz." Armand answered the query as though he had announced a commonplace outing to Versailles.

" To Metz ! "

" Where else ? Did you not say that you wished me to help you in the hunt for Ribou ? Come, monsieur, you do not yourself do justice to the wine. Fill up ! "

" I drank some—some Burgundy the other evening that disagreed with me. But why Metz ? "

" Ah, you should be careful. There are many varieties of red wine. Now, Argonne, as you know——"

" Is marvellous in its effects at times. But pray tell me, why Metz ? "

" Where else would you seek traces of Ribou ? In Berlin, possibly, but surely not in Paris."

Folliet puzzled his brains until he thought he had caught the drift of Armand's philosophy.

" Well, perhaps," he said, " it was a good idea to get hold of Ribou's German acquaintances. They might know more than we. Were you successful ? "

Armand laughed boisterously as he called for another bottle. " Metz is a mere figure of speech. I passed my spare hours there in ordinary sightseeing. With others, I gaped at the Kaiser, who awaits the conference of mayors. That is a very clever idea of Vansittart's, I can tell you. Those fellows will think more of trading facilities than of manœuvres."

" Do you mean to say, then, that you did not even try to get hold of one of Ribou's agents—that fellow Hans Schwartz, for instance ? "

The other looked steadily at Folliet, with amused cynicism in his bright eyes. " No," he said; " I did not see Schwartz. I hardly spoke to a soul. Yet you are shrewd, Folliet. You plod along the track of a comet in the effort to discover its direction. Why do you never soar into the empyrean ? I told you that the champagne of '73 gave wings to genius."

" Then you learnt nothing of Ribou at Metz ? "

" Not a word. I never mentioned his name. Indeed, I hardly thought of him."

" But why the devil did you go there ? "

" Merely to oblige you, my friend. You asked me to help you, so I went to Metz and here I am."

" *Mille tonnerres!* I see that. But where is Ribou ? "

Armand drank another deep draught. " I will tell you," he said slowly, " before eleven o'clock to-morrow, if it is a clear day. If it is misty, no. But before eleven o'clock on the first clear day."

Notwithstanding all previous experience this was too much for Folliet. He laughed sarcastically :

" Do you require a telescope, then, monsieur ? "

Armand pondered. He answered the question at random.

" No, hardly a telescope ; it is a difficult instrument to adjust rapidly, and covers too small a field—but good opera-glasses, yes."

" This is beyond a joke," growled Folliet, now quite sure that Duprés was mad, and that his former powers of divination were the last glowing embers of the fire that illumined his strange soul.

" My husband never jokes," purred Marie, complacently. " At least, never when he speaks seriously."

The angelic Marie made her awkward confession of faith with an air of conviction that was galling to the Prefect.

" Opera-glasses ! " he cried. " Nonsense ! Why not a microscope, or a kite ? "

Armand toyed with his glass. " Poor Folliet," he murmured. " There will ever be a Didymus who does not believe because he cannot see."

And not one other word on the subject near to his heart could the Prefect draw from him during the course of the meal.

At last the visitors rose to go. Folliet allowed his anxiety to master his growing wrath.

"Tell me, at least," he said, "what I may expect to-morrow."

Duprés turned upon him suavely. "You had nearly lost Ribou, M. Folliet. I am glad to learn that you still trust me. Have you one of those maps of Paris in which the larger buildings are indicated by small profile drawings?"

The Prefect, still anxious to probe the mystery that hung round Armand's utterances, sent out an attendant, and the man soon brought the sheet described.

Armand examined it closely for some moments, paying special heed to the heights marked opposite each notable structure. He marked several of these and placed the map in his pocket, saying :

"To-morrow, Folliet, at nine o'clock, I will be here. I hope you will meet me, or, at any rate, detail eight of your smartest men to await my instructions. Let them be men of keen eyes, and—yes—see that they possess good opera-glasses. But only if it be a clear day. If the atmosphere is dull and hazy I do not come. At 9 A.M. on the first clear day. Good-bye."

Marie tucked her arm under Armand's and they trotted off, the happiest and queerest couple in Paris.

Folliet fumed a good deal, yet he drew his blinds early next morning with eager outlook for the weather. It was superb. Slight rain overnight had cooled and clarified the air. Smokeless Paris was bathed in bright sunshine.

Curiously enough, the pleasant aspect of nature restored Folliet's confidence. He remembered Armand's apparently miraculous deductions from the mere appearance of a bottle of wine on the table of a country inn, and he reflected that he had not paid sufficient heed overnight to the harmless variety of this enthusiastic compound of genius and poetry. So it was in humbler frame of mind that he awaited Armand's arrival at the Prefecture. A few minutes later Duprés appeared, followed by a cabman who carried a large wicker-work crate.

Folliet gazed fixedly at the basket as the man dumped it down on the floor ; from its interior came the flutter of wings and the soft cooing of pigeons. Then the clever policeman thumped his head viciously. At last he understood.

" So," he said, " if you did not see Herr Schwartz, you saw his house."

" Yes. I listened with interest to your story of the Rue Pigalle. It escaped you that the pigeons at Gravelotte might fly to other quarters of Paris than Montmartre."

" It did."

" And that pigeons might yet fly from Paris to Gravelotte."

" Trust me, I will never doubt you again."

Folliet was humbled. He now knew how news could travel so rapidly between the frontier and the capital at a time when every known source of communication was wholly in his power.

" As a matter of fact," laughed Armand, " Schwartz visited his farm nightly and fed his pigeons. The supply of grain showed that. He would swear badly last night, for I brought them all away."

" Oh, yes, I want to hear no more. Let us be quick, quick."

" Then lead me to your staff of assistants."

In the bureau Armand addressed the detectives.

" You will each go at once," he said, " to the buildings I will allot to you individually, mount to the top, and at 10.15 sharp keep a careful lookout for a solitary pigeon that may fly towards you from the Eiffel Tower. Should you see such a bird, watch intently to see where it goes. Mark the building with the utmost exactitude. If you cannot distinguish the building, note the direction taken by the bird. In either event, return here at once. Those who see no bird at all can return at eleven o'clock."

The men signified their full comprehension of their instructions, and started in cabs for their posts. Folliet and

Armand drove at spanking pace to the Tour d'Eiffel. Here the Prefect's authority secured them a quick ascent. They reached the public summit, and climbed thence by a ladder and trap-door to the topmost point of that remarkable structure.

Armand sniffed the keen air jealously. "How it invigorates!" he cried. "No wonder the Tibetan Buddhists have won fame for their capacity of taking thought. Marie and I must buy a villa in the Alps."

"Oh, come, help to liberate these birds." Folliet was scrutinising his watch and it was nearly the appointed time.

Armand sighed. "I shall never make a philosopher of you, Folliet." Yet even he bent to the crate with some show of eagerness, for his theory was about to be put to the test.

Folliet secured a pigeon, tenderly caressed its wings, and threw it out from the Tower. The graceful bird, dazed by its imprisonment and unexpected height from the ground, fluttered uncertainly for a few seconds. It then began a gradually increasing spiral flight, and after a few wide sweeps made off towards the chapel-crowned hill of Montmartre.

Both men ejaculated : "The Rue Pigalle !"

In the second essay the pigeon, keeping high in the air, darted swiftly eastwards. Through their glasses they could distinctly see it covering the districts of Charonne and Montreuil.

"To Gravelotte !" cried Folliet.

"Possibly. Let us try again."

The third messenger also fled eastward, but, as they watched, it paused in its flight, and circled gradually lower over the Temple district.

"Glorious !" roared Folliet. "Let us be off."

But Armand was visibly annoyed. He resented Folliet's encouraging grasp on his arm. "Associating with you," he growled, "has had a deteriorating effect. Fool that I am !"

" Why ? " gasped the other.

" I should have doubled or trebled the men stationed to the east. That man on the Hotel de Ville tore off to the Prefecture long before the second pigeon passed."

" Well, well, we have localised Ribou. We will try again from the Hotel de Ville."

" True ; but I said eleven o'clock. It will be noon, or more, before you lay hands on Ribou."

This fine point of honour was lost on the excited Prefect. They descended, with the remaining birds ; Folliet flushed with anticipation, Armand sulky and careless of developments.

When they reached the rendezvous it was exactly as Duprés had predicted. The detective could only report the pigeon that soared off to the familiar loft near the Bois d'Oignons, nearly two hundred miles away.

Armand refused to go to the roof of the Hotel de Ville. He had an appointment with Marie for *déjeûner* at the Grand Hotel. The fate of Ribou weighed little in the scale against Marie's deferred breakfast.

He was glad afterwards that he escaped the scene that took place later.

From the leads of the Town Hall it was an easy matter to learn the exact harbour of the second pigeon that hovered over the Temple.

" La Rue des Fourmiers, the third house from the end ! " shouted Folliet and one of his men simultaneously. They rushed thither, calling to their aid every policeman they passed on the way.

It was a tall, dingy building, with close-shuttered windows, locked door, and the significant placard *To Let* on its walls.

" Smash in the door," said the Prefect, and a crowd gathered like dust in a whirlwind at the unusual spectacle of a number of policemen furiously butting at the solid planks.

Soon the door yielded and the men poured inside, each striving against the other for distinction beneath the eye of the Prefect. They dashed up the dark and narrow stairway, but Folliet paused a moment to leave a guard on the door, and to see that there was no available exit to the rear.

It was well for him that he did so.

Shots resounded in quick succession down the well of the stairs, with wild trampings on the loose boards, and the cries of wounded men.

Springing up and up, until his breath was almost spent, Folliet heard more firing, and oaths, whilst a familiar voice bellowed :

"Where is Folliet? Send him here. I yield to none other."

Stumbling over the corpse of one policeman and the wounded bodies of two others, the wiry little Prefect gained the topmost landing. Through the open door of the attic he saw Ribou, standing with his back to a wide casement, whilst the last of the detectives crouched, watching him, behind the jamb of the door.

"Be careful, sir," cried the man. "I am unarmed, and he has two chambers of his revolver loaded."

But Ribou's furious tones rang out. "Ha, ha, my friend. You are there. Let me greet you!"

He fired and Folliet's preliminary jump just saved his life.

Ribou swore coarsely when he saw he had missed. He advanced to make sure of the next shot. But the crouching detective was a man of resource. He had taken off his boot, and now hit the infuriated murderer in the chest with this heavy missile.

Involuntarily Ribou's hand clenched, and the last bullet spent itself harmlessly in the plaster.

Folliet and the detective sprang forward simultaneously. Ribou was too quick for them.

He gave a fierce yell—half-laugh, half-groan. "Not yet, Folliet," he roared, and jumped bodily through the window.

For an instant Folliet thought that his enemy had devised some means of escape. But a glance in the street showed that the unfortunate conspirator had sought the last solace of desperate humanity. He had thrown himself from the attic of a six-story house, and the gaping crowd in the street were now gazing alternately at the ghastly lump on the pavement and up into the air as though they expected another body to come hustling downwards.

In such a matter the Prefect of Police was case-hardened.

" He has saved much trouble," he murmured, turning to give aid to the men wounded by the Communist leader. Whilst crossing the room he heard a rustle of wings, and for the first time saw two pigeons tremulously perched on a closed cage.

The first bird had puzzled Ribou ; the second alarmed him. Two minutes after its arrival he heard his death-knell in the police assault upon his door.

Folliet called at the Grand Hotel to acquaint Armand with the details.

The great man had breakfasted well. A café and cognac had restored his equanimity. He listened unmoved to the description of Ribou's terrible plunge through space.

" Ah, Folliet ! " he said, leaning back contentedly in his chair, " neither of you had wings ! "

CHAPTER XXXVII

THE selection of the twelve mayors who were to constitute the world-renowned Council of Metz was not
such an easy matter when the representatives of
France and Germany came to tackle it in earnest.

In the first case it was necessary that the six Frenchmen
should speak German, and the six Germans French, to insure
a thorough exchange of ideas preparatory to the compilation
of a joint report.

When the bilingual lists were drawn up, giving the names
of every man thus qualified, the leaders on both sides passed
some anxious hours in picking out those dignitaries most
likely to preserve a judicial frame of mind. Thus, it was
discovered, at the eleventh hour, that the excellent Mayor
of Cretonne was an enthusiastic Alsatian. His admitted
prejudices hopelessly barrred him. The Germans learnt,
too, that the esteemed Burgomaster of Schatsalp-von-Dumpf-
stück, a local magnate of admitted merit, was an ardent
Socialist. He was ruled out.

At last, amidst much speculation by their fellow-country-
men, and objects of close attention by Europe and America,
the chosen twelve assembled in the Town Hall of Metz.

Here they were received by Vansittart and the two monarchs. After the worthy gentlemen had been hospitably
entertained, the millionaire addressed them.

"Gentlemen," he said, "the problem submitted to your
devoted attention is perhaps the most serious that any human
conclave was ever yet asked to solve. Two great nations,

which geographically and ethnologically are wholly distinct, have lived for a generation in hourly dread of the war which has just been brought to a close. Why? Because of the constant rankling in the breast of each of the wound left open by the campaign of 1870–71. Other considerations I sweep aside. I do not admit that so-called social or hereditary feuds can live in the electric glare of modern progress. The world is more than big enough for every Frenchman and every German. I am absolutely convinced that the heart's desire of every true patriot in both countries is to see his land prospering in peace and freed from the curse of militarism."

An unmistakable burst of applause from the delegates encouraged Vansittart, whilst Wilhelm II. took a keen interest in the shape of his left boot.

"I am glad to think that you are with me in this belief. I look to you with confidence to justify the trust I reposed in you when I asked the King of France and the German Emperor to submit to your arbitration the vital questions in dispute between them."

The King of France and the German Emperor both tried to look as though Jerome's way of putting the matter was strictly accurate. But the Mayor of Leipsic, who was a bit of a wag, winked solemnly at his *confrère* of Lyons, an old and valued business correspondent.

"What we propose—I speak with their Majesties' approval," went on Vansittart—"is that you shall meet forthwith in the apartments prepared for you. There, unfettered by diplomacy, unchecked by treaty or precedent, supplied only with writing materials and some excellent maps, you will proceed to draw up what I hope will be a unanimous decision as to the best means of finally settling the question of the natural frontier between France and Germany. You are a judicial tribunal, not a collection of special pleaders. The industrial masses of Germany have as much faith in the representatives of France as the people of

France have in those of Germany. Show neither fear nor favour. Your recommendations in the interests of peace cannot go too far, your guarantees cannot be too binding."

Vansittart's voice became unconsciously stern, almost menacing, as he uttered the last sentences. The assembled mayors looked at him only now, whilst Henri and the Kaiser wondered what he would say next. To their relief he added:

" Beyond this general counsel I cannot now proceed. Did I not hold a brief for France in this quarrel I would gladly assist at your deliberations, but the circumstances of the case render it impossible. I appeal to you to approach your grave duties in the spirit of traders rather than statesmen, as pioneers of progress, and not as soldiers holding back civilisation at the point of the bayonet. You have, on the honour of French and German ministers, been summoned hither without advice or instruction. You will remain so until you communicate to me that you have arrived at a unanimous agreement, or as near such a consummation as may be attainable. During your sitting, or sittings—for you may remain together for some days if you so desire—no one will be permitted to visit you nor hear from you. To all intents and purposes you will be a jury dealing with the most noteworthy verdict that ever yet jury was convened to consider. Strong in the conviction that the mayors of twelve enlightened cities will readily settle a vexed question which two terrible and disastrous wars have utterly failed to decide, I dismiss you to your task."

There was a moment's pause, when the strong staccato accents of the German Emperor sounded through the room :

" I have nothing to add to what M. Vansittart has said. May the spirit of" (by sheer force of habit he nearly said " my grandfather ") " of wisdom abide with you. Hoch ! "

Henri V. thought it incumbent to make his voice heard. " I drink to the frontier of peace and brotherly relations," he said, and the little King's happy phrase won general approval.

But the Mayor of Hamburg, a portly man who had enjoyed his *déjeûner*, had something on his mind.

" Do I understand you rightly, M. Vansittart," he inquired, " that we should be supplied with *nothing* but maps, pens, ink, and paper ? "

" Yes ; that is our intention."

" What ? Nothing *to eat ?* And we may sit for a week ! "

A general, if somewhat uneasy, laugh ran through the room. But Vansittart explained that, of course, ample provision would be made for meals and sleeping accommodations if such should be found necessary.

He thought he knew his men far too well for this contingency to arise. In the event he was right.

The mayors retired at one o'clock. At five the same evening the Mayor of Marseilles, who, by reason of seniority in years, had been elected spokesman for the others, sent messages to both camps to the effect that the council was ready with its report.

The intense curiosity that prevailed in the breasts of French and German statesmen brought them rapidly to the Hotel de Ville. Not alone Vansittart and the two monarchs, but every minister and prominent official who had the slightest claim to be present, put in an appearance, and the grand Salon of the Town Hall was filled with a brilliant and animated throng when the mayors solemnly filed in from their memorable conclave.

The exceeding brevity of their meeting, considering the vital nature of the questions at issue, excited general surprise, and no one could form the least idea as to the extent or nature of their findings.

" Have you unanimously agreed upon your recommendations, gentlemen ? " said Vansittart, and the query induced a profound silence in the crowded room.

" We have," said the Mayor of Marseilles.

Stepping forward he read, with clear and emphatic voice, the following :

" We, the undersigned mayors of twelve French and German cities, in pursuance of the great trust committed to our care, are unanimously of opinion :

" 1. That the province of Lorraine, as marked out by a reasonably straight line drawn from Donon in the Vosges Mountains to, but not including, the town of Saargemund, shall in future be French territory, the legal boundary to be fixed by a properly constituted commission.

" 2. That the province of Elsass, naturally defined by the watershed of the Vosges Mountains, shall remain German territory, with the addition of the small portion of Lorraine lying to the east of the line indicated in paragraph 1.

" 3. That all fortresses and defensive works of military significance within the limits of the said provinces of Lorraine and Elsass be forthwith levelled to the ground.

" 4. That all so-called strategic railways in both provinces shall be speedily linked together, and joined, where practicable, to the main lines of France and Germany, for the better development of commerce and the promotion of mutual intercourse.

" 5. That no officer of the army shall hold administrative positions in either of the provinces.

" 6. That no troops shall be stationed in large numbers, nor military stores or armaments collected, within 100 French kilometres of the new frontier line.

" 7. That the Customs and Police authorities of France and Germany shall be solely entrusted with the conduct of frontier regulations, which shall be framed only in regard to revenue and legal necessities.

" 8. That in all other respects there shall be free and uninterrupted passage between the two countries."

Then the Mayor read the names and designations of himself and his colleagues.

At once a buzz of eager comment arose.

" It means the dismantling of Strassbourg and Mulhausen," cried the Kaiser.

" We get Metz shorn of its defences, whilst Belfort, Verdun, and every fortress in the east of France must be torn to pieces," vociferated Henri.

" Preposterous," growled the German officers.

"Ridiculous," cried the Frenchmen.

Then everyone looked to Vansittart, who had meanwhile secured the report from the Mayor of Marseilles and had perused it with the aid of a small map.

Raising his head he obtained a hearing.

"I am glad to note," he said with a smile, "that nobody seems to be satisfied. There is no surer sign that these excellent gentlemen have tried to be just. Nay, more, they have succeeded in their efforts. Their award exceeds my utmost hopes, whilst it more than justifies the confidence I placed in them. They have given to France French Lorraine ; they have secured to Germany German Elsass. And because they have arrived at a conclusion outlined for them by natural law, they take stringent precautions lest the power of men to do ill deeds makes ill deeds done. Surely they have well acquitted themselves. If ever men deserved honour, these do. In a few hours, aided only by their common sense, they have achieved triumphs which two generations of statesmen and generals, backed by millions of soldiers, have wholly failed to achieve. My friends, think what it means. There are no longer Lost Provinces or hostile principalities. Let us marvel at their work rather than cavil at its methods. If we do, the whole world will join in our chorus of praise."

Such was the magnetism of Vansittart's character that his words evoked enthusiasm, and a hearty cheer broke out as he paused. Taking advantage of the moment he cried : "But the Mayor of Hamburg must be hungry. Let us dine !" And two hours later the Kaiser proposed his health with three "Hochs,"—a sign of complete and fraternal agreement.

The banquet had a bright feature in the presence of many distinguished ladies. The German Empress had come from Berlin to join her Royal Consort, and was now chatting amicably with the King of France on her right and Jerome on her left. The Kaiser, of course, did the honours to

Honorine, but he took care that the disposition of guests brought Evelyn to his left hand.

He entertained both with a vivacious account of Marie's memorable interview with him during Madame Vansittart's captivity. Nor did he spare himself.

" It was a great temptation to me to leave you in durance vile," he said. " But pray remember that I had not then seen you."

" What would have been the result if you had ? " laughed Evelyn.

" Well, to tell the honest truth, I would have known at once of your adventures ; your instant release would be ordered, and, hey, presto! the war must have ended sooner."

" Why ? "

" Because your husband is as irresistible in the field as you are in the Court. Were it not for the grace he gave me for a few days, I should probably have been beaten on the Rhine instead of in the interior of France."

" So the French troops count for nothing ? " Honorine's question savoured ever so slightly of resentment.

" No. Please do not so construe my intent. It was with French troops that M. Vansittart broke up the picked soldiers of Germany. But in these great wars the leader counts for more than army corps. Battalions are the chessmen ; it is the brain that directs their movements on the board that wins the fight."

Evelyn glanced lovingly at Jerome, who was at the moment entertaining the Empress with a lively account of the fat Mayor of Hamburg. " Yes," she said, " Jerome is the greatest man living."

" And I must add that you always believed in him." Honorine, much as she owed to the American, wished in her heart that Henri had done something, if ever so little, towards bringing the campaign to its glorious close.

The Kaiser was tactful enough to feel this. " After all, Madame Vansittart, the King of France and I had not your husband's opportunities. We were tied by convention and precedent ; he, by sheer might of intellect, sweeps obstacles from his path, whilst we have to find a way round them."

" I only know," replied Evelyn, " that he dreaded you as an opponent quite as much as he valued the wonderful assistance given to him by the King of France. He could never have done so well at the frontier had not the King sacrificed his own desires by remaining in Paris to control the important operations at the base."

Wilhelm stole a glance at meek little Evelyn. She had rounded his point so neatly that he changed the conversation.

When the royal party broke up, they acceded to the clamorous cries of the crowd in the street, and stood for a few moments on the balcony of the Town Hall.

The people cheered them vociferously, and small wonder. Dwellers in peaceful cities can never realise what the conclusion of hostilities means to the inhabitants of a town like Metz, the shuttlecock of mighty players at the awful game of war. The sentiments of every adult being in that frowning frontier fortress were those of a man who, condemned to torture and perhaps death, is suddenly set at liberty.

But in the crowd was one who nursed very different feelings.

Gazing with baleful eyes at Vansittart, whilst he fended the excited passers-by from off his maimed wrist, Hans Schwartz had the aspect of a demon. All his plans thwarted, himself a hopeless cripple, this revengeful plotter was no longer the quietly determined man who faced the German Emperor. He then hoped that the march of events might enable him to restore his name and position—perchance to square accounts with Folliet. The collapse of the revolution and the end of the war had come upon him like a bolt from the blue. There remained but the mad hope of revenge. He still knew how to strike Vansittart in a way that no council could alleviate, no king or emperor gainsay.

Now it befell that the citizens of Metz had organised a

26

torchlight procession. Arizona Jim, mingling with the crowd, took up his position, unnoticed, on the doorstep of a shop, and as the torch-bearers passed, the light illumined the evil face of Schwartz, standing a few paces to the right. Bates came as near to staring with surprise as he ever did in the course of a placidly eventful life. He saw imprinted on that animated page but one design, murder, and a second glance revealed its object.

" Phew," whistled Jim, hitching round his revolver. " There 's more trouble."

At last the group on the balcony disappeared, the crowd thinned, and Schwartz moved off with Jim after him. Through some narrow lanes they passed until they came to a square, with a large enclosed garden beyond, and dense trees. The night was clear and fine—one of those delicious continental evenings when people are tempted to stroll about long after ordinary hours. Bates saw the other climb the high iron railings with muttered curses, because of the pain thus caused to his injured limb. Once over, the man dived into the shrubbery. Bates, running like a deer, gained the fence in time to catch sight of Schwartz turning a laurel-shrouded corner. A quick climb, and a stealthy run on the grass, enabled the pursuer to get close to his quarry. The lights of a large building glittered close at hand and Schwartz hid behind a tree with thick brushwood at its roots.

" Gee whiz !" said Jim. " The Hotel de Ville ! I must get the drop on him, cert."

In this sort of business Arizona Jim was an expert. Many a time had he crawled over the prairie to take an Apache in flank. And here was a vicious Indian if ever there was one. " A good Injun is a dead Injun," and Hans Schwartz was surely dead if he attempted mischief. A minute after he had taken up his position the next tree in his rear sheltered an enemy who once before had tricked him when he apparently held the winning hand.

Schwartz was right in his surmise. Not many minutes

elapsed before doors were thrown open, stalwart men and beautiful women came trooping out over the lawns and paths, the scent of cigars and cigarettes mingled with more delicate perfumes came floating on the gentle breeze, and the pleasant jingle of spurred heels mixed with the frou-frou of silk. Quiet laughter and merry converse bubbled through the air. French and Germans were fraternising as though such things as battles did not exist. At last a group appeared before which all others unostentatiously melted. In front, Vansittart talked with Evelyn and the Countess von Gossler. Close behind came the others, blithely unconscious of the black death that lurked beneath the trees. Strolling unconcernedly onward they neared Schwartz's hiding-place, and Jim fingered the trigger of his revolver.

Said the Countess : " How glad you must be, Madame Vansittart, that this distressing conflict is done with ! We both must have suffered, but you, I am sorry to learn, far more than I."

" Yes," said Evelyn ; " it is so indeed. In your case, as in mine, the one person most thought of in the world was exposed to the risks of a severe campaign. But when I was carried off into Argonne, my keenest grief came from the knowledge that Jerome had to undergo the——"

A dark figure suddenly sprang from the leafy shades, a knife glittered in the rays of a distant lamp, a shot rang out, and a man doubled up on the pathway at the very feet of the affrighted women. The fallen assailant still clutched the knife, so Jerome put his foot on the weapon before he bent over him. As he did so, Jim Bates's well-known accents sounded close to him :

" Sorry to disturb the ladies, guv'nor, but I guessed he was up to mischief, so I followed him here." Coming closer, Jim said: " He's handin' in his checks this time, all right."

The whole scene had transpired so rapidly that Evelyn, half fainting, and the terrified Countess were hurried off before they were well aware of what had happened.

The Kaiser, stooping to look at the dying man's face, ex-claimed, " *Gott im Himmel*, it is Schwartz."

Schwartz tried to speak, but died in the effort.

" Well," said Wilhelm II., as he walked back to the house with Vansittart, " the incident has taught me a lesson. The next time I order a rascal to be hanged I will not change my mind. What a wonderful fellow this re-tainer of yours is ! By the way, why is he called Arizona Jim ? "

CHAPTER XXXVIII

A FAMILY MATTER

LEAVING Prime Minister Liancourt and Chancellor Hohenlohe to wrestle with budgets—for they who choose such tunes as a European war must pay many pipers—Vansittart transferred himself and his belongings across the Channel, to spend a quiet autumn at Evelyn's country home.

Tears stood in the eyes of Dick Harland and his sister when they gazed once more on the beautiful cottage in a little Devonshire village where they had passed their youthful years. But they were tears of thankfulness. This peaceful spot offered a delightful refuge after the turmoil of life during days of strife and nights of restless anxiety.

Besides, to gladden Evelyn's heart, were there not certain chubby Vansittarts shrieking with joy at the sight of " daddy " and " mammy " once more ? As for Jerome, he declared emphatically that for two solid months he would do nothing but smoke, read, eat, and sleep.

He kept his word. When the period of incubation was passed, he announced his intention of running over to New York, "just to see how things were getting on." So his dutiful wife gave orders to the servants, and the cottage— it would pass as a mansion in the suburbs of London—became a centre of activity.

On the eve of departure, Vansittart was sitting in a favourite nook of the garden, when Jim Bates sauntered up to him.

Jim's manner had not that air of perfect self-assurance which generally fitted so easily upon him. He was chewing a cigar, having forgotten to light it, and there was a subdued *timbre* in his voice as he uttered the familiar :

" Good evenin', guv'nor."

" Good evening, Jim. Have n't you got a match ? "

" Why, yes, but, Great Scott, how *kin* you hit upon a thing straight off like that ? "

" Like what ? I only wondered why you were carrying about an unlit cigar in your mouth."

" Eh, goldarn me, boss, but you 're a slick one." Jim struck a vesta, and puffed vigorously until he had burnt a quarter of an inch of tobacco.

Vansittart looked at him curiously. " What 's the matter, Jim ? There 's something on your mind."

" Well, guv'nor, I don't mind allowin' as how you 're right. You generally air right."

" Getting tired of this quiet life, eh ? Cheer up. We 're off to-morrow, and after I have seen to things in New York, Mr. Harland and you will come with me for a nice little winter shooting-trip in Canada. I am simply dying for a smell of the pine-woods once more."

Bates kept on smoking prodigiously, but he stammered :

" 'Tain't 'xactly that. You see, guv'nor "—then finding, Vansittart's eye on him, he failed in his resolution, and said : " Hev you heerd the news ? They say as how the Kaiser is dead stuck on goin' to Paris and knockin' the Tsar's visit sky-high."

" Look here, Jim ! " said Jerome. " It is not to tell me gossip about the Kaiser you have come. Sit down, and out with it."

Jim desperately threw away his cigar, sat down, clasped his sombrero to his right knee with both hands, and commenced :

" It 's this way. There 's a pore ole widder down there " —jerking his thumb towards the neighbouring village—" as lives very quiet an' homelike. I 've took quite a likin' to her, an'——"

" How old is she ? "

" Gettin' on for sixty, if she 's a day. Now, don't you grin, guv'nor. I ain't marryin' widders of sixty. No, sir."

" Did I smile ? Sorry."

" Well, this pore ole widder, she 's awful skeered about bein' left alone in the world. She hez a son, who 's somewhere in the Colonies, an'——"

" What does she want, Jim ? Just tell me the best thing I can do for her and it 's done, if you ask it. You know that well enough, without all this beating about the bush."

Arizona Jim took thought for a moment. He smiled weakly as he answered : " I 've a sort of idea, boss, that you can't fix this business, nohow."

" Who on earth is she ? "

" Elsie—Mrs. Brook—yes, that 's it."

" Mrs. Brook ! Why, that 's my wife's old nurse. She has lived here half a century. I must tell Evelyn to go and see her at once if she is in any sort of trouble. We will delay our departure if necessary. My wife will be quite concerned about it."

Vansittart half rose, but Bates detained him.

" You 've not quite got the hang of it yet, boss. As I was sayin', there 's a son."

" Yes ? "

" An' a daughter."

" Oh ! " After a pause, " Not that pretty girl whom I 've seen you talking to occasionally ? "

" Now you 've hit it, as the man said when his wife hammered her thumb instead of the tack."

Another pause. " Jim," said Vansittart slowly, " have you been telling me this cock-and-bull story about a poor old woman in order to let me know that you were going to marry her daughter ? "

" That 's about the size of it. Yes, sir."

" Have you quite made up your mind ? "

" Not 'xactly."

" What do you mean, you rascal ? "

" You see, boss, I 've been rollin' about the world many a year now, an' the wildest cuss as ever left the West wants to settle down, peaceable like, some day. There 's somethin' in his buzzum what tells him he oughter have a fireside of his own, an' a wife, an'—an'—other things."

" Who knows that better than I ? But you are not quite certain that this girl—she comes of excellent stock—will make you a good wife ? "

" Sure as death."

" Then what on earth *is* the trouble ? "

Jim fumbled about a good deal before he went on : " Elsie 's got a powerful grip on me, an' I 'm clean gone on her. So that 's all right as far as it goes. But you and I, guv'nor, hev bin tumblin' about together so long that I can't bear the thought——"

" My dear friend," said Jerome, taking Jim's rough hand in his own, " my one trusty companion. Did you think I would let you leave me ? Never ! Next to my wife and children I value you more than any living soul. Bring Elsie along, too, when you 're ready."

Jim's voice shook somewhat as he said : " Guv'nor, what you sez goes."

And that is how Vansittart and Arizona Jim parted for a little while.

THE END

THE HUDSON LIBRARY

Registered as Second-Class Matter.

16°, paper, 50 cts. ; 12°, cloth, $1.00 and $1.25.

I. Love and Shawl-Straps. By ANNETTE LUCILE NOBLE.

"Decidedly a success."—*Boston Herald.*

II. Miss Hurd : An Enigma. By ANNA KATHARINE GREEN.

"Miss Hurd fulfils one's anticipations from start to finish. She keeps you in a state of suspense which is positively fascinating."—*Kansas Times.*

III. How Thankful was Bewitched. By J. K. HOSMER.

"A picturesque romance charmingly told. The interest is both historical and poetic."—*Independent.*

IV. A Woman of Impulse. By JUSTIN HUNTLEY MCCARTHY.

"It is a book well worth reading, charmingly written, and containing a most interesting collection of characters that are just like life. . . ."—*Chicago Journal.*

V. Countess Bettina. By CLINTON ROSS.

"There is a charm in stories of this kind, free from sentimentality, and written only to entertain."—*Boston Times.*

VI Her Majesty. By ELIZABETH K. TOMPKINS.

"It is written with a charming style, with grace and ease, and very pretty unexpected turns of expression."—DROCH, in *N. Y. Life.*

VII. God Forsaken. By FREDERIC BRETON.

"A very clever book. . . . The characters are well and firmly drawn."—*Liverpool Mercury.*

VIII. An Island Princess. By THEODORE GIFT.

"A charming and often brilliant tale."—*Literary World.*

IX. Elizabeth's Pretenders. By HAMILTON AÏDÉ.

"It is a novel of character, of uncommon power and interest, wholesome, humorous, and sensible in every chapter."—*Bookman.*

X. At Tuxter's. By G. B. BURGIN.

"A very interesting story. The characters are particularly well drawn."—*Boston Times.*

XI. At Cherryfield Hall. By FREDERIC H. BALFOUR (Ross George Deering).

"This is a brilliantly-told tale, the constructive ingenuity and literary excellence of which entitle the author to a place of honor in the foremost rank of contemporary English romancists."—*London Telegraph.*

XII. The Crime of the Century. By R. OTTOLENGUI.

"It is one of the best-told stories of its kind we have read, and the reader will not be able to guess its ending easily."—*Boston Times.*

XIII. The Things that Matter. By FRANCIS GRIBBLE.

"A very amusing novel, full of bright satire directed against the New Woman and similar objects."—*London Speaker.*

XIV. The Heart of Life. By W. H. MALLOCK.

"Interesting, sometimes tender, and uniformly brilliant. . . . People will read Mr. Mallock's 'Heart of Life,' for the extraordinary brilliance with which he tells his story."—*Daily Telegraph.*

G. P. PUTNAM'S SONS, NEW YORK AND LONDON

THE HUDSON LIBRARY

XV.   The Broken Ring.   By ELIZABETH K. TOMPKINS.

" A romance of war and love in royal life, pleasantly written and cleverly composed for melodramatic effect in the end."—*Independent*.

XVI.   The Strange Schemes of Randolph Mason.   By MELVILLE D. POST,

" This book is very entertaining and original . . . ingeniously constructed . . . well worth reading."—*N. Y. Herald*.

XVII.   That Affair Next Door.   By ANNA KATHARINE GREEN.

" The success of this is something almost unprecedented. Its startling ingenuity, sustained interest, and wonderful plot shows that the author's hand has not lost its cunning."—*Buffalo Inquirer*.

XVIII.   In the Crucible.   By GRACE DENIO LITCHFIELD.

" The reader will find in this book bright, breezy talk, and a more than ordinary insight into the possibilities of human character."—*Cambridge Tribune*.

XIX.   Eyes Like the Sea.   By MAURUS JÓKAI.

" A strikingly original and powerful story."—*London Speaker*.

XX.   An Uncrowned King.   By S. C. GRIER.

" Original and uncommonly interesting."—*Scotsman*.

XXI.   The Professor's Dilemma.   By A. L. NOBLE.

" A bright, entertaining novel . . . fresh, piquant, and well told."—*Boston Transcript*.

XXII.   The Ways of Life.   Two Stories.   By MRS. OLIPHANT.

" As a work of art we can praise the story without reserve."—*London Spectator*.

XXIII.   The Man of the Family.   By CHRISTIAN REID.

" A Southern story of romantic and thrilling interest."—*Boston Times*.

XXIV.   Margot.   By SIDNEY PICKERING.

" We have nothing but praise for this excellently written novel."—*Pall Mall Gazette*.

XXV.   The Fall of the Sparrow.   By M. C. BALFOUR.

" A book to be enjoyed . . . of unflagging interest and original in conception."—*Boston Times*.

XXVI.   Elementary Jane.   By RICHARD PRYCE.

" A heartfelt, sincere, beautiful love story, told with infinite humor."—*Chicago Times-Herald*.

XXVII.   The Man of Last Resort.   By MELVILLE D. POST.

" The author makes a strong plea for moral responsibility in his work, and his vivid style and undeniable earnestness must carry great weight with all thinking readers. It is a notable book."—*Boston Times*.

XXVIII.   The Confession of Stephen Whapshare.   By EMMA BROOKE.

" Its psychology is delicate and acute ; the tragedy of it poignant and sustained ; all the characters are clearly conceived and drawn with firmness and precision."—*London Chronicle*.

XXIX.   Lost Man's Lane.   By ANNA KATHARINE GREEN.

XXX.   Wheat in the Ear.   By ALIEN.

XXXI.   As Having Nothing.   By HESTER C. OAKLEY.

XXXII.   The Chase of an Heiress.   By CHRISTIAN REID.

G. P. PUTNAM'S SONS, NEW YORK AND LONDON.

Three Notable Books

The Red Republic. A Romance of the Commune. By ROBERT W. CHAMBERS, author of "The King in Yellow," etc. *Second edition.* Large 12° $1.25

"With all its rush and excitement there is a solid basis of painstaking and thoughtfulness in 'The Red Republic.' Mr. Chambers is wholly free from self-consciousness ; indeed his gifts seem to be little short of genius. Wonderfully vivid and graphic."—*N. Y. Press.*

"Mr. Chambers shows great familiarity with the many dreadful days of 1871, and Mr. Thiers' policy is critically examined. 'The Red Republic' abounds in action."—*N. Y. Times.*

"'The Red Republic' has the healthly ring of a young man's book. Mr. Chambers can do what few men can do, he can tell a story." *N. Y. Journal.*

"I do not think that one need hesitate to call 'The Red Republic' the best American novel of the year."—VANCE THOMPSON in *N. Y. Morning Advertiser.*

"The book will commend itself not only for its strength and vividness, but for imagination and fancy. . . . Glow with gentle beauty and romance, putting in striking contrast the barbarity of war."—DROCH in *N. Y. Life.*

A King and a Few Dukes. A Romance. By ROBERT W. CHAMBERS, author of "The Red Republic." Large 12° $1 25

"No superior fiction has appeared in months. . . . . It is a charming love story, attractively told in a way that is essentially Mr. Chambers' own."—*N. Y. Times.*

"A more charming, wholly delightful story, it would be difficult to name in the whole range of English fiction. That is saying much, but not one bit more than the book deserves. . . . The characters are wonderfully well drawn."—*N. Y. World.*

"This latest of Mr. Chambers' stories is written in a very charming manner, and with all the grace and finish that have made the writings of the author so popular during the past."—*Albany Union.*

The Maker of Moons. By ROBERT W. CHAMBERS, author of "A King and a Few Dukes." Large 12°, gilt top . $1 50

"Mr. Chambers writes with the irresistible fluent vigor that characterizes the born story-teller. . . . His stories are in great part as improbable as the famous 'She' by Rider Haggard, but the reader having once begun it is impossible for him not to continue to the end. In the present volume there are also three stories which, on a basis of probability, develop a series of incidents illustrated with humor and pathos which makes them distinctively American."—*Boston Literary world.*

G. P. PUTNAM'S SONS, New York and London

www.ingramcontent.com/pod-product-compliance
Lightning Source LLC
Chambersburg PA
CBHW020859130726
47900CB00014B/1109

* 9 7 8 3 7 4 4 6 6 5 8 5 8 *